THE MEDIEVAL STAINED GLASS OF
Herefordshire & Shropshire

Fig. 1 Eaton Bishop, St Michael: Madonna and Child (c.1330–35)[1]

The Medieval Stained Glass of Herefordshire & Shropshire

Robert Walker

LOGASTON PRESS

First published in 2023 by Logaston Press.
The Holme, Church Road, Eardisley HR3 6NJ
www.logastonpress.co.uk
An imprint of Fircone Books Ltd.

ISBN 978-1-910839-54-6

Text copyright © Robert Walker 2023.
All images copyright © Robert Walker unless otherwise stated beneath each image.

All rights reserved.
The moral rights of the author have been asserted.

Without limiting the rights under copyright reserved above, no part of this publication may be reproduced, stored in or introduced into a retrieval system, or transmitted, in any form or by any means (electronic, mechanical, photocopying, recording or otherwise), without prior written permission of the copyright owner and the above publisher of this book.

Designed and typeset by Richard Wheeler in 10.5 on 14.5 Minion.
Cover design by Richard Wheeler.

Printed and bound in Poland.

Logaston Press is committed to a sustainable future for our business, our readers and our planet.
The book in your hands is made from paper from sustainable sources.

British Library Catalogue in Publishing Data.
A CIP catalogue record for this book is available from the British Library.

CONTENTS

	PREFACE & ACKNOWLEDGEMENTS	*vii*
	ABBREVIATIONS & BIBLIOGRAPHY	*xi*
	GLOSSARY	*xiv*
	KEY TO WINDOW REFERENCE NUMBERING	*xv*
	MAP OF THE CHURCHES IN THE GAZETTEERS	*xvi*
PART ONE	The History and Iconography of Stained Glass in the Diocese of Hereford	1
PART TWO	Gazetteer of Churches in Herefordshire and the Diocese of Hereford	33
APPENDIX ONE	Gazetteer of Churches in North Shropshire	209
APPENDIX TWO	Other important Stained Glass in the region of the Welsh Marches	249
APPENDIX THREE	Notes on Conservators & Restorers	251
	NOTES & REFERENCES	257
	LIST OF FIGURES	273
	INDEX OF PLACES	279
	GENERAL INDEX	282

For Rachel, Emily and Meredith

PREFACE & ACKNOWLEDGEMENTS

One of the pleasures of living in the Welsh March is discovering its heritage of churches in landscapes of timeless beauty. The first view of Abbey Dore in its ancient valley, the silence surrounding Michaelchurch Escley in the shadow of the Black Mountains and the narrow cut through the market square façade to soaring Perpendicular glory in Ludlow; such encounters haunt the memory. Beyond those first meetings, delight is found in every detail of churches and their churchyards, for they enfold almost all that survives of medieval art in carving, wall paintings and stained glass, and they speak still of our common history – perhaps the last real, enduring, holy thing we share.

Published surveys of stained glass tend to be prepared on a county basis. However, the diocesan boundaries are arguably more important than county boundaries because they define compartments of administration which were in force when the medieval glass was being installed and which, through the Diocesan Advisory Committees, map out the present-day administration of care and conservation. The principal focus of this book is therefore the Diocese of Hereford, but some outliers have been included in Part One because they bear a strong affinity with glass in the diocese. During the preparation of the text relating to the diocese, the churches in the remainder of Shropshire were visited and the glass photographed. Notes on the churches in north Shropshire are included here in a gazetteer in Appendix One.

Many antiquaries have taken an interest in the churches of Herefordshire and Shropshire, sometimes seeming obsessional in their recording of heraldry, monuments, stone mouldings, churchyard crosses and fonts. There is, however, a single-mindedness or inconsistency about some of them which can be infuriating:

Richard Symonds taking a moment away from civil war, sketching the arms in a church window, but making no note of the saints and angels; or Sir Stephen Glynne describing a church in erudite detail but seeming not to see beauties in the glass. Even William Mytton, who recorded and drew numerous figures in Shropshire windows, can be silent when his help is most needed to understand the survival and restoration of windows.

Several churches of the diocese have glass of outstanding importance, which has attracted more recent attention. George Marshall (d.1950), a president of the Woolhope Club, wrote about Eaton Bishop, Madley and Ross-on-Wye, and left some useful notes and photographs. His contemporary, Henry Weyman, wrote a seminal account of the Ludlow glass. The fourteenth-century glass at Ludlow and at Madley were the subject of an important essay on Tree of Jesse windows by Christopher Woodforde.[2] He proposed the existence of a Midlands workshop, a theory that was examined in the monumental PhD thesis of Peter Newton (Newton P., 1961), which provides a detailed description of most of the medieval glass in Shropshire.[3] The survey of churches in Shropshire by David Cranage (published in episodes between 1894 and 1912) is also a key reference.

More recently, another Woolhope Club president, Joe Hillaby, wrote about the glass at Abbey Dore and the Chapel of St Katherine in Ledbury, and focussed attention on stained glass during his presidency. In 1970, one of the leading authorities on English stained glass, Madeline Caviness, wrote about the glass which was sold away from Hampton Court. It was the first building studied in this survey, and her influence has remained throughout. In 1995, the British Archaeological Association visited Hereford and published papers by Sarah Brown and David O'Connor on Madley and Ross,[4] which have also been inspirational in this survey. This book owes much to these writers and to Richard Marks, whose broad survey of English medieval glass and work on Abbey Dore has been drawn on many times.[5]

Sarah Brown is chair of *Corpus Vitrearum Medii Aevi* (CVMA) which maintains an online resource for researchers, that has also been used in this survey. Only 23 out of the 104 churches in this survey were represented in that image library, and this book began as a photographic project to fill the gaps with new images and thorough research papers. This full photographic record and associated research have been given to CVMA and other national and local archives.[6]

This book exists for the pleasure of discovering bright and beautiful shards of the past – colourful, fragile and rare – among the other pleasures of ancient churches; but it is not just about pleasure and has a serious purpose too. It is indebted to the people who have care of our churches and especially those in the rural areas where the burden of responsibility falls on diminishing numbers of churchgoers. As, seems likely, more rural churches go out of ecclesiastical use, it is crucial that the significance of their stained glass is known and can be given weight in decisions about funding and uses. Certainly, important glass should not become a private possession or be threatened by the inappropriate use of a church.

I must thank many people who helped with this work. Those who let me into the churches they care for, especially in the difficult years of Coronavirus, must come first. The staff of the county archives of Herefordshire and Shropshire, and the libraries of Hereford Cathedral, the Society of Antiquaries and Birmingham University were ever courteous and patient. Heather Hurley advised about John Scudamore and Catherine Beale made a significant difference to the account of Hampton Court.

Hearty thanks are due to Bishop David Thomson for his scholarly help and encouragement which came at key moments, and to Trevor Cooper who made an important contribution to the accounts of Abbey Dore and Sellack. Sarah Brown's support was decisive in obtaining funding for publication.

The Marc Fitch Fund made a significant grant towards the costs of publication.

Finally, this book would have been impossible without Logaston Press and the skill and enthusiasm of Su and Richard Wheeler.

Robert Walker
October 2022

Fig. 2 Eaton Bishop, St Michael: Archangel Gabriel (c.1330–35)

ABBREVIATIONS & BIBLIOGRAPHY

BoE H	Brooks, A. and Pevsner, N., *The Buildings of England: Herefordshire*, Yale University Press (2012).
BoE S	Newman, J. & Pevsner, N., *The Buildings of England: Shropshire*, Yale University Press (2006).
Botzum, R. & C., 1997	Botzum, R. & C., *The 1675 Thomas Blount Manuscript History of Herefordshire*, Hereford (1997).
Brown, S., 1994	Brown, S., *Stained Glass: An Illustrated History*, London (1994).
Brown, S., 1995	Brown, S., 'The Fourteenth-Century Stained Glass at Madley' in *Hereford: Medieval Art, Architecture and Archaeology*, ed. David Whitehead, London: British Archaeological Association (1995).
Cole, W., 1993	Cole, W., *A Catalogue of Netherlandish and North European Roundels in Britain*, OUP for CVMA (1993).
Cowan, P., 1985	Cowan, P., *A Guide to Stained Glass in Britain*, Michael Joseph, London (1985).
Cranage, D.	Cranage, D., *An Architectural Account of the Churches of Shropshire*. This was published in parts. Part number, date and page are given.
Dingley, T., 1864	Baker, C. (ed.), Thomas Dingley: *An Account of the Progress of his Grace Henry the first Duke of Beaufort through Wales, 1684*, London (1864).
Dingley, T., 1867	Dingley, T., *History from Marble*: Volume I, Edited by Thomas Winnington, Camden Society (1867).
Duncumb, J.	Duncumb, J. The ragbag of volumes of John Duncumb and his successors between 1804 and 1913 are referred to here by volume and page. All the volumes sit together on an open shelf at HARC.

Faraday, M., 2012	Faraday, M., *The Herefordshire Chantry Valuations of 1547*, Privately Published (2012).
Ganderton, E., 1961	Ganderton, E., & Lafond, J., *Ludlow Stained and Painted Glass*, Ludlow (1961).
Glynne	Leonard, J., (ed.), *Herefordshire Churches through Victorian Eyes: Sir Stephen Glynne's Church Notes for Herefordshire*, Logaston Press (2006).
Hillaby, J., 1997	Hillaby, J., 'The Beauty of Holiness' in Shoesmith, R. & Richardson, R. (eds), *The Definitive History of Abbey Dore*, Logaston Press (1997), pp. 185–194.
Hillaby, J., 2003	Hillaby, J., *St Katherine's Hospital, Ledbury c.1230–1547*, Logaston Press (2003).
Iles, P., 2000	Iles, P., 'The Stained Glass' in Aylmer, G. and Tiller, J. (eds), *Hereford Cathedral: A History*, London (2000).
Marks, R., 1986	Marks, R., 'Cistercian Window Glass in England and Wales' in Norton, C., & Park, D. (eds*), Cistercian Art and Architecture in the British Isles*, Cambridge University Press (1986).
Marks R., 1993	Marks, R., *Stained Glass in England during the Middle Ages*, Routledge (1993).
Marshall, G., 1922	Marshall. G., 'Some Remarks on the Ancient Stained Glass in Eaton Bishop Church' in TRANS (1922).
Morgan, F.C., 1979	Morgan, F.C., *Hereford Cathedral Church Glass*, Hereford (1979).
Mytton	The Mytton Papers, Cadbury Library, Birmingham University, Ref. MYT.
Nelson, P., 1913	Nelson, P., *Ancient Painted Glass in England*, Methuen (1913).
Newton, P., 1961	Newton, P., *Schools of Glass Painting in the Midlands 1275–1430*, London University PhD Thesis (1961).
O'Connor, D., 1995	O'Connor, D., 'Bishop Spofford's Glass at Ross-on-Wye' in *Hereford: Medieval Art, Architecture and Archaeology,* ed. David Whitehead, London: British Archaeological Association (1995), pp. 138–149 and plates B, XXIV–XXVIII.
RCHM 1	Royal Commission on Historic Monuments, An Inventory of the Historical Monuments in Herefordshire: Volume I, South West, HMSO (1931).
RCHM 2	Royal Commission on Historic Monuments, An Inventory of the Historical Monuments in Herefordshire, Volume II, East, HMSO (1932).
RCHM 3	Royal Commission on Historic Monuments, An Inventory of the Historical Monuments in Herefordshire, Volume III, North West, HMSO (1934).

RUSHFORTH, G., 1936	Rushforth, G. Mc. N., *Medieval Christian Imagery, as illustrated by the painted windows of Great Malvern Priory Church, Worcestershire, together with a description and explanation of all the ancient glass in the church*, Oxford, Clarendon Press (1936).
SALZMAN, L.F., 1952	Salzman, L.F., *Building in England Down to 1540*, Oxford (1952).
SAUL, N., 2020	Saul, N., *Decorated in Glory*, Logaston Press (2020).
SYMONDS, R., 1859	Symonds, R., 'Diary of the Marches of the Royal Army During the Great Civil War', Charles Edward Long (ed.), Camden Society (1859). The notebooks of Symonds in the British Library include many sketches omitted from the Camden Society publication.: BL Harley MS 944.
TRANS	*Transactions of the Woolhope Naturalists' Field Club*.
WEAVER, P., 2015	Weaver, P., *A Dictionary of Herefordshire Biography*, Logaston Press (2015), 310.
WEYMAN, H., 1905	Weyman, H., *The Glass in Ludlow Church*, Ludlow (1905).
WHITEHEAD, D., 1995	Whitehead, D. (ed.), *Hereford: Medieval Art, Architecture and Archaeology*, London: British Archaeological Association (1995).
WOODFORDE, C., 1931	Woodforde, C., 'English Stained Glass and Glass Painters in the Fourteenth century' in *Journal of the British Society of Master Glass Painters*, Vol VI (1931).
WOODFORDE, C., 1935–7A	Woodforde, C., 'Glass painters in England before the Reformation' in *Journal of the British Society of Master Glass Painters*, (1935–7).
WOODFORDE, C., 1935–7B	Woodforde, C., 'A Group of Fourteenth Century Windows showing the Tree of Jesse', *Journal of the British Society of Master Glass Painters*, (1935–7).
WRIGHT, T., 1869	Wright, T., *Churchwardens' Accounts of the Town of Ludlow in Shropshire from 1540 to the end of the Reign of Elizabeth*, Camden Society (1869).
WRIGHT, T., 1856	Wright, T., *Historical and Descriptive Sketch of Ludlow Castle and the Church of St Lawrence, Ludlow*, Ludlow (1856).

GLOSSARY

Abrading	Mechanical etching of flashed glass (see below) to reveal the base glass.
Annealing	Controlled cooling of fired glass or the application of jewel bosses by firing.
Cames	The H-section strips of lead used to hold pieces of glass together. Early cames are cast, but after about 1600 milling machines were in use.
Diaper	A background of patterns or foliage.
Enamel	Paint including ground glass which is fired onto the surface of the glass. The technique was developed after 1500 and allows intricate draughtsmanship and painterly colouring and shading.
Ferramenta	Supporting ironwork.
Flashed glass	Plain glass onto which a thin film of molten coloured glass is applied.
Grisaille	Panels of white glass on which patterns are made with the lead cames and/or paint. The term is also used for panels of white glass painted with a single medium, usually silver stain.
Ledbury border	
Medallion	A round or vesica-shaped panel.
Pot metal	Glass of uniform colour formed in the kiln by the addition of metallic oxides.
Quarry	A rectangular or diamond-shaped piece of glass.
Roundel	A single round painted pane.
Smear shading	Shading with thin layers of glass paint (akin to watercolour washes).
Vidimus	A drawing showing a proposed panel or window.

KEY TO WINDOW REFERENCE NUMBERING

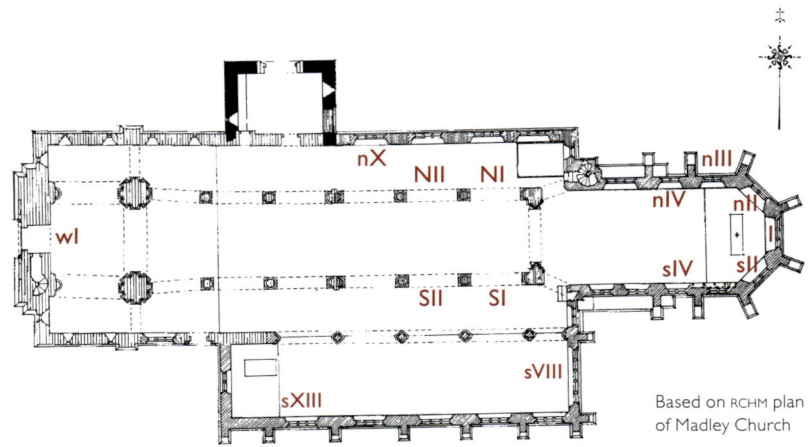

Based on RCHM plan of Madley Church

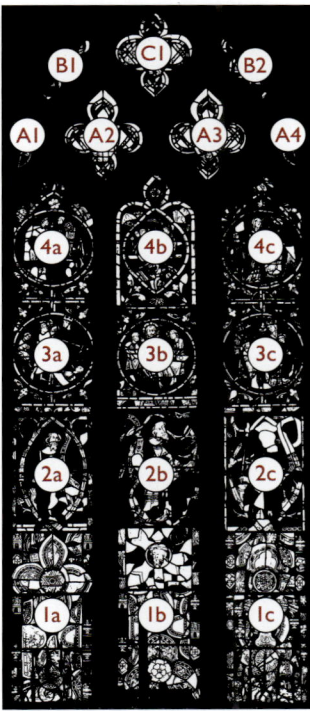

LOCATING WINDOWS IN A CHURCH
In the system favoured by the CVMA (*Corpus Vitrearum Medii Aevi*) the east window is numbered 'I' on plan and the others numbered in Roman numerals prefixed by 'n' (north) or 's' (south) in ascending order to the west. Clerestorey windows follow the same principle but have capital letter prefixes, e.g. 'SIII'.

IDENTIFYING PANELS IN A WINDOW
The panels in the principal lights of windows are numbered by rows in ascending order, with height and the lights lettered from left to right. In the tracery the rows are given ascending capitals and the panels numbered from left to right.

XV

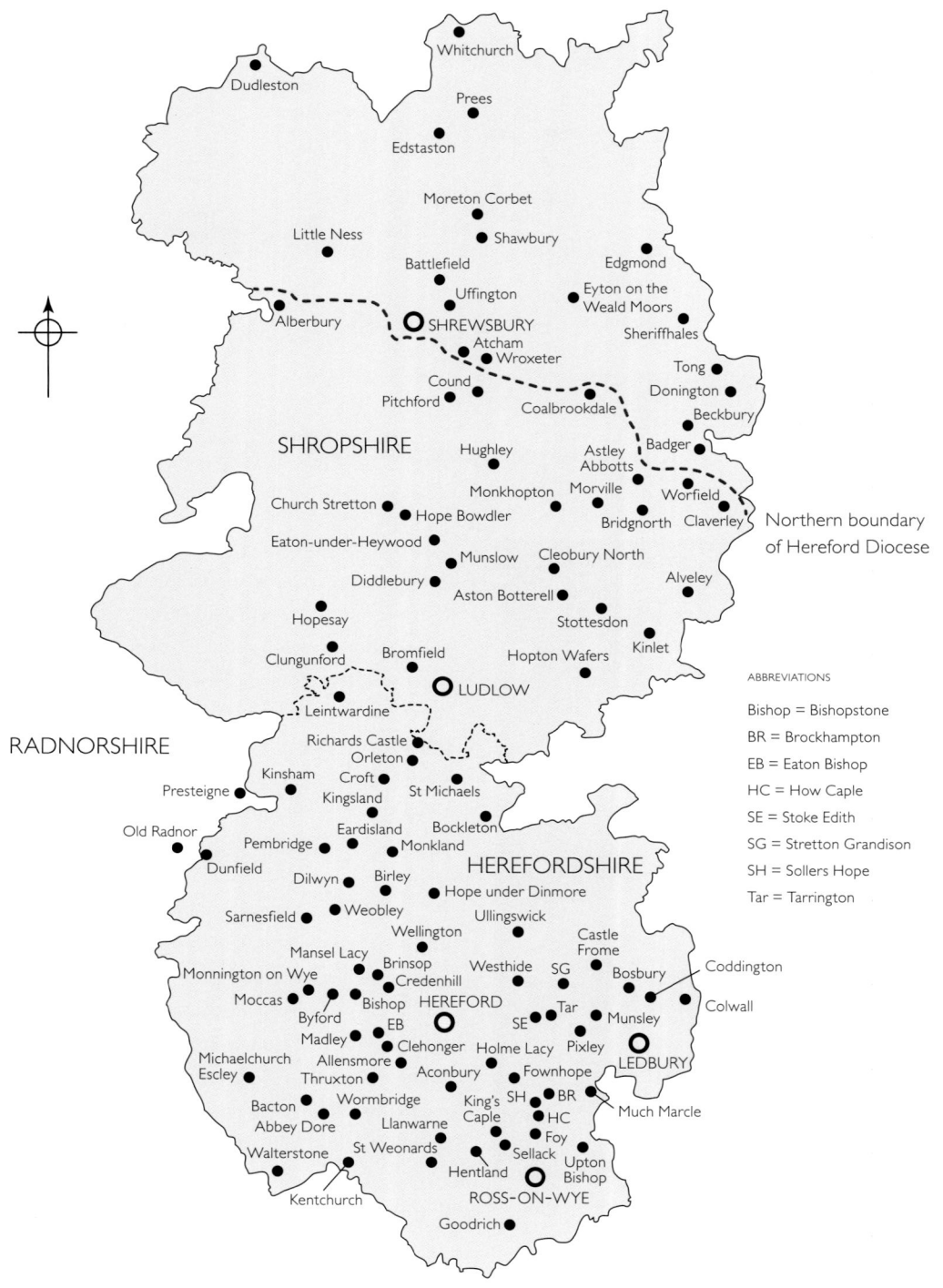

Map of Shropshire and Herefordshire, showing the locations of the churches included in this study, together with the diocesan boundary

PART ONE

The History and Iconography of Stained Glass in the Diocese of Hereford

GLASS is a mysterious, magical material, being solid and waterproof and yet translucent. It allows light into buildings while keeping the weather out, so that the evolution of glass-making technology has been a defining factor of architectural history. Here at the end of history we are used to seeing whole buildings clad in vast sheets of glass, but for this study we must look back to a time when glass suitable for making windows could only be made and finished in much smaller pieces.

The earliest pictorial glass in this survey dates from the thirteenth century (Fig. 33) but more than a millennium before that, the Romans used glass to make windows, beautiful everyday objects and magnificent works of art such as the Portland Vase. The revival of glass manufacture and the craft of glass-shaping and glazing in western Christendom was not seen until the sixth century, and the earliest known pictorial windows of substantial scale and endeavour were made around 1100 for Augsburg Cathedral.[7] The panels depicting the ancestors of Christ in Canterbury Cathedral have been dated using a new, non-destructive technique which indicates that they may date back to the mid 1100s.[8]

The earliest surviving glass in Britain is at Monkwearmouth and Jarrow (Northumbria), dating from *c*.675, where through-coloured glass has been found but no painted glass. Glaziers from Gaul were engaged by Benedict Biscop, the Abbot of Monkwearmouth, and they are said by Bede to have taught the craft to the Saxons.[9] Other glass-works at monastic sites have been found,[10] leading to the conclusion that there was an association between the early development of glass-making in England and Christian communities.[11]

Insofar as the process could be controlled and imperfections minimised, glass could be made in various degrees of translucency, and could be coloured by controlling the firing or by adding metal oxides to the crucible; the resulting molten material was known as 'pot metal'. It is generally held that the through-coloured glass – the reds, blues, yellows and greens – of the windows in this survey would have been imported and that English manufacturers, including some not far away in Shropshire and Staffordshire, would only have supplied plain glass – and even that was considered inferior to glass from France and the Low Countries.

The idea that only coloured glass originating from outside England was used is based on two documents. The first concerns the attempt by Henry VI in 1449,

… to encourage the local production of coloured glass to install beautiful windows like those of the Sainte Chapelle [in Paris]. He granted a 20 year monopoly to John Utynam from Flanders, 'who has returned of late to England at the Kings command', in order 'to make glass of all colours for the windows of Eton college and the College of Saint Mary and Saint Nicholas [King's College] because the said art has *never been used in England*' [author's emphasis].[12]

The second document is the contract of John Prudde of Westminster, made in 1447 for the glass in the Beauchamp Chapel in Warwick, which specified, 'Glasse beyond the Seas, and with no Glasse of England.'[13] This has been read as there being no English glass at this date; however, a more accurate interpretation would be that there was English glass, but it was not to be used, perhaps because it was considered to be of inferior quality.

Louis Francis Salzman was unable to find the use of English coloured glass in his survey of important building accounts before 1540.[14] And yet it seems unlikely that an industry that had mastered the technology of manufacture in glassworks at, for example, Rugeley (Staffs), the Weald and several religious houses, and produced glaziers of great ability who were able to adapt to other new technologies such as silver staining, provided none of the considerable quantities of coloured glass that were used in the fourteenth and fifteenth centuries in England, when they would have had a clear commercial advantage over imports.

At its simplest, the process of making stained glass involved heating sand to which a flux (normally soda, or potash in the form of wood ash) was added to lower the temperature required to fuse the ingredients together. Other additives such as lime were needed to improve strength and durability, and processes of heating were manipulated in kilns to obtain different qualities and colours. The flat pieces of glass for windows were made either by blowing a cylinder (muff glass), which could be cut open and flattened, or by spinning a disc of molten glass (crown glass). Sheets made from cylinders were 250 x 300mm or smaller, and the discs up to 450mm in diameter. Discs produced glass of varying thickness, which got stouter towards the centre or 'crown' of the disc.[15] After forming, it was important to anneal the glass in a separate oven, to prevent uneven cooling and cracking. There were also special techniques used in manufacturing, which can be seen in this survey, for example 'flashing' a thin coat of molten coloured glass onto white glass, which was useful if the coloured pot metal glass would otherwise have been too dark.

The essential design problem was how to make a window from a mosaic of small pieces of glass without a solid background to provide support. The solution is the use of H-section strips of lead (cames) into which adjacent pieces of glass are fitted. Lead is very flexible, which means that it can hold together complex shapes. The panels of composite glazing can then be fitted into the stone frame of the window and be given additional support by attaching them to iron 'saddle bars' or *ferramenta* by means of copper ties incorporated into the leading. In surviving churchwardens' accounts, the ironwork was invariably provided by a blacksmith, not the glazier. To make the panel waterproof, the junctions of the cames are soldered, and the joints between the cames and the glass filled with glazing 'cement' based on whiting, linseed oil and lampblack. In the Ludlow accounts for 1592–93, this is referred to as 'lyme to dresse the windowes.'[16]

Fig. 3 Assembly of a leaded window over a cartoon

If glaziers wanted to produce panels with patterns and pictures, rather than a glassy equivalent of crazy paving, a cartoon had to be drawn as a template for the making of the window. Before that, a *vidimus* might be drawn by the glazier or an artist (Fig. 26) in order to agree the design with the client, from which a full-size cartoon could be made.

Richard Marks suggests that before 1350 cartoons were drawn directly onto tables or boards, but after that time paper cartoons came into use.[17] The cartoon was fixed to the table on which the panel was to be made so that the individual pieces could be shaped, painted, and assembled over it (Fig. 3, above).[18] It was crucial that the lines of the lead complemented the picture, reinforcing the composition and, ideally, not cutting across faces and other important details. A cartoon is the best way to work this out and decide on the scale of the cames, which can be varied in width.

The individual pieces of glass had to be shaped, usually with a pointed red-hot iron which cracked the glass. This was not precise, and the edges of the pieces were adjusted by nibbling away with a 'grozing iron'. Grozing left a rough edge which was hidden by the lead cames. Diamond cutters were not in use until the late fifteenth century.

It is possible to make multiple images or flipped images from the same cartoon. A good example can be found at Dilwyn (Fig. 50) where the two angels are the same but flipped.

Much of the surviving early glass is 'grisaille', in which the cames create complex geometrical patterns (Fig. 67). These patterns could be enriched with coloured glass and with further geometrical or naturalistic patterns painted onto the glass (see Hereford Cathedral, Figs 70a & 70b). The individual pieces, called 'quarries', were often decorated with abstract floral designs, flowers, birds or animals.

To make complex patterns and to make pictures, with subtlety of line and shading, several painting techniques were needed to create an image. Glass paint was made from a variety of materials and binders such as metallic oxides and gum arabic. The black 'matt' for line and shading incorporated oxides of copper and iron, pulverised glass and gum in a liquid such as wine or urine. From the late sixteenth-century, paints were developed which included ground glass which fused with the base glass in a process called 'enamelling'. These paints allowed fine draftsmanship which can be seen, for example, in the roundels at Bromfield (Figs 40a & 40b). Usually, the painting was done on the inside surface of the glass, but 'back-painting' is sometimes encountered. Modelling could be achieved by 'badgering', that is applying a thin film over the whole surface and taking out the highlights with a badger-hair brush. Smear shading and stippling were also used. The former involved building up thin washes for shadowed areas and the latter dabbing with a stiff brush. Effects such as cross-hatching could be achieved by scratching out pale lines in a dark ground.

After painting the piece would be fired. This was a risky operation, because the pieces could crack, and the painter would try to ensure that the drawing and shading could be fixed in one firing.

At the beginning of the fourteenth century a new painting technique emerged, using solutions of silver oxide or nitrate which turn golden yellow on firing. Early in the fourteenth century this might be used for details such as hair, crowns or heraldry (for example at Madley, Fig. 10) but by the end of the fifteenth century whole panels were painted with silver stain with exquisite modelling and variations of hue (see the Golden Window at Ludlow, Fig. 98, and the panels in the north transept of Hereford Cathedral, Figs 65 & 66). Other highly-skilled techniques were developed, for example at Ludlow, where the jewel bosses, which add richness to the decoration of the figures in the fifteenth-century chancel windows, are set into holes drilled in the body of the leaded glass.

GLAZIERS

There is little evidence of glass having been made in the diocese in the medieval period. There was a glass-making site in Shropshire in 1349, which supplied glass to Westminster.[19] This was probably near Wroxeter or Ruyton where evidence for Roman and medieval glassworks have been found.[20] The more favourable commercial conditions and the combination of sand and wood (and lime) which resulted in the establishment of an early industry close to London, in the Weald, might not have been found in Herefordshire; however, later, at the end of the sixteenth century, there was glass-making in the parish of St Weonards. The glass-makers were Huguenots, and they are remembered in the name of Glass House Farm and four field-names in the parish.[21] There was a much larger and well-documented Huguenot enterprise at Newent, which continued into the seventeenth century. Archaeologists found window glass amongst the waste there.[22]

Other than the surviving glass, the glaziers' craft has left little evidence about how it was organised in the medieval March. The most substantial work surviving from an early date is the collection of late thirteenth-century medallions at Madley (Fig. 105). It is suggested in the gazetteer below that this could be the work of French glaziers under the patronage of a French bishop of Hereford. Only two later medieval documentary references have been found and they both relate to William of Hereford. He was employed as a glass painter among the many glaziers mustered to work on St Stephen's Chapel, Westminster in 1350, and he supplied glass at St Weonards in 1355.[23] The possibility of a workshop in Hereford in the fourteenth century is considered in more detail in the chronological survey below, but Woodforde noted that:

> As we have the names of many glass painters whose place of origin or sphere of activities are not known, so there are counties in which we can place no centre of glass painting with certainty. There is no school of any great importance to be found in the south western counties – Wiltshire, Somerset, Gloucester, Worcester and Hereford. Yet these counties can still show magnificent windows of glass …[24]

The record has yielded no names of glass painters in the later fourteenth and fifteenth centuries other than the suggestion of a signature in the glass at Sellack. The inscription in black letter reads: *Ele - - sine me fecit* (Fig. 135) which could, however, be part of the word 'Eleemosyne', meaning alms.[25]

There are similarities with the work of known artists in the International Style, such as the fragments of Oxford-work at Madley, and there are numerous schemes in the diocese and adjacent counties that appear to be related to glass from John Thornton's York/ Coventry enterprises. Some of these relatives of York – at Ludlow, Hereford (see Hampton Court) and Great Malvern – were substantial projects. Richard Marks points out that the stars of the time, such as John Thornton and John Prudde (Figs 97a & 97b), worked all over England, but the sum of the work that might be associated with Thornton on the grounds of style suggests the existence of a local atelier of York-trained glaziers. In 1482 two painters accomplished in the International Style, Richard Twygge and Thomas Wodeshaw of Malvern, worked at Tattershall, Lincolnshire.[26] They were engaged on other important projects, including the nave of Westminster Abbey, and they might have served their apprenticeship in such a workshop in the Malvern area.

PATRONAGE

Who paid for glass and why they paid for it determined where glass was placed, its subject matter and who was commissioned to make it. More importantly for art historians, where donors can be identified by name or their heraldic imprint, the work can usually be dated, and its iconography can be better understood. It might also ensure the survival of at least part of a window in times of iconoclasm because heraldry and the images of donors and their children were not forbidden. Even so, many lost images of donors, their arms and their inscriptions are preserved in the notes of seventeenth- and eighteenth-century antiquaries (Fig. 4).

Bishops and Deans could afford the best glaziers in their palaces and cathedrals. Hereford

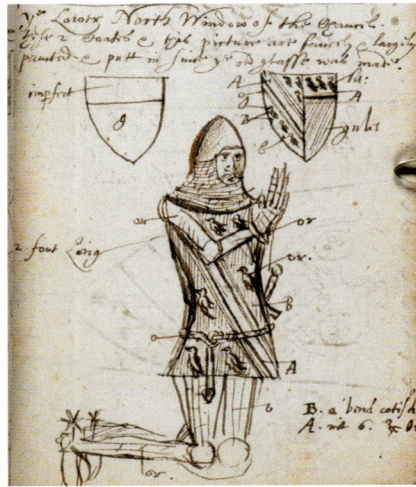

Fig. 4 Antiquarian sketches: Richard Symonds (ABOVE) and Thomas Dingley (BELOW) of lost glass depicting an armed figure in the 'lower north window of the chancel' at Dilwyn (the Richard Symonds image is by kind permission of the British Library)

Cathedral has lost most of its medieval glass, but the chapel of Bishop Audley (1492–1502) retains a few pieces, and Bishop Spofford (1421–48) probably commissioned glass that survives in museums (see Hampton Court). He commissioned fine glass for his palace at Sugwas, which was moved to Ross-on-Wye at the end of the eighteenth century. This includes his portrait with his adopted saint, Anne (Figs 129 & 130). He also appears with her in the tracery of the east window at Ludlow, not as donor but with the thanks of the parishioners for resolving difficulties with their rector over the rebuilding of the chancel. Spofford had roots in York, and so it is not surprising that the glass is associated with York glaziers.

Little has survived from the monastic churches and chapels. The most interesting fragments of glass are at Abbey Dore, including the white-robed figure of a Cistercian Abbot (Fig. 20). Excavations at the site of Craswall Priory yielded a head of early date which is now in Hereford Museum (Fig. 73), and Aconbury retains a few fragments of grisaille. There is a head of a white-clad abbot at Wellington (Fig. 143) representing perhaps one of the monastic saints with local connections, such as Owen or Guthlac.

A bishop or the Dean and Chapter might commission glass in the parish churches where they had responsibility for the fabric. Madley's chancel, which was developed as a place of Marian pilgrimage, still displays the fourteenth-century arms of the Deanery, and its (relocated) medallions of thirteenth-century glass might be associated with the bishopric of Peter of Savoy (1240–66). Lesser clerics were also patrons of parish church windows. In the east window at Eaton Bishop (Fig. 55), the image of Adam Murimuth, cantor, flesh-coloured, tonsured and bearded, kneeling in prayer and wearing a long-sleeved surplice, is prominent among several other figures who might have been donors of other, now lost, windows.

Not quite so prominent but also over the high altar, at Ledbury, two of the Ledbury portionists who shared the living (Fig. 87) occupy tracery lights in the east window. At Hentland, Richard Rotherham, an important cleric and a protégé of Bishop Spofford, kneels amiably in the east window. At Munslow is the inscription, 'Of yr charytye pray for the soul and state of Johne Lloydde which glasing was done at hys cost.' He was the last rector before the Reformation.

The windows of parish churches were funded by the builders of chantries, by guilds and other associations, and by individuals, often in their wills or in commemoration of family members. Several of the windows in this survey are or were in chantry chapels, such as the Jesse Tree at Madley (Fig. 104). Perhaps the most important examples of guild windows in the country are at Ludlow where the Palmers Guild, dedicated to the Virgin Mary and St John the Evangelist, commissioned a Jesse Tree window in the Lady Chapel (Fig. 95), and the visualisation of its own foundation myth involving the Evangelist, in its guild chapel (Figs 100 & 100a). There are also records of a window provided by the shearers' guild and several illustrations of private donors. At Weobley, a newly-founded Chapel of the Holy Rood was provided with a splendid Perpendicular window with angels carrying Instruments of the Passion (Figs 144–144b).

There are a few surviving examples of memorials to lay people, inspired by the belief in the benefits of perpetual prayers for the souls of the departed. Richard Marks points out that glass was an expensive way of making a memorial compared to the alternatives of a brass or ledger slab, so it is not surprising that it is mainly the leading families who are represented in glass and also in antiquarian records of glass.[27]

An important difference between glass and other types of monument is that the donors of glass usually appear only as lesser figures, perhaps represented by their arms or inscriptions, leaving the larger field to images of saints or narrative scenes. The Golden Window at Ludlow (Fig. 98) is a good example, where the donors are pictured with their name saints below (one of the great catechetical images for which Ludlow is famous). The donor might choose the subject or be guided by the parish, but it seems likely that these windows were gifts to the church in its teaching endeavour as well as personal memorials.

Among these monuments to aristocrats, there are several examples of armed figures, usually kneeling in prayer to the crucified Christ or a saint. The east window at Kinlet, though much restored, is a good example (Fig. 83). Richard Symonds and Thomas Dingley drew armed figures in several churches, notably Dilwyn, where they both showed the same kneeling figure of one of the Delaberes (Fig. 4). The glass in St Katherine's Hospital Chapel, Ledbury, was part of a reconstruction programme of c.1335–40 under the patronage of Bishop John Grandison, who intended the window to be a memorial to his parents. The arms of his father, William Grandison, are in the central panel of the principal east window.[28]

The arms of important local dynasties are often found – Mortimers (15 occurrences in glass and record), Bohuns (6), Talbots (5), Cornewalls (5). Whether they paid for all the buildings in which their arms were placed is not certain, but Nigel Saul demonstrates that one Mortimer, Margaret, can be directly connected with at least four churches where the Mortimer arms are recorded – Pembridge, Kingsland, Orleton and Presteigne. In other cases, lesser gentry might place the arms of aristocrats as a mark of allegiance. But perhaps the most famous example of a memorial provided by a grateful heir is the east window at Sellack, commissioned by John Scudamore in 1630 in memory of his uncle Roland, who kneels like the knights of old, though robed and not armed (Fig. 58).

Recent research into the funding of glass through wills has revealed many examples of windows paid for, in whole or part, by will.[29] Many include specifications of the content of windows, and Sally Badham[30] describes a will requiring the image of the donor to be placed with the Crucifix, the Virgin and St John, which brings to mind the much-restored example at Munslow, paid for by Richard Sheppard who, in the inscription, asks for prayers for his soul and that of his wife.

Some of the most charming images in glass are the civilian couples accompanied by their children, many of which may well have been paid for by wills. Outstanding among these, at Atcham, in glass moved from Bacton, are Miles Ap-harry (or Parry) of Newcourt in Bacton, and his wife Joan, daughter of Sir Henry Stradling of St Donat's Castle near Cardiff, with their 19 children (Fig. 34). At Munslow there is a kneeling donor and four daughters, all robed in deep purple and carrying rosaries, except for the smallest. There is a banderol in black letter asking for the prayers of Mary (Fig. 119).

CHRONOLOGICAL SURVEY
Before 1300

The oldest glass in this survey is a figure at Astley Abbotts (Inset 1 & Fig. 33). Richard Marks suggests that this figure is Christ, presumably because the nimbus is cruciform.[31] The completely rearranged assemblage of gloomy grisaille glass in the south aisle of Abbey Dore is thought to date from between 1180 and 1250. Had this been in its original state, it would have had great significance as the only known example of English Cistercian grisaille.

The medallions in the east window at Madley (Inset 2 & Fig. 105) have been dated to around 1250. Narrative medallion programmes from the thirteenth century are mostly found in cathedrals; only a handful of medallions remain in parish churches. There seem to be medallions from two schemes at Madley – the Life of Christ and the Life of St John the Evangelist. The panels showing St John and the poison, and his death, are unique in English churches, and the Last Supper with John reclining against the doomed Christ is among the most moving scenes in this survey. Madley is the only parish church that shows a scheme reminiscent of the great English and French cathedral medallion windows. It is impossible to overstate its importance.

From later in the thirteenth century is the small amount of grisaille glass at Aconbury (Fig. 28) which can be dated to *c*.1275. This takes the trefoiled form of Early English stiff-leaf decoration, which is also found at Hughley, where thirteenth-century fragments are re-set in the tracery of a fourteenth-century window, including the feet of the crucified Christ and two figures with huge vesica eyes (Inset 3 & Fig. 78b).

In the lady chapel of the cathedral are panels which were taken from St Peter's Church in the city, which Richard Marks suggests are, 'among the principal monuments of the years 1250–90.'[32] They have a dark, forceful, primitive appearance (Figs 70a & 70b) but the quality of composition and draughtsmanship of the head and face of Christ (Inset 4), which is certainly original, suggests a date late in the thirteenth or even early fourteenth century. The historiated panels must have been part of a larger scheme of medallions depicting the Life or Passion of Christ. Comparison with Madley is inevitable: both are remarkably local survivals of medallion programmes, but the composition, expression and draftsmanship of the Hereford panels, where they can be distinguished from the restoration of the nineteenth century, suggest a later date or more confident hand than those at Madley.

The difficulty of dating images around 1300 is further illustrated by the depiction of the Slaughter of the Innocents at Ledbury (Fig. 90b) in which the soldier has mail armour similar to the fourteenth-century image of St George at Brinsop (Fig. 37). The Ledbury soldier is accompanied by other large-eyed, somewhat clumsy figures (Inset 5) of Herod, a Crucifix and Mary and the Child in the Flight into Egypt (Fig. 90a), which suggest a date before 1300. The same scene of slaughter at Wormbridge (Fig. 149) can be confidently placed in the fourteenth century.

The Decorated style: 1300–50

A recently published survey of fourteenth-century church building in Herefordshire[33] describes the flowering of the Decorated style in the half-century before the Black Death:

> Intense church building took place in these years in other parts of the Midlands … Nowhere however was quite so much building undertaken, nor that building activity quite so widely distributed, as in Herefordshire and the neighbouring areas of South Shropshire. And nowhere have quite so many fabrics of the period come down to us for the most part almost unaltered.

This remarkable intensity of building in Herefordshire is not obviously reflected in the survival of glass. The proportion of churches with surviving fourteenth-century glass is not significantly higher in Herefordshire than in the surrounding English counties, although it is considerably higher than in counties further east, such as Gloucestershire and Norfolk, where the Perpendicular style is more strongly represented. There is, of course, a problem with counting surviving glass in that there are many intervening variables determining what remains. The sometimes seemingly random impact of iconoclasm, the ability and will to maintain glass in later centuries and the progress of restoration and rebuilding weave different stories in different areas. It must, however, be true that there was an increase in the local demand for glazing in the diocese, corresponding with the increase in building activity that Nigel Saul identifies, and one of the radically new characteristics of the Decorated style was the use of larger windows of multiple lights which presented glaziers with projects of unprecedented scale and artistic opportunity.

It might, however, be a mistake to think that the Decorated building boom gave rise to armies of glaziers setting up workshops in the diocese. Nigel Saul's gazetteer of Decorated projects[34] lists 21 buildings in which a significant amount of work occurred in the fourteenth century, which, on a rough count, involved fewer than 200 new windows. There would also have been many minor projects of one or two windows, reglazing and repair work, but over the period of 50 years this would probably average out at fewer than 20 per year, some of which would have had plain or grisaille glazing.

The decades from 1320 to 1350 might have seen a greater intensity of work, but even so a modest number of glaziers could have kept up. The possibility of a local or West Midlands workshop in the fourteenth century is 'suspected' by Nigel Saul[35] and, as long ago as 1935, Christopher Woodforde thought that the surviving Jesse windows (see below) in the region were from a single source.[36] Richard Marks also argued for a fourteenth-century West Midlands workshop:

> The West Midlands ... contain a large corpus of major monuments dating from the late 1330s to the 1350s ... They include Tewkesbury choir clerestory, the East window of the choir of Gloucester cathedral and a series of Jesse Trees at Tewkesbury, Bristol cathedral, Ludlow and Madley in Herefordshire, as well as some of the glass at Eaton Bishop and Moccas ... They are all by the same workshop, but the entire group would repay detailed investigation, not least as to its relationship to the Wells Choir clerestory glass. There is a close similarity between the canopies at Wells, Eaton Bishop, Moccas and Tewkesbury; on the other hand, the affinities in figure style appear to be less clear.[37]

The findings of this survey suggest several masters were responsible for the glass listed by Richard Marks. Whether they worked in a single or separate workshops cannot be known. It is, however, possible to see some patterns in the details and distribution of the surviving glass, although some common themes in the first half of the fourteenth century reflected national fashions and obscure the differences between individual makers. In this time, Lombardic script was the norm, and elaborate niches and canopy-work were developed as the setting for figures, for example at Eaton Bishop (Fig. 55) and Moccas (Fig. 110), with a much more sophisticated approach to colour, line and shading to give faces and drapery a more naturalistic appearance. After about 1320, silver staining took on ever greater importance, latticed backgrounds appear, and more precisely drawn diapering and prominent borders using motifs such as crowns, castles, vines and fleurs-de-lis became de rigueur (Eaton Bishop and Madley).

Against this common background of fashion there are, however, several significantly different strands to follow in the glass, which are distinguishable by idiosyncrasies of drawing.

Fig. 5 Credenhill: Bishops Thomas Becket and Thomas Cantilupe (sIV), before 1320

Strand 1: Extending the thirteenth-century tradition

The two-dimensional line drawings of the thirteenth century, depicting people with large eyes, pinched brows, drooping mouths and simplified drapery, continue with increasing sophistication and richness of colouring into the 1330s and probably later. This is typified by the two bishop saints at Credenhill (before 1320) (Fig. 5) and two crowned figures at Donington (Inset 6 & Fig. 52) in which flesh is tinted but not much modelled with shading. This conservative thread can be seen elsewhere in the Midlands, for example at Stanford-on-Avon, Northamptonshire (1320–30) (Fig. 6).[38] In this tradition are figures at Orleton (Figs 122a & 122b), Brinsop (Figs 37 & 38) and in the tracery (Figs 81a–81d) and a figure of a bishop at Kingsland. The bishop at Eaton Bishop on panel I.2b (Fig. 55), and other figures can also be counted here, while at Richards Castle (Figs 7, 127a & 127b), Alberbury (Figs 29a & 29b), Allensmore and Cound (Fig. 47), yellow stain and shading are added to essentially conservative figures. Most of the surviving Crucifixes are in this strand: for example, Allensmore (Fig. 30), Thruxton (Fig. 141) and the north chancel window at Eaton Bishop. Other images of Christ have an icon-like consistency and deceptive simplicity – as seen, for example, at Kingsland (Fig. 81a) and Donington (Fig. 8).

Fig. 8 Donington: Christ with a cruciform nimbus (nIII)

Fig. 6 St Barnabas, Stanford-on-Avon, Northamptonshire (nIII), c.1320–30

Fig. 7 Richards Castle: Christ with a cruciform nimbus (sIV)

Strand 2: The master of the Madley Mouth

One of the loveliest of Herefordshire's fourteenth-century church extensions is the south aisle Chilstone Chapel at Madley. Its east window, with reticulated tracery, held a Tree of Jesse, the remains of which are now in the chancel east window (Figs 9a & 10). It is the work of a great and original artist whose command of composition, colour and draughtsmanship was revolutionary. His signature is in the way he draws mouths like a stretched letter H, with the lips either side of the bar (Insets 7–10 & Fig. 10). Sarah Brown

Fig. 10 King Ozias from the Madley Jesse window (I.2a)

Figs 9a–9c Kings from Jesse windows. **Fig. 9a**: Madley (TOP); **Fig. 9b**: Ludlow (ABOVE LEFT); & **Fig. 9c**: Merevale (ABOVE RIGHT)

describes his figures as having, 'long faces, foxy features, sidelong glances, pointed beards, and elegant, expressive hands.'[39] They have also been described as 'Mannerist' because of their strong, bold composition, deep colouring and stylised figures.[40] The artist drew other figures at Madley, Kempsey and Abbey Dore, with square jaws and stubble beards (Insets 8 & 9, Figs 106a & 106b), which share the same confident eyes and mouths as the Jesse figures, and he can be seen to have been experimenting with line and silver stain in striking figures with flowing beards in several places (Inset 10).

The Madley Master painted another Tree of Jesse in the diocese, in the Lady Chapel at Ludlow (Figs 9b & 95), and a third in Clehonger. Jesse Tree windows are strongly associated with Lady chapels, and this was indeed the function of the Madley south aisle, otherwise called St Mary's Chapel. This was probably completed in the early 1340s.[41] The Madley Jesse has been compared with other versions of the subject in the Midlands, the suggestion being that they are the product of a single workshop.[42] The details of the windows suggest it is very unlikely that all these Jesse windows were made by the same hand, but some firm associations can be seen between some of them. The heavily-restored Jesse at Ludlow is a close relation to Madley (Figs 9a & 9b) sharing the 'Madley Mouth', the vine stems decorated with fleurs-de-lis, the blue backgrounds and the Lombardic capitals. Some of the Ludlow faces have distinctly different, spurred eyebrows (Inset 11). Ludlow is thought to have been commissioned after a bequest in 1330, and the Madley window is *c*.1340.[43] This may explain the more mobile, swaying figures and more mature, confident and simplified composition at Madley, with the greater use of silver stain for hair and beards. Ludlow has some important features which are not seen at Madley, in that its vine leaves are not only green but also white (as at Merevale, Warwickshire), and there are birds among the foliage; however, this may be because less medieval glass survives at Madley.

Merevale shares some features with Madley (Fig. 9c). Some but not all faces have the Madley Mouth, or a slightly different, full-lipped version; but the background, though blue, has a vine pattern and the fleurs-de-lis make a double-row on the stems. The lettering is black letter and not Lombardic. It is possible that the Madley Master was one of the team there, but responsible for only part of the picture. Merevale and Ludlow seem more obviously related in style and character (note the spurred eyebrows) than Madley and Merevale.

Tewkesbury Abbey vestry south window is fragmentary, but part of a Jesse Tree can be discerned. This has nothing in common with Madley and Ludlow, but some other fragments, probably from another subject, have faces with the Madley Mouth, Lombardic capitals and a blue background, which together resonate with Madley. Considering other Jesse trees which have been compared with Madley, there seems to be little common ground with St Mary's, Shrewsbury (see p. 226), Lowick (Northants) or the Bristol Cathedral east window. Fragments at Fillongley, Warwickshire, have the Madley Mouth but a wholly different treatment of the nose. It could be that the Madley figures are the successors of Ludlow and Merevale in that they represent the development of the subjects to a more Mannerist perfection. The suggested dates of these works would support that assertion. Ludlow was, as noted above, probably given in 1330, Merevale is a work of 1324–40[44] and the Madley Chilstone Chapel was started *c*.1340.

There are other images in this survey which are the work of the Madley Master. At Abbey Dore (Inset 9 & Fig. 23) and Clehonger (Figs 45a & 45b) are heads with the Madley Mouth and grizzled beards. At Clehonger there are also pieces of stem from a Tree of Jesse. At Worfield (Figs 145–147), in a heavily-restored window depicting the Crucifixion and groups of onlookers, the king in the right-hand panel is clearly by the Madley Master. The grace, inventiveness and colouring of the canopy-work, and the composition of a single scene across all three panels, is decades before its time. The canopy-work is related to the surviving panels at Moccas (Figs 110 & 111) which have a lightness, depth and colouring which surpasses even those in the greater churches at Tewkesbury and Gloucester Cathedral. At Moccas, the device of installing standard-bearers and their standards in the canopies, is inspired and adds colour and rhythm, greatly increasing the visual impact of the work. The standard-bearers have the Madley Mouth.

There are further links to Madley at Thruxton, where a fragment of cup-and-cover border matches those at Madley exactly; and at Pembridge, where a censing angel has the Madley Mouth. Outside the diocese are further convincing relatives: the heads of saints at Kempsey, Worcestershire (Fig. 11a), a Virgin at Worcester Cathedral[45] (Fig. 11b) and a Virgin of the Annunciation from Hadzor, now in the Ely Stained Glass Museum (Fig. 11c), seem to be wholly

Figs 11a–11c: C14 faces. **Fig. 11a**: Kempsey (TOP LEFT), **Fig. 11b**: Worcester Cathedral (TOP RIGHT) & **Fig. 11c**: Hadzor (ABOVE)

Figs 12a–12c: comparison of C14 faces. FROM TOP: **Fig. 12a**: Christ Church, Oxford, **Fig. 12b**: Ledbury Church, **Fig. 12c**: Ledbury, St Katherine

in the Madley style. The Hadzor Annunciation has the unparalleled grace, colouring and style that might be expected from the Madley Master. Perhaps the swaying figure of St Catherine at Kempsey (Fig. 11a) is the prototype?

Further afield, the figures in the Latin Chapel of Christ Church Cathedral, Oxford (Inset 12 & Fig. 12a) have been suggested as possible affinities,[46] and there is one remote relative at Worpelsdon in Surrey. Otherwise, the Madley Master's work clusters in or on the border of the diocese. Merevale, which is also remote, has an obvious connection with Abbey Dore in that they were both Cistercian houses. Two other strands are yet to be considered, but if there is a case for a local workshop, and a possible glimpse of the hand of William of Hereford, who was master enough to be called to work at Westminster, then this is made by the Madley Master's oeuvre.

The relationship between glaziers and masons in the fourteenth century is difficult to understand given the paucity of evidence. An obvious question is: did master masons favour particular glaziers? William of Hereford was almost certainly employed at (and got his name from) the cathedral, the great building project which cast an influence over a wide area. But if he is the Madley Master, his hand cannot be seen in the scant remains of cathedral glass. Richard Morris identified several master masons working in different parts of Herefordshire in the fourteenth century, and there does, at first glance, seem to be one possible correlation between the strands in glass painting and the pattern of masonry where the Madley Master's work overlaps with Morris's master mason of Allensmore.[47] Both executed several commissions in the Wye valley west of Hereford. They certainly worked together at Madley and Clehonger, and probably at Moccas. However, that is not evidence of an exclusive working relationship because they did not work together at Allensmore and Eaton Bishop as we will see in the next strand of painting.

Strand 3: The Master of Archangels

George Marshall believed that the glass at Madley and Eaton Bishop were from the same workshop because they both have panels with lattice backgrounds (only in the tracery at Madley) and borders with cup-and-cover decoration.[48] However, both forms of decoration are only similar, not exactly alike, and are found throughout England. Sarah Brown has dismissed any direct connection:

> The paucity of figural glass ... at Madley makes a direct comparison problematic, but even at a superficial level it is not altogether convincing. The ecclesiastics' heads at Madley display broad foreheads, full cheeks and a prominent jaw line modelled with smear shading. The Eaton Bishop heads have rather naïve, almost childlike gentleness with little modelling ...[49]

Most of the figures in the composite east window at Eaton Bishop belong in the first strand of essentially traditional or conservative character, but the two archangels and the Virgin and Child (Figs 1 & 2), with their curved stances, piecrust nimbi and lipless, sardonic smiles, are strikingly fresh and utterly beautiful (Inset 13). The faces are fuller and more rounded than the Madley Master's, and the palette of more sombre olive green and ochre is very unlike his deep and vibrant colours. (Several related images are compared in Figs 12a–12c.) The Master of Archangels probably drew the image of another archangel in the tracery of the east window at Ledbury Church, which may be as late as 1370 (Fig. 88); and, nearby, in the figure of St Margaret in the chapel at St Katherine's Hospital, which Joe Hillaby also compared with the figures of the Virgin and Gabriel in the Latin Chapel in Christ Church Cathedral, Oxford (Fig. 12a). He suggests that the glass at St Katherine's Hospital,

> Can be attributed to a workshop active in the West Midlands 1330–50. Some of the most noticeable products of this workshop are to be found in the 3 windows of the Latin Chapel, that is the north eastern chapel of Christ Church Cathedral, Oxford.[50]

Insets showing the changes in the portrayal of faces from the thirteenth to the fifteenth century

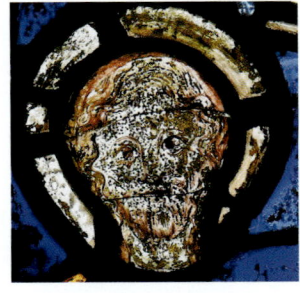

1. Astley Abbotts (I): the face of Christ (C13)

6. Donington (nIII): the figure of a king (c.1300)

2. Madley (I.3b): detail of medallion showing the Last Supper (late C13)

7. Madley (I.2a): a face by the Madley Master (c.1340)

3. Hughley (nII.A3): detail of fragments (probably C13)

8. Kempsey, Worcs (nIII.2b): a face by the Madley Master (C14)

4. Hereford Cathedral (sV): the Crucified Christ (c.1250–90)

9. Abbey Dore (sIX.4a): a face by the Madley Master (C14)

5. Ledbury (nX.1d): King Herod from The Slaughter of the Innocents (c.1300)

10. Madley (sII.6a): the Madley Master experimenting with silver stain and matt shading (C14)

11. Ludlow (sV.A2): A head from the Tree of Jesse window (c.1330)

16. Tarrington (sII): female figure (c.1400)

12. Latin Chapel, Christ Church Cathedral, Oxford: the Virgin (C14)

17. Madley (nII.4b): figure possibly by Thomas of Oxford (c.1380)

13. Eaton Bishop (I): Archangel Michael (c.1330)

18. Weobley (nV.C2): an angel (c.1400)

14. Fladbury: the Virgin (C14)

19. Presteigne (sIII): a bearded face (C15)

15. Wormbridge (sII): St Peter (C14)

20. Old Radnor (nIII): St Catherine (C15)

Fig. 13
Deerhurst, Gloucestershire: St Catherine (sIX)

Strand 4: The Master of the Chinless Madonna

There are two pictures of the Madonna and Child, close to Herefordshire, at Fladbury and Warndon in Worcestershire, which are well-known examples of the use of a single cartoon to make multiple images (Inset 14, Figs 14a & 14b). They are distinguished from the other styles of drawing by their strangely distorted, chinless faces with mouths that appear to be stapled shut. A possible connection with the Madley Master can be seen at Moccas, where,

There are other local relatives of the Eaton Bishop archangels, notably the angels at Dilwyn (Fig. 50) and St Catherine at Deerhurst, Gloucestershire (Fig. 13), and more tenuous relatives at Orleton (Figs 122a & 122b) and Donington (Figs 51 & 52). The tantalising idea of a local workshop, occurring to other writers, is met with again in Herbert Read's analysis of the work at Eaton Bishop,

> There is still in England survivals of early Gothic glass-paintings which exhibit not merely English, but even more localized characteristics. The splendid glass at Eaton Bishop, is a pre-eminent example. It is not strictly comparable with any glass in France, nor even with any other glass in England, and one can only suppose that it emanated from a local school at Hereford.[51]

However, the small number of local survivals might argue for an Oxford, rather than Herefordshire, base when further examples of similar work are plotted.

Figs 14a–14b: Madonna and Child figures from the same cartoon:

Fig. 14a Warndon, Worcestershire

Fig. 14b Fladbury, Worcestershire

among the bannermen, most of whom have the Madley Mouth, is one chinless figure. The small number of images in this style might suggest that the Madonnas are an experiment of the Madley Master because they have the energy of pose and sureness of line that characterises his other work.

There is fourteenth-century glass, identified in the following gazetteer, that cannot be attributed to these masters, the most pleasing of which are the small roundels and tracery lights painted in silver stain against a black background. The saints and prophets at Wormbridge (Inset 15 & Figs 150a–150d) and the angels at Sarnesfield (Figs 133a & 134) are particularly memorable.

THE INTERNATIONAL STYLE

The so-called International Style departs from the rich colouring and lively drawing of the Decorated style in that windows display less and less pot metal colour, and show instead drawing and modelling with silver stain. The faces have beautifully expressive round eyes with fine, curved crease-lines from their outer corners, small mouths, well-defined noses and quizzical expressions. The Weobley angels, for example, are all seen full-face, but where figures are shown in profile – for example, at Tarrington (Inset 16 & Fig. 139) and Ross (Figs 128–130) – the noses are elongated and have bulbous tips.

There are several panels of glass that can be placed in the half-century after the Black Death. The puzzling glass in the east window at Ledbury seems to continue the Decorated style into tracery of a Perpendicular window which can be dated by the identity of donors to *c*.1370. Two faces at Madley, probably from the 1380s, are by Thomas of Oxford, an early proponent of the new style (Inset 17 & Figs 107a–107e) which, in his glazing of New College, Oxford, achieves unprecedented realism by skilful line and shading. Fragments of canopy-work of an unusual form, which Thomas used at New College, are found at Madley, Pixley, Abbey Dore (window sVIII), Allensmore (panel I.C2) and Tarrington.

The new style breaks through more clearly at the turn of the fifteenth century, at Weobley, where the window noted above was inserted in the north aisle as a reredos to an altar dedicated to the Holy Rode (Inset 18, Fig. 144) *c*.1400. In Perpendicular architecture, the windows often have multiple tracery lights which are ideal for small figures. Angels were a favourite subject for these lights.

The Ross glass was commissioned by Bishop Spofford for the east window of the bishop's palace at Sugwas. He was bishop between 1421 and 1447, and is probably associated with three important projects. At Ross, the bishop himself is seen presenting his heart to St Anne and her daughter, the Virgin Mary. He had a lifelong devotion to St Anne and is pictured with her in the east window at Ludlow (1444). He has also been associated with glass formerly at Hampton Court, which depicts his saint teaching the Virgin to read. This glass, which might have been associated with an altar to Anne in Hereford Cathedral, is now in Canada. The Hampton Court Chapel also held images of the Annunciation and the Assumption (Figs 15 & 16, overleaf), now in the Burrell Collection, and the cathedral has retained important fifteenth-century glass in the re-set panels in the north transept (Figs 65 & 66), in the panel of fragments in the south aisle (Fig. 69) and in a few fragments in the care of the cathedral library.

There are well-known and documented masters and workshops of the fifteenth century associated with cities such as London, York, Coventry and Oxford. John Thornton of Coventry, who also had a crucial presence in York (where he made the great Apocalypse east

Fig. 15 Chapel of Hampton Court: the Assumption of the Virgin, now in the Burrell Collection (used with the kind permission of the Burrell Collection)

Fig. 16 Chapel of Hampton Court: the Annunciation, now in the Burrell Collection (used with the kind permission of the Burrell Collection)

window of the Minster) cast his influence, if not his hand, over much of England, and all the schemes associated with Bishop Spofford, who was a Yorkshireman, have been attributed to him. The panel of fragments at Presteigne (Inset 19, Fig. 126), which includes several characterful faces, can be associated with York/ Coventry; and at Hentland, where the donor was connected to Spofford, the faces also seem to have Thornton's imprint. Part of the head of an angel with a tiara at Brockhampton by Ross (Fig. 39) might also be included in the York/ Coventry oeuvre. At Ludlow there is an assemblage of important windows by different workshops. The great east window, and other glass in the chancel, may be by painters from York (Fig. 101a) who also worked at Battlefield and Tong (see pp. 212 & 240).

The Creed and Golden windows in the north chapel at Ludlow (Figs 97a–99b) are, perhaps, by another star, John Prudde of Westminster, who glazed the Beauchamp Chapel in Warwick (see the gazetteer entry below). There is an even larger assemblage across the border, at Great Malvern Priory, where glass dating throughout the fifteenth century survives in profusion. Birtsmorton and Little Malvern Priory also display fine fifteenth-century glass – the former being the work of the York glaziers and the latter probably by the Malvern glaziers, Richard Twygge and Thomas Wodshawe. They are probably the painters of the pale, elegant glass at Atcham, which was formerly at Bacton (Fig. 34).

THE EARLY SIXTEENTH CENTURY AND THE REFORMATION

There is a trend in the fifteenth century towards strong line and colour, and the embellishment of figures with jewelled bosses seen, for example, in the north aisle east window at St Weonards (Fig. 131). There is a tendency towards mannered draughtsmanship, caricature, grotesque and the growing influence, and eventual presence, of glass from the Low Countries and Germany. The St Catherine at Old Radnor (Inset 20 & Fig. 120) is a stage in that development which finds its climax in the imported German glass at Coalbrookdale with its Dureresque Apostles (Fig. 46). The saints and angels of c.1500 in the clerestory at Alveley (Fig. 31) have a strong presence achieved by vigorous line drawing and lashings of silver stain, while glass at Munslow, heavily restored by Betton & Evans (which can be dated by the image of John Lloyd, rector 1506–28, Fig. 118), bristles with jewelled bosses.

John Lloyd's images of saints and the Crucifixion were old-fashioned. By his time Flemish talent had flourished at Fairford (worth cycling the 60 miles from Hereford in a head wind) and was at work at King's College, Cambridge. The foreign glaziers used glass enamels and set their characters in landscapes and interiors that ignored the inconvenience of mullions and transoms. John Lloyd's glass is also a late example of a Catholic tradition of images which were about to be declared superstitious and forbidden.

DOWN TO 1700

There is a glass memorial to Blanche Parry at Atcham (Fig. 35) which is dated 1589. It is carefully devoid of any superstitious imagery and is a great rarity for, 'By the time of Elizabeth's death in 1603, the craft had dwindled to a core of glass painters in London and York, fulfilling mainly heraldic commissions and working in quite a different way from their mediaeval predecessors.'[52] The Cecil arms at Walterstone and Hereford Museum (Figs 74a & 74b) with their strident orange colouring, typical of the time, are also from the end of the sixteenth century.

It is against this background of a craft, at least locally, at a low ebb, that makes John Scudamore's glass of the 1630s at Sellack (Fig. 58), Abbey Dore (Figs 24a–24c) and Much Marcle (Fig. 114) seem so startling. There was a significant flowering of religious glass painting nationally as Archbishop Laud's influence was felt, but the 'beauty of holiness' was at that time confined to a relatively small number of buildings, notably college chapels, and was predominantly in the hands of foreign enamellers such as the van Linge family. Their work could have been seen locally in a small panel dated 1629 from Hampton Court Chapel, now in the Victoria and Albert Museum (Fig. 61). John Scudamore's glass is utterly unlike it.

IMPORTED PAINTED GLASS

If glass painting was at a low ebb after the Reformation in England, this was not the case in Europe, and production continued in the sixteenth and seventeenth centuries. The monasteries of the Low Countries, France and Rhineland did have their own reformation, but not until the end of the eighteenth century. This resulted in the sale of large quantities of glass, a significant amount of which came to England by the agency of dealers and glaziers, sometimes changing hands many times before being installed in churches here.

> In the first half of the nineteenth century, a group of clergy from the diocese of Lichfield, together with the glass-painter [John Betton] of Shrewsbury, imported and installed Continental stained glass in Lichfield Cathedral in 1802, the triumvirate of Archdeacon Woodhouse, the Rev. Hugh Owen and the Rev. William Gorsuch Rowland. Rowland design[ed] the installation ... John Betton of Shrewsbury being contracted to repair and install the glass. Owen, Rowland

and Betton [with Evans after 1815][53] were responsible for numerous installations of stained glass in Shrewsbury, particularly the church of St Mary, mainly after 1825.[54]

Shrewsbury is considered in Appendix One. In Herefordshire, the Last Supper at Coalbrookdale and accompanying roundels were part of this trade, and the roundels at Church Stretton and Bromfield were supplied and installed by Betton & Evans. There are two significant collections of roundels in the south of the diocese, at Bishopstone and Llanwarne, and an interesting Netherlandish panel at St Weonards.[55] The most spectacular assembly of foreign glass is at Kentchurch Court where sixteenth-century Swiss panels depicting the arms of the cantons were installed in the 1920s (Fig. 79).

The trade in medieval glass continued into the twentieth century with glazier-dealers acquiring and exporting English medieval glass. The famous (some might say infamous) Roy Grosvenor Thomas and his partner Wilfred Drake were also glaziers and could arrange for the re-leading of windows once valuable glass had been removed. They worked on behalf of collectors, including Sir William Burrell of Glasgow, and had strong connections to America. They were responsible for the dispersal of the glass from Hampton Court Chapel, details of which, along with hundreds of other windows, are listed in their sales books in the library of the Society of Antiquaries.

ICONOGRAPHY

By studying the stories, characters and symbols depicted in the windows of the diocese, we might hope to understand something about the religion of the people of the past; what occupied their devotions and inspired their spiritual lives, and whether the Marches nourished devotion to particular cults. The surviving glass, however, is such a small part of what they made, and has been so brutally diminished by iconoclasm and restoration, that few meaningful conclusions can be drawn. The following is a sketch of the subjects that survive or are known by record (there is a full list of subjects in the Index).

It is difficult to reconstruct a picture of how churches looked and whether there was any sense of programme or didactic scheme among the windows and between the windows, and other decoration, such as wall paintings. Ludlow, as in so many other respects, stands out with its series of Catechism windows, its guild window and its great east window showing the life of St Laurence, which was substantially remade in the restoration by Betton & Evans of Shrewsbury. Munslow was also heavily restored by the firm, but retains a significant assemblage which can be traced back to the eighteenth century in unusually detailed antiquarian records.

There are few surviving Old Testament subjects except in the collections of post-Reformation roundels. The Commandments window at Ludlow (Figs 103a–103c) is of national importance, and so too are the Tree of Jesse windows here and at Madley. In Hereford Cathedral is the fragmentary image of Joseph in the well, a subject also found at Great Malvern, where relatively large amounts of glass have survived, and about a sixth of all panels display Old Testament images.

Bishop Spofford had a deep devotion to St Anne, the mother of the Virgin Mary. She is often shown teaching the Virgin to read, prefiguring the images of the Annunciation, which show Mary holding a book. Mother and daughter appear with the supplicant Spofford at Ross, where her normally shy husband, Joachim, is also found. They are also found on a panel from Hampton Court which is now in a private collection, and in the east window at Ludlow. There was another depiction at Stottesdon, recorded in the eighteenth century but now lost.

The Annunciation was a popular subject, adaptable both to large panels and small tracery lights. There are small fourteenth-century images of the Archangel of the Annunciation at Allensmore and Sarnesfield, and a fifteenth-century Annunciation in tracery lights at St Weonards. A much-restored fourteenth-century panel in the east window at Kingsland shows Mary and Archangel Gabriel face-to-face, but a panel of *c*.1400 in the Burrell Collection, previously at Hampton Court, is distinguished by the way in which the Virgin faces away from God and the archangel in a manner which is more commonly seen in art of the Low Countries, much later in the century. In the clerestory at Alveley, of *c*.1500, the Virgin holds a book, while another lies open on the floor (Fig. 32), but the most beautiful portrayal is in the north chapel at Ludlow (Fig. 98), in a complex fifteenth-century image which symbolises the Incarnation and the nature of God.

In the eighteenth century, Hereford All Saints still retained a series of panels depicting the Annunciation and the Nativity, which have since been lost. There is an early image of the Magi in a medallion at Madley (Fig. 105) and a fifteenth-century trio, possibly by the York/Coventry craftsmen, in the chancel at Ludlow (sIII).[56] They are not met with again until the seventeenth century in glass at Sellack (Fig. 58) and Foy (Fig. 57).

The story continues with two rare depictions of the Slaughter of the Innocents. At Ledbury (Fig. 90b) glass of *c*.1300 depicts the Slaughter, and Flight into Egypt, while at Wormbridge there is a later fourteenth-century Slaughter (Fig. 149). The Virgin and infant Christ are seen together in a Madley medallion of the Presentation in the Temple (Fig. 105) and in several beautiful panels at Eaton Bishop (Fig 1), Wormbridge (Fig. 148), Ullingswick (Fig. 142), Atcham (Fig. 34) and the north transept of the cathedral (Fig. 66). Dingley recorded a fine image of the Virgin and Child in the old library at the cathedral, which was demolished in 1737 (Fig. 17).

Fig. 17 Hereford Cathedral old library: Dingley's sketch of the Virgin and Child

The New Testament narrative is lost until the Last Supper, depicted touchingly with John reclining on Christ's breast in a Madley medallion (Fig. 105). In another (much-restored) early medallion in the cathedral (Fig. 70a), Christ carries the Cross. That medallion is accompanied by other Passion scenes, the Crucifixion and the Empty Tomb (also seen at Madley). F.C. Morgan[57] described the green cross in the Hereford medallions as 'an unusual feature'; however, if there is a distinctly local (but not unique) characteristic of the Crucifix, it is Christ on a green Cross.

There are 20 surviving Crucifixions, most of which are of the early fourteenth century and earlier, and most of which follow, icon-like, a pattern of the Christ describing a Y with his arms and a reversed S with his body. His head droops to the observer's left and his knees point to the same side. The green cross (or *arbor vitae*) is a symbolic link to the Tree of Life in Eden, which stands for eternal life. It is found in manuscripts from an early date and, though pale, the Crucifix on the Mappa Mundi is also green.

There are three Crucifixions at Eaton Bishop, two of which have latticed backgrounds (also found at Mamble in Worcestershire). The Crucifixion in the east window, in which the Virgin and St John are also shown, is particularly beautiful (Fig. 55). A later fourteenth-century panel at Morville (Fig. 113), which is executed entirely in silver stain, carefully retains the form of the earlier images, and it is only the much later and heavily-restored pictures at Munslow and St Weonards which show a straight-bodied Christ. The seventeenth-century version at Sellack (copied at Foy) goes back to the fourteenth-century form, but at Sellack there is also a beautiful fifteenth-century version of the 'Throne of Mercy' in which the seated Father holds the crucified Son (Fig. 135).

The only surviving image of the Ascension is in the extravagant seventeenth-century east window at Abbey Dore (Fig. 27a), but there are several versions of the risen Christ in other guises, as the Man of Sorrows displaying his wounds (six versions), and as Christ in Majesty (six versions). The image of sorrow is deliberately harrowing, and nowhere more so than at St Weonards (Fig. 18), in a late fifteenth-century panel. Earlier representations at Eaton Bishop and Kingsland are less gory. Christ in Glory is splendid in the cathedral, surrounded by the symbols of the

The Assumption from Hampton Court is now in the Burrell Collection (Fig. 15), but Coronations survive at Donington (Fig. 51), Kingsland (Fig. 81d) and Richards Castle (Figs 127a & 127b). The east window at Aston Botterell still had part of a picture of the radiant, crowned Virgin surrounded by angels when William Mytton visited in c.1730.

The Apostles are found together with their attributes in the fifteenth-century Creed window at Ludlow (Figs 99a & 99b). Creed windows existed at Hampton Court (in glass formerly in the cathedral or Leominster Priory and now exported to America) and in lost glass in the north chapel at Dilwyn. There are few images of Apostles elsewhere, but St John the Evangelist was the subject of special regard and survives in several places. He was the patron of the Palmers' Guild in Ludlow and appears in the east window of their chapel. He is also the subject of much earlier medallions at Madley, where a unique representation of his death is found (Fig. 105). There is a beautiful early fourteenth-century image at Cound (Fig. 47), and he stands with Mary at Atcham (Fig. 34) and Munslow (where he is represented three times in different windows). He was a favourite of his namesake John Scudamore and appears in the viscount's windows at Abbey Dore (Figs 24a–24c) and Sellack (Fig. 58).

Fig. 18 St Weonards: the Man of Sorrows (nIII)

Evangelists (Fig. 70a), and on a smaller scale at Brinsop (Fig. 38), blessing with his right hand and holding the *Orbis Terrarum* globe in his left.

Images of the Trinity are scarce. There is only one Trinity shield (nV at Munslow) and, other than the Throne of Mercy at Sellack noted above, only one attempt at illustrating the Trinity in the magnificent work of a fifteenth-century imagination in the north chapel at Ludlow (nVIII, Fig. 98). The east window at Atcham, with glass from Bacton, includes a figure of God from a Trinity, adapted by the restorer to stand as Christ.

The Virgin Mary has fared a little better, surviving in scenes of the Crucifixion, the visit of the Magi and the Presentation noted above.

Among the other 30 or so saints, St Catherine was by far the most popular. Devotion to her flourished in the later Middle Ages and this is reflected in the surviving glass, which is mostly of the fifteenth century. Her images at Old Radnor (Fig. 120) and St Weonards (Fig. 131) are most striking and include all her attributes – crown, sword and wheel. Exquisitely beautiful, crowned heads at Tarrington (Fig. 139) and Sarnesfield are probably intended to be St Catherine. John the Baptist figures in a similar

Fig. 19 Ludlow: the Nine Orders of Angels in the chancel (nIII)

number of churches and is seen, for example, with his mother in a small fifteenth-century image in the cathedral north transept (Fig. 65).

There are some memorable images of popular English saints. The fourteenth-century Credenhill image of Thomas Cantilupe and Thomas Becket (Fig. 5) standing side by side is well known. Cantilupe is seen in the mid fifteenth-century east window at Ross (Fig. 129) and *c*.1500 panel at Munslow (nIV). Becket appears in tracery lights at Wormbridge and a much-restored fourteenth-century window in the north aisle of the cathedral. Perhaps the most famous local images of England's saints are the fourteenth-century St George at Brinsop (Fig. 37) – an utterly satisfying mail-clad warrior decorated with the red cross on shield, surcoat, and banner – and the benign, bearded Edward the Confessor in the Palmers' Chapel window at Ludlow (Fig. 100).

The company of heaven includes the angels. These are a gift to the glass painter, and silver stain might have been invented just to display their feathery luminance. The substantially renewed fourteenth-century east window at Kingsland is a great rarity in that it shows all four Archangels – Michael, Gabriel, Raphael and Uriel. Gabriel and Michael are beautifully drawn at Eaton Bishop (cover picture). Michael, holding scales, is in his guise as the Judge of Souls, in which he also appears at Ledbury (Fig. 88). Later in the Middle Ages the idea that there were nine orders of angels gained credence. Angels were organised into three hierarchies:[58] at the top, the seraphim, six-winged and burning red; and in the lower tier, archangels and angels. The late fifteenth-century tracery of a chancel window at Ludlow (Fig. 19) attempts to distinguish them, but a journey to Great Malvern Priory is required to see them full-size. There are many angel images, but the cherubim, holding Instruments of the Passion in the tracery lights of a window that lit an altar dedicated to the Holy Rode at Weobley, stand out with their peacock wings and their feathered bodies (Fig. 144). The thurifers at Dilwyn (Fig. 50) and Ledbury (Fig. 89) are charming, but the most arresting angelic image is Gabriel in the Guild Chapel at Ludlow (nVIII, Fig. 98).

HERALDRY

Arms are an important key to understanding patronage and they can often be quite accurately dated because they evolve with different generations and alliances. Shields of arms were placed in windows, often in the tracery lights, for several reasons. They might represent donors of the window, and that is probably true of most of the 85 shields which only appear once in the survey. The de Frenes of Moccas are a good example of this (Figs 110 & 111). It was 'their' church, it served as a mausoleum, and they must have paid for the extravagant display of their arms in fourteenth-century windows made by the Madley Master.

When Richard Symonds visited Madley in the seventeenth century, the fourteenth-century arms of the Deanery (now lost) were in a south window of the chancel, to record the investment of the Dean and Chapter in a building under their patronage. The arms of England, Warrene and Bohun remain there (Fig. 104), but these powerful families were not necessarily donors; rather, these arms were probably placed out of respect or fealty for the established social and political order of their time.

Several different motives are also illustrated by three shields of the Grandisons. At Ledbury, the arms of the Grandisons in the chapel of the Hospital of St Katherine mark their patronage.

Their arms, now lost, were also recorded in the north transept at Pembridge, where their only known association with the church was the marriage of Sir Peter de Grandison to Blanche, the daughter of Roger de Mortimer IV and Joan de Geneville, not long before 10 June 1330. There was another lost shield in the south transept[59] of the cathedral, where it was among the arms of other great local families, which might suggest patronage or a roll-call of the body politic.

ICONOCLASM

When John Price wrote about Leominster Priory towards the end of the eighteenth century, he said,

> The windows were of painted glass, some brilliant remains of which are to be seen at this time about the town, which may have given the church the gloomy appearance Leland describes.[60]

Leominster had a reputation as 'Little Geneva' and so it is not surprising that iconoclasm bit deeply there. The formal expression of iconoclasm, the published rules and orders of the Reformation[61] and Commonwealth,[62] are well-known, and their effect can be read in churchwardens' accounts, such as Ludlow's in the sixteenth century.[63] The focus of the sixteenth-century injunctions was the prevention of idolatry and the prohibition of images which were the subject of pilgrimage, offerings and adoration such as kissing. At least once a quarter, ministers were required to preach on the Scriptures and against the fantasies of the adoration of idols and pilgrimage. Ministers and parishioners were exhorted to remove and destroy images, and monuments that were accessories to idolatry. The Parliamentary

Ordinances of the following century required the removal of images whether or not they were used for idolatry, and in 1644 became even more hostile to stained glass by the addition of angels to the lists of images which were to be destroyed:

> That all Representations of any of the Persons of the Trinity, or of any Angel or Saint, in or about any Cathedral, Collegiate or Parish Church, or Chappel, or in any open place within this Kingdome, shall be taken away, defaced, and utterly demolished; And that no such shall hereafter be set up …

Robert Harley of Brampton Bryan headed the parliamentary committee for the destruction of superstitious images:

> Having been a member of the committee which drew up the order against innovations in September 1641, Harley used the parliamentary recess which followed to ensure that it was carried out in the parishes neighbouring his estate at Brampton Bryan. This involved the removal of the church cross at Wigmore, and the breaking of windows at Leintwardine … (where) the offensive windows were first demolished, then the glass 'broke small with a hammer' and thrown into the River Teme, allegedly 'in imitation of King Asa 2 Chronicles 15:16: who threw the images Into the Brook Kidron.'[64]

Despite such implacable fervour, medieval glass survives in almost 100 churches in the diocese – and in some places, such as Ludlow, Eaton Bishop and Madley, a great deal remained after the noise of war had subsided. It seems probable that the iconoclasms were not as utterly devastating as is sometimes thought, and that a good deal of the loss we ascribe to iconoclasts came about later. The Restoration was more than 350 years ago, and leaded glass requires regular maintenance. Most windows would have needed re-leading at least twice in that time, and there were long periods when money and skills were in short supply, and there was no inclination to repair weathered Virgins.

Trying to explain how 'superstitious' glass survived is, perhaps, more interesting than trying to tot up what was lost. Some high-profile targets of iconoclasm, such as roods, could not easily be ignored. A rood could also be removed at little or no cost, and might even be sold.[65] The powerful factor encouraging the retention of glass was the simple fact that the destruction of images in glass was both costly and inconvenient. A Crucifix or saint in glass would leave a hole which needed to be made good, and the glass removed was unlikely to have monetary value. This alone must have discouraged compliance beyond defacement, but where a church – particularly one backed by an important figure or body – chose to resist (as was probably the case in the 'cavalier stronghold' of Ludlow)[66] they might well be successful.

The survival of several Crucifixes (including three in Eaton Bishop Church) points to another way in which images survived – by being placed out of reach. The cathedral seems to be a common factor in some of these and might have collected such images, distributing them to Allensmore, Thruxton and Eaton Bishop in less troubled times.

CARE AND RESTORATION

Churchwardens were not universally neglectful of windows after the Reformation. In 1575 the Ludlow accounts record annual payments of '*XXs*' (20 shillings or £1) to Thomas Season for 'mending the glass.'[67] In 1607, the same accounts record the substantial payment of '*XXXVij.s*' (37 shillings or £1.85) to Mr Bonde for 'puttinge the glase in order and soe keepinge them the whole yeare'. Bond also received annual payments, increased several times when it was 'a great wyndye yere'. Bond was a plumber and he and his son Edward appear in the accounts down to 1662–63.[68] In 1624–25, there is an unusual record of repairs to windows being enforced by a consistory court. The wardens had to appear first to explain why the previous wardens had erroneously stated that repairs had been done, and secondly to get a certificate to say that they had been done.

Wherever churchwardens' accounts survive from the seventeenth and eighteenth centuries, they show that money was regularly spent on glazing. In the villages, the sums often appear modest and, in most places, keeping the windows weatherproof was probably done by parishioners. In the towns, the maintenance of bells was always the greatest expenditure, but glazing usually comes second, and substantial reglazing projects are not unheard of. In a few cases – for example the cathedral, Ludlow and Abbey Dore – a glazier was retained on an annual basis (an account of the maintenance of the cathedral glass is given in the following gazetteer).

On a smaller scale, a similar story is told at Abbey Dore, where the churchwardens' accounts for the late seventeenth and eighteenth centuries are sketchy but illustrate an exceptional year in 1784 when Richard Powall (probably *Powell*, who worked at the cathedral 1784–92) received three payments.[69] In 1838 the Dore churchwardens made an agreement in the sum of 20s annually (the same sum paid to Bond in Ludlow in the seventeenth century) with William Holman, 'Painter & Glazier', which is the only written record of such an agreement found in this survey. Elsewhere, such agreements can be inferred from the regular employment of some glaziers for the same annual payment, and occasionally from a note referring to an agreement in the accounts. At Abbey Dore, the wardens were to provide the support of a mason for pointing, and Holman's duties did not include the repair of deliberate damage. The subsequent accounts record the annual payment down to 1853 when Mr Bosworth took over the contract.[70]

The picture that emerges is not one of wilful neglect, but of the windows of the cathedral and churches in the care of tradespeople who, almost certainly, had no conservation intent and were often employed to do far less than was required. The result was obvious in the great east window at Ludlow, which, prior to its restoration, was described as, 'particularly defaced and wantonly broken.'[71]

In 1830, Betton & Evans of Shrewsbury were engaged to repair the window, and they are the first and, in their subsequent impact on the windows of the diocese, the most important of the nineteenth-century glass painters. They were involved in the importation of glass from Europe, and they worked on important medieval glass in several churches. Sarah Brown has written about Betton & Evans,

> Much work remains to be done on Betton & Evans, but it is hard to escape the conclusion that the growing dominance in the company of the talented draughtsman and glass painter David Evans (1793–1861), who became a partner in 1815, had a transformative effect on the company's practice, especially after Betton's retirement in 1824. The almost total replacement of medieval glass at Winchester College seemed like the only way of satisfying

the college's expectation for legible, brilliant, and translucent windows. However, the company's methodology would have been unthinkable, and indeed unachievable, without a mastery of glass painting and firing techniques, and would have been judged a failure without Evans's skills as a copyist.[72]

Restoration by replacement, especially of heads,[73] was the consequence of increasing skill in painting at a time when techniques for repair and cleaning were undeveloped. New glass became cheaper with the removal of taxes, and old glass became valuable as antiquarian interest developed, encouraging the replacement of old glass with new. These processes are illustrated by the head of St Laurence, which Mytton sketched in the east window of Ludlow church (Fig. 155b). The head is now in Battlefield, and that in Ludlow is a copy. A further head is illustrated in Fig. 155d, which was removed to Sundorne Castle. At Munslow, Mytton recorded several partial and complete figures, including a donor and the Archangel Michael, which were lost in the restoration by Betton & Evans.[74]

Such practices were bound to spark a reaction, and the movement towards conservation rather than restoration began with Charles Winston, who published a seminal paper in 1844:[75]

> Whenever a glass painting, although in other respects perfect, appears to bag, or bulge out in places, that is a symptom that its leading requires reparation or renewal. If the latter, the restoration ought to be most carefully conducted. The pieces of glass of which it is composed should be retained in their original positions, and the forms of the ancient lead-work preserved as much as possible. When the work is complicated, it is better to have it re-leaded by a regular glass painter, than to trust it to the tender mercies of an ignorant glazier; but even this is better than to suffer it to fall to pieces without an effort to save it. If the painting should be already much shattered, no time ought to be lost in repairing or renewing the leads, and in replacing the missing pieces with new glass. And here we condemn the practice of what is called restoring an ancient glass painting, by supplying its defects with modern painted glass. It may be allowable, in some cases, to fill the place of what must have been plain colour with a corresponding plain piece of coloured glass; or even perhaps to restore a portion of ornament, or other matter, where sufficient authority exists for the restoration; but in all other cases, it is safest to make up the deficiency with a piece of plain white glass, slightly dulled.[76]

Later schemes of reglazing embraced these principles to differing degrees. The work undertaken in 1864 at the cathedral by William Warrington[77] seems to have preserved medieval glass, but Warrington 'restored' faces and other parts of the figures. There was extensive reglazing of the east window of the north aisle of St Weonards *c*.1870 according to the records of Thomas Baillie, which include 'before' photographs.[78] In 1912, John Matthews noted in the sixth volume of Duncumb's *Collections*,

> Thomas Blount ... has left interesting particulars concerning the ancient stained glass of this church. A considerable portion of the old glass had escaped Reformation and Revolution, but most of what then survived has since been swept away by the ravages of Restoration.[79]

Below the tracery lights, little old glass remains, but parts of the figures in the upper part of the window can be dated to 1521 and form an important corpus of work of the period. The criticism is probably harsh. The principal figures are restored but the window was in poor condition before the work was undertaken, and to follow Winston's principle of plain glass would have left highly fragmentary images. The same company reglazed the east window at Ross at about the same time. David O'Connor described this as,

> ... extremely skilful, producing a window which was not only aesthetically pleasing but looked authentic. So good is the copying, reinforced by a certain amount of antiquating with paint to suggest corrosion, that careful examination of both sides is needed to establish the authenticity of every piece.[80]

This approach might be called 'conservative restoration', making every effort to preserve the smallest fragment of medieval glass, but also making a coherent picture by painting new glass to imitate old.

About 50 years later, in 1927, Walter Tower of Kempe & Co. corresponded with the antiquary George Marshall concerning the re-leading of the east window at Eaton Bishop. It is a revealing correspondence which shows that the conservation ideals of Winston had become common good practice almost a century after his *Archaeological Journal* paper.

David King of Norwich, probably the foremost conservator of his time, re-leaded the window in 1967 and remarked,

As stated in my earlier letter Mr. Walter Tower's 1928 rearrangement of the glass was most carefully worked out, the donor panels were reset at the base of the window and the borders balanced, with some new painted glass. The South window glass was considerably adjusted but the false position of the rood panels, designed for the 3-light north window, with the crucifixion between Saint John and the Virgin was retained.[81]

UNFOUND AND UNSEEN

The antiquarian records of Herefordshire include several churches where small amounts of glass were noted, which have not been included in the following gazetteer. William Mytton's notes include a further 40 churches in the Shropshire part of the diocese with shields of arms or fragments which are no longer in place, and which are not included here.

The Royal Commission recorded medieval glass in two houses which were not visited because of the Coronavirus restrictions, or failure to get permission. At Wharton Bank (un-listed) near Leominster, fragments from Ford Church were in place in *c*.1933; and at the Old Vicarage, Much Dewchurch (listed Grade-II) the Commission also reported unspecified fragments.

The Commission reported fragments of glass in churches at Birley, Garway, Llangarron, Mathon and Norton Canon, all of which were visited, but the glass was not found.

The chancel of Abbey Dore, showing Scudamore's east window (1634)

PART TWO

Gazetteer of Churches in Herefordshire and the Diocese of Hereford

ABBEY DORE
St Mary (SO 3871 2872, HR2 0AA)

The abbey was founded in 1174 for Cistercians from Morimond, and substantially built in two campaigns between *c.*1175–80 and *c.*1210–20, although not consecrated until 1275.[82]

Richard Marks considered the Cistercian glass to be important:

> Of all the major religious orders the Cistercians suffered the most severe losses in buildings and furnishings during the Dissolution … of more than 100 Cistercian houses … only one, Abbey Dore, retains any medieval glazing in its windows. For the rest, we have to rely on fragments found in excavations …[83]

The abbey was suppressed in 1537 and, significantly for the later history of the glass, the Crown receiver was John Scudamore (d.1571).[84] Most of the claustral buildings and the nave were demolished, leaving the crossing and chancel with its ambulatory to serve as the parish church. Ownership of the buildings and tythes eventually passed to John, 1st Viscount, Scudamore (d.1671). He was an Oxford graduate and High-Church protégé of Archbishop William Laud who made the young viscount uncomfortable about the profit his family had made from their acquisitions at the Dissolution. With Laud's encouragement the viscount repaired the remaining chancel and transepts of Abbey Dore and several other Herefordshire churches, and restored tithes and property to them (see Sellack and Holme Lacy). Scudamore's repair work at Dore, involving the famous carpenter/ architect John Abel, is well-documented from surviving contracts and accounts – except for the glazing and the screen. Finding the name of the glazier of Scudamore's great east window (dated 1634) would be a great prize.

For the later history of the stained glass, the churchwardens' accounts for the late seventeenth and eighteenth centuries are sketchy, but there was an exceptional year in 1784 when Richard Powall (spelt thus but probably the Richard Powell who worked at Hereford Cathedral) received three payments.[85]

1784: January fifteenth
Pd Richard Powall Glazier for
   repairing church windows   £3.17s.4d
Pd Richard Powall's bill for
   glazeing 2 years before   10s.6d

> *November 8th*
> Pd the Glazier's bill for glazing
> the church windows and
> Repairing the lead of the do.   £3.4s.7d

In the next century, as with several other churches in this survey, the repair of the glazing was put on a regular basis. In 1838 the churchwardens made an agreement in the sum of twenty shillings (£1) annually with William Holman, painter and glazier. Elsewhere, such agreements can be inferred from the regular employment of some glaziers, and occasionally from a note in the accounts referring to an agreement, but the Abbey Dore accounts have the only surviving written agreement in this survey.

There were two interesting conditions: the wardens were to provide a mason for pointing, and Holman's contract excluded the repair of deliberate damage. The subsequent accounts record Holman's payments down to 1853 when Mr Bosworth took over the contract.[86]

The architect Roland Paul said that there was no pre-seventeenth-century glass to be seen when restoration was started under his supervision in 1903. Paul, a scholarly architect, found many glass fragments under the ambulatory floors:[87]

> More medieval glass than has been rediscovered from any other Cistercian site in Britain. This was carefully sorted into 3 categories: early grisaille and later grisaille, the so called grey glass, and coloured and figured glass ... the best preserved pieces were reset in the south east chapel.[88]

South choir aisle: window sVII

This holds the oldest glass. During the thirteenth and fourteenth centuries, Cistercian rules against embellishment were increasingly disregarded. This can be seen in the wealth of beautiful carved decoration that survives at Abbey Dore, and in the glass fragments in the south-east chapel, which speak of sumptuous glazing employing glaziers of importance. At an earlier date, the rule against pictorial or brightly-coloured glass, led to the development of sophisticated patterns formed with tinted glass and painted leaf scrolls.

Roland Paul gathered the earliest grisaille glass into this window and created a panel which Richard Marks described as containing 'two rows of white glass with scale-like pattern formed by concentric overlapping semicircles.'[89] The pattern was more likely to be from Paul's mind than from the minds of the early monks and their glazier, as Richard Marks recognised:

> There are several problems with the grisaille glass. It was not in situ, for the pieces revealed clear signs of de-vitrification through contact with the soil. The glass was placed in this window around 1904 [and] as the leading was carried out at this time even the ornamental arrangement is open to doubt. Furthermore, the de-vitrification was so far advanced as to make it impossible to establish from an on-site examination whether there was originally any painted decoration. The date is equally uncertain ... [and] could ... have been made at any time between 1180 and the middle of the thirteenth century.[90]

The present window contains fragments from Roland Paul's window, but in a regrettably clumsy re-leading in 1973 his design was utterly disregarded.[91] This window now contains three roundels with a few dots of plain colour and a predominance of grey glass, some fragments of which have waterleaf drawing. This type of stylised foliage, 'ending in a trefoil, on long and curling stems and set against cross-hatched grounds', was found in excavations at the Cistercian house of Rievaulx.[92]

South-east chapel windows (sVIII) (east) & (sIX) (south) (Figs 20–23)

At the top of window sVIII, almost hidden by the ferramenta, is the figure of a Cistercian monk wearing a white habit (Fig. 20). Marks notes that the glass at Merevale 'provides firm evidence that at least from the middle of the fourteenth century lay people were giving stained glass to Cistercian houses.'[93] Joe Hillaby describes how Abbot Straddell established strong connections with the most important families in the Marches and subverted Cistercian prohibitions on sepulture and the accumulation of churches.[94] It therefore seems likely that some of the surviving glass was commissioned by prominent lay-people.

Below the white monk is a group of four small pieces drawn with silver stain. Two are quarries showing a pear and a strawberry(?) fruit, while the others, from the lobes of a quatrefoil, show the tetramorphic symbols of Mark (lion) and Luke (ox). About halfway down the window is a composite figure wearing vestments. The hands are tucked into the breast of the robe. Could these be the hands of Abbot Richard Straddell (d.1346) who, far from being cloistered in ascetic confinement, walked on the stage of international diplomacy? The head of this composite figure is a woman's, wearing a coif (Fig. 21). She is in the International Style and is contemporary with the quarries at the base of window sIX.

At the top of window sIX (Fig. 22, overleaf) are the remains of a finely-drawn, feathered angel holding the chain of a thurible (Fig. 23, overleaf). Around the angel are three heads which are probably of Abbot Straddell's time (1305–46).

LEFT:
Fig. 20 Abbey Dore: south chapel. A white-robed Cistercian possibly Abbot Straddell (abbot 1305–46) (sVIII)

BELOW:
Fig. 21 Abbey Dore: south chapel. At the centre, the coif-capped head of a woman (sVIII)

LEFT: **Fig. 22** Abbey Dore: south chapel (sIX)
ABOVE: **Fig. 23** Abbey Dore: south chapel (sIX), detail of upper part of window

These are by the master who worked at Madley and Ludlow.

Roland Paul's glazier tried to make a coherent form for the mitred figure: the body of the figure is made of rich blue and red fragments of diapering and drapery; the belt is a quatrefoil border, and the single hand holds an *Orbis Terrarum*,[95] normally seen in the hand of Christ or God.[96] The robes are formed with rich brown fragments and the 'feet' comprise fragments on a black and white geometrical pattern of paving. The lowest panel has quarries of three types, one of which, in the form of an eight-point star, is found in the work in the International Style at the cathedral and at Hampton Court.

CHANCEL EAST WINDOW (I) (Figs 24a–27a)
The composition is a simple one: in the central light is the Ascension surmounted by Moses and the Baptist. The two side-lights have two tiers of figures which are related to each other side-to-side. In the lower tier are the four Disciples who head the list of Disciples in Matthew 10.2. In the upper tier are the four Evangelists each holding an inscribed book, and each accompanied by his tetramorphic symbol.

On the left of the lowest tier, the figures of St Peter and St Andrew stand bare-footed on a chequerboard floor holding books and their familiar attributes (keys and a saltire cross).[97] On the right of the lowest tier are the figures of St James and St John bearing books and their attributes (the pilgrim staff and chalice). Each Apostle has a caption describing his death.[98] The date 1634 appears below the figures.

On the left of the upper tier, are the figures of Matthew and Mark (Fig. 25, overleaf) holding their Gospels and pens. Matthew is distinguished by an angel at his left shoulder while Mark has a lion. Both figures have gold nimbi. The books have inscriptions.[99]

On the right of the upper tier are the figures of Luke and John, which are the most damaged of the ten figures in the window. Luke is only identified by his name given at the base of the panel. John can still be identified by the eagle on his right shoulder. His head has been lost but the book, pen and inscription remain.[100] Among the fragments of medieval glass used to repair the panel are part of a harpist and a head of Christ crowned with thorns.

Figs 24a–24c: Abbey Dore: Viscount John Scudamore's great east window of 1634 (I)
Fig. 24a: the central light (RIGHT)
Figs 24b & 24c the two flanking lights (OVERLEAF)

Fig. 24b

Fig. 24c

Fig. 25 Abbey Dore: the figure of St Mark in Viscount John Scudamore's great east window

At the centre of the window is the Ascension (Fig. 27a, overleaf). It is starkly different from the rest of the window; a Renaissance Christ in a Gothic gathering. Above are the figures of Moses and John the Baptist, both labelled.[101] Moses holds a rod and John a book on which the Paschal Lamb and flag are displayed. Between John's feet is the head of a beast, probably a camel.

The window was installed during Viscount John Scudamore's restoration of the Abbey. The glass comes from the same hand as the east window at Sellack (Fig. 58), which is associated with John Scudamore and dated 1630,[102] and a Royal Arms at Much Marcle (1628–35) (Fig. 114) with which John Scudamore can also be connected. The glass is conspicuously distinct from the general tenor of glass-painting at this time, which is better represented by Abraham van Linge's 'Deposition' of 1639, commissioned by another Herefordshire noble for the chapel of Hampton Court (Fig. 61).

The influences on Scudamore are difficult to untangle.[103] Joe Hillaby points to the friendship between John Scudamore and William Laud, and the likelihood that he was familiar with windows installed in Oxford college chapels in the early seventeenth century. However, these Oxford windows could only have influenced in a general sense, showing that stained glass could enhance the setting of worship ('the beauty of holiness' propounded by Laud) and more particularly the setting of the altar of a church or chapel. The singular form and content of the Dore windows, with their figures in niches, are backwards-looking and out of kilter with Oxford windows of the time, which display painterly figures and scenes spreading across whole windows regardless of their mullions and transoms.

There is a possibility that John Scudamore was himself involved in their making. Matthew Gibson, writing about Abbey Dore in 1727 says, 'The fine East-window, over the Communion Table, was made by the Lord Scudamore; and the Glass so painted by him, as I have been told, at the expense of one hundred pounds.'[104]

It is hard to imagine the viscount making the windows with his own hands,[105] but there is another connection between him and the design in the form of a vidimus in the Scudamore papers in the Hereford Library (Fig. 26, overleaf).[106] The vidimus is accompanied by a drawing of the tracery of a window in Perpendicular style;[107] however, none of the handwriting can be matched with known signatures of John Scudamore.[108] It also seems that the drawing of the vidimus and the glass, even allowing for the fact that a vidimus would probably be sketchier than the finished product, are by different hands. Richard Marks suggests that, by this time, glass-painting and assembly became separate from design. An artist, or an

Fig. 26 Abbey Dore: vidimus for Viscount Scudamore's great east window (by permission of Herefordshire Libraries)

artist's work in the form of a print,[109] would be employed to produce a vidimus.[110] The vidimus in Fig. 26 seems to be a commission to be copied, but the possibility of a glazier-viscount is still difficult to accept.

There were glaziers capable of large projects in the early seventeenth century, as can be seen in the Tewkesbury accounts for 1611–22 when John Paynter was paid for 'glassinge the upper windows one [on] both sides of the churche.'[111] Two local possibilities are James Jaggard, who worked at the cathedral between 1617 and 1666, and Thomas Morgan who worked at the cathedral and at Madley between 1613 and 1626. A further possibility, which resonates with the singular character of this glass, is that it was made by the Huguenots who had glassworks at St Weonards and Newent.[112]

The substantial east window of Wadham College, of 1622, employing the foremost glazier of the time, Bernard van Linge, cost £113. It is a large work of enormous complexity, which makes it difficult to accept that the east window at Dore cost the £100 suggested by Gibson, especially if it were a 'DIY' project. The £100 figure is probably sufficient for the reglazing of the whole church, relative to John Paynter's charges at Tewkesbury.

There are many differences between the vidimus and the finished glass. The saints and Old Testament figures are in the positions shown in the vidimus, but one of the most striking differences is the introduction in the window of border- and canopy-work such that the full-length figures stand in niches in the medieval fashion not seen in the early seventeenth-century work in Oxford and elsewhere. The niches left no room for the angels at the tops of the side lights. The other obvious difference (as noted above) is the treatment of the Ascension, which, in the vidimus, takes the traditional form of the bereft Disciples looking up at Christ's cloud-wreathed feet, yet is given a contemporary expression in the glass.

Joe Hillaby suggests that the composition of the window was influenced by a brand of Laudianism tempered by the prevailing spirit of the day, which was against Romish and superstitious pictures.[113] He points to the fact that the Virgin is absent from the Ascension;[114] that John's cup is without the usual dragon or Devil; and that James is denied his full panoply of pilgrim symbols.

However, the church had extreme Laudian furnishings including a mensa, an image of the five wounds of Christ on the screen and an image of the Crucifixion behind the altar,[115] and the slightly earlier window at Sellack had no such reserve, containing both the Virgin and the Crucifixion.

Fig. 27a Abbey Dore: the Ascension in the central light of Viscount John Scudamore's great east window (I)

Fig. 27b *The Ascension* by Egbert van Panderen (1581–1637) published in Haarlem by Theodore Galle (1571–1633)

The green *arbor vitae* Crucifix at Sellack is a medieval trope found at Eaton Bishop, a church John Scudamore would have known; and the framework of borders and niches there might also have influenced the composition of the Abbey Dore window. Sellack is an exploration, both in terms of theology and drawing (Fig. 58), and the framework of borders and canopies is simpler than that at Dore. There is also an attempt at shading and flesh tones in the figure of St John at Sellack, which seems to have been abandoned for the black line-drawing on white glass used throughout the Dore window (except for the image of Christ).

The Abbey Dore Ascension (Fig. 27a) abandons the Gothic style of the rest of the window and embraces the Renaissance. The two arches over the panels suggest that the original bipartite design was commenced, but at some point (possibly after the window was complete) it was changed. Perhaps that change was the result of the time John Scudamore spent as ambassador in Paris between 1635 and 1639, where he would have been exposed to the full blast of French and Italian art. He was a close friend of Viscount Basil Fielding, the English ambassador to northern Italy, and he may well have visited Brescia and seen – or seen copies of – the Ascension altar of Bernardino Gaudino (1587–1651), which bears close comparison with the Dore picture. However, inspiration probably originated closer to home, in the plentiful engravings circulating from London and Continental publishing houses.

The Dore window has a good deal of text, while Sellack only bears its date and the initials 'RS'. The Dore Evangelists have verses in the books they hold, which follows a fashion of the time for verses at the foot of images in engravings of the Evangelists. These paeans are not fine poetry and appear to be the work of the engravers. The Dore verses can be found in engravings of the Evangelists by the publisher William Peake of Holborn.[116] William Peake was associated with Archbishop Laud, and produced the 'Archbishops Bible' of 1633, packed with 'superstitious' imagery, which was extremely controversial when it was published. It became damning evidence at Laud's trial, which led to his execution in 1645.[117]

The Peakes' engravings were widely distributed. They were bound or pasted into Bibles and used, for example, by the Little Gidding community in their hand-made concordances. In the concordance of the Acts of the Apostles in the British Library is an image of the Ascension which is undoubtedly the model for the figure of Christ in the Dore window.[118] It is part of an Ascension by Egbert van Panderen (1581–1637) published in Haarlem by Theodore Galle (1571–1633) (Fig. 27b).[119] George Henderson suggests that a publisher, Francis Ash,

> … was a papistical focus of activity in picture Bibles in the West Country before 1642, probably a good while before 1642, involving the use of Peake's prints and a large importation by a clever active trader of other prints …

Perhaps Ash was the contact between Scudamore and the world of London publishers.

EAST AMBULATORY WINDOW (SIII)
The panel of *c*.1600 depicts the 'arms of Carwarden with two wild-men and some mantling.'[120] The arms are: *sable a staff-sling bendwise between two pheons argent*.[121] Wild-men were introduced into heraldry as supporters in the fourteenth century and were popular in the succeeding centuries.

WEST WALL, SOUTH WINDOW (SXII)
The border contains a few pieces of seventeenth-century glass.

ACONBURY
ST JOHN THE BAPTIST (SO 5167 3348, HR2 6PQ)

The church was originally the chapel of a small nunnery[122] dating, mostly, from the second half of the thirteenth century. George Gilbert Scott oversaw the restoration of the church 1862–63.[123] The report of the reopening of the church in the *Hereford Times* in June 1863 suggests that both two-light windows on the north side had old

Fig. 28 Aconbury: quatrefoil using glass of c.1270 (nIII)

glass, and that they had been re-leaded as part of Scott's scheme.

The surviving early glass is in the middle window on the north side, and consists of two quatrefoils and three other small panels of grisaille glass from *c*.1270 (Fig. 28). Although little glass survives, and not in situ, this glass has great significance because of its relatively early date, and because it is seen in combination with an extensive wall-painting scheme also of the thirteenth century.

The two matching quatrefoils with curling waterleaf decoration terminating in a trefoil and a dot, resemble grisaille glass of *c*.1275 at Stanton Harcourt (Oxon) and Salisbury Cathedral.[124]

ALBERBURY
St Michael and All Angels
(SJ 3586 1444, SY5 9AH)

The south aisle Loton Chapel, built *c*.1330, has some fourteenth-century glass in the tracery of the south-east window (sV). In the upper light a king and a queen face each other. This image has been described as the Coronation of the Virgin,[125] but neither figure is nimbed. However, it is possible that the figures are not in situ and the halos have been lost. The figures are in a conservative style with pot metal garments and simple line-drawing of the features without shading (see Richards Castle, Figs 7, 127a & 127b). The hair and crowns are painted in silver stain, which gives these figures a strong resemblance to some at Stanford-on-Avon where the early use of silver stain can be dated to 1320–30.

In two trefoil lights below the Coronation (Fig. 29a illustrates one of them) are censing angels against backgrounds of oak leaf and acorn grisaille.

The main lights are filled with highly-regarded Art Nouveau glass by Barbara Sotheby, to commemorate her father, Sir Baldwyn Leighton, who died in 1887. She was a friend of Burne-Jones. The retention of the medieval glass displays a degree of sensitivity often lacking earlier in the nineteenth century.

Fig. 29a Alberbury: a censing angel (sV)

Fig. 29b Alberbury: the Coronation of the Virgin (sV)

ALLENSMORE
St Andrew (SO 4662 3588, HR2 9AG)

The church was substantially altered early in the fourteenth century, most obviously through the insertion of new windows in the Decorated style, including the reticulated tracery of the east window which holds the surviving medieval stained glass.

Silas Taylor visited but made no report of arms here in the mid seventeenth century,[126] and when James Hill visited, roughly a century later, he only noted what might be the existing Crucifix in glass – 'A crucifix over the altar entire.'[127]

About a century after that, Duncumb made a sketch of the east window, which contains some elements which are recognisable, notably the Crucifix positioned where it is now. He saw, 'a female in the attitude of devotion' and 'a male in a monkish habit resting his left arm on an altar.' This does not seem to describe the existing figures.[128]

Philip Nelson included Allensmore in his county-by-county list of glass,

> In east window are xv century Crucifixion, two saints and two shields brought from Hereford Cathedral.[129]

He could not have seen the glass because the date he gives is clearly wrong. F.C. Morgan also suggests that the glass is from Hereford Cathedral, but gives no information as to when and from where in the cathedral the glass was taken.[130]

East window (I)
This was reglazed and the stained glass in the main lights installed in 1876, 'probably by Gibbs and Moore'.[131] The restoration of the glass in the tracery was probably done at the same time.

Fig. 30 Allensmore: Crucifixion in the east window (I)

Two of the tracery lights have composite figures. In one (panel B2), fragments are made into the figure of an Apostle with a book and bare feet. The head and feet might go together, and there is a tentative use of yellow stain. The hand and book are inverted. Everything else about the figure is modern, but the setting is made from old fragments of border and vine grisaille which resemble vine grisaille at the cathedral, Eaton Bishop and Madley. In the other (panel B3) is the Archangel of the Annunciation, probably of similar date to the Apostle but by a different artist applying marked shading to the eyes. The angel's hand is raised in greeting and the banderol reads *AVE GRACIA PLENA* in Lombardics. The background is, again, of old fragments including some deep-green vine leaves.

The principal panel at Allensmore is the Crucifixion (A3) (Fig. 30). The figure of Christ is of a type seen in several places in this survey, nailed to a green cross with a reversed S-curve to His body, and His arms forming a Y. It seems that only the head and torso are old; the background, Cross, nimbus, limbs and rays of light are new. At the head of the Cross is a reversed 'IHS' monogram[132] in rays of yellow, which is of later date. There is a border of heavily-pitted and darkened fragments of grisaille.

The church was a possession of the Dean and Chapter whose arms with blue and gold chevrons are to the left of the Crucifixion. The shield is entirely new, but the arms were present at the top of the window in Duncumb's sketch. The shield to the right is also new and seems to be an invention of the glazier. At the top of the window now is a seventeenth-century strapwork cartouche with a belted shield and a background of architectural fragments.

ALVELEY
St Mary (SO 7596 8454, WV15 6ND)

The Alveley glass is exceptionally interesting. It is relatively late in date (after 1500) and is associated with Sir John Blount (*c*.1484–1531), the father of Bessie Blount, mistress of Henry VIII and mother of the illegitimate prince, Henry Fitzroy. The arms of Sir John were recorded by Richard Symonds in 1645:

In a south window, next the south door of the church, three times this escutcheon, and underneath coat, helme, mantle, and crest … 1, *Barry nebuly of six or and sable* [Blount]; 2, *Argent, a lion rampant gules within a bordure sable, bezanty* [Cornwall]; impaling, *Quarterly per fess indented azure and argent, a lion passant in the first quarter* [Croft]; the whole surmounted by a helmet.[133]

A slightly different version of the arms was recorded by William Mytton (d.1746)[134] and remains in the tracery of the clerestory (see below) which was built late in the fifteenth century. In the south-east window of the clerestory are four large panels and eight tracery lights with medieval glass. The glass is probably in situ judging by the good fit between the pinnacles of the canopy-work and the cusping of the tracery, although substantially restored in 1878–79 when Blomfield 'ruthlessly renewed' the church.[135]

The two eastern panels of the south-east window are characterised by scruffy and imprecise drawing, large pieces of coloured glass for garments, niches of crocketed pinnacles and an overall sepia tone (Fig. 31, overleaf). There are numerous reused fragments in these figures, illustrating architecture, angel wings and borders. In the easternmost panel (1a) is St Armel, mitred and nimbed, with a serpent coiling around his staff (Figs 31 & 31a). Armel is found in glass of the fifteenth century at Merevale (Warks), where he is armoured but bears the same attributes. At Merevale the serpent or dragon is wrapped in a shawl. He is also in a large company of saints (*c*.1475) on the screen at Torbryan (Devon) where he is bearded and tonsured and has an open book in his left hand and a dragon tethered by a chain.

Fig. 31 Alveley: clerestory window with St Armel and St Anthony in the larger lights (SII)

Fig. 31a Alveley: clerestory window, detail of the left-hand light, showing St Armel (SII)

Madeleine Gray has shown that St Armel was important in the Marches, and that he is associated with the Tudors.[136] Henry VII was devoted to St Armel who, he claimed, saved him from shipwreck. He is in the company of the stone saints in Henry VII's Lady Chapel at Westminster Abbey, at the east end of the north aisle and in the third bay of the south triforium.

The conscious revival of the cult of St Armel had a clear political charge. Many of these depictions – like the stained glass at Merevale Abbey and the statue on Cardinal Morton's tomb in Canterbury Cathedral – occur in contexts which demonstrate a link between devotion to St Armel and conspicuous loyalty to the Tudor dynasty.'[137]

The saint stands on a dark blue ground of diapering patterned with paterae. Three suns, symbols of the dynasty of York, have been carefully placed in the background as if eclipsed by the chosen saint. This is Tudor symbolism, blatant and confident.

In the adjacent panel (1b) is the figure of St Anthony (Fig. 31), full-lipped and bearded; his blue mantle forms a cowl, and his head is nimbed. In his left hand is a long staff with a T-shaped head, which forms a Tau Cross, a common attribute of Anthony. He is also found in Henry VII's chapel with a T-staff and his better-known attributes of a bell and a pig (see Richard Croft's tomb at Croft c.1509). Anthony was a popular saint locally and can also be seen in glass at Munslow, and in William Mytton's notes for Aston Botterell, where he shared the east window with the Virgin and St George.[138]

In the four tracery lights above these two saints are a broad, round, bearded and nimbed head, drawn in fine line, silver stain and sepia;

Fig. 32 Alveley: the Virgin Annunciate (SII)

St Catherine, crowned, nimbed and with the pommel of her sword just visible; another crowned royal saint; and a composite figure with a mannered and heavy-featured face. If these lights are in situ the window is a gathering of saints with Tudor connotations. Catherine would be a natural choice (the name of the Queen), while the royal figure might be Edward the Confessor, a king admired by the Tudors.

The two west panels depict the Annunciation drawn almost entirely in black line and silver stain with smear shading (Fig. 32). Much has

48 THE MEDIEVAL STAINED GLASS OF HEREFORDSHIRE & SHROPSHIRE

been renewed including the faces of both figures. However, the composition is probably as originally intended, with sumptuous settings and clothing. The familiar symbols remain: the lily and the Old Testament lying discarded on the floor.

Above these panels, in the tracery, are an angel drawn with heavy line and distinctive features – large eyes, strong jaw and pointed chin – and two angels wearing tiaras and holding incomplete shields of Blount quartered with Cornwall and impaling Croft. The angels are by the same hand as one at Claverley (Fig. 43).

In the west window of the tower, there are three roundels which were at nearby Coton Chapel when Mytton visited *c*.1730.[139] All three are exercises in silver stain and fine line depicting the Crucifixion, a ciborium with the host, and Christ in Majesty.[140]

ASTLEY ABBOTTS

SAINT CALIXTUS (SO 7086 9623, WV16 4SW)

At the beginning of the twentieth century, the east window was described by Cranage:

> In the east window are a few fragments of old glass. The figures have rake-like feet and no iris to the eyes: these combined with the natural foliage indicate a fourteenth or late thirteenth century date.[141]

EAST WINDOW (I)
There is now a single small panel in the east window (I) of early date (Fig. 33). The nimbed figure is greatly restored, but the composition is probably as originally intended judging by the remains of the capitals of the niche and the survival of the head and feet of the saint. The feet

Fig. 33 Astley Abbotts: an Apostle or Christ in the east window (I)

are bare, suggesting an Apostle rather than the dedication saint, Calixtus, who is usually shown dressed in the mitre and robes of a pope. Richard Marks suggests this figure is Christ, presumably because the nimbus is cruciform,

> A figure of Christ at Astley Abbotts in Shropshire [window I] is set under a pointed trefoil arch resting on capitals. This is comparable with a canopy over the figure of Noah from the Canterbury choir clerestory, which is possibly the first appearance of a canopy in stained glass. Although similar enframing devices occur in French stained glass of the first half of the thirteenth century, as in the cathedrals at Chalons-sur-Marne and Troyes and in the parish church at Norrey-en-Auge [Normandy], they are also present in English manuscript illumination from the 12th century and are found in contemporary wall painting.[142]

ASTON BOTTERELL
St Michael

In the east window of the chancel, William Mytton drew three splendid figures depicting George and the Dragon, Mary crowned and surrounded by angels and St Anthony with a pig. There were also shields of arms, including the black lion rampant of Botterell, monograms and a black letter *'orate'* inscription for Thomas [blank] of the city of London, and his wife Alice.[143]

BACTON
St Faith, Herefs. (SO 3708 3238, HR2 0AR)
now at ATCHAM
St Eata, Salop (SJ 5409 0919, SY5 6QE)

Bacton has two significant Elizabethan artefacts, both connected to Blanche Parry who was close to Queen Elizabeth. Blanche's tomb, uniquely, has an image of Elizabeth as well as Blanche herself. The tomb is depicted in the glass at Atcham (Fig. 35). Further west, on the north wall, is an altar cloth which recent research has identified as fabric from one of Elizabeth's dresses, and which is the only substantial remnant from her wardrobe.

In 1811 Mrs Burton, wife of the Revd Henry Burton, vicar of Atcham, paid a visit to Bacton in search of memorials of the Parrys of Newcourt. She found the stained glass in poor condition and had it moved to her husband's church, where it can be found in the east (Fig. 34) and the north-west (Fig. 35) windows. The glass at Atcham consists of the Bacton glass from an unknown number of windows, medieval glass already in Atcham church, and old and new glass from the glazier's stock.

Gordon McNeil Rushforth (d.1938) wrote about the Bacton glass in 1935.[144] He argued that the glazier who installed the glass at Atcham was William Eginton, and that in 1811 the Shrewsbury firm of Betton & Evans was not sufficiently established for the project. However, William Eginton had no convincing Gothic credentials,[145] while Evans joined Betton in 1808 and became crucial to the Gothic revival in stained glass. The Atcham window is entirely in the manner of Betton & Evans, of restoration accurately copying the style of the original. Some details can be associated with the Evans restoration of Munslow: for example, the broad borders at the hems of robes decorated with pearl-encrusted ovals and lozenges, and panel borders with toothed leaves curling round a pole. These could also be medieval survivals, but their fresh appearance betrays the hand of Evans.

East window (I)

The east window at Atcham (I) (Fig. 34) has a striking, pale appearance because it is an exercise in silver stain (see Figs 65 & 66 – Hereford Cathedral north transept for an earlier example). At the base of the window are the donor, Miles ap-Harry or Parry of New Court in Bacton, and his wife Joan, with 19 children, kneeling at a prayer desk. Parry's will was proved in 1488, the approximate date of the medieval glass. Rushforth considered these lower panels to be almost entirely renewed in 1811, and so too most of the principal subjects, which he identified as the Virgin and Child, Christ with a communion cup and St John, holding a sceptre and palm rather than the cup which is his usual symbol. Evans could be casual about the traditional attributes of saints,[146] but here their unusual allocation says something about how the glass was arranged at Bacton.

Fig. 34 Atcham: glass from Bacton in the east window (I), restored by Betton & Evans

Fig. 35 Atcham: memorial window to Blanche Parry of Bacton (nV)

The 'Christ' figure is unconvincing. He appears too elderly and benign, and there is a bird in front of his chest, which suggests that this image is really two-thirds of a Trinity or Throne of Mercy (see Sellack sV, Fig. 135), with the Father, and the Spirit represented by the bird. At Bacton, the Trinity flanked by Mary with the Child and John in a single window would have been an unusual composition, and it is more likely that the east window there was a Crucifixion flanked by Mary and John. The Throne of Mercy must have been in another window. The Revd Burton and Betton & Evans, the glaziers, faced with windows from Bacton in poor condition, may have taken inspiration from Munslow, where Mary, Christ and John stand together in the east window (also much restored by Evans). At Atcham the window is a reredos, so they gave emphasis to the Eucharist by placing the cup in the hand of the central figure.

There is a great deal of medieval work in the border crowns and lozenges in the east window, and possibly some of the quarries are ancient. At the top are the nimbed, helmeted head of St George, the crowned St Catherine and shield-bearing angels.

North-west window (nV)

In the north-west window, the angels in the tracery are of the late fifteenth century and probably in situ. They are a good example of a cartoon being reused several times. In the central light are a collection of fragments including some heraldry and a black letter inscription: *Orate pro anima] d(o)m(ini) Joh(a)n(ni)s Rosse V(icarii ?) [… qui istam] Fenestram fieri fecit*.[147]

There are panels depicting the Blanche Parry tomb at Bacton and an inscription recording her death in 1589 (Fig. 35). Rushforth was of the view that this was entirely the work of the 1811 restorers working to Mrs Burton's brief because such a memorial would have been unnecessary at Bacton where the pictured tomb existed.[148] However, it is possible that the Bacton tomb was made in advance, for it contains no details of Blanche's death, while the glass, now at Atcham, was commissioned after her death and completes her story.

BIRLEY
St Peter (SO 4536 5336, HR4 8ET)

Only a few plain fragments remain in the tracery of the west window of the south chapel. James Hill recorded the arms of Burley but did not say in which window of the chapel he saw them.[149]

BISHOPSTONE
St Lawrence (SO 4159 4390, HR4 7JG)

The church underwent a thorough restoration in the early years of the incumbency of Archdeacon Richard Lane Freer, rector of Bishopstone and vicar of Yazor from 1839 until his death in 1863. It is likely that the glass in the south chancel window (sII) was introduced by him. In 1934, the Royal Commission reported the panels which can be seen today. Its record cards include five images of panels which show that the window has been reglazed since 1934.[150]

D.A.L. MacLean, in his survey of Royal Arms, drew attention to arms in the north window of the north chapel, which represent Henry IV or his son, Henry V.[151] They are, however, a modern copy, perhaps based on some pre-existing fragments.

Figs 36a–36b: Bishopstone roundels (sII): **Fig. 36a**: Crucifixion (TOP), **Fig. 36b**: the Marriage of Tobit (BOTTOM)

Window sII
1a: The adolescent Baptist with the lamb.
1b: Christ and the Baptist as children playing with the lamb. The banner reads 'ECCE AGNUS'.
2a: A roundel with the Return of the Prodigal. There are also two small panels with vine leaf and heraldic canons. This panel has faded since the Royal Commission photographed it c.1930.
2b: A roundel with (probably) the Marriage of Tobias and Sarah (possibly from the 'burst of popularity of the Book of Tobit as the subject of silver-stained roundels during the first two decades of the sixteenth century'.)[152] (**Fig. 36b**) There are also two small panels with fleurs-de-lis.
3a: The Crucifixion (**Fig. 36a**).
3b: The young Baptist. Images of the young Baptist are uncommon and there are three in this window.
4a: A roundel with the monogram of Mary set on the sun. There are two small panels with fragments of decoration.
4b: A roundel with the IHS monogram on a rayed sun with the three nails of the Passion. Also, two small panels with fragments of decoration.

SOUTH CHANCEL WINDOW (sII)
Compared to Llanwarne, the panels have been expertly set in a background which does not overwhelm them. The window is not included in William Cole's national catalogue.

BOCKLETON
ST MICHAEL (SO 5930 6143, WR15 8PX)

There is a small and almost illegible panel in the north-east window of the nave. Mary Green described the panel in 1933:

> Reset in the centre light of the south east window of nave: the Blessed Virgin is seated in a green chair and wears a red gown and yellow mantle [pot metal]. Possibly the child on left arm. Or the whole may be St Anne teaching the Virgin to read. A small piece of grisaille with Ivy leaf design. This seems to be the remains of the thirteenth or early fourteenth century grisaille window with square panel; it is poor glass and in very bad condition.[153]

The window has been reglazed since then but remains an unrewarding sight.

BOSBURY
HOLY TRINITY (SO 6955 4344, HR8 1QT)

The beautiful and richly-decorated Morton Chapel (south chapel), which was added c.1511–28, must have had splendid glass. A few fragments survive, scattered through the east window, including sacred initials, foliage, a breastplate of armour and a bird beak.

BRIDGNORTH
ST LEONARD

Richard Symonds drew several coats of arms and a kneeling donor in mail armour. In a north window he saw a saint with a cross-head staff and a shield *argent with a cross formy throughout gules*[154] (St George?). Mytton visited the church and recorded arms in a window, but none of the arms or figures seen by Symonds.[155]

BRINSOP
St George (SO 44233 44790, HR4 7AT)

It has been suggested that, 'at the end of the 18th century every window was filled with ancient glass, which was taken out and sold by the churchwardens.'[156] However, important medieval glass survives in two windows.

East window (I)
The east window (I) was reglazed in 1867[157] and again in 1923 under the direction of the architect, Ninian Comper. The two uppermost shields of arms represent Chandos – *or a lion rampant double queued gules* – with obvious replacements to the gold ground, and Dancey or Dauncey impaling another. Both shields were seen by James Hill in the eighteenth century[158] and were lower down the window in 1867. They are now set partly among Comper's modern quarries (with the donor's initials) and partly on old grisaille quarries with a vine motif.

Richard Symonds visited in 1645 and recorded the two shields seen today, plus the Talbot arms – *Gules, a lion rampant, a bordure engrailed, or* – which is also found at nearby Credenhill. St George caught Symonds' eye, together with a donor figure: 'A lady kneeling. On her robe these arms, viz. *Argent, a chevron gules between three hurts.*'[159] These are the Baskerville arms; the Baskervilles held property in Brinsop from the fourteenth century.

In his book about the cult of St George, Jonathan Good lists 37 examples of the saint

Fig. 37 Brinsop: St George in the east window (I)

depicted in stained glass, two of which are in Hereford Diocese at Brinsop and the cathedral.[160] To these two can be added the image recorded by William Mytton at Aston Botterell[161] and the head of St George at Atcham (I). About half of the 37 images show St George without the dragon, and these seem to be from the earlier fourteenth century.[162] The Brinsop St George (Fig. 37, above) is from *c.*1330–40.[163] He stands in a niche against a lattice background between heraldic borders of France on the left and England on the right. The drawing of the figure seems conservative, but the artist has conveyed a powerful man who dominates the whole window. Brinsop's St George wears mail without the plate armour seen in the later figures at Wells, Tewkesbury and Gloucester. David O'Connor described the panel for the 'Age of Chivalry exhibition in 1987':

This is a powerful secular image of the soldier saint who enjoyed a widespread cult in the later Middle Ages, especially in court circles. Edward III showed particular devotion to the saint, who became one of the patrons of the Order of the Garter in 1347. The image at Brinsop does not include a dragon and is perhaps designed to stress the saint's role as patron and protector of England. The borders may well be an allusion to Edward's claim to the French throne.[164]

St George may be in situ – the one piece of the window traceable in the records back to the mid seventeenth century. It is not difficult to envisage the shields that Symonds counted gathered round, for they were the arms of the king's local supporters. Talbot, Edward's chancellor, was there and Roger de Chandos another favourite who flourished in Edward's reign. The window is a display by the Baskervilles, less favoured yet ambitious, raising their colours in support of a powerful and successful martial king and his court.

Above St George is the Virgin in a blue mantle, possibly from a Crucifixion scene. The face is modern, and reminiscent of William Warrington's restoration of the fourteenth-century windows at the cathedral. The battlemented plinth on which the Virgin stands is Comper's work. The crocketed pinnacles at the top of the main lights, framed by vine borders, are typical of the earlier fourteenth century, shown in flat elevation with no attempt at perspective. The Virgin and Child (top of the central light) and St Michael with a dragon (bottom), are Comper's work, as too are the four lower shields in the outer lights.

Fig. 38 Brinsop: Christ in Majesty (nV)

NORTH-WEST WINDOW (nV)
In the quatrefoil tracery of the north-west window (nV) is Christ, nimbed, seated and with His right hand raised and His left hand holding an *Orbis Terrarum* globe. He is drawn in black line on white glass and the background is deep red diapered with vine (Fig. 38). The globe is a reminder of Hereford's Mappa Mundi, which is based on the *Orbis Terrarum* globe surmounted by the seated Christ in Majesty displaying his wounds on raised hands. This is a delightful fourteenth-century piece, probably similar in date to St George in the east window.

BROCKHAMPTON
ALL SAINTS (SO 5941 3215, HR1 4SD)

The present church, breathtaking in its English rural beauty, was built in 1901–02 to the design

Fig. 39 Brockhampton: angel (sV)

of William Lethaby. The medieval glass, probably from the closed church of Holy Trinity nearby (SO 5980 3161), was inserted in a south window of the nave when it was first glazed. It is drawn with black line and silver stain, and the principal piece depicts the upper part of the head of an angel wearing a tiara crowned by a cross (Fig. 39). She has the eyes and long nose of the International Style, and has a good deal in common with panels in the north transept of the cathedral, possibly from the York/ Coventry milieu.

BROMFIELD

St Mary the Virgin (SO 4820 7680, SY8 2JP)

A window in the vestry, which was added to the church as part of the restoration of 1889–90 by C. Hodgson Fowler,[165] contains roundels and panels of imported glass from the Low Countries. There is a modern panel made of pieces of border leaf scroll by David Evans of Shrewsbury, but the vestry post-dates his death. If this attribution is correct, it means either that the roundels might have been in another part of

Figs 40a–40b: Bromfield, Netherlandish roundels in vestry window. **Fig. 40a**: the Nativity

Fig. 40b: the Crucifixion

the church prior to the building of the vestry, or the glazing in 1890 was by Evans's sons who were successors to the stock left by him. William Cole recorded the panels, with the dates given here being his:[166]

Vestry window

1a: Moses striking the rock c.1525.
1b: Abraham and Lot parting c.1540.
1c: The Mount of Olives c.1550.
1d: Panel of pieces by David Evans.
2a: Pharaoh in the Red Sea c.1540.
2b: Abraham and the angels c.1540,
2c: Abraham and Lot dividing the land c.1540.
3a: Death of the Virgin c.1540.
3b: Joseph retelling his dreams c.1540.
3c: Abraham and Lot travel to Canaan c.1540.
3d: A woman touches Christ's robe.
A1: The Nativity (**Fig. 40a**).
A2: The Crucifixion (**Fig. 40b**).

Fig. 41 Castle Frome: donor's head (sIV)

BYFORD
St John the Baptist (SO 3972 4291, HR4 7LD)

There are a few fragments of fourteenth-century border and diaper-work in the tracery of the south-east window of the nave.

CASTLE FROME
St Michael (SO 6675 4587, HR8 1HQ)

South nave window (sIV)
Fragments of glass have been gathered into three panels in the south nave window (sIV). The glass (Fig. 41) appears to be from a single scheme, by a hand not encountered elsewhere in this survey, except for being reminiscent of glass at Alveley. The drawing is of high quality but heavy-lined and the features of the principal figure large-eyed, deeply creased and firmly shaded. The head may belong to William Devereux II of Frome who died in 1384. He was sketched as the kneeling donor in 'the eastern window' by James Hill before 1725.[167]

All three panels have fragments of a crocketed style of architecture, confidently and precisely drawn, highlighted in silver stain and strongly shaded sepia/ grey. The original scheme probably comprised three canopies with angels among the pinnacles. Three angels survive in the side panels. They share the large eyes and firm shading of the principal figure. The three lights probably held saints, including John the Evangelist who, according to James Hill, was called upon by the donor with the black letter plea, '*ora p[ro] nobis*'. A pair of feet below an embroidered hem can be seen at the base of the central panel.

CHURCH STRETTON
St Laurence (SO 4524 9366, SY6 6DQ)

The thorough church history by Douglas Grounds[168] is uncertain about the date of the acquisition of the roundels in the chancel. He suggests that they may have been the gift of Robert Pemberton, *c*.1820 – possibly connected with the Betton & Evans east window of 1819. He also suggests that a collection in 1885–86 might have paid for the installation of the glass. The backgrounds of the three smaller chancel windows are by Betton & Evans, and the use of imported roundels ties in with their work at Lichfield Cathedral and St Mary's Shrewsbury (from 1825). Some of the glass is said to be from St Mary's where Evans, whose work extended over a long period, installed roundels.

The roundels are included in William Cole's catalogue, and the dates given here are his:[169]

Fig. 42 Church Stretton: Netherlandish roundels (nII). The Circumcision and Crucifixion

Window nII

1a: Labours of the Months: November, *c*.1550.
1b: Crucifixion *c*.1540 (**Fig. 42**).
2a: Unidentified saints, late sixteenth century.
2b: Circumcision, late sixteenth century (**Fig. 42**).
3a: Idolatry in the time of Josiah *c*.1550.
3b: David brought to Saul *c*.1550.
3c: St Mark, seventeenth century.
3d: St John the Evangelist, seventeenth century.
4a: Acts of mercy, welcoming a stranger, late sixteenth century.
4b: Two men with an ox, late sixteenth century.
5a: Circumcision, late sixteenth century.
5b: The Beatitudes – the peacemakers, late sixteenth century.
6a: A man reading a book *c*.1550.

Window sIII

1a: Slaughter of the Innocents, late sixteenth century.
2a: Christ washing the Disciples' feet, late sixteenth century.
3a: A king ordering a man to prison *c*.1550.

Window SI

A panel of Betton & Evans fragments.

CLAVERLEY
ALL SAINTS (SO 7926 9342, WV5 7DT)

William Mytton (d.1746) recorded saints, angels, a Crucifixion and numerous black letter inscriptions and images of donors with their family members.[170]

Fig. 43 Claverley: an angel in the north aisle (nIV). (See **Fig. 32**)

CLOCKWISE FROM LEFT:
Fig. 44 Clehonger: fourteenth-century glass gathered in a nave north window (nVI).
Figs 45a–45b Clehonger: two heads in the nave north window (nVI)

North aisle, north-east window (nIV)

In this window is glass from the early sixteenth century. The head of an angel is by the same hand as two angels in the clerestory at Alveley (Fig. 43), and there is a roundel with a kneeling angel holding a banderol with 'St Mathe' in black letter at the top of the window. This roundel was previously in the east window of the south aisle, with another containing the lion of St Mark.

Chancel north (nII) & south (sII) windows

In these windows are more fragments, mostly of the fourteenth century, including dark yellow vine with red roses and yellow quatrefoil flowers at the heads of the main lights, which are probably in situ.

CLEHONGER

All Saints (so 4655 3795, hr2 9se)

Silas Taylor 'viewed' the church on 23 May 1656[171] and recorded several shields which have now gone. In the north nave window he found two escutcheons, one of which was inside out and displayed Pembridge impaling de la Barre. Another shield of de la Barre was in the north chapel. In the chancel, Taylor found two shields in glass, one of de la Barre and the other of Pembridge – this could be the Pembridge shield now in the north nave window.

The north chapel, built by Sir Richard de Pembridge as a chantry dedicated to St Anne, was endowed in April 1342 to be served by a single chaplain. Richard died in February

1337/8.[172] All Saints houses important monuments to the Pembridges and would almost certainly have had high quality glass (as at other churches of important families, such as Moccas). It has two windows of three lights, which would have been glazed with, among other things, St Anne and the Virgin, and the genealogy of the Virgin in a Tree of Jesse (see below). Sir Richard or his wife commissioned glass which remains in fragments in the north nave window (nVI). The important windows at the nearby churches of Madley and Eaton Bishop were glazed about the same time that this chapel was built.

Among the papers of George Marshall, are monochrome photographs of the north nave window, taken by the architect Roland Paul in 1927.[173] This was in poor condition and much of the glass was inside-out. The church guidebook (dated 1998) says that the window had deteriorated to such an extent that it was completely reglazed in 1980 by Mr D. Morrish of Eardisley. At some point in the process, an angel, noted by the Royal Commission in 1931, disappeared.[174]

The north nave window (Fig. 44) holds important fragments from the fourteenth century. There are two heads (Figs 45a & 45b) which are by the master who worked at nearby Madley. The crowned figure at the top of the panel (Fig. 45b) is one of the most pleasing in this survey. It could be the Virgin, or perhaps St Catherine who was popular in the Marches.

A Tree of Jesse can be inferred from some stems and a Lombardic inscription for Jeremiah Prophet which are like those at Madley and Ludlow.

The shields contain some medieval material: the upper shield, *barry of eight azure and gules*, is not de la Barre (*gules: three barres gobony* according to Taylor) or recognisably local. The red bars have thin diapering. The Pembridge shield has different patterns of diapering for the two colours. The strident colour of the modern glass at the top of the shield stands out.

CLEOBURY NORTH
St Peter & St Paul (so 62329 86995, wv16 6rp)

In the SOUTH AISLE EAST WINDOW are several quarries of a type associated with York/Coventry work of the fifteenth century (see Figs 71a–71d for a similar fragment in the Hereford Cathedral library, and Fig. 126 for several pieces in the Presteigne south aisle east window). David and Charles Evans installed the window and Apostles in the chancel in 1861,[175] and it is likely that these quarries, which are not well-preserved, were in their father's stock, perhaps from Battlefield or Ludlow.

COALBROOKDALE
Holy Trinity (sj 6705 0446, tf8 7ns)

The church was paid for by the ironmaster Abraham Darby IV and consecrated in 1854. The glass in the SOUTH AISLE EAST WINDOW (sII) was given to Adelaide Darby as a wedding present in 1852.[176] The panels are described as 'Flemish' in every publication except for the two editions of Pevsner's 'Shropshire', where they are described as 'important early sixteenth century German painted glass.'[177] The Darby dynasty of industrialists had trade connections with Germany, and they also gave German silver to the church. Two of the three panels of the main lights depict the Last Supper, and the third has Christ washing Peter's feet (Fig. 46). It looks as though both scenes have been cropped, perhaps because the glass was part of a larger triptych.

Fig. 46 Coalbrookdale: the Last Supper and Christ washing Peter's feet (sII)

There are clear affinities with German glass of the time. The use of an architectural frame rather like a grand fireplace surround, with niches in the pilasters occupied by saints and prophets, is seen, for example, in *The Kiss of Judas* by Everhard Rensig of Cologne, dated to 1522–26 and now in Cleveland Museum.[178] The nimbus of Christ in the Coalbrookdale window, with its elegant Cross, is also related to images from the first half of the sixteenth century, such as the Cedron Brook picture of 1534 from the Lower Rhine, now in the Victoria and Albert Museum.[179] The approach in line, form and mannerism which celebrates, with exaggerated realism, the grotesque,[180] has parallels with the Cleveland picture and much German work of the time. This can be particularly engaging in images of groups of Apostles, such as the Foot Washing of 1533 in the Victoria and Albert Museum.[181]

The trade in glass from Rhineland and the Low Countries to Shropshire is a fascinating story.[182] In the early decades of the nineteenth century, monastic houses were closed on both sides of the shifting German/ French border, and their treasures sold. A significant amount of glass came to England through the agency of dealers and glaziers, sometimes changing hands many times before being installed in churches. Coalbrookdale Church was being built sometime after glass from Altenberg and St Apern was installed in St Mary's Shrewsbury by Revd William Gorsuch Rowland. He acquired a large quantity of glass from Betton & Evans, which had arrived in England nearly half a century after it had been removed. Evans probably installed the Coalbrookdale glass, and it might have been part of the same consignment. It is unlike anything in St Mary's and therefore may not have found a place there, inspiring Rowland to give it to Adelaide Darby as a wedding present. There is no recorded connection between Rowland and Adelaide in her diary[183] but her mother's doctor was 'Mr Rowland' and they must have been in the same social circle. If he was the donor, the glass was probably from Altenberg or St Apern.

Immediately above the main subjects are three rectangular grisaille panels depicting The Annunciation and The Adoration of the Magi, probably from the same hand; and John the Baptist pointing to the Lamb of God (from John 1.36). In the tracery light are five roundels from three different hands. The upper two show the building of an altar and the anointing from the life of King David, drawn in black line with sepia colouring of hair and flesh. Two of the other three are in black line and yellow stain, and depict scenes from the Life of Joseph, in which Joseph, now a prince in Egypt, deals with his brothers. The third roundel, a dark monochrome piece, depicts St Peter in chains. The roundels are not in William Cole's national inventory.

CODDINGTON
All Saints (SO 7183 4268, HR8 1JJ)

There are fragments of fourteenth- and fifteenth-century glass gathered in the SOUTH-EAST NAVE WINDOW, depicting crocketed pinnacles and vine leaves.

COLWALL
St James (SO7391 4230, WR13 6HE)

The NORTH AISLE was added in 1881, reusing two medieval windows. In 1932, the Royal Commission reported glass, 'In N. aisle – in N.E. window, foliated roundel, fourteenth or fifteenth century; in third window, similar roundel, and fragments, fourteenth century.'[184] The remaining fragments are in four north aisle windows and, in addition to the fragments noted above, include borders, a piece of angel wing and part of a fifteenth-century viola da gamba.

COUND
St Peter (SJ 5582 0499, SY5 6EW)

William Mytton recorded glass in two chancel windows. In a north window, he found a quartered shield and full-length figures of a bishop and a saint. In a south window, he saw canopy-work and a full-length figure with a spear.[185]

East window of south aisle (sV)
The surviving medieval glass now in this window (sV) cannot be identified with Mytton's sketches and might have been introduced later. Peter Newton considered it to be of the fourteenth century.[186] The border pieces are of typical quatrefoils and a single fragment of cup-and-cover.

The figure of St John (Fig. 47) in a green mantle is probably from a Crucifixion. He is an exceptionally beautiful figure despite having lost his feet.

Fig. 47 Cound: St John the Evangelist (sV)

CREDENHILL
St Mary (so 4503 4389, hr4 7dl)

The Credenhill bishops, Thomas Becket and Thomas Cantilupe (Fig. 5), in the CHANCEL SOUTH-WEST WINDOW (sIV) are among the most familiar figures in English glass. They are probably in situ and were seen by Silas Taylor when he visited in the seventeenth century, at which time there was more heraldic glass (of the Talbots) in the church and an image of the Virgin with a soldier.[187] These figures were also recorded by James Hill a century later.[188]

The figures stand side-by-side in episcopal dress, each holding a crosier, and over them in Lombardic characters are the words CANTUAR – THOMAS – CANTELUPE, emphasising their common Christian name. The right hand of each is raised in the act of giving benediction. Henry Cooke noted that the hand of Becket of Canterbury (CANTUAR) is raised higher, and suggested that the drawing showed individuality and an attempt at portraiture. If that is so, the Credenhill image of Cantilupe is the only near-contemporary image of Hereford's saint, who died in Italy in 1282.[189]

In 1886 Francis Havergal published a description of the two bishops[190] and suggested a precise date of 1328 for the window. Cantilupe was canonised in 1320 and Havergal thought the window could not have been made before then on stylistic grounds. He argued that the window was sponsored early in his episcopacy by Bishop Thomas Charlton, who was installed in 1327. David O Connor argued for an earlier date:

> Havergal and subsequent writers dated the panel to after the official canonization process of 1320. However, this would make it an exceptionally conservative piece on grounds of style and technique. Representations of unofficial saints are not that rare, and the ambivalence suggested by the absence of halos and sanctus inscriptions presupposes an image designed to stimulate a cult, rather than the celebration of a successful canonisation ...[191]

Richard Marks suggests a date of c.1300[192] which would place the work in the time of Bishop Swinfield (bishop 1283–1317) who was a strong proponent of the canonisation of Cantilupe – a campaign which strengthened as his cult grew and the numbers of pilgrims to Hereford increased. The Credenhill window shows the revered local bishop standing shoulder to shoulder with the greatest English archbishop saint. Nigel Saul[193] suggests that a Talbot, not Swinfield, was the sponsor,

> Not only is there the evidence of the Talbot heraldry [but] in style and technique the surviving panels of Cantilupe and Becket, which were clearly part of one and the same scheme, belong to the opening years of the fourteenth century, the years of Talbot's incumbency.[194] Since Cantilupe's canonization was not actually to be approved until 1320, we are afforded a striking example of unofficial canonization – that is, the elevation of the respected local figure to sainthood by popular acclaim. Quite possibly, [the Talbots were] active in promoting the cult locally, given the family association with the see and the cathedral.

Nave north-east window (nIII)
This window was installed by Morris & Co. in 1918, retaining, at the top of the window, old glass described by Taylor and other antiquaries. The shield with a lion in an engrailed bordure represents the Talbots who held the manor at Credenhill. Philip Talbot, rector, founded a chantry of St Mary and built a chapel on the north side, which remained when Silas Taylor visited in 1649–50. The Talbot lion was recorded by Taylor in that chapel and other places in the church, and Phillip Talbot was named in the glass then. The chapel on the north side, dedicated to the Virgin and 'Our Lady Service' was still in existence at the suppression of the chantries.[195]

Fig. 48 Credenhill: detail of the nave north-east window (nIII)

Next to the Talbot shield is a composite panel (Fig. 48) which shows a woman holding a baby and reaching for a flower held by a crowned figure. The woman wears a scarf which looks like a wimple, and is smiling. The child is almost indiscernible. The other figure, wearing an out-sized crown, also smiles and there is a suggestion of the soldier mentioned by Taylor in the amber grip and pommel of a sword between the two figures. The shield has a deep blue diapered background and is set on a ground of medieval vine grisaille. These figures could be the Virgin and a soldier noted by Taylor, and were probably part of a Crucifixion scene or cycle. It seems likely that the glass seen by Taylor had already been cobbled together from a more extensive glazing scheme and was further rearranged by Morris & Co. The top light of the window has more fourteenth-century border and grisaille fragments.

CROFT
St Michael and All Angels
(SO 4499 6543, HR6 9PW)

In the tracery lights at the heads of the nave windows, there are late fourteenth-century roundels of suns, stars and a scallop shell drawn in yellow stain.

DIDDLEBURY
St Peter (so 5084 8537, sy7 9dh)

Chancel north window (nII)
This window contains a fourteenth-century Crucifixion in a tracery light (Fig. 49). It was seen by Cranage c.1900[196] and is probably in situ. The crucified Christ is drawn in the curved, hanging pose common to almost every Crucifixion image in this survey. The Cross is white, rather than the more usual green. Christ's loin cloth and long hair are painted in yellow stain and the Cross stands on a sepia ground. Behind the Cross there is red diapering with three lobed flowers, and in the lower parts of the trefoil panel diapering of white ivy leaves on a grey ground around green four-petalled flowers. The whole panel has a border of yellow discs on a black background.

Fig. 49 Diddlebury: Crucifixion (nII)

DILWYN
St Mary (so 4152 5467, hr4 8hr)

Richard Symonds sketched a kneeling donor in armour and saw Apostles in the north window of the fourteenth-century north chapel.[197] Such a gathering suggests that this might have been a Creed window and begs the question whether Dilwyn was the source of the Apostles which were in the windows of Hampton Court Chapel for a time. The window lights are wide enough (840mm), and tall enough for four tiers of saints, but not tall enough to accommodate the canopy-work that surrounded the figures at Hampton Court.

South window of chancel (sIII)
The chancel south window contains angels with thuribles. The original location of the angels is given in a newspaper report of Heaton, Butler and Bayne's reglazing of 1867, as the tracery of the north window of the north transept chapel.[198] The border of the panel, with lions and fleurs-de-lis, was recorded by Silas Taylor in the same window.[199]

The two figures are from the same cartoon reversed (Fig. 50). They are drawn in black line with silver stain for hair, apparel, wings and metalwork. Their robes are white with a single deep dark red band decorated with trefoil, and they stand on a deep green ground. Their nimbi are dark blue. The background is red with ivy leaf diapering. The figures are surrounded by stars (probably by Heaton, Butler and Bayne). The framing quatrefoil is defined by a border with a white band and a yellow band of pellets. The quatrefoil is surmounted by two crocketed pinnacles.

In the upper part of the panel, the pellet border is used to define a roundel with a tail

Fig. 50 Dilwyn: angel thurifers (sIII)

(resembling garter arms). Enclosed are six red roses linked by curved stalks. There is green trefoil vine diapering and a finial of large crockets embracing a rose.

The faces of the figures resonate with angels at Eaton Bishop and Ledbury. These two angels were probably inserted as soon as the reticulated tracery was finished and can be dated to *c*.1320–30.

DONINGTON
St Cuthbert (SJ 8089 0465, WV7 3EP)

Donington is in Lichfield Diocese but is included here because it relates to other important fourteenth-century work in this survey. The two two-light CHANCEL NORTH WINDOWS contain collections of fragments including shields and incomplete figures.

Chancel eastern window (nII)
The upper light holds a sixteenth-century crowned fleur-de-lis in rich yellow stain. The top of the east light has two heads of vested angels in the International Style and three pieces with hands. Lower down in the same light is a lozenge-shaped panel which comprises fragments from borders and deep red and blue seaweed backgrounds. The west light has an inverted monogram, 'nicy', below which are several fragments of architecture and angel's wings in the fifteenth-century International Style. In the same style of pale-yellow stain, at the bottom of the light, are two demi-figures from a Doom window. Both are naked, one is crowned, and they look skywards in the hope of heaven (Fig. 52, overleaf). In the centre of the light is a lozenge of fragments including black-letter inscriptions.

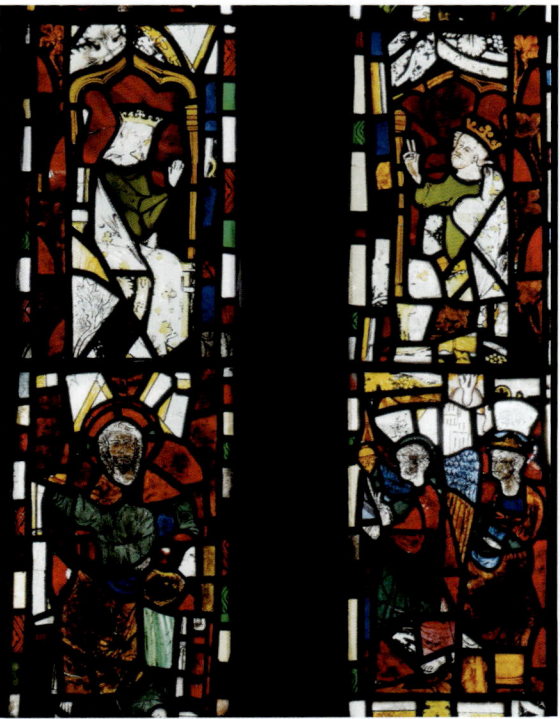

Fig. 51 Donington: fourteenth-century glass collected in a chancel north window (nIII)

Chancel western window (nIII) (Fig. 51)
This belongs almost entirely to the fourteenth century. There is yellow stain, but the predominant impression is of deep red, green and blue pot metal. At the top of the east light is a fifteenth- or sixteenth-century head of a woman in a pedimented headdress among fragments of architecture and borders. At the top of the west light is the fourteenth-century face of Christ. There are two similar shields set among oak leaf grisaille, vine leaves and architectural fragments which William Mytton drew *c*.1730.[200] Peter Newton identified these as the arms of Zouche – *gules bezanty or, a chief ermine*.[201] Below the shields are a crowned man with his hand raised in benediction and a crowned woman holding her hands prayerfully. They face each other from similar cusped, ogee-arched niches. These

Fig. 52 Donington: figures from a fifteenth-century Doom (nII)

are probably the Virgin and Christ from an Assumption or Coronation picture, but neither figure is nimbed. The figures are from the same hand, similar in style and with the same green robes and mantles decorated with fleurs-de-lis. The outer borders of both lights are typical fourteenth-century vines, and in this part of the panel (and above) there are pieces of vine stem with fleurs-de-lis which are reminiscent of the stems in Jesse windows at Ludlow and Madley. At the base of the lights are three fragmentary figures; to the west, Christ in Majesty, and to the east a censing angel and a seated, crowned and nimbed female – probably the Virgin.

This is an interesting window in that it seems to include glass from either side of a stylistic boundary in the fourteenth century. The Zouche line ended in 1314 but the name, estates and arms were taken by William (formerly Mortimer) de Zouche. The arms could pre-date 1314, being purely Zouche and undifferenced, and there is a case for that date in the other glass. The lower three figures are simply drawn, devoid of yellow stain and shading and with features which seem rooted in the thirteenth century. The two figures above show the developing use of silver stain and shading in the more vigorous, sinuous and colourful style of, for example, the Jesse figures at Ludlow and Madley, which were made two or three decades after 1314.

EARDISLAND

St Mary (so 4205 5852, hr6 9bp)

Thomas Dingley (d.1695)[202] and James Hill (d.1727)[203] made records of glass in the church (Fig. 53). In the CHANCEL NORTH WINDOW (nII) the arms of Mortimer and in the CHANCEL SOUTH WINDOW (sII), *argent a lion rampant sable*

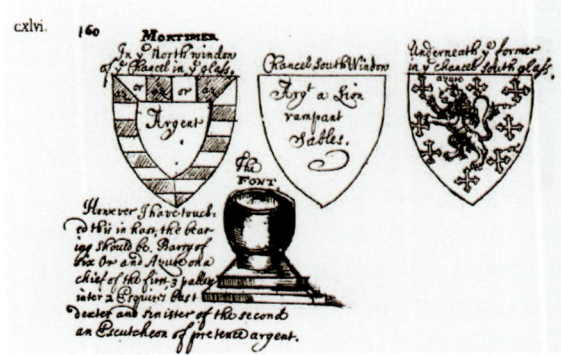

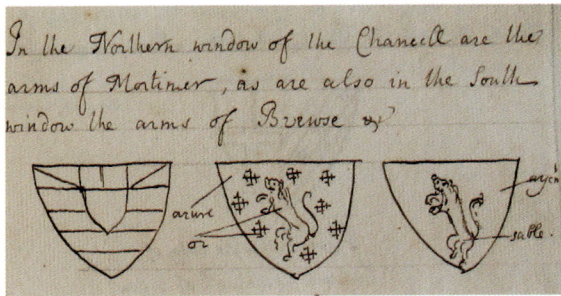

Fig. 53 Eardisland: records of heraldry by Dingley (ABOVE) and Hill (BELOW)

(possibly Mortimer)[204] and *azure a lion rampant inter crosse crosslets or*[205] which are the arms of de Braose. In the NAVE SOUTH WINDOW (sIII), *or three bars gules* representing St Owen of Burton Court.

Of these, only the St Owen shield survives. The church, like other victims of the nineteenth-century coterie of local architects, was severely restored by Henry Curzon in the 1860s. An over-exposed photograph in Leominster Museum shows the east window between the Curzon restoration and the reglazing of the window by Burlison and Grylls in 1902.[206] There was only plain glass and borders in the larger tracery lights and the main lights. However, the cartoon made by Burlison and Grylls[207] suggests that original glass survived in a small light at the centre of the lowest tier of small tracery lights. A note on the drawing dates it to the thirteenth century but it was more likely to have been early fourteenth-century, given its setting within reticulated tracery.

In the NAVE NORTH-EAST WINDOW (nII) there are a few pieces of lozenge border in black and yellow stain with quatrefoils. In the NAVE SOUTH-EAST WINDOW (sII) there are a number of fragments of border lozenges with fleurs-de-lis and quatrefoils in the apexes of the main lights. There is a small yellow flower in a fragment, which may be the model for flowers used in Burlison and Grylls's reglazing. In the tracery quatrefoil are the arms of St Owen (as seen by Dingley and Hill), a good deal of fourteenth-century border and some border lozenged with quatrefoils and fleurs-de-lis. The five-petalled yellow flowers are plentiful, mostly by Burlison and Grylls.

EATON BISHOP
St Michael (so 4431 3910, hr2 9qd)

The Eaton Bishop glass is exceptionally beautiful. Some of it can be dated to c.1330–40 from the Lombardic inscription which refers to Adam Murimuth, 'Cantor'. He was probably a Herefordshire man by birth and appointed as Cantor of Exeter Cathedral in 1328. Between 1312 and 1318 he practised in the papal curia at Avignon, and King Edward II was among his clients. He held canonries at Hereford, Wells and St Paul's, as well as the precentorship of Exeter Cathedral. He retired to Buckinghamshire and devoted himself to writing an important chronicle of his own times in 1331, which might be considered the *terminus ante quem* for the glass. His connection with Eaton Bishop is unknown, but it is not surprising, given his rank, that the glass, some of which he presumably donated, is of high quality.[208]

There was a tradition that the Eaton Bishop glass came from the chapel of the nearby palace of the bishops of Hereford at Sugwas, which was demolished in 1792. George Marshall[209] debunked this idea by referring to descriptions of the Sugwas Chapel by the antiquaries, James Hill and Thomas Blount, and was able to establish that the Sugwas glass is now in the chancel east window at Ross-on-Wye, where the Hereford bishops also had a palace. He quoted a letter from the daughter of Canon Musgrave, the incumbent who oversaw the re-leading,

> I am sorry I can give you little help about the glass, but of one thing I feel positive, that it was always in the church, and that my father had it collected and rearranged. I feel sure I have heard him say that the old glass was found in the church hidden away somewhere, I believe, and collected.[210]

It seems almost impossible that three Crucifixions should have survived the iconoclasm of the sixteenth and seventeenth centuries, but maybe the bishops' patronage was a protection, or perhaps the glass was removed and stored. That would account for the persistent stories that the glass was collected at some later date. However, Silas Taylor[211] noted in the seventeenth century, 'In ye windows of ye chancel are many paintings but mostly of figures of priests that contributed toward ye glazing as by ye writing under their pictures is knowne.' This suggests that much of the glass was in situ not long after iconoclastic times.

The eighteenth-century churchwardens' accounts tell a similar story to that found in the accounts of other churches. There are regular but mostly small items of expenditure on glazing. Quite modest sums appear in about one in four years, with an exceptional, but still relatively small, sum in 1725 of £2 12s 9d for 'Glazing ye windows and six frames and lattice to do.'[212]

John Duncumb[213] visited c.1810 and Thomas Bird[214] visited on 19 July 1827 and found the contents of the windows broadly as seen today. The nineteenth-century churchwardens' accounts record increasing expenditure on repairs from 1806. In 1819 John Rogers was paid at his day rate of three and six for re-leading two lights. In 1840 a very much larger sum of over £10 was paid out by the churchwardens, which was also the subject of a vestry minute. It seems likely that the work done in 1840 resulted in painted glass being removed and put in storage because a further scheme, possibly around 1850, was overseen by Canon A.W. Musgrave who became rector in 1841.

The earliest pictures of the east window are the photographs taken by Alfred Watkins before George Marshall wrote about the glass in 1922.[215] These images show the same content as can be seen today but arranged rather differently (Fig. 54, overleaf).[216] Marshall also described a different arrangement of subjects from that described by Bird in 1827. This must have been the result of Canon Musgrave's reglazing. In Marshall's time, the row of donor figures in the east window was above the archangels and the bishop, and not below as now (Fig. 55).

In 1927, Marshall received a copy of a letter from Walter Tower, of C.E. Kempe & Co.,[217] to Canon A.T. Bannister[218] which described poor leading, 'the leaf of this leading being flat and very thin,' and inadequate saddle bars. Walter Tower's thoughts on the original arrangement of the glass are of interest:

... this East window is a collection of beautiful fragments from at least four windows.

The borders and grisaille work in the heads of the three central lights, as well as the three upper canopies in these lights are I think in their original position as also the central group of the Crucifixion. The figures of Saint Michael [front cover] and Saint Gabriel [Fig. 2] were probably placed immediately on either side of the Crucifixion, where the second row of canopies now are in these lights. But it is well-nigh impossible to say with real assurance how the rest of the glass was originally arranged. For instance, there is the interesting figure of the Bishop in the base of the centre light -- in all probability representing St Thomas of Hereford. I think this figure was probably placed under the canopy that is now wrongly placed immediately on the right of the Crucifixion panel [i.e., in the fourth light] and that it was possibly originally in the first or fifth light, or even in another window of this church.

... any drastic rearrangement will fail to produce a real gain on the present arrangement. The fact that there are portions here of some four windows forces this conclusion, however disappointing it is to say so.[219]

It seems, despite these reservations, that there was significant rearrangement of the subjects, aimed at giving the donor figures less prominence and returning to the arrangement described by Bird in 1827, with the archangels closer to the Crucifixion. Tower gave a quotation for re-leading of £250. Canon Bannister raised this sum by an appeal,[220] and the work was carried out in 1928.

Fig. 54 Eaton Bishop: Alfred Watkins's photograph of the east window (I) before 1920 (courtesy of HARC)

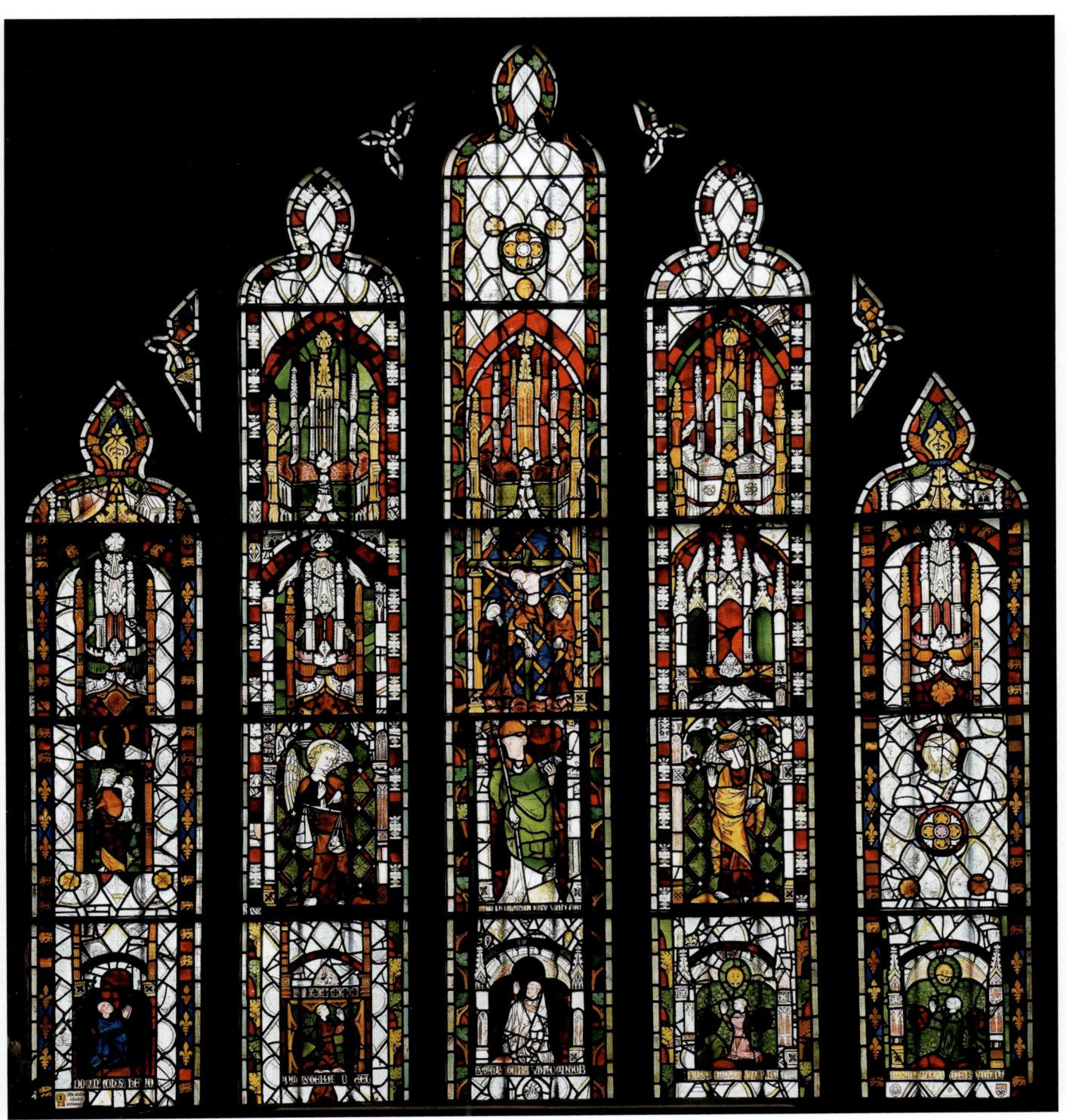

Fig. 55 Eaton Bishop: east window (I) in 2019

The south chancel window has also been rearranged. The Royal Commission found in 1931,

> In S.E. window in trefoil of tracery, a Majesty set in fragments; in E. light panels with figures probably of the Virgin and St. John belonging to the crucifix in the W. light, below crucifix, panel with kneeling figure of priest with a scroll inscribed 'Ave Maria', all set in fragments with canopies and borders, early fourteenth-century.[221]

The glass was removed for safe-keeping during the Second World War and not securely refixed. In 1967 its condition, and the need to repair the masonry of the window, led to a further complete re-leading by G. King & Sons of Norwich. Denis King wrote,

> Unfortunately, upon its reinstatement after war safety removal new copper ties were not fitted for tying to the saddle-bars and in consequence the weight of the unsupported glazing, plus heat distortion, has caused buckling of almost every panel ... I have decided to recommend complete re-leading now. We can then restore loss of definition, colour and brilliance where possible, e.g., the face of the bishop, and joining important cracked pains e.g., the Virgin's head, with modern adhesives and butyl mastic sealing to an external clear plating only. No major rearrangement of glass seems called for unless it be the introduction of the balancing subject into the central panel of the South light.[222]

The project was completed by 1970 with grants from The Worshipful Company of Glaziers and The Pilgrim Trust.

EAST WINDOW (I) (Figs 54 & 55, previous pages)
The east window has five principal lights and four small trefoil tracery lights (Fig. 55). The low sill of the window and its breadth suggest it was designed as an altar piece, a reredos, and the earliest descriptions of it tend to confirm this idea. The donor figures, almost always present in painted or carved altar pieces, were still there in the mid seventeenth century when Silas Taylor visited, and some are probably an original part of the design. Taylor does not record the Crucifixion at that time, but the omission may be explained by his preoccupation with pedigrees and inscriptions. The Crucifixion was there in 1810 and would be expected in a medieval altar piece. It is the one panel where there is a good fit between the niche and the canopy-work above.

The notes of the glazier Walter Tower (quoted on p. 71) suggest that the glass came from four different windows. He believed that the Crucifixion was in situ (as now) and that the tops of the lights (above the first three rows of panels) were also unchanged. He also thought that the figures of the Archangels Michael and Gabriel were probably placed immediately on either side of the Crucifixion. Marshall argued that the archangels had originally been in the window over the chancel arch, where Michael is often found in Doom paintings weighing souls. It is likely that the composition of the window was like others of the same period, with figures in niches surrounding the Crucifixion. A good example is the south aisle east window at All Saints, North Street, York.[223] The large quantity of surviving grisaille in the east and south windows suggests that the original design was a looser composition with greater areas of grisaille and fewer figures.

There are figures which are clearly by the same hand. The Crucifixion and archangels share the lattice backgrounds, and the drawing of the faces and diapering are closely related. The least conforming figures in the window are the green-coped bishop, and the full-face head of Christ. These are considered further below. Comparing the images in all three windows there are some minor coincidences in individual fragments of the backgrounds, and obvious similarities in style, but the details of the figures betray different hands. Perhaps the most important aspect of the window is the early use of silver stain, as noted by Herbert Read[224] and Heather Gilderdale.[225]

The inscriptions have been rearranged several times. That in panel 1a, to *DOM:N: JOHS: KENT* (Master John Kent), probably belongs with the figure in the panel. John Kent is not found in the Hereford bishops' registers.

In the other panels, the words 'Magister' (twice), 'Adam' (twice complete and twice initially), 'Murimuth' (once complete and twice as 'UTH') and 'Cantor' (once complete and once in part) seem to indicate that Adam Murimuth Cantor was the donor. The words 'PATER' and 'FRA' can also be seen, which may relate to Murimuth's relatives or to his clerical roles.

East window (I)

1a: There is an inscription at bottom left with the garb and tower mark of Walter Tower, recording the re-leading of 1928. The tonsured priest kneeling in prayer wears a dark blue habit and is set in a niche with a deep red background with various diapering patterns. The detail of the face differs from the other figures in the drawing of the mouth.

1b: The panel shows a tonsured priest kneeling in prayer. He wears a dark brown habit and is set against a deep green background of diapering characterised by lobed flowers with protruding pistils. The top part clearly belongs with the niche but there are other inserted patterns, one with clover leaves.

1c: The niche, of mainly white and yellow, has broad pilasters with Decorated tracery, and a cusped, segmental arch surmounted by battlements. The image of Adam Murimuth, flesh-coloured, tonsured and bearded, kneels in prayer, wearing a long-sleeved surplice and an almuce with fur tassels (possibly with a separate hood attached by clasps).

1d: The kneeling, praying figure is tonsured, clean-shaven and wears a deep pink habit. The background has green diapering of lily of the valley flowers. There are three paterae, in the top of the niche a lion mask and each side of the figure a deep red plain disc.

1e: The kneeling, praying female figure wears a coif cap and dark green gown. The background has the same green diapering of lily of the valley flowers as 1d. There are three paterae (also as 1d). In the top of the niche a lion mask and each side of the figure a deep red plain disc.

2a: Madonna and Child (**Fig. 1**): This panel was previously at 1a where it had cup-and-cover borders. The subject was a popular one in the early fourteenth century, and there are surviving examples not far away at Fladbury and Warndon in Worcestershire. These are well-known for their remarkable similarity, but are clearly not by the same hand as the Eaton Bishop scene. Madley had a representation in the north aisle[226] which James Malcolm described as, 'the blessed Virgin with the infant on her left arm and the lily in the right, the colours and drapery of this figure are rich and graceful.' The Eaton Bishop Virgin fits this description, and is the only surviving version in glass of the period which does, and it suggests that the Eaton Bishop Virgin came from Madley. This is supported by the fact that the dark green background is composed of several different patterns, including the lily of the valley, which can be found in 1d and 1e, and the pointed quatrefoil found in the two lattice panels of window sII, suggesting that the panel was not complete when it was installed.

2b & 2d: Archangels Michael (**cover**) and Gabriel (**Fig. 2**): These two figures are among the most beautiful of their period. They were previously in 1b and 1d but moved to their present positions in the reglazing by Walter Tower. Representations of both figures are common in medieval art, but they are rarely shown together in stained glass. There is an even rarer local ensemble of all four archangels in an east window at Kingsland and there were archangels in the glass at the bishop's palace at Sugwas.

It has been suggested that these figures are not an original part of the east window, but Walter Tower thought they stood either side of the Crucifixion in 3c (they were there in 1827 in Thomas Bird's description), and examination of the top of the Gabriel panel shows a short section of cresting that would match the canopy-work above 3d. One of the reasons for thinking Michael was above the chancel is his association with Doom paintings, but it must be remembered that the church is dedicated to him, and it is not surprising that he should be found in pride of place in the east window (as at Ledbury).

Heather Gilderdale suggested that the whole group of Crucifixion and archangels was originally located elsewhere, but made the following comments about the intended iconography, which holds good for their present position:

> The dedication ... to St Michael no doubt rendered a depiction of the saint an attractive option, particularly if it was displayed in the prominent position high in the wall separating the chancel from the nave. Certainly, it was common practice in medieval England to incorporate an image of the patronal saint, whether in glass, wood or stone sculpture, into the fabric and furnishings of a church. However, the St Michael image was almost certainly originally incorporated within an iconographical arrangement that suggests he was also selected for purposes more complex than a general evocation of protection from a church's titular saint. He was most probably accompanied by depictions of the Archangel Gabriel and the Crucifixion, now also housed in the chancel east window, which share a number of stylistic and design features, most prominent of which is their dramatically coloured trellis-work backgrounds.[227]

Trellis backgrounds with quatrefoils at the intersections are also used at Madley, Brinsop and Credenhill. This lattice motif was 'beloved' of Continental glass painters – as can be seen, for example, in the Trades Windows at Freiburg in Germany,[228] at about the same date as the Eaton Bishop glass. There are much earlier examples: for instance, a panel from Trier of c.1270 in the Victoria and Albert Museum.[229] In England, this motif is not unique to the small area of Herefordshire churches named above, or to stained glass. The fourteenth-century sedilia at Tewkesbury are decorated with the lattice, and it appears in glass in the tracery lights there and in places as far apart as, for example, Beer Ferrers in Devon[230] and York.

Michael is most often illustrated in one of two roles, as the destroyer of the Beast (as at Kingsland) or as the judge, weighing souls at the Crack of Doom. Here Michael, robed not armoured, is shown weighing a soul. The pleading soul is beautifully drawn, but there was almost certainly a demon trying to tip the balance, which has been missing since before the Watkins photograph. The east window at Ledbury (**Fig. 88**) contains an image of Michael that shares much with Eaton Bishop's Michael.

2c: The figure of a mitred bishop with a flesh-coloured and bearded face. He holds a crozier with a foliated head in his right hand and a book in his left. He wears an alb and an apparel is visible at the foot. His amice has yellow apparel and his chasuble green. His left wrist has a yellow maniple. Marshall firmly rejects the idea that this might be Thomas Cantilupe and suggests St Barnabas. However, Barnabas is a rare saint in medieval art, and it is difficult to see why he should be in Adam Murimuth's window. Arguably this is more likely to be a local celebrity saint, such as Thomas or Dubricius.

2e: The face of Christ: The panel was formerly at 1e. It consists of a grisaille background with two yellow, petalled paterae near the base and a geometrical design in a ring towards the centre. At the top a stern, bearded face, probably of Christ in the guise of 'Man of Sorrows', of a type still to be seen at Merevale and Tewkesbury. The full-face figure is unlike any of the surviving fourteenth-century work at Eaton Bishop or Madley and therefore difficult to compare, but the technique of strong flowing line and wavy yellow hair suggests affinity with other figures in the east window. James Malcolm recorded in the north aisle (nIX) at Madley:

> In the next window is the Saviour seated under a canopy with a globe at his feet in a purple mantle trimmed with gold, the face destroyed, the hands elevated and pierced with wounds from which the blood flows in plenteous streams.

Perhaps this is the destroyed face seen by James Malcolm in Madley nIX, brought here by one of the glaziers working in the eighteenth or nineteenth century?

The panel displays a good deal of the two forms of grisaille found throughout the window. These are a sprig of three lilies, and more commonly a vine with lobed leaves. The strapwork is yellow and draws four-lobed figures with a central boss against a lattice background (best seen in 5c). There seems to be a strong affinity with the fragments of grisaille at Madley and Weobley.

Canopy-work: There are two forms of canopy-work in the third row of panels. The details of 3a, b and e are similar; the brown buttresses and pinnacles distinguish them from the canopy in 3d, which is also wider. These three were part of a window with more than three lights, with the same details, because at the top of 3b, between the birds, is a misplaced arch finial with a trefoil poppy head which is the same as those at the base of each crowning pinnacle. These canopies were probably taken from the window over the chancel arch. The form, with an octagonal drum and a niche flanked by buttresses, is very reminiscent of the work in the choir clerestory at Tewkesbury. The canopy in 3d is three lights wide and, apart from the birds, is wholly different from the three described above.

Crucifixion in 3c: There are three representations of the Crucifixion at Eaton Bishop. The Crucifixion in the east window has features which appear frequently in glass of the early fourteenth century and are based on even earlier painted glass and manuscript images. The arms of Christ slope down to His shoulders and His torso is curved into a reversed S, while His head droops and His eyes are closed. This depiction is found in all other Herefordshire examples.

An exception in another medium is the Mappa Mundi image in which Christ has a raised head and open eyes. Most Crucifixions in this survey have a green Cross, with the example in the adjacent north window being an exception. The green Cross represents life – the Tree of Life – which persists in the face of death. It is a deep-rooted image in stained glass as far back as Chartres in the twelfth century, and is found in illuminated manuscripts. There is a representation in a psalter of *c*.1260 from Liege,[231] which shows that the Eaton Bishop scene follows a European tradition practised for almost two centuries.

Upper canopy-work: These panels are in situ. A pleasing feature is the inclusion of little buildings among the pinnacles in 4a and 4e.

CHANCEL SOUTH-EAST WINDOW (sII) (Fig. 56)
No description by local antiquarians has been found before George Marshall's paper of 1922.[232] Silas Taylor referred to windows (plural), with donor figures in the chancel in the seventeenth century, but in 1832 Thomas Bird mentions only the north-east window ('North aisle E window remains of stained glass'),[233] which suggests that there was nothing of interest in the south-east window. It is probable that the tracery light is in situ, much-restored, but the four pictorial panels and the grisaille in the main lights come from other windows. The photograph of *c*.1931 in the Royal Commission survey shows that the two main lights have been swapped. The Crucifixion and donor were in the west light, which meant that the Virgin was looking in the wrong direction, away from Christ.

The three-light window in the north transept is the most likely source of the Crucifixion with the Virgin and St John. The panels share lattice backgrounds and mannered figures with the east

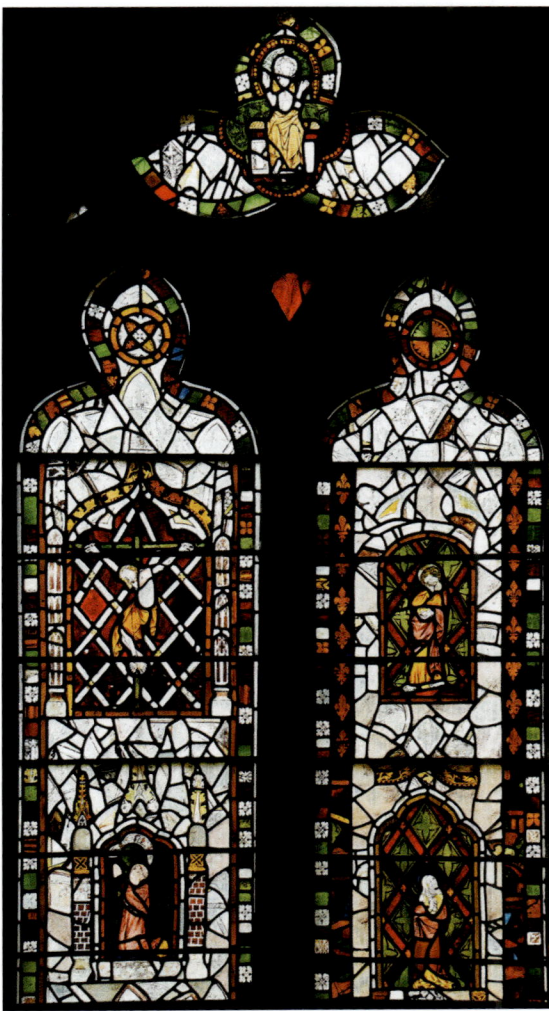

Fig. 56 Eaton Bishop: The chancel south-east window (sII)

window and are probably contemporary. The images of St John and Christ in the two windows are so similar that they must be related. The images of the Virgin are different in form but not in style. The donor figure has a scroll with *AVE MARIA*. It would be tempting to link this donor with the Virgin and Child in the east window, but the drawing does not match.

At the top of the window is an image of Christ in Glory. This figure seems to be earlier than others in the window. There is no hint of yellow stain, and the drawing is relatively crude. The border may be in situ, but the grisaille probably comes from another window. Christ's pose is a conflation of the familiar Christ in Glory and Christ of the Five Wounds, in that the seated Christ displays the wound in his left hand while raising his right in blessing.

Chancel north window (nII)

This panel, in the tracery light, is incomplete and the Christ disjointed. The standing figure appears to be a female, with her head covered, but she is on the wrong side for Mary.

Eaton Bishop and Madley

The Eaton Bishop glass tends to attract comparison with the fourteenth-century glass at Madley (1.5 miles away by the old track via Wormhill). There exist similarities between the grisaille vines in some panels of both churches, and at Eaton Bishop there are a few fragments of the 'Oxford' canopy-work found at Madley. However, these might be explained by the fact that, in the mid eighteenth century, Thomas Gough, Samuel Fisher, James Parry and John Rogers worked at both churches, and it might be supposed that they had stocks of glass they used in both, or that glass was transferred from one church to the other. It is suggested above that the Man of Sorrows (I.2e) and the Virgin and Child (I.2a) could have been transferred from Madley. There was also a Crucifixion in the north aisle at Madley, now lost. It is possible that the fragments in nII or the panel in sII are from Madley.

Marshall thought that the work at Eaton Bishop was by the same workshop as that found at Madley. They share motifs which are widespread, but Sarah Brown (making the comparison from the Madley standpoint) considered that details do not tie up sufficiently to support Marshall's suggestion.[234] It is worth listening also to Herbert Read who wrote about the glass almost a century ago,

> At Eaton Bishop the … figures have a background of trellised quarries, but here the colour is so diverse and fresh, and the drawing of foliage pattern on the quarries so free and individual, as to be in no sense comparable with the French practice.
>
> There is still in England survivals of early Gothic glass-paintings which exhibit not merely English, but even more localized characteristics. The splendid glass at Eaton Bishop, is a pre-eminent example. It is not strictly comparable with any glass in France, nor even with any other glass in England, and one can only suppose that it emanated from a local school at Hereford.[235]

EATON-UNDER-HEYWOOD
St Edith (SO 4997 9002, SY6 7DH)

There are fragments of fourteenth-century grisaille glass from several schemes with vine leaf and tulip motifs in the tracery of a north nave window (nIII).

FOWNHOPE
St Mary (SO 5809 3428, HR1 4PQ)

This large Norman church was greatly altered during the early fourteenth century when most of the windows were made. In 1846 Sir Stephen Glynne found 'the east window is of three lights and has some stained glass.' Glynne rarely mentions glass, so it was perhaps of more significance than the cursory note suggests.[236]

In 1932 the Royal Commission recorded fragments of fourteenth-century glass in the east window and the middle window of the south aisle.[237] The glass in the south aisle has gone, possibly to be incorporated into the east window. The glass now in the EAST WINDOW (I), is as the Royal Commission described, but it must be said that the formal geometrical design gives no pleasure, and a random jumble – as, for example at Holme Lacy – would have been preferable. Most of the fragments are fourteenth-century with vine leaf grisaille and 'Ledbury borders'.

FOY
St Mary (SO 5979 2835, HR9 6QY)

The church was reordered in the fourteenth century and the windows changed. One of the survivals from this time is the CHANCEL NORTH-WEST WINDOW (nIII) which retains fragments of fourteenth-century glass.

The EAST WINDOW glass is dated 1675 and is a copy of the window of 1630 at nearby Sellack. Marshall was of the view that Paul Abrahall, who died in 1675 and whose monument is in the chancel, was responsible for commissioning the window:

> In 1675 the east wall of the chancel was pulled down and re-erected with the present perpendicular four-light window. Above the window is a plaque with the arms of Abrahall and 'I.A.' and '1675'. It is said that Paul Abrahall in 1675, by his will, directed this window to be erected. It contains glass of the period and is a copy of the east window in the adjoining parish of Sellack, which dates from 1630. In the glass is a monogram 'P.A.' for Paul Abrahall, and the date, 1675.[238]

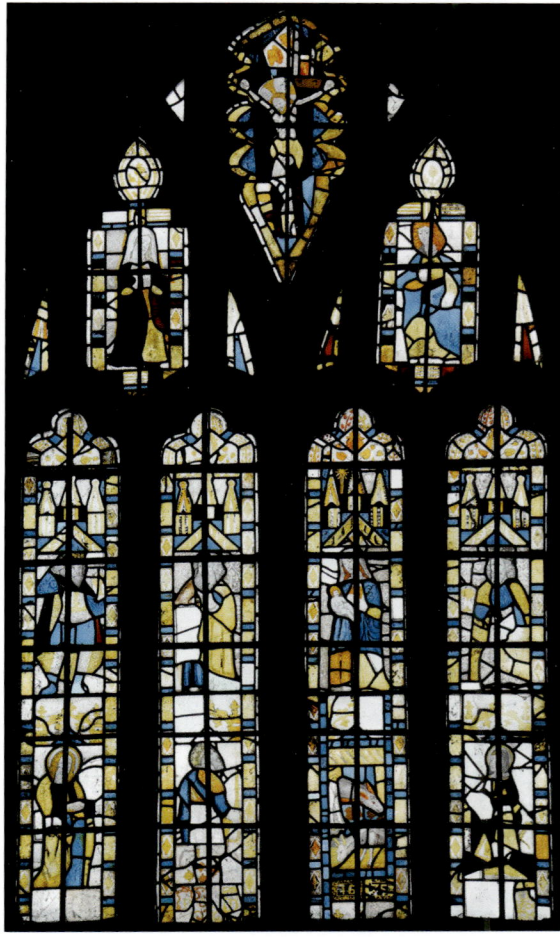

Fig. 57 Foy: east window (I)

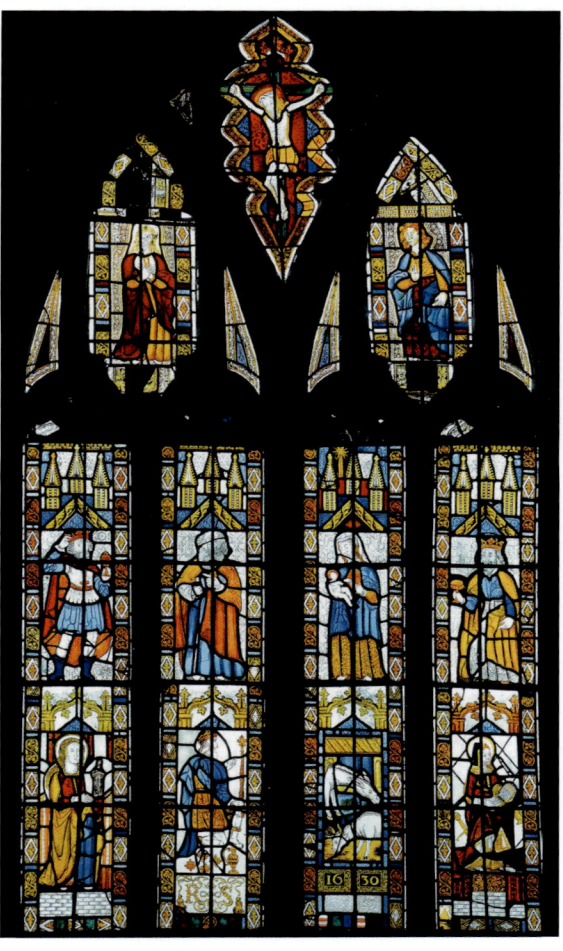

Fig. 58 Sellack: east window (I)

More recent texts suggest that the idea of the window, if not its execution, belonged to John Abrahall who died in 1640 (without issue) and that it was:

> executed according to the will of John Abrahall [died] 1640. He bequeathed lands, goods and stocks for a 'fayer windowe containing three lights and there place the same after the same manner as such is placed in the church of Sellack.'[239]

The church website supports this view:

> In the early fifteenth century the Abrahall family appear as lords of the manor, their principal residence being at Ingestone, located at the tip of the Welsh Foy peninsula.
>
> John Abrahall was the greatest lay benefactor of the village. He (…) left money to rebuild the east wall, putting in it stained glass deliberately copied from Sellack's East window – a bequest delayed for 35 years by defaulting executors. His initials and the date 1673 are on the East gable.

Perhaps the wrangling was over the wording of the will, which required a three-light window like that at Sellack – which is a four-light window. Paul, rather than usurping his cousin's monument, may have ordered and financed its completion, sharing the honours with John who is named on the gable. It may also have simply been the result of the decades of unrest and uncertainty in Church and State. The Abrahalls were Royalists, and the window might still have been considered to have superstitious imagery. The decades after 1640 were not favourable ones for members of the minor gentry to be putting Crucifixes in their chancels.

The lives of the Scudamores and the Abrahalls were bound together in the life of the Wye peninsula. Rowland Scudamore, who is commemorated in the Sellack window, purchased his house, Caradoc Court, from the Abrahalls. From this point the Scudamores became the more prominent and powerful dynasty, while the Abrahalls took to the church and held the benefice successively (with only two interruptions) from 1642 until 1937.[240] The Abrahall hold on the church was guided by the same Laudian spirituality that Viscount John Scudamore expressed in his churches. At Foy the sanctity of the chancel is preserved through the survival of the screen, and a new pulpit was placed in the nave – in the same position as that at Sellack.

The EAST WINDOW (Fig. 57) was poorly made and has weathered badly. As noted, the window was repaired shortly before 1912 and, 'It has recently been re-leaded, and the faces painted in.'

The Royal Commission volume of 1931 included a photograph which shows little difference from today's window. However, it is noted in Pevsner that the window was 'repaired and lightened' by Hardman in 1933.[241] Close comparison suggests the leading pattern was unchanged, but some larger, darkened pieces – for example above the Magdalene's jar[242] in panel 1a and above the head of the figure in 1b – were replaced with plain glass.

One striking difference between the two windows is the figure intended to be St Catherine with her attributes of a sword and barbed wheel. At Sellack she is a nimbed figure with a black, gabled hood of the fifteenth century or later. She holds a book and wears a deep red cloak over a white robe edged in gold pellet borders. The two figures at Foy and Sellack face in opposite directions because the Sellack figure was inside-out and has been reversed since 1931.

GOODRICH
St Giles (SO 5722 1906, HR9 6JA)

Silas Taylor, visiting the church in the mid seventeenth century, recorded the arms of Talbot with the kneeling figures of John and Mary Bry and William and Sibilla Sindusby, the donors of the window. In the east window of the north aisle, where medieval glass can still be seen, Taylor recorded the arms of Talbot and Lisle, which remain today. The Lisle arms were recorded about 200 years later by the herald Thomas King (1802–72).[243]

In December 1859, a meeting was held in the vestry room of the church, to begin the task of repairing and reordering the church.[244] The restoration of the NORTH AISLE EAST WINDOW by Burlison and Grylls was unveiled in the October of that year.[245]

There are four shield-bearing angels in the lowest row of tracery lights. To the left (A1) (Fig. 59) the shield, the angel and the upper part of the wings are in situ. The lower part is much-repaired, with the replacement pieces being

Fig. 59 Goodrich: the Lisle arms in the north aisle (nII)

York glaziers were working for Bishop Spofford at Sugwas at about the same time as this window was made (see Ross-on-Wye, p. 177).

In the next panel (A2), the early nineteenth-century Royal Arms must be by Burlison and Grylls. The angel is complete, except for the head which is by Burlison and Grylls. The chequerboard plinth also appears to be intact. The next panel (A3) is also restored: the head of the angel and the shield – Cantilupe's arms adopted by the diocese – are Burlison and Grylls's work. The floral diapering stands out in this panel.

The fourth panel (A4) holds the arms of Lisle of Kingston Lisle. John Talbot's wife, Margaret Beauchamp, inherited Kingston Lisle. Their son, John, was granted the baronetcy in 1444. Both Johns were killed in France in 1453. Presumably, the arms appear in the window in her right, since John II did not use them, and that right would have been extinguished in 1444. This would give a range of dates for the window: between 1424, when Talbot's Garter arms came into use, and 1444, when Margaret's Lisle arms were given up. The panel has been much weathered and repaired, and the upper body and possibly the head of the angel are replacements. The two pieces do not fit at the neck below the amice.

In the row above, are angels bearing Passion symbols. In the left panel (B1) is an angel bearing the Crown of Thorns and a stave. The wings, robe and diapering are old glass but the head, sponge, and part of the Crown of Thorns are modern replacements. The middle panel (B2) is the work of Burlison and Grylls. Again, shading and distressing result in new work which sits comfortably with the old glass. In the right panel (B3) is an angel bearing the three nails and a stave. The head and spear are modern replacements.

obvious. A good deal of the chequerboard plinth remains. The angel holds the arms of Talbot and Strange. Sir John Talbot, sometimes known as the English Achilles, acquired the baronies of Talbot and Strange when his niece died in 1421, but the quartered arms were probably not adopted until after his appointment to the Order of the Garter in 1424. The angel has the oval face and eyes with curlicues in the corners typical of the International Style. The rather fluffy, droopy wings don't echo so strongly with the York school, but the two long streamers from the wings do. David O'Connor suggests that the

GREETE
St James

In 1733 William Mytton sketched a complete Crucifixion in the east window, with Mary, John, an angel and a saint.

HAMPTON COURT CHAPEL, HOPE UNDER DINMORE
The Chapel (so 5207 5242, HR6 0PN)

The windows of the chapel presently display shields, mainly of the Coningsby family with their distinctive rabbits. In the EAST WINDOW are five panels in a row. One of these has three small roundels linked by a black letter inscription. The roundels represent the arms of England quartered with France, the helm of England surmounted by a lion and the swan badge of the Bohun Earls of Hereford. The arms of Devereux, with a *red fess and three red torteaux* (discs), were seen by Silas Taylor in the seventeenth century and are combined with the *starred black bend* of the Lenthalls in another shield.

The quartered arms of Coningsby rabbits with lions display a conjunction which can also be seen above the dining hall fireplace. It was not recorded by antiquarians and might have been in another part of the house. The *lion rampant* (red on gold) *with engrailed bordure* is associated with the Cornewalls, but there is no Coningsby/Cornewall union in the line of occupants of the Court. The Court was purchased by Humphrey Coningsby from the Cornewalls, but there is no marriage until his great-great-granddaughter, Anne Lyttelton (d.1656), married Thomas Cornewall (d.1635).

A shield with three harts on a blue background, of unknown relevance to the

Fig. 60 Hampton Court Chapel: before the sale of the glass in 1924 (by permission of Mr Michael James)

Coningsby line, may have been introduced at the reglazing following the sale of the medieval glass in 1924 (see below).

The THREE WINDOWS ON THE NORTH SIDE have Coningsby arms. In the EASTERN WINDOW, the arms of Thomas Coningsby impaling Fitzwilliam with the cypher of Thomas Coningsby and Phillipa Fitzwilliam. The panels are dated in successive years, 1613 and 1614. The arms and the quarries with the cypher appear jammed in and are surrounded by fragments which are probably of similar seventeenth-century date, given their depiction of classical architectural elements, and were probably taken from other panels of the north windows.

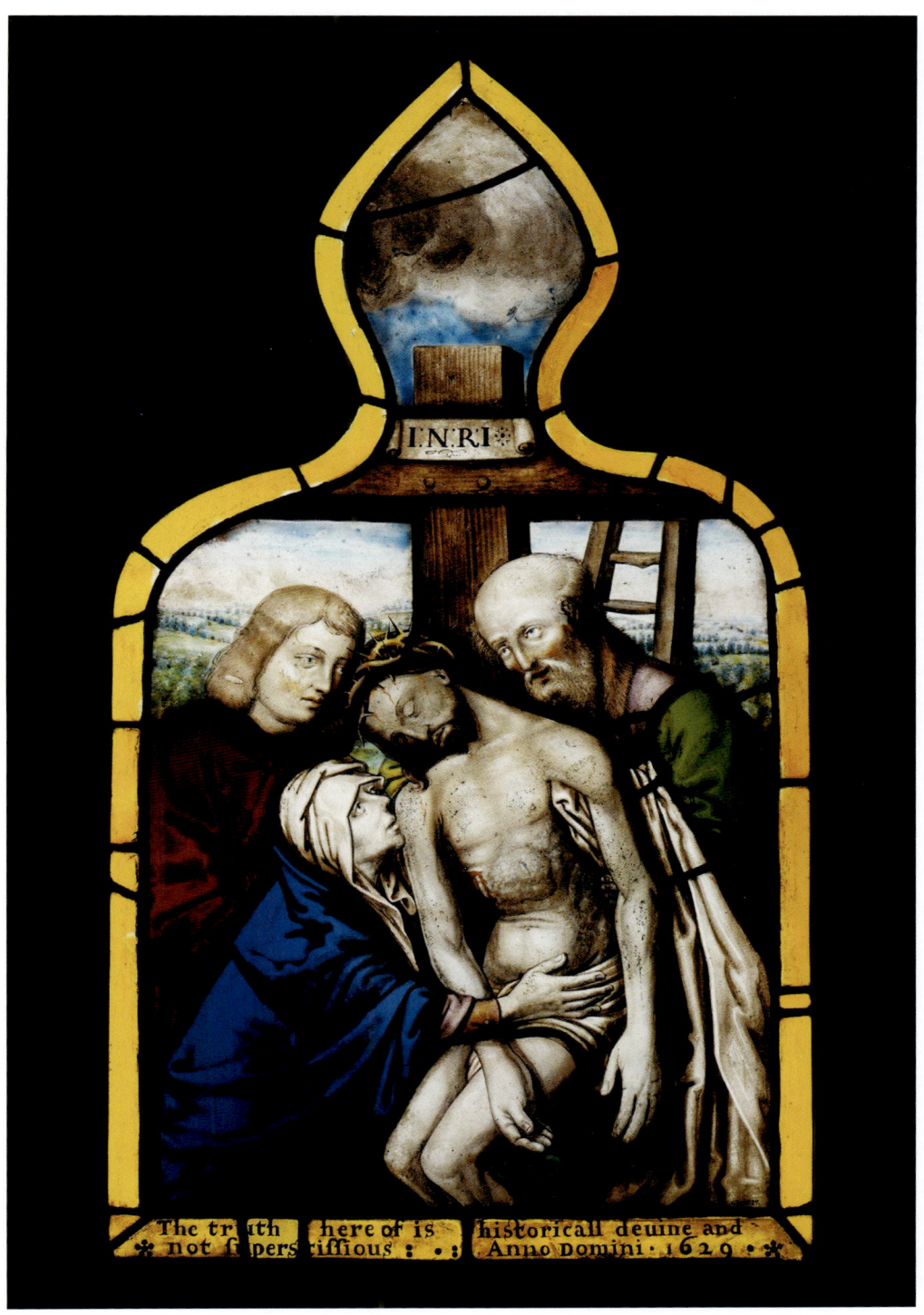

Fig. 61 Hampton Court Chapel: the Deposition by Abraham van Linge
(by permission of the Victoria and Albert Museum)

The middle window has two shields connected to the Lenthalls which must be part of the first glazing of the chapel; the shields are set among mainly later fragments. The western window has two shields which contain the arms of Ann Fereby, or Ferby, who married Sir Humphrey Coningsby in the 1480s (*a fess ermine between three goat heads*). Several different quarries have been incorporated in the 1924 reglazing. Some are probably medieval, but a substantial number look fresher and may be copies. Exotic plants and roses are found in the east window, and in the north windows, a distinctive owl.

The existing glass is a small part of the glazing that adorned the chapel from the seventeenth century until 1924, when it was sold to the dealers Roy Grosvenor Thomas and his partner Wilfred Drake.[246] They were the leading figures in a trade which seems at best dubious, and they were also glaziers and could arrange for the re-leading of windows once valuable medieval glass had been removed. They worked on behalf of collectors, including Sir William Burrell of Glasgow and many museums and wealthy clients in America. There is a photograph by Richard L. Warham, 1851–1926,[247] taken just before the sale in 1924, which shows what a profound loss the sale was to Herefordshire (Fig. 60).

It is known that by 1683, when Dingley visited, there were Apostles with Creed articles, a Deposition, an image of the Virgin, the 'prophets' and saints including Francis, Winifrida, Anne, John the Baptist and Stephen.[248] Just over 30 years later, James Hill made a more detailed record of 18 figures[249] which were augmented, possibly after 1786, by panels of glass now in Hereford Cathedral (nXVIII & nXIX).

The important recent publications about the glass, by Madeline Caviness,[250] suggest that the Apostles were taken from the west window of the south transept of Hereford Cathedral during the Civil War or Commonwealth. The cathedral window is six lights wide and each light is 2ft 7½ins (800mm) wide, so a comfortable fit for the panels now in Boston, which are 1ft 7in (485mm) wide, in two tiers. In her earlier paper, Caviness envisaged a reconstruction of the original arrangement in two tiers, which produces harmony in the poses of the figures and the colours of their seaweed backgrounds, and continuity in the Creed articles.

There are eight Apostles now in Boston, but it is known that Philip was also in the chapel, and one seventeenth-century description suggests there were more, perhaps even twelve. The question must be asked as to why all the surviving Apostles were not assembled in the chapel east window? The photograph (Fig. 60) from before the sale, shows that the centre light was occupied by two scenes from the Life of the Virgin (Figs 15 & 16) and two male figures – St Laurence and a prelate. This arrangement reflects the Marian devotion of the Coningsbys, but it might also reflect the arrangement of the original window from which the glass was taken.

An alternative source for the Apostles could be the great west window at Leominster Priory. The Leominster window, with its buttressed mullions, is influenced by work of the fourteenth century at Gloucester and was intended as a costly statement of the pride and growing wealth of the town. The six side lights at Leominster are 2ft 2ins (660mm) wide and probably a better fit for the Boston panels than the lights at Hereford Cathedral. There was probably a Creed window in the north transept at Dilwyn, but this can be ruled out for having insufficient height.[251]

The Leominster west window could have had the Creed series in two tiers in the side lights (of which there are exactly twelve), and scenes from the Life of the Virgin between the buttresses, which is how they were subsequently arranged in the Hampton Court Chapel. These two programmes are clearly linked because the floral ground on which Mary kneels in the Annunciation is the same ground on which the Apostles stand. This firm link between Apostles and Virgin suggests that the two themes shared a window like the Leominster great west window, rather than being in separate windows in the cathedral as Caviness suggests. The twelve side lights of the Leominster window are the ideal setting for the Apostles and would have placed the catechetical image of the Creed prominently in the parish nave.

Joe and Caroline Hillaby say,

> Originally [the window] would have been filled with the remarkable stained glass of the era, and on sunny afternoons the parish's south nave would have been suffused with its colours. Given Leominster's reputation during the Commonwealth as 'little Geneva', it is hardly surprising that every trace of the original glazing has been lost.[252]

The idea that the Hampton Court glass was at Leominster is further supported because both the window and the glass can be similarly dated to c.1425–35. The Priory seems to be a church which has been deliberately cleansed of all 'superstitious' glass, whilst it is not certain that Hereford Cathedral was. Hereford retained 'superstitious' medieval glass in the south transept, where Caviness suggested the Apostles were. When Dingley visited after the Civil War, even the Virgin survived there.[253]

There is another possibility – that the glass was not a casualty of iconoclasm but of age. The glass would have been in place for well over 200 years by the mid seventeenth century and was probably in a poor state. The Hereford Chapter might have had reasons for disposing of the glass, but perhaps the burghers of 'little Geneva' had a stronger inclination to dispose of painted glass, which meant nothing to them theologically, and which would have raised some cash towards a new, simpler glazing scheme. It happened again just over 200 years later in 1924, when the Apostles and other glass were sold away from Hampton Court and the present simpler glazing scheme was installed. (The same approach to medieval glass can be seen at Brinsop where the wardens sold much of the pictorial glass.) When John Price wrote about Leominster Priory towards the end of the eighteenth century, he said,

> The windows were of painted glass, some brilliant remains of which are to be seen at this time about the town, which may have given the church the gloomy appearance Leland describes.[254]

This suggests a sell-off rather than a smash-up, and it would not be a surprise to find that the Royalist Thomas Coningsby of Hampton Court (1550–1625) or his successor, Fitzwilliam (c.1596–1666), had been a purchaser. They were prominent in Leominster affairs, and it is only five miles from the Priory to the Court. The later Thomas represented Leominster in 14 parliaments, was Lord of the Manor and eager to wield the authority once vested in the Prior.

The origins of the Creed Apostles may be supposition, and the exact content of the windows in the seventeenth century remains unclear, but it is certain that Thomas Coningsby did some reglazing in 1613–14, as can be seen from dated arms in the tracery of north windows. The full extent of the work is not known, but it is possible that the Apostles and other medieval glass were installed at that time. The Deposition, with its plea to iconoclasts (see below), is dated 1626 which suggests it was commissioned in the year of Thomas's death – or perhaps it was an addition by Fitzwilliam Coningsby making a plea in the wording of the inscription to protect his late father's glazing project.

It is certain that the glass which was sold in 1924 was in place by the time James Hill made his notes early in the eighteenth century. He counted 23 different panels not including the armorial glass. The arrangement probably remained unchanged until the addition of glass in nIII from Hereford Cathedral, which has since been returned to the north transept there (nXVIII & nXIX). In the cathedral accounts for 1737 a large sum was paid to William Reese for 'glazing and painting the west window' which might be the source of those panels.

John Arkwright undertook substantial alterations to the main house between 1830 and 1845, when the south window of the chapel was blocked. The photograph in Fig. 60 and Grosvenor Thomas's list have the figures of Becket and St Francis moved to the upper lights of the east window, while the Pietà, the Baptist and Winifreda were moved to north windows. A panel showing St Anne teaching the Virgin cannot be accounted for.

In 1912, Richard Arkwright[255] sold Hampton Court to Mrs Nancy Burrell (not related to the collector William Burrell). In 1923 she began to dispose of the estate and a sale was held by Knight Frank. The house and park (Lot 45) were not sold and remained with Mrs Burrell until 1925. The glass was acquired by Thomas and Drake in 1924. No doubt Knight Frank, who sold many country estates at that time, were aware of Thomas and Drake and made the necessary arrangements for a scheme which not only raised money but solved a repair problem which could have been discouraging prospective purchasers of the house.

The glass was sold to several collectors, museums and galleries. The table opposite is a summary of the panels other than those in Hereford Cathedral.

Only one of the panels can confidently be described as having been commissioned for the chapel from the artist, and that is the Deposition, now in the Victoria and Albert Museum (Fig. 61). It is a rare, dated panel and a moving monument to troubled theological times with its plea to those who oppose imagery. 'The Beauty of Holiness' was Laud's ideal and he was an acquaintance of Coningsby whose circle of connections included Viscount Scudamore who reglazed Abbey Dore and Sellack. It has been called 'one of the most remarkable pieces of religious glass to survive from the period.'[258] The Victoria and Albert catalogue describes the panel:

> This panel is characteristic of the stained-glass making techniques of the early seventeenth century. Coloured glass was scarce owing to the destruction of glasshouses in Lorraine – the chief source of supply. In its place, white glass was cut into panes and painted with enamels in the manner of a translucent canvas. Both stained and painted glass have been used in this panel.
>
> This window can be attributed to Abraham van Linge (active in England from about 1625 to 1641). His initials are painted on the top rung of the ladder leaning against Christ's cross. The glass was painted, probably in Herefordshire, from a composition by Rogier van der Weyden.[259]

PANEL	IN THE CHAPEL	PRESENT WHEREABOUTS
Apostles with Creed articles: St Peter, St Andrew, St James Great, St John, St Bartholomew, St Simon, St James Less (called Thaddeus in some accounts), St Matthias	From Leominster Priory or Hereford Cathedral. Earliest reference, Dingley 1683. In the photo of the east window prior to sale.	Boston, Museum of Fine Arts.
Apostle with Creed article: Philip	Part of the Creed series above. Described by Hill before 1727 in a north window.	Not known.
Other Apostles	Dingley and Coningsby suggest that there were more than 8 Apostles, the additional saints being in north windows.	Not known.
St Laurence	Described by Hill before 1727 in the east window.	V&A Museum. These two items were sold by Grosvenor Thomas to Arthur Sachs in 1925, repurchased, and sold to the V&A Museum in 1931.[256]
St Stephen	Earliest reference, Dingley 1683. Described by Hill before 1727 in a north window.	
St Benedict	Described by Hill before 1727 in the east window. In the photo of the east window prior to sale.	Smithsonian Institute, Washington.
Annunciation	Described by Hill before 1727 in the east window. In the photo of the east window prior to sale.	These two items were first sold to the industrialist Charles Myron Taylor. He died in 1959 and they were purchased by the Dirk de Leur Collection, Switzerland in 1960. Purchased by Burrell Collection, Glasgow in 1979.[257]
Assumption of the Virgin	Described by Hill before 1727 in the east window. In the photo of the east window prior to sale.	
Deposition	Earliest reference, Dingley 1683. Described by Hill before 1727 in the east window. NOT in the photo of the east window prior to sale.	V&A Museum.
'Adrianus'	Described by Hill before 1727 in a north window.	Not known.
St Catherine	Described by Hill before 1727 in a north window.	Not known.
St Thomas Becket, St Winifreda and St Anne and the Virgin (3 panels)	Described by Hill before 1727 in a south window. In the photo of the east window prior to sale.	Sold to J. McConnell of Montreal and now in Montreal Museum of Fine Arts.
Pietà	Described by Hill before 1727 in the south window.	Boston, Museum of Fine Arts.
St Francis and St John Baptist (2 panels)	Earliest reference, Dingley 1683. Described by Hill before 1727 in the south window.	Boston, Museum of Fine Arts.
St John Evangelist and St Barbara (2 panels)	In the photo of the east window prior to sale (topmost lights).	Bought by Myron Taylor Collection. Now owned by Madeline Caviness.
Quarries with floral designs	Associated with the above two panels	King's College Chapel, Cambridge and private collections (S. Thomas, personal communication, November 2022)

Table summarising the panels from Hampton Court Chapel, including their original placement within the chapel, and present whereabouts

HENTLAND

Saint Dubricius (SO 5429 2639, HR9 6LW)

Silas Taylor saw the EAST WINDOW (I) and made the following note:

> In ye chancel of ye church wch is now a small though ancient building is ye remainders in ye east window of some effigies under written thus: orate pro anima Ricardi Roderham doctoris in Theologia … & peri bendiary Ecclie cathedralis Herefordie & rectoris de Ross qui … fieri fecit.[260]

The inscription was still in place in 1837 when it was reported (with somewhat different wording from the above) by Charles Robinson: 'The east-window contains the figure of an Ecclesiastic, with the legend – "Orate pro anima Ricardi Rotheram, D.D."'[261]

Fig. 62a Hentland: the donor Richard Rotheram in the east window (I)

Fig. 62b Hentland: unidentified figure in the east window (I)

90 THE MEDIEVAL STAINED GLASS OF HEREFORDSHIRE & SHROPSHIRE

Rotherham (or Roderham) was an important cleric, a protégé of Bishop Thomas Spofford and a fellow Yorkshireman. He was presented as prebendary by Spofford at the end of 1430, and to Canonical House (as Chancellor of the Choir) two months later. In 1434 he was presented to the Ross rectory,[262] and his relationship with Hentland probably starts after that date. He resigned as treasurer of the cathedral in the same year. He remains in the Hereford record until 1454 when he resigned his positions at Ross and as prebendary of Huntingdon.[263] He continued to serve in Exeter Diocese and died in 1455.[264]

The window, in which Rotherham appeared as donor, must have been commissioned after 1434, and was probably in place by the time he retired from clerical life in Hereford in 1454. This period overlaps the decades when Bishop Spofford was glazing the chapel at the Bishops Palace at Sugwas with glass that is now in the east window at Ross. There is a strong possibility that Spofford engaged a workshop of John Thornton, so the question arises as to whether the Hentland glass is of the York School. It is quite different to the Ross glass, and yet there is something of York in the face of Mary, with the curlicues from her squarish eyes and the stark, slashed hairline with its rolled edge.

The three figures (Figs 62a–62c) are probably not in their intended relationship and appear to contain fragments of clothing from more than one figure. The outer figures also appear to be of a different scale to the central character. At the centre is the donor, Ricardi Roderham – possibly a rare, accurate portrait.

The other two figures are both nimbed and have curly, yellow hair and both have been shortened at mid-thigh level. The Royal Commission suggests that they represent the Annunciation, but the standing 'Gabriel', whose robes appear to be original, holds a book (the hand having been replaced) which doesn't fit with Annunciation iconography. The left arm of this figure is missing

The surviving part of the figure in the south light, holding her hands in prayer, was probably kneeling. She is distinguished from the other nimbed figure by her long hair and her yellow lined and hemmed robe. Her demeanour offers a more convincing argument for this having been an Annunciation scene.

Fig. 62c Hentland: unidentified figure in the east window (l)

HEREFORD

Cathedral of St Mary and St Ethelbert
(SO 5100 3980, HR1 6NG)

At the end of the nineteenth century, the writer of a history of the cathedral was only able to note that, 'The stained glass has survived only in a few fragments, scattered about the eastern end of the cathedral.'[265] When the Royal Commission reported in 1931, the amount of medieval glass had been increased by the addition of the panels in the north transept taken from the chapel at Hampton Court (near Leominster) in 1924. The report also noted the collections of fragments in the south aisle, the Audley Chapel heraldic glass and some fragments in the upper storey of the north porch.

The antiquaries who provided an insight into the glazing of churches such as Madley, recorded little pictorial, rather than armorial, glass in the cathedral. James Hill (d.1727), for example, devoted his long report to monuments.[266] The most extensive accounts before 1800 are the 1634 Visitation by the College of Arms,[267] the diary of Richard Symonds (1645),[268] and the notes of Silas Taylor (before 1675).[269] All omit any reference to the south aisle of the nave. Taylor's work was copied by Richard Rawlinson in his description of the cathedral, published in 1717,[270] and by James Malcolm and John Duncumb[271] in the following century.

At the west end of the nave there was a large window in Perpendicular style which still held images of kings and princes, including the Henrys from IV–VI, and the arms of Mortimer, the Templars and France quartered with England. The kingly figures would probably have occupied each of the six lights at the same level, forming a row of royals standing shoulder to shoulder, perhaps with coats of arms at the base of each panel. This recalls the fourteenth-century glass in the choir clerestory of Tewkesbury Abbey or the great east window of Gloucester Cathedral, but some if not all the Hereford glass would have been considerably later in date than those windows.

Paul Iles suggests, 'The window was inserted before 1435 by William Lochard [d.1438], canon residentiary and precentor, whose memorial brass was at the west end of the nave. The brass was lost after the collapse of the west front.'[272] David Whitehead says, 'Lochard was a prebendary in the Chapel Royal at Windsor and had benefitted from Royal patronage. Thus, the glass in the window celebrated his noble and royal patrons with the figures of Richard II, Henry IV, Henry V and Henry VI.'[273]

In the nave aisles, shields remained in the heads of every window, forming a roll call of the great families of the fourteenth century. The Mortimers, Beauchamps, Bohuns, Mountfords, Cornewalls and Clares were represented more than once. The windows with their famous ballflower carvings, are of the second quarter of the fourteenth century, and the south aisle (sXVIII & sXIX) held the arms of Bishop Charlton (bishop 1327–44).

Dingley described stained glass images of Thomas Cantilupe, the Virgin, King Ethelbert and St Dennis of France in the south transept,[274] where Rawlinson and Symonds found numerous shields including those of the See, the Deanery and the Beauchamps. The south transept may have been the location of important fifteenth-century glass of the York School. Madeline Caviness, in two papers,[275] argues that glass was removed from the cathedral by Thomas Coningsby during the Civil War and subsequently installed in the windows of the chapel at Hampton Court (see Hampton

Fig. 63 Hereford Cathedral: Dingley's drawing of the Virgin in the old library

Court, p. 84). The west window of the south transept and the vault were made during Bishop Spofford's time, as part of the founding of a chapel to St Anne, his favourite saint. His connection with York and with the glaziers there was strong, which makes a case for the York connection with the Hampton Court glass. That connection is confirmed by some of the glass fragments in the cathedral archive (see below) which show characteristics of York painting. However, none of the Hampton Court glass can be correlated with written accounts of the cathedral.

Hill described paintings in the Chapter House and noted that, 'over several of these figures were coats of arms such are in the windows of St Ann's Isle [sic].'[276] That is the south choir aisle where arms can be seen today following restoration in the nineteenth century.

Rawlinson[277] described 'several mangled Inscriptions and Images' in the old library above the Bishop's Chapel. His account was copied by Duncumb:[278]

> ... in the upper light on the left hand, was the figure of the Virgin Mary, with an infant in her arms, and with the letters M. A. and R. frequently repeated. This was recorded and drawn by Dingley 'during the reign of Charles II.' [**Fig. 63**][279]

Below was a person kneeling before a desk and holding a book with this inscription: 'Orate pro aia Johis Kinge, --London:'

ICONOCLASM IN THE CATHEDRAL

The single-minded focus of Silas Taylor on coats of arms is well-known, but he does occasionally refer to pictorial glass. It is possible that no pictorial glass was left in the 15 windows of the cathedral, which he described as only having heraldic glass. Certainly, that was the case at the end of the eighteenth century when Duncumb described the nave as having,

> ... grandeur which, on the other hand, loses much of its force by an uninterrupted glare of light, and the almost total absence of appropriate ornament.[280]

This would represent a very great and assiduous destruction by will or neglect during the Reformation and Civil War; but, without further evidence, it must also be allowed that Taylor's and Rawlinson's accounts are simply incomplete. Part of the answer to that puzzle lies in questions about the care and maintenance of the windows during and after the Reformation. David Whitehead says of the first iconoclasm in the Reformation,

> Apart from the destruction of the Cantilupe shrine and the defacing of the mourning knights on his tomb chest there seems to have been little deliberate vandalism at Hereford. The letters and papers of Henry VIII 1538 refer to a holy water stoup and an image of the Trinity being removed and a further letter in 1547 required the removal of all images including stained glass.[281]

Whether that Henrician injunction was carried out can only be surmised, given the lack of iconoclastic zeal which David Whitehead identified, and which is illustrated by the survival of the Mary panel, noted above, in the library.

There was a period of much greater expenditure on the fabric after 1617: a calm before the storm of the Civil War. In the second period of iconoclasm, Caviness suggests that a substantial amount of medieval glass was removed from the cathedral by Fitzwilliam Coningsby while the Royalists held the city between December 1642 and December 1645. Again, David Whitehead finds no strong evidence for systematic iconoclasm.

> Neglect and not wilful damage posed the greatest threat to the fabric between 1645 and 1660. There are no fabric rolls surviving from this period during which the cathedral became the meeting house for the city on the abolition of the dean and chapter in 1649 … The only casualty of the era was the chapter house 'being beat down in the rebellion'.[282]

Iconoclasm was not inevitable – Ludlow, Great Malvern, Fairford and York testify to the possibility of survival. The glass in those places is predominantly of the fifteenth century, which meant the windows were younger and in better condition through the turbulent times in the sixteenth and seventeenth centuries than the Hereford windows. The glass in the Hereford nave was a century older than the glass at Malvern, for example, and its condition would probably have been poor when imagery was at its most unpopular. Avoiding the cost of re-glazing was a reason for preserving imagery but the higher cost of the careful repair of pictorial schemes, if a skilled glazier could be found, was a reason for their replacement with plain glazing which was within the capabilities of the plumber-glaziers of the time.

MAINTENANCE AFTER THE MID SEVENTEENTH CENTURY

The cathedral fabric accounts for this period tell a similar story to that encountered in the churchwardens' accounts of parish churches. The Dean and Chapter paid for repairs to keep the windows weatherproof every year, and sometimes spent substantial sums. As with parish churches, glaziers could be retained over quite long periods, and some were paid a retainer or salary. The plumber-glaziers seem to have been the elite of craftsmen, at times being the only men employed, and taking a significant share of the fabric budget. Their retainers exceeded even the allowance of the surveyor of the fabric.[283] Nearly all the glaziers were also plumbers, and it is not certain that every entry in the fabric accounts, beside their names, are wholly for glazing, rather than other plumbers' work; however, in many cases the nature of the work is given.

The fabric rolls from the early seventeenth century record only a very few items for glazing. The earliest, in 1613, refers to Thomas Morgan glazing the school. In the following year an allowance of 13s 4d was paid to an unnamed plumber (listed alongside the allowance to the clock-keeper). In the rolls for 1616 and 1617, Morgan was paid for glazing on the north side and the east window. Hill noted that £2 13s 4d was paid to the 'plummer and Glasier' in 1636.[284]

There is a gap of about 50 years in the accounts, but when the rolls speak again in 1660–66[285] there is recorded a substantial sum of £22 paid to James Jaggard, 'for glazing and mending the church windows.' This might include the window in the south aisle with its collection of ancient glass. From 1687 to 1728 William Griffiths was employed and paid an annual fee of £2 13s 4d. In 1719–20 he undertook considerable work, totalling over £180, which would have been more than enough to reglaze several large, aisle windows. From 1729, the work was undertaken by William Dubberley who received relatively modest sums in 1729–30 and 1731–32. He was a typical plumber-glazier and continued to be engaged for plumbing work after William Reece became the glazier of choice for the Dean and Chapter.

From 1734 to 1781 the glazing was looked after by William Reece who carried out the reglazing of the west window. His death notice in the *Hereford Journal* on 12 April 1781 describes him as the 'eminent' glazier – perhaps a hint of the regard that skilled men once enjoyed.[286] Reece was still remembered as the 'late' Plumber and Glazier in 1787, when the *Hereford Journal* reported the death of his son, an apothecary in Essex.[287] Reece, unlike the later glaziers, never advertised in the local newspapers, and cannot be found in local trade directories. He made a good living from the cathedral and church work (for example at St Peter's in Hereford) and that was probably enough for him.

A Mr Mason was engaged for two years, then in 1784 Richard Powell was engaged at an annual salary of £8 8s. It appears that the Dean and Chapter helped Powell to establish his business by paying part of the legal costs of some dealings with Francis Knill, another Hereford glazier.[288] In 1814–15, a glazier named Price came to prominence in the accounts, and interestingly the name is attached to a woman, Rachel Price. In 1792, Mr Price, glazier, was living in Church Street.[289] This may well be Rachel Price's son, who is referred to in a newspaper advertisement of 1819 as having died, and it is possible that he began the work at the cathedral in 1814. Rachel Price continued to work at the cathedral until 1822, when she advertised her retirement due to ill health.[290] In 1823 she advertised again in the newspaper as a part of winding up the business.[291] During that four-year period she received three of the four highest annual payments in the accounts between 1700 and 1865.

In the accounts for 1822–23 Matthew Williams appears as glazier, and continues in the account until 1835. He was a Londoner who set up in Hereford in 1807, by purchasing the business of Francis Knill. In 1822 his man Charles Childs inscribed his name on a plain quarry in the Audley Chapel, recording the reglazing for which Williams was paid £64 9s 10d in the following year (Fig. 64, overleaf). In 1836, William Williams took over until 1840. There is no entry for glazing in the accounts after then until 1843, but William Williams died in November of that year aged 58.[292] The 1843 payment was made to David Evans of Wyle Cop (see Lady Chapel below and Ludlow) for 'repairs to painted windows', and Evans was succeeded by James Williams who was paid more than £15 in 1845.[293] It is not known

GAZETTEER OF CHURCHES IN HEREFORDSHIRE AND THE DIOCESE OF HEREFORD   95

Fig. 64 Hereford Cathedral Audley Chapel: quarry signed by the glazier in 1822

whether these three glaziers with the name of Williams were related.

In 1848 William Rowberry was paid for glazing at the west end of the cathedral. Rowberry was probably introduced to the Dean and Chapter by John Goode, who had been employed by them on the chancel at Madley.[294] When Goode died in 1838, Rowberry bought the business from his brother Samuel Goode. Rowberry had his yard in St Owen Street, and continued to work at the cathedral until 1867.[295] In 1851 he was paid a large sum of £111,[296] but the accounts do not say where this was expended.

In 1869 Stephens & Sons were employed. They were a long-established plumbing dynasty and probably continued in the employ of the Dean and Chapter. The account book down to 1878 has two further items in relation to windows. James Bowers was paid £115 in 1877 for the restoration of a window and Henry Welsh £40 for restoration of the south-east window of the south-east transept. Both men were builders not glaziers, so the necessary glazing work was probably subcontracted.

THE REPLACEMENT OF THE WINDOW AT THE FORMER WEST END

In 1735 the replacement of the medieval west window was put in hand. The Chapter book records in August 1735:[297]

> On this day they agreed with Avery Hunt of Ross for the taking down of the great window at the west end of the church and setting up a new one in the place and stead thereof ...

Hunt was a blacksmith and was paid a goodly sum for ironwork in the following year. In October, the Dean and Chapter decided that they should seek the advice of an architect, and the chapter clerk was ordered to speak to Hunt and defer the taking down of the old window.[298] Mr John Wood (the Elder) of Bath or Mr William Townsend of Oxford were to be called for, but did not respond, so in December 1735 it was decided to seek the advice of Francis Smith of Warwick. In March 1736, the Chapter had heard nothing and resolved to put the work in hand unless a better scheme was found in time for their June meeting. In June 1736, an estimate was given by Francis Smith of Warwick for a new window. The window was of considerable size and was to be filled in with a Y-tracery design (a drawing is preserved in the archives).

The glazier, William Reece, had been working for the Dean and Chapter in 1734 and 1735,[299] and was chosen to work on the west window. There is a bill in the archives which seeks payment for glass in October 1735, on which a note is written to the effect that payment must await the approval of the Dean and Chapter.[300] The bill is curious in that it gives a price for the glass and then reduces it by more than half, leaving a sum of £7 5s 10d. In the fabric accounts, and in the Chapter Book for July 1736, this sum is referred to as Reece's 'loss' in crown glass 'prepared' for the west window.

David Whitehead says,[301]

> There was no mention of the medieval coloured glass but the account of William Reese, the glazier, allows him interest on the glass which the Chapter have reserved for themselves. This may suggest that the old glass, perhaps traditionally the property of the glazier, was being kept by the Dean and Chapter.

David Whitehead's conclusion led Paul Iles to comment that,

> In 1737 the Chapter deliberately and carefully retained the medieval glass from the window and some of it, together with other fragments, is believed to have made up the two panels of fifteenth century glass (now in the north transept).[302]

It could, however, be argued that the scraps of evidence relied on betray no such care on the part of the Chapter. The bill is for an additional cost to the glazier in the provision of the glass, and more probably means that the new glass was bought by the glazier with money from the Chapter and that it cost more than the original estimate, requiring Reece to pay a further £7 5s 10d from his own pocket. Crown glass was the most expensive glass in the eighteenth century and its price fluctuated such that a variation in the contract is not surprising. The accounts for 1735–36 show that both Reece and Smith were paid.[303] Hunt also received a substantial sum.

Reece was paid a further sum of £9 16s 9d 'for glazing and plumbing' in the same year, presumably for work at the west end.[304] The work continued for at least two years. In 1736–37, Reece received £10 9s 10d, then in 1737–38 a further substantial payment for 'glazing and painting at the West window'. Reece remained in the Chapter's employ, receiving significant sums of £68 in 1740–41 and £45 in 1742–43. These payments may represent the clearing out of medieval glass that lead to Duncumb's disappointment.

There is also a tradition that important glass of an earlier period was given to Allensmore Church, one of the churches that the Dean and Chapter are patrons of. This glass, possibly of early fourteenth-century date, includes a Crucifixion (Fig. 30).[305]

North transept west windows (nXVIII & nXIX)

There are two panels (nXVIII & nXIX, see overleaf, Figs 65 & 66) which were in a north window of the chapel at Hampton Court prior to 1924. The Hampton Court glass, described as being among the most important of its period in England,[306] was acquired by a dealer, Roy Grosvenor Thomas,[307] and sold to museums and private collectors. Grosvenor Thomas and his partner Maurice Drake retained these two panels and gave them to the cathedral in 1925.[308]

There is a tradition that the glass in the two panels was originally in the west window of the cathedral and was removed to Hampton Court when the west window was replaced or following the collapse of the west front in 1786.

Fig. 65 Hereford Cathedral: north transept (nXVIII) glass from Hampton Court

Fig. 66 Hereford Cathedral: north transept (nXIX) glass from Hampton Court

Caviness[309] points out that none of the glass now in the north transept matches published descriptions of glass in the west front, and the tradition is therefore doubtful. However, the figures described in the west window in the seventeenth century could only have occupied a part of the whole window, and it therefore remains possible that the glass came from there. An alternative possibility is that the glass came from another building, and it is suggested that at least some of the Hampton Court glass may have been at Leominster Priory. It is more likely that the painted glass, if it was in the west front window, was simply disposed of by the Dean and Chapter in order to allow its replacement with plain crown glass by William Reese, thus saving on repair costs.[310]

When the glass (Figs 65 & 66) was first installed in the cathedral, the two panels were placed in a single light, one above the other.[311] They have since been repositioned and repaired by Jim Budd (for example, the nimbus in the Virgin and Child in nXIX is now complete, compared to a drawing made by Sidney Eden in 1925).[312] The first impression is one of uniformity of style and execution. There is almost no coloured glass, and the panels are painted in black line and silver stain. There is strong reason to suggest that the workshop of John Thornton of York/ Coventry was responsible for much of this glass – the figures share the hallmark eyes, noses and hair of this workshop, and a similar style of drawing and shading. Strong affinities can be found for the armed figures and the nimbed figures in York, Great Malvern and the now dispersed glass from Hampton Court.

North transept, window nXVIII
From the bottom of the window:
- A hand holding a disc with an exotic cypher, which Eden suggests is the hand of Judas holding a coin and the infamous purse.[313]
- A male head has a nimbus with trefoiled cusps in contrast to the forked cusps of most nimbi, and is drawn more freely and with subtler shading. The aquiline features are highly distinctive.
- The head of a soldier wearing a bascinet with a visor on side pivot mounts with the edge of the camail (a hood or neck guard) just visible. This figure has a strong affinity with figures in Thornton's east window at York.
- A small figure, possibly an angel, from canopy-work. Small figures in canopy-work are a favourite device of Thornton (York east window).
- Two nimbed female heads with a mitre between them. The one on the left wears a kerchief and is, perhaps, St Veronica; the other is an angel.
- The nimbed head of an archangel with a tiara with a Latin cross *bottonee*.
- The nimbed tonsured head of a saint bishop with the crook of a crozier (Becket?)
- At top left the infant John the Baptist with Elizabeth. On his lap the Lamb of God and a reed cross. He wears a hair shirt and she a white kerchief.

NORTH TRANSEPT, WINDOW nXIX
In the lower part of the window are the Virgin and Child. The overwhelming impression is of flowers – in the nimbi, on the child's shawl and decorating Mary's robe. Mary holds a stem of lily flowers. Both are distinguished from all the other figures by large eyes and ears, and thin mouths. The smiling child fondles the hem at the throat of Mary's robe. The nimbus of Mary has been restored since 1925.

In the upper part of the window is an important subject group of seven female figures (Fig. 66). The largest and central figure is crowned and holds a book in her left hand, but she and her two flanking companions are not nimbed. The four women in the back row are all nimbed. The 'Queen' listens intently with her right hand over her heart, as the figure on her right, with her left hand raised, speaks to her as if whispering. On the left of the crowned figure, stands an anxious looking woman with a chaplet and her left hand clasping the skirt of her robe. To her left a detached hand is raised in emphasis. The women in the back row alternately wear bourrelets or are bare-headed. They have anxious expressions.

Several explanations have been advanced for this subject. Eden[314] thought it was St Catherine of Alexandria debating with the philosophers. There are parallels for depicting Catherine with a book and crown, but the Queen's company are surely women. If they were men, they are too young to represent important academics of their time.[315] Wilfred Drake thought the subject was the Virgin Mary with six virgin saints,[316] for which it is difficult to find parallels, but an alternative title might be 'The Queen of Heaven' and there are several depictions of Mary thus, crowned and without the Christ Child.[317]

Madeline Caviness suggests St Ursula surrounded by some of her entourage of 11,000 virgins.[318] It is unusual for Ursula to be depicted without both of her attributes – a book and an arrow – and the virgins are not generally shown nimbed, except when their detached heads lie nimbed upon the ground following martyrdom; however, this is the most plausible suggestion.[319]

NORTH-EAST TRANSEPT WINDOW (nVIII) & SOUTH CHOIR AISLE WINDOW (sX)
Symonds[320] recorded the six coats of arms which can be seen in these two windows, but found them in the two windows of the south choir aisle. Duncumb also found them there.[321] These windows were re-made in 1864 by William Warrington who was an important stained-glass artist during the nineteenth-century Gothic Revival. The firm, known as William Warrington, Warrington & Co. or Warrington & Son, worked until c.1905.[322] Warrington had worked at the cathedral before, when he made a window for the private chapel of the Bishop's Palace in 1845, and installed the north chancel aisle north-east window and a window in the north nave aisle of the cathedral in 1862.

In June 1862, the Chapter Book[323] records a letter signed 'Evans, brothers', whose father, David Evans, had been storing the glass for the Dean and Chapter. These brothers were the successors of Betton & Evans,[324] glaziers of Shrewsbury, who installed glass in the Lady Chapel, which was taken from St Peter's in Hereford. David Evans died in November 1861. Presumably there had been an earlier proposal for David Evans to undertake the work and he had taken the glass to his studio for closer examination prior to giving his estimate. David Evans undertook 'repairs' to 'painted windows' at the cathedral in 1843,[325] and that may be the date of the removal of this glass to Shrewsbury. The Evans brothers said in their letter that the glass

Fig. 67 Hereford Cathedral: north choir aisle (nVIII)

matter was settled because the next mention of the glass in the Chapter Book follows completion of the installation in November 1864,

> The account of Mister Warrington for old glass adapted and restored in two windows in the cathedral viz. one in transept and one in south aisle containing altogether eight canopies and eight figures besides 8 coats of arms and geometrical grounds with borders composing the whole as described by Sawyer as agreed: £150. Other expenses to fixing the same complete as agreed: £20.[326]

The glass was in two boxes which suggests that the two large windows made by Warrington are predominantly new glass.

The NORTH CHOIR AISLE WINDOW (nVIII) is shown in Fig. 67. Considering the principal lights, the canopy-work is ambitious, compared even to that in the chancel of Tewkesbury; it is also unusually uniform because Warrington was using a technique that he developed for giving new glass an aged appearance. The grisaille in this window is entirely of vine form and related to part of window sX, which has similarities with ancient vine pattern grisaille in the locality. Much of the grisaille in sX appears to be made with old glass, while the grisaille in nVIII looks new.

The SOUTH CHOIR WINDOW (sX) is more difficult to see than nVIII but contains rather more medieval glass. The composition, with individual figures framed by canopy-work, combined with deep, rich colours and strongly stylised drawing, places these remains in the early fourteenth century (Fig. 68). The figures are those of Mary Magdalene, St Ethelbert, St Augustine and St George. Comparison with work of a similar date at Tewkesbury, Ledbury, Credenhill and Brinsop reveals no specific similarities in the

had been forwarded some years previously to the architect of the cathedral, J.N. Cottingham, together with the account which the Dean and Chapter owed for the warehousing of the glass for many years. The glass had been passed from the architect to William Warrington without the knowledge of the Dean and Chapter.

In November 1863, the Dean and Chapter ordered Warrington to send the glass to Gilbert Scott, their new architect. This order was restated more firmly in December. It seems that the

Fig. 68 Hereford Cathedral: Mary Magdalene from the south choir aisle (sX)

Fig. 69 Hereford Cathedral: south aisle (sXIV). Joseph being lowered into the dry well

drawing of the figures or the rather distinctive Lombardic lettering. The relative crudeness of the drawing, the sad mouths, and the sideways dip of the head of Magdalene seem more like the early glass at Madley than the fourteenth-century work there and at Eaton Bishop. The figures and their labels appear to be made of old glass except for the figure of George, which is by Warrington. The heads of Mary Magdalene and Ethelbert are incomplete, but Augustine's face is original (although his mitre is not).

The three coats of arms in the larger tracery lights are set among fragments of old grisaille and canopy-work. The arms in C1 are those of the Deanery, and the shield may be the one recorded by Taylor on the south side of the nave (but see window sXIV, below). The arms of Braose appear to be old.

Nave south aisle window (sXIV)

This window has a multitude of fifteenth-century fragments. The source of the glass and the date of its installation are not known for certain, but William Sawyer writing *c.*1835 noted, 'The easternmost of these [south aisle] windows is filled with un-arranged fragments of painted glass; below is a doorway leading to the bishop's cloisters'.[327] The window was repaired in 1935[328] and in 1984, when a coat of arms and date were inserted in panel 1c.

There are four lights in the window but no clear horizontal banding. In the left panel (a) there is a good deal of modern glass including parts of a date for Marc(h) (1)939 with three modern faces and part of a robed figure. In the middle of the panel is a very pleasing deep-blue sky with sun, moon and stars, reminiscent of the Creation of Luminaries panel in the St Anne Chapel at Great Malvern. There is also a striking group of three heads with yellow stain hair combed to a fringe.

In the second light from the left (b), there is a significant amount of modern drapery and architectural scraps; however, the centre of the panel contains one of the most important images in this survey. The reclining figure under a wooden structure is thought to represent Joseph being lowered into the dry well (Genesis 37.23 & 24) (Fig. 69). This is a rare subject in glass and, compared with other known representations (such as that at Great Malvern), it is probably without parallel.[329] There are five incomplete figures. At first sight they seem different from the York School work seen in the north transept (p. 100). The heads are sharply drawn with a good deal of fine line, and the expressions are taut. Modelling and the tones of flesh and hair are executed without silver stain, which is reserved for the details of the garments. However, there are similarities with some figures in the east window at Great Malvern, in the drawing of eyes and hair.

In the right-hand panel (d) is a substantially complete kneeling figure in a blue robe. The figure has yellow hair and does not appear to be related to the figures in panel b above. The body and hand of a civilian and a female head with a white kerchief are also there.

The LADY CHAPEL SOUTH WINDOWS (sV & sVI) contain the oldest glass in the cathedral. This glass was removed from the Church of St Peter in the city. Duncumb saw some of the glass in St Peters around 1800,

> The East window of the North aisle still has some remains of painted glass, in an imperfect state. The centre light contains the Crucifixion, with the pious women standing near the cross, and above is part of a portrait, having the right hand raised, as if to command attention … In the light towards the North are the words 'Orate Pro', and in others are flowers and ornaments of various colours.[330]

On 19 May 1847, the churchwardens of St Peter's advertised in the *Hereford Journal*, offering 'several feet of ancient painted glass' which could be viewed in situ in the east window. In 1847 the wardens at St Peter's spent more than £15 on glazing (with two glaziers, Vaughan and Leach).[331] The gift of the glass to the cathedral is recorded on a brass plate in the Lady Chapel, below the windows. It says that Biddulph Phillips presented the glass to the cathedral in 1849. Paul Iles suggests that it was taken to the workshop of Betton & Evans in Shrewsbury and not installed in the cathedral until 1898, when its installation was paid for by W. Henry Barneby (this date is also on the brass plate).[332]

There is, however, evidence for the earlier installation of the windows. David Evans undertook 'repairs' to 'painted windows' at the cathedral in 1843.[333] The wording of the plate can be read as simply recording the date of the plate itself, and that must be the case because glass cannot have been in storage with Evans & Sons until 1898. David Evans died in 1861 and there is no record of his sons carrying on the business to the end of the century. Fortunately, the John Murray guide to the western cathedrals, which was published in 1864, has an illustration on which the historiated window, glazed as now, can be clearly seen.[334] The installation therefore took place between Dean Merewether's death in 1850 and the publication of Murray's guide in 1864, which points to David Evans as the glazier some time before his death in 1861.

Richard Marks, in his national survey of medieval glass, places the Hereford windows, 'amongst the principal monuments of the years

1250–90.'³³⁵ Both Morgan and Iles suggest that the glass comes from a workshop in Munich, but there seem to be no strong reasons for asserting this. The original installation was generally thought to be a rather harsh restoration and the windows were reworked in 1935, and some of Evans' more extreme choices of colours (see the east window at Ludlow) 'toned down'.³³⁶ Duncumb only described two panels: the Majesty and Crucifixion, which remain in the relationship described by him. The other panels are the work of David Evans, who was a master imitator of medieval styles.³³⁷

It is difficult to find English parallels for the overall composition here. However, there is a thirteenth-century window at Poitiers which, on a grander scale, places the Majesty above the Crucifixion and narrative scenes, including the Empty Tomb. In that window the strong blocks of colour also resonate with the Hereford panels (except that there is little blue glass in the Hereford windows).³³⁸

WINDOW sV: CHRIST IN MAJESTY (Fig. 70a)
This image is mostly composed of medieval glass; Christ's head and some of his robes are new.³³⁹ Christ is seated in a vesica with the right hand raised in blessing and the left holding an orb (Inset 4). He is surrounded by the tetramorphic symbols, each in its own small vesica. At the base of the panel in a roundel is the Lamb of God, which is the invention of David Evans.

Christ in Majesty is a familiar figure in the ancient art of Herefordshire. Upton Bishop has an early figure, probably contemporary with a detached capital in the Hereford retrochoir. The Herefordshire School of Romanesque Sculpture has left more typical representations at Shobdon and Rowlestone. In these images (in common with contemporary images in other media),

Figs 70a–70b: Hereford Cathedral Lady Chapel lancets. **Fig. 70a**: window sV (LEFT), **Fig. 70b**: window sVI (RIGHT)

Christ holds a book in his left hand, and is surrounded by angels. The Rowlestone Christ is framed by a rather elliptical vesica but shares the same pellet decoration with the window here.

The window is somewhat different from these familiar pictures, in that Christ holds an orb, not a book, and is surrounded by the Evangelists' symbols rather than angels. The composition is strikingly like that on the tympanum just over the border at Pedmore, which has strong Continental affinities. There is another image in which these elements come together and that is the Vision of Ezekiel; and the tetramorphic figures appear in other Apocalyptic literature, notably in Revelations. In this type of picture, the deity is the Father not the Son, a possibility reinforced by the presence of the orb rather than the book more frequently associated with Christ in Majesty.

The interpretation of the 'Majesty' must influence the interpretation of the other mostly medieval panel in the window, the Crucifixion. The conventional interpretation is under the heading of 'Life of Christ', but it might well be called the mystical 'Death of Christ'. The subject matter is of little help in dating the window or identifying its origin. There are examples of this subject in the arts of the Munich area, notably in manuscript illustration, but these images are commonplace throughout the medieval period and throughout Christendom.

The Empty Tomb: this panel is completely Evan's work.

The Crucifixion: this is mostly ancient glass, including all the heads. The scene is enclosed in a quatrefoil with a thin red border. The green Cross, once thought to be unusual, is in fact the more common representation and the S-curve of Christ's body and the down curve of His arms is in a tradition which stretches from Chartres in the twelfth century to the end of the medieval era.

The lower panel is Evans' work, apart from the left side border.

The historiated panels, which were taken from the top of the east window of the north aisle at St Peter's, must have been part of a larger scheme of medallions depicting the Life or Death of Christ. Examination of the head and face of Christ, which is certainly original, suggests a date late in the thirteenth or early fourteenth century. Comparison with Madley is inevitable:

it is a remarkably local survival of a medallion programme. However, the composition, expression and draughtsmanship suggest that the Hereford panels were made after c.1300 and they are not contemporary with the Madley medallions.

As for the suggestion by Morgan that the glass is from Munich, both the subject matter and the draughtsmanship could be English. It might be suspected that the Munich suggestion comes from the bold and confident composition of each medallion and the colouring of the panels. The liberal use of strong red, particularly in the Majesty panel, has German affinities. However, there are examples of strong red backgrounds in English work of the thirteenth century, as at Canterbury and Dorchester Abbey, so this is not conclusive.[340] The red background at Hereford has vine grisaille which seems to be of a competence and neatness of finish absent in earlier work of the thirteenth century, adding further weight to a date of around 1300.

Window sVI

The Friends' report of 1937 noted that, 'The second lancet was in rather better condition. It is a grisaille with a leaf border, ruby with green stems and four fine knot designs in yellow, as medallions set on the grisaille.'[341]

The design consists of large, oblong, eight-lobed figures with a central eight-lobed interlace separated by paired demi-figures of quatrefoil form with a central patera and an outer ring. There is no secondary or imposed geometrical pattern, as normally found in larger windows, nor does the background vine scroll form a continuous pattern. The background of vine takes two main forms. In the large central figures, lobed leaves with three main lobes, and on some leaves between one and three smaller lobes. In the demi-figures the main lobes appear toothed. The outer border is uniform and of five bands. The principal feature is a vine of three-lobed leaves on a green stem and a red ground.

The innermost, narrow band is of four different forms, again, reflecting the source of the glass from several lights. Grisaille presents limitless opportunities for patterns, which makes it difficult to find affinities. However, the strong vine border, and the dominant theme of lobed panels, can be seen in windows at Exeter Cathedral (St Gabriel Chapel) and Norbury in Derbyshire from the period 1300–10.

The AUDLEY CHAPEL was probably started before 1502, when the eponymous bishop moved to Salisbury; however, the inclusion of the arms of one of Audley's successors, Bishop Mayew, in glass and stone suggests it was not finished until later.[342] There are five windows in the upper chapel, three of three lights wide and two (to east and west) of two lights wide. The west window has no painted glass.

Dingley recorded the arms seen today, but also found the initials BB which referred to Bishop Booth.[343] A signed quarry (Fig. 64) records that the chapel windows were re-leaded in 1822 by Charles Childs. They were re-leaded again about a century later. The Friends reported in 1935 that the five windows in the Audley Chapel, containing heraldic shields set on plain quarries, and a few fifteenth-century painted quarries, were in bad condition. The leading was perished, the lights were buckled and had to be completely taken out, re-leaded and replaced. It seems that Childs had no cause to be proud of his workmanship, for the tracery of the windows had been patched in a most unsightly manner with common sheet glass held in place with cement, the shape of the tracery openings consequently being much disfigured. The heraldry was repaired, and the old crown quarries carefully preserved and rearranged to enhance the effect of the stained glass.

Audley was a Yorkist serving Lancastrian kings. This is reflected in the imagery surviving in the glass of the chapel. In the upper panel of the left light SI, is a group of four quarries each with a pinned 'sun in splendour' retainer badge in yellow stain. The badge is a Yorkist symbol which derives from the apparition called a parhelion which gave rise to the legend of three suns shining on the battlefield of Mortimer's Cross, where the Yorkists enjoyed their last victory. Here, long after the Tudors prevailed, and Audley had been testator to Henry VII's will, the York sun rises in many lights of a bishop's chapel. The white rose can be seen in the lower part of the window but is a modern piece.

WINDOW SI has three shields within oak wreaths in the upper lights, two of which were recorded by Dingley. That on the right, *Gules, a frette, or*, represents Audley himself, and can be seen on the plinth within the Lady Chapel. That on the left has a winged figure that was thought by Dingley to be the arms of Henry de Wingham, though it is difficult to find any reason for Wingham arms to be on Audley's memorial. The middle shield, with a red background and three objects, may be intended as the arms of the See of Hereford. The lower lights hold two lozenges each made of four 'sun in splendour' quarries. The third, on the right, is a collection including part of a feathered costume which is similar to some fragments in the cathedral archive.

WINDOW SIII displays the arms of the deanery, flanked by geometrical roundels in the outer panels and three lozenges of 'sun in splendour' quarries.

WINDOW SIV has further sun quarries. A few pieces of original glazing remain in the tracery lights. That in SIII is part of an elaborate letter, but impossible to decipher. It might be expected to be E or A, the bishop's initials.

In the BOOTH PORCH, the Royal Commission found, 'In upper storey of outer N. porch – in E. window, fragments with oak-leaf and border, early 16th-century.'³⁴⁴ These fragments have gone, and all that remains of painted glass is a fragment in a north tracery light.

In the cathedral archives there are two boxes of carefully packed and wrapped fragments.³⁴⁵ There is no record of when or how the glass was obtained, or where it came from. If it were certain that it came from the cathedral at all, some important conclusions could be reached about the surviving glass.

The following are tentative suggestions about a few of the 55 pieces.

Instruments of the Passion (Fig. 71a): the largest fragment shows a hand with coins on its open palm, depicting the 40 pieces of silver given to Judas Iscariot, which suggests that it probably comes from a programme of Instruments of the Passion. The most important such programme in this survey is at Weobley (window nV) (Figs 144 & 144b). The smaller piece, showing a hand grasping a shaft, strongly resembles the hands in that window, and the fragments of feathered wings are also remarkably like those at Weobley. The Weobley glass probably came from the workshop of John Thornton, and, as indicated above, that workshop is associated with the cathedral. However, the affinity between these fragments and the glass at Weobley is so strong that they might have come from there, perhaps found locally and entrusted to the cathedral archivist.

Heads with marked hairlines and curved lines from the corners of eyes (Fig. 71b): these pieces are characterised by their hair, drawn in thick strands of black and two shades of yellow with a very even edge. They also share the way their

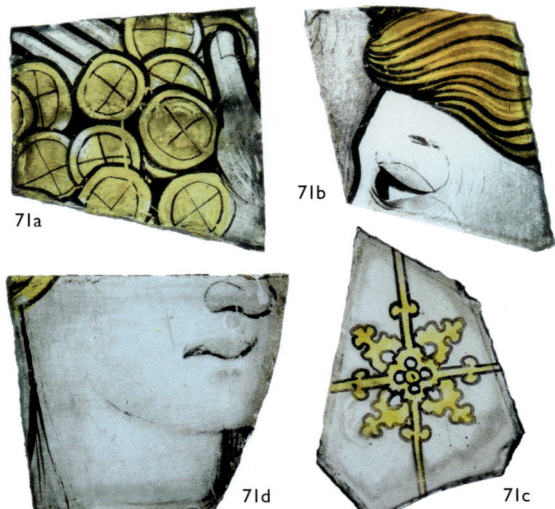

Figs 71a–71d: Hereford Cathedral: fragments in the Cathedral Archives

eyes are depicted, particularly the fine curving lines from the outer corner of the eye up to the understated eyebrow. The fragments bear a strong resemblance to parts of the collection of ancient glass in the south aisle window (sXIV). There are also similarities with some figures in the east window at Great Malvern.

Floral Quarries (Fig. 71c): these quarries are related to the two panels of fifteenth-century glass in the north-east transept. Their importance is that, if they have been in the cathedral since their removal from windows, they suggest that the glass previously in the chapel at Hampton Court could have been in the cathedral.

Madley Face (Fig. 71d): one fragment bears a resemblance to faces in the east window at Madley. Madley chancel was the responsibility of the Dean and Chapter, and it would not be surprising to find that fragments discovered there found their way to the cathedral archive. Examination of the Madley glass suggests that the workshop of William Glazier of Oxford might be the source of these distinctive faces.

HEREFORD: THE TOWN CHURCHES
ST PETER'S

No medieval glass survives in the church, but, as described above, the Lady Chapel of the cathedral (windows sV and sVI) contains important early glass which was probably taken from the east window of the north aisle.

ALL SAINTS CHURCH

All Saints has a marvellous collection of medieval carpentry and furnishings, which makes the absence of medieval glass disappointing, and doubly so because James Hill recorded much of interest:[346]

> In the windows are a few inscriptions, scattered over the religious painting. In the eastern window of the northern aisle, is the Salutation of the B. Virgin lively represented, in the hand of the Angell is a scroll thus inscribed *AVE: MARIA: GRACIA: PLENA: DNS TECCVM*.
>
> In the same window are the kneeling Magi offering their presents to our infant Jesus, with all the circumstances of the Epiphany naturally described. In other windows of this ancient fabric are persons represented kneeling. Under them are their names subscribed ... Some are putting up petitions inscribed upon painted labels.
>
> About this church I find the following arms: In the east window of the north aisle, two, coats of Pitchard.

It seems likely that all the old glass had been removed by 1800, for Duncumb had nothing to say about medieval glass in All Saints.

ST NICHOLAS

Thomas Dingley recorded a kneeling donor in a north window in this church.[347] This represented 'Eoger Beele, who died 19 Hen. VIII', then mayor of Hereford. Dingley also noted another similar figure and a Crucifixion in the east window.

HEREFORD
The Chapel of Coningsby Hospital
(SO 5112 4045, HR4 9HN)

In the NORTH WINDOW, the arms of Thomas Coningsby impaling Fitzwilliam, with the cypher of Thomas Coningsby and Phillipa Fitzwilliam dated 1614 (Fig. 72), by the same hand, and the same date as arms in Hampton Court Chapel.

In the SOUTH WINDOW, a detached panel of quarries formerly in the east window (which now has glass by Hardman from the chapel at Harewood). These include the cypher and the Coningsby crest with a rabbit among ostrich feathers sprouting from a ducal coronet.

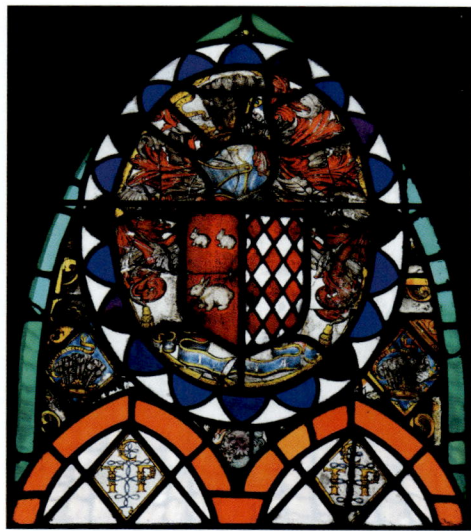

Fig. 72 Hereford: Coningsby Hospital Chapel (nII)

HEREFORD MUSEUM

The museum holds a small collection of fragments, many of which have come from archaeological digs. Most of the fragments are shards and, as is normal with buried fragments, illegible.[348]

Fragments from Craswell Priory

Craswall Priory was founded c.1220 by Walter II de Lacy. Some lead cames and an important glass fragment showing part of a face, were found during excavations undertaken by C.J. Lilwall in 1904. The face is on display in the Museum in Broad Street (Fig. 73). The Craswall Priory website quotes Richard Marks as saying the 'fine head looks early thirteenth century'.[349] If so, this would potentially be the earliest image on glass in this survey.

The Arms of William Cecil

The cartouche (Fig. 74a) was originally at the Cecil family house, Allt yr Ynys, in a room off the hall.[350] A similar cartouche remains in Walterstone Church (Fig. 74b, see below), but they are not exact copies: the quartered shields are quite similar but the strapwork surrounds are significantly different.

The museum glass is labelled, '374 Heraldic glass 16th century from Allesynis. The arms of William Cecil, Lord Burghley quartering Winston, Caerleon, Heckington. Donor: Mrs Rosser'. This must refer to the Roshers who owned Trewyn from 1772 until 1895, undertaking significant restorations in the 1870s, directed by Isobel Bernadette Rosher, an amateur architect.[351] The Woolhope Club *Transactions* reported in 1918 that 'Mrs Rosser [sic] has now presented the [panel of glass] to the Hereford Museum. It hangs in the Reference Library.'[352]

Fig. 73 Hereford Museum: fragment from Craswall Priory

Fig. 74a Hereford Museum: arms of William Cecil

Fig. 74b The arms of William Cecil in Walterstone Church

So, the cartouche left Allt yr Ynys some time before 1872 and was retained at Trewyn as a detached panel. It would then have gone to Mrs Rosher's home in Abergavenny, Ty Berlwyn, before being given to the Museum. Mrs Rosher died in 1927.[353]

The arms were formed by the time of William Cecil, 1st Baron Burghley (d.1598). His heir, Thomas, used the straightforward *Barry of ten argent and azure, six escutcheons sable, each charged with a lion rampant of the first, 3, 2, 1 seen in the 1st and 6th quarters*.[354] His second son, Robert, used the arms but with a crescent cadence mark (as befits a second son), and so it would be safe to presume the two Herefordshire cartouches are pre-1598.

HOLME LACY
St Cuthbert (SO 5684 3474, HR2 6LP)

The glass was gathered into one window on the north side of the chancel (nIII) (Figs 75a–75c) from the east window in 1915. James Hill (d.1727) wrote about the east window of the north transept chapel in which were two large crosses, one red and the other blue.[355] Sir Stephen Glynne visited in 1860 and found, 'The east window of the chancel is Perp. and contains some old stained glass.'[356] The Woolhope Club visited in 1918 and reported, 'The east window of the north nave has been filled quite recently with new stained glass, and the fragments of ancient glass and the original bordering which was in situ removed into another window adjoining.'[357]

There are some details which appear throughout the window: lozenge borders and crowns with letters I and P. The letters are not a familiar sacred monogram but may have a royal connotation (see Eaton Bishop for association with Eleanor of Castile): Philippa (d.1369), Queen of Edward III, and her mother Joan perhaps? Among the many other subjects are fragments of fifteenth-century black letter and numerous architectural fragments in which are embedded some interesting faces.

Figs 75a–75c: Holme Lacy heads (nIII) (CLOCKWISE FROM ABOVE): Fig. 75a head of Edward the Confessor(?), Fig. 75b woman wearing a horned headdress, Fig. 75c bearded head with liripipe hood

Near the top of the left-hand lights is a composite, bearded figure wearing vestments with a broad amice (Fig. 75a). This could be Christ (a conclusion supported by the cruciform nimbus); however, the combination of crown, nimbus, cross staff and vestments might represent Edward the Confessor and account for the rather human expression. At the same level in the right-hand light is a woman's head executed in silver stain, wearing a horned headdress of the fourteenth century (Fig. 75b), with a gold chain at her throat. Below the horned woman is a roundel of *c*.1320–40[358] (Fig. 75c) with a grotesque, bearded face topped with a liripipe (long-tailed hood), and one with a six-pointed star.

HOPE BOWDLER
St Andrew (SO 4758 9239, SY6 7DD)

In the NAVE NORTH-WEST WINDOW is glass installed in 1967 from the collection of Riou George Benson (1834–96), a former rector.

Nave north-west window (nVI)
(**1**) At the base of the lancet, the dedication.
(**2**) A seventeenth-century rectangular panel in black paint, silver stain and enamel, of the four Fathers of the Church with two female figures. Pope Gregory and Ambrose sit in St Peter's throne while Jerome, in a red, flat-top cardinal's hat, and Augustine look on.
(**3**) A mid sixteenth-century roundel of John the Baptist in black paint and silver stain.[359]
(**4**) A rectangular panel and two quarries of fragments including part of a strapwork cartouche and part of a feathered wing.
(**5**) A seventeenth-century roundel of St Martin cutting his cloak in half to give to a naked pauper (back cover) with two quarries showing a fleur-de-lis and a stag.[360]
(**6**) A cartouche of Fitton impaling(?) c.1600.

HOPESAY
St Mary (SO 3893 8328, SY7 8HD)

Fig. 76
Hopesay: Fitzalan coat of arms, 1390–97 (sIX)

William Mytton recorded four coats of arms of Mortimer and Fitzalan in several windows, cobbled together into one shield (Fig. 76). The parts date from the 1390s and refer to Richard Fitzalan, earl of Arundel and his second wife Philippa, daughter of Edmund Mortimer, earl of March. Fitzalan was lord of the Manor of Hopesay and owned the advowson of the church. They were married in 1390 and he was executed in 1397. Peter Newton notes that, 'The artist has not given the correct tinctures of the Fitzalan and Mortimer coats. The Fitzalan *gules a lion rampant or* is represented by a lion painted in black enamel on white glass. The 'or' parts of the Mortimer coat are represented by plain white glass.'[361]

HOPE UNDER DINMORE
St Mary the Virgin

There is a single foliated quarry of the thirteenth or fourteenth century in a window of the tower.

HOW CAPLE
St Mary & St Andrew (SO 6115 3055, HR1 4SR)

There are a few fragments of fourteenth-century borders in the chancel north-west window, and some silver stain floral and architectural pieces in the quatrefoil of the nave north-west window. The lower lobe has the chequered *or and azure* of a Warrene shield.

HUGHLEY
St John the Baptist (SO 5647 9794, SY5 6NT)

Hughley seems remote, and the church modest, and yet it was lavishly furnished by Reginald de Leye and his successors in the fourteenth and fifteenth centuries with fine woodwork, tiles and stained glass. The church belonged to Wenlock

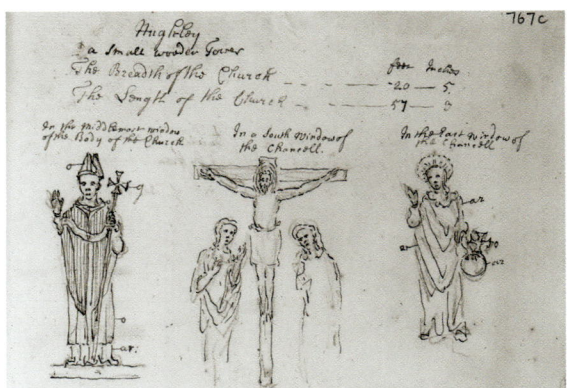

Fig. 77 (TOP) Hughley: William Mytton's sketches of the glass (by permission of the Cadbury Library, University of Birmingham). **Figs 78a–78b** (BELOW) Hughley: faces in the tracery of the chancel north window (nII)

Priory, but the de Leyes held the manor, and Reginald presented Hugh de Leye to the living in 1313.[362] Little remains of the glass, but what survives is of high quality. In the eighteenth century, William Mytton sketched a Crucifixion in a south window of the chancel (Fig. 77), fragments of which are presently in the north chancel window. He also saw a full-length image of a bishop holding a cross staff in a north window of the 'body of the church' – and, in the east window, a nimbed and robed figure bearing an orb.[363]

In the top tracery light of the EAST WINDOW (I) is an apparently seated figure, blue-robed with a gold mantle and holding an orb. The face is obscured, but this is probably Mytton's third figure (on the right in Fig. 77) and almost certainly meant to represent Christ in Glory. The Cross over the orb is clearly as Mytton drew it.

Christ is set among cinquefoil flowers which are found elsewhere in this part of the diocese and which appear in profusion in the main lights. The flamboyant tracery dates the window to the mid fourteenth century.

In the main lights, the borders with a continuous thread around which foliage and lion masks wind, are of a form found elsewhere in Shropshire (at nearby Munslow for example). The canopy-work with pinnacles and tracery and its bright reds and blues is reminiscent of Moccas. These fragments are set against a rich green foliage diapering. The background of cinquefoil quarries, 'Ledbury borders' and diagonal lattice work are fourteenth-century.

The CHANCEL NORTH WINDOW (nII) has simpler, earlier tracery, although later than the thirteenth-century lancets in the nave. The remains of the Crucifixion sketched by William Mytton are discernible (Figs 78a & 78b). The figures with large eyes and exaggerated mannerisms suggest a date no later than c.1300. The green Cross is typical of most Crucifixes in this survey.

KENTCHURCH COURT
PRIVATE HOUSE CHAPEL
(SO 4232 2590, HR2 0DB)

The glass is in the chapel at the mezzanine level of the great staircase on the south side of the tower. This part of the house, with its huge Perpendicular window, is the work of John Nash in 1795–96.

The Royal Commission recorded glass in the window as follows:

Re-set in the window of the Chapel is some 16th-century glass consisting of four roundels

(1) in a circular chaplet of foliage a shield-of-arms, Capel impaling party fessewise argent and vert three leeks counter-coloured; (2) feathered chaplet enclosing a shield of Baskerville; (3) chaplet of foliage with shield-of-arms, Baskerville impaling (or) gules a fesse (or) between three scallops argent; (4) chaplet of guilloche pattern alternating with four roses, enclosing shield with Baskerville impaling Nanphan. In addition, eight rectangular and one circular panels of Swiss glass with the arms of the Cantons, have recently been placed here; one of the panels has the date 1521.[364]

Fig. 79 Kentchurch Court: arms of the Canton of Zurich

The Swiss glass 'recently placed here' must have formed part of the refurbishment and redecoration of the house between 1927, when Sybil Lucas Scudamore (née Webber) moved into the house after it had been rented out for a long period.[365] Her arms – with Scudamore and Lucas quartered and Webber inescutcheon – are at the top of the window.

It is not presently known where the glass was acquired. Maurice Drake, who wrote about Swiss glass[366] and who was a dealer in glass, is a good suspect, but no connection has been found. The panel in Fig. 79 shows the arms of the Canton of Zurich and is typical of the whole group in its dramatic drawing style and rich colours. Three of the panels are dated 1521.

KING'S CAPLE

St John the Baptist (SO 5589 2884, HR1 4XT)

James Hill (d.1727) visited the church[367] and noted the arms of Baskerville in the windows – these have been lost. The present collection of fragments was in place by 1912 when it was noted in the sixth volume of Duncumb's *Collections*.[368]

Fig. 80 King's Caple: head of Christ with crowns (nV)

The surviving medieval glass is gathered in the Aramstone Chapel north window (nV), an extension of c.1400.[369] The common theme is black line on white glass with silver stain to represent metal and hair and Christ's nimbus. These are like the borders at Thruxton, which are associated there with a fourteenth-century Crucifix. At the centre of the panel here is the nimbed head of Christ crowned with thorns (Fig. 80). This must be later than the Thruxton image as there is shading and modelling, and the crown is drawn with confidence and verve. This image, with its bifurcated beard, bears a remarkable likeness to the Christ in the nave south window at Sellack.

Figs 81a–81d: Kingsland: upper tracery lights of east window (I) (FROM TOP) **Fig. 81a**: Christ seated on a rainbow; **Figs 81b & 81c**: crowned figures; (photographed in the workshop of Jim Budd in October 2021); **Fig. 81d**: tracery lights in situ

KINGSLAND
St Michael & All Angels
(SO 4468 6129, HR6 9QW)

The church was probably started late in the thirteenth century and the chancel was built c.1300–40.[370] In the seventeenth century, Silas Taylor recorded arms, some of which remain, but in 1826 the east window was 'much mutilated' and the shields were jumbled together.[371] Forty years later, Baillie & Co. re-leaded the east window.[372] Jim Budd recently cleaned and repaired the east window which, he thought, from details of the leading, had been re-leaded again about 1950.

East window (I)

The east window (I) (Fig. 82, opposite) is of outstanding interest. At the top (Fig. 81a), is Christ seated on a rainbow, displaying his wounds, his head surrounded by a red and gold Cruciferous nimbus. His left hand cups the wound in his side, while the right hand holds a green Cross, the *arbor vitea*, which places it

Fig. 82
Kingsland: four archangels in the tracery lights of the east window (l)

within a strong tradition in local representations of the Crucifixion. The drapery on Christ's left shoulder is obviously renewed. In the tracery panels below (Figs 81b & 81c) are two crowned and nimbed figures with similar thrones and backgrounds. The nimbus of the bearded male figure is cruciform and suggests the scene is the Coronation of the Virgin.

In the main lights are four archangels, not simply standing with their attributes but engaging with people. These are set on a background of geometrical grisaille with a vine pattern based on overlapping quatrefoils and lozenges. All four archangels are set in niches defined by narrow frames of white glass, which the archangels' wings overlap in places. The tracery lights seem to retain a good deal of old glass including the heads of the figures, but the main lights are predominantly the work of Baillie & Co. In a recent cleaning and setting in isothermal glazing, Jim Budd found that the four principal figures were almost entirely renewed.

George Marshall wrote about the archangels, pointing out the rarity of the company of four in any medium.[373] Angels were extremely common in stained glass, and their classification into nine orders, in which archangels occupy the penultimate niche, can be seen at Great Malvern and Ludlow (see Fig. 19). However, they were also a prime target for iconoclasts, and the survival of the Kingsland figures in the most prominent window is doubly unexpected.

In the upper tier of the main lights, between two shields, is the Annunciation with Gabriel and Mary. This image is somewhat sparse, placing the angel and Mary almost face-to-face without any of the common accompaniments – a scroll, a dove or the hand of God. In the lower tier are Raphael, Michael and Uriel. The story of Tobias, Raphael and the fish is found in the apocryphal Book of Tobit.

Tobit, the father of Tobias, was blind, but the boy had to go on a quest with Raphael to find a woman called Sarah who was so cursed that her husbands always died on their wedding night. During the quest, while crossing a river, Tobias caught a fish and Raphael instructed him to preserve parts of it, including its eyes. These were eventually used to cure Tobit of his blindness. This is a rare subject – probably the only image of its kind in medieval glass until a much later period when it is found in Netherlandish roundels. Some of the drapery, parts of the dark red background and crocketed gable and Raphael's left wing are probably original.

The Archangel Michael is shown driving his spear through the worm, the spearhead passes out of the niche into the surrounding grisaille. St Michael appears in various guises in medieval imagery: dressed in robes, armour or feathers in the roles of beast-slayer or the judge of souls. In the West, there appears to be a preference for the robed Michael. The head of Michael is modern, but much of the rest of the panel is original.

Just as images of Raphael and Tobias are hard to find in the Western tradition, so Uriel is a mere shadow in the record. Uriel was the archangel present during the expulsion of Adam and Eve from the Garden of Eden. The Kingsland subject comes from the apocryphal book of Esdras or Ezra, in which the writer, Esdras, has several visions of meetings with the archangel. The heads appear to be renewed.

Marshall noted, 'As regards the two shields of arms, the Braose coat is partly original, but the other with the arms of the See of Hereford is modern, though a few pieces of old glass appear to be used in the field.'[374]

Grisaille is difficult to date and there are few substantial survivals locally. The pattern in the south aisle of the cathedral, in a much larger window, adopts the same geometrical quatrefoils and lozenges as Kingsland. However, the most striking characteristic of Kingsland, which sets it apart from almost all of the grisaille in this survey, is that the foliage is simple and stylised rather than naturalistic. Nearly all the fourteenth-century examples in Herefordshire, including those in the cathedral, use the lobed vine or ivy leaf; Kingsland seems to look back into the thirteenth century. The two views about the date of this chancel seem to come into focus with this grisaille: Marshall suggests 1300; Morris 1320–40. The drawing of the figures and faces in the tracery lights, the form drawing and colouring of the figures in the main lights and the grisaille, all point towards the earlier date.

Baillie & Co. reglazed the CHANCEL NORTH WINDOW in 1868 but the glass in the trefoil tracery light appears to be of early date, with simple, stylised grisaille. At the centre is a leopard mask of the fourteenth century.

The CHANCEL SOUTH-EAST WINDOW was also reglazed by Baillie & Co. In the centre is a red rose patera with a border of gold pellets, but here the grisaille is naturalistic. It is possible to hypothesise an order of making and glazing the chancel windows as follows: north side – east – south side based on the details of the grisaille.

Marshall wrote of the CHANCEL SOUTH-WEST WINDOW:

> In this last window is a small figure of an archbishop, partly a restoration. This is probably a figure of St. Thomas of Canterbury and may be compared with the figure of that saint at Credenhill, and another similar figure at Saintbury St. Nicholas, in Gloucestershire.[375]

The panel is greatly restored, probably by Baillie & Co., and shows many fragments of the earlier, stylised grisaille. The Kingsland bishop bears a strong resemblance to the Credenhill Becket, placing it closer in date to 1300 than to 1320, let alone 1340. This window contains another image: a small roundel with a drawing of St Helena (mother of Constantine and finder of the True Cross) in black line with yellow stain for the robe, crown and border. This is a charming piece of the fourteenth century.

THE ORGAN CHAMBER: The window in the north wall behind the organ in the chancel, was removed from the north chancel wall when this chamber was built some years ago. It contains early nineteenth-century glass, including shields of arms.

KINLET

St John the Baptist (SO 7107 8103, DY12 3AY)

In 1814, THE EAST WINDOW (I) was filled with painted glass by Betton & Evans of Shrewsbury.[376] 'The design was intended to represent the several families through which the manor has descended, and the pattern of the tabernacles was made out from the remaining fragments of the former work.'[377]

In the main lights there are two tiers of figures. In the centre of the upper tier is a martyr bearing a palm and a bird, which has some old glass in the lower part of the palm frond and the bird. The truly awful head and Cambridge blue nimbus must be by Evans. Can this be St Francis with a strange conflation of attributes?

The knights in panel I 2a, 2d, 2e, appear to be entirely of 1814 but the kneeling knight in panel 2b (Fig. 83, overleaf) is one of the most important armoured figures in this survey; much of his body is old glass. He wears a combination of mail and plate armour with a pointed bascinet over a mail mantle or aventail. The bascinet has no visor but has the unusual (possibly unique) feature of upward-pointing metal lion claws around the brow. His surcoat is charged with the crowned lion of the Cornwalls. The Revd Blakeway, who oversaw the work, suggested this is the last of the Kinlet Cornwalls.[378] Kinlet was passed through the Cornwalls, to Sir John Cornwall on the death of his father, Sir Brian Cornwall in 1391. Sir John died in 1414. This armour seems to fit more comfortably with 1391 than 1414 and is probably earlier still. Edmund Cornwall died in 1353, and a similar date for the glass is supported by the date of building of the chancel early in the fourteenth century,[379] by the inscription in black letter with a Lombardic capital, which is consistent with a date of 1350, and by the

LEFT: **Fig. 83** Kinlet: donor knight restored by Betton & Evans (I). RIGHT: **Fig. 84** Birtsmorton: donor knight (sII)

details of the canopy-work, for which Richard Marks suggests a date of around 1365,

> … gradually these embellishments were eliminated, together with the pitched roofs. Examples of the fully developed solid platform canopy can be seen in the west window of Winchester Cathedral, dating from the time of Bishop Edington (d.1366), Maxey in Cambridgeshire of 1367–8, Lacock Abbey, and east windows of Kimberly in Norfolk and Kinlet, Shropshire.[380]

At Birtsmorton is a knight in a bascinet with aventail and visor, which has been dated to 1380–1400[381] (Fig. 84). It seems unlikely that the Kinlet knight is much later than this and the figure cannot therefore be the last of the Kinlet Cornwalls.

The NORTH (nII) AND SOUTH CHANCEL WINDOWS (sII) have arms in the tracery lights. In the north chancel window, the arms of Lacon quartered with Peshall, Harley, Brampton and Corbett. In the south, the Royal Arms of England and France quartered, which was the usual form between 1461 and 1603, except during the reign of Mary I. The closed crown is uncommonly tall with almost straight arches and is flanked by white roses. Much, if not all, of this is the work of Betton & Evans.

In the SOUTH TRANSEPT the tracery lights have old glass. In the east (sIII), two small panels with cusping and rose paterae. In the south (sIV), good quality glass of *c*.1350, drawn in silver stain and fine line which is probably in its original setting. The trefoil panels have roundels with flowers and borders of black and yellow with lozenges and quatrefoils scratched out. The quatrefoil panels have tetramorphic figures – an eagle and a winged bull – which occupy roundels from which lobes filled with vines radiate.[382] In the upper light, the face of a stern Christ with a bifurcated beard and a cruciform nimbus (Fig. 85): a fitting companion to the beautiful alabaster Trinity on the east wall.

The tracery of the NORTH TRANSEPT (nIII & nIV) is like that of the south, but the glass seems to be of earlier date. There are plain green and red borders sometimes mixed in the same panels. In the quatrefoils, three forms of simple water leaf and vine leaf grisaille. In the trefoils, scrollwork.

Fig. 85 Kinlet: the face of Christ (sIV)

118 THE MEDIEVAL STAINED GLASS OF HEREFORDSHIRE & SHROPSHIRE

KINSHAM

All Saints (so 3644 6490, ld8 2hr)

In 1934 the Royal Commission reported a 'jumble of fragments including border with fleurs-de-lis and towers, parts of figures, etc., probably fourteenth-century.'[383] Since then, the jumble has been rearranged into a geometrical form in the tracery of the EAST WINDOW. The fragments are small; among them simple leaf grisaille, hands blessing and praying, and border castles and fleurs-de-lis.

LEDBURY

St Michael (so 7128 3772, hr8 1dl)

Ledbury has glass from several periods and the fabric accounts are relatively complete.[384] From 1687 to 1696 William Pillinger was employed and, in 1689–90 charged '4d per foote of glass' for repairing 24 foot of glass. He also charged for 68 bags of moss at 2d per bag.[385] Other glaziers were also engaged in this period, including James Symonds for 'coloringe the windows.'[386]

John Dubberley (various spellings) was engaged, almost annually, down to 1765, both on the church and the schoolhouse, but mostly for small sums. In 1698 his bill came to nearly £9. The later payments to Dubberley might have been to William (perhaps John's son) who worked at the cathedral in 1730. During Dubberley's association with the church, other glaziers were employed. In 1700 the accounts show:

Richard Phillips for his work to a window	£7.10.0
Paid the same time to John Tomlins for glasing	£1.18.0
Paid for poles for the window scaffold at the church	£0.06.8
Paid John Dubberly for glasing the schoolhouse	£0.06.2
Paid for 27 foot of glass for sash windows at 6d p. foot	£0.13.6

The Ledbury accounts are unusual in giving rates for the work. A further example from 1715 is shown in Fig. 86.

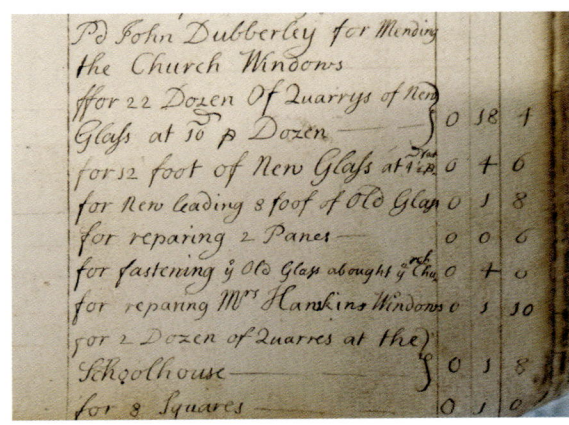

Fig. 86 Ledbury: extract from churchwardens' accounts

Joseph Nott was engaged from 1765 and the amounts spent annually were significantly greater.[387] His son Samuel took over in 1796 and expenditure continued to increase until the end of the century. From 1784 another glazier, John Nicholas, was also employed. He received the highest payment in any one year of the eighteenth century of £19 19s 2d in 1799, in a three-year period of exceptional spending on the glass from 1799 to 1802, amounting to almost £50.

From 1800 until the end of the account book in 1849, expenditure continued to rise. In 1812–13 the exceptional spending of £86 7s 1d is recorded against the name of John Nicholas. He continued to be employed until 1818, but Samuel Nott was still employed in 1845 – a long association which is not unusual among the well-paid elite craftsmen glaziers (see Hereford Cathedral). There are two unusually early references to putting up wire guards in the chancel and elsewhere in 1826–27 and 1828–29.

East window (I)

The east window was reglazed by Kempe & Co. in 1895.[388] A slightly earlier photograph shows the survival of ancient glass in the tracery lights, which Kempe & Co. retained in the new work.[389] The window is, according to the Royal Commission survey, 'a late 13th or early 14th-century opening with a 15th-century filling of four trefoiled and sub-cusped lights with vertical tracery in a two-centred head.' It also dated the glass to the fifteenth century, but both the window and the glass are earlier.

There are two donor figures in the tracery. Both are priests and both named on banderols (Fig. 87):[390] Nicholas Heth (Hethe or de Hethe) is prominent in the bishops' registers of the later fourteenth century. Nicholas and his brother Humphrey were so-called 'portionists' in 1359.[391] The benefice of Ledbury was shared; that is, divided into 'portions' to which portionists were appointed. Nicholas was presented by the king for the Overhall portion in 1387,[392] only three years before his death in 1390.[393] John Lutteley was a portionist in 1371.[394] The donors kneel in prayer. Both are bearded and tonsured with long hair at the sides. The figure labelled 'Johannes Lutteley', wears a cassock with buttoned cuffs which are of the period,[395] but are probably the work of Kempe & Co., along with most of the cassock and the ground. The figure of Nicholas de Hethe is similar and has also been restored, with the cassock below the arms also being by Kempe & Co. If these two were the donors, the time when both men were in position, around 1371, would seem to be the most likely date for the glass.

The form of the tracery, subarcuated into two main parts, is found at Weobley and is thought to be based on windows at New College, Oxford, with a date of around 1385. The Ledbury window has some unusual features for which it is difficult to find local affinities. The heads of the main panels have a stilted appearance, and the use of straight bars in the formation of the smaller lights looks ungainly. Perhaps more telling is the presence of quatrefoils which look back to the earlier fourteenth century. These features suggest an early and not entirely successful experimental work in the style which has roots not far away in Gloucester. Stephen Hart classifies this type of tracery as 'alternate supermullioned' and describes examples as early as *c*.1360.[396]

The glass seems closer in character to the work at Eaton Bishop (thought to be *c*.1340) and at St Katherine's Hospital nearby (*c*.1335–40)[397] than to the later fourteenth- and fifteenth-century work of the York/ Malvern/ Coventry School found

Fig. 87 Ledbury: two portionist donors (I)

in this survey. The Ledbury church figures still have significant quantities of pot metal for the drapery, while the Hospital figures are wholly in silver stain and smear shading. Although quite different, they share the same 'Ledbury border' designs.

If the images of the Archangel Michael in Ledbury and Eaton Bishop are compared (Fig. 88 & front cover), the Ledbury figure is slightly less stylised and more natural – a difference which might be accounted for by the 40 or so years between the two panels. The Ledbury work seems to still have one foot in the Decorated style, but it seems too far-fetched to see Ledbury Church and Hospital and Eaton Bishop as the work of the same local atelier.[398]

The comparison of the heads of the surviving figures and the panel borders in the east window, shows that the medieval glass in the window is by one hand. The overall programme of the window cannot now be known, but its purpose as a reredos would suggest it included more donors[399] and a Crucifixion. However, that would be hampered by the unresolved duality of the composition of the mullions, which forces the eye to fix on the thick central column. In the late fourteenth century, and throughout much of the medieval period, the church was dedicated to St Peter[400] and changed to St Michael and All Angels by the eighteenth century.[401] Is it mere coincidence that the images of these two survive so complete? Perhaps the small repair job of 1700, which required pole scaffolding for John Tomlins the glazier (see above), was their salvation.

St Michael is a familiar figure in wall paintings, manuscripts and even bench ends, yet it is hard to find affinities in glass for the Ledbury panel, other than the Eaton Bishop picture – and, in terms of dress, the image at Kingsland (Fig. 82). In these local examples, the archangel is winged, nimbed and robed rather than clad in armour. Perhaps this is a west of England tradition, seen in the early fourteenth-century representation at Dorchester Abbey, of a robed figure killing the dragon; and the detached panel at Meysey Hampton (Glos), with a robed St Michael holding a balance and pointing like the Ledbury figure.

Opposite St Michael is a bishop, a stern figure wearing a mitre with low, slightly outward-sloping sides typical of the later fourteenth century. The mitre has a long tasselled *infula* (ribbons) visible at the neck and halfway down the left side of the figure. Held up in his right hand is a book, the details of which are indistinct. The robes are mostly the work of Kempe & Co.

Fig. 88 Ledbury: Archangel Michael (l)

GAZETTEER OF CHURCHES IN HEREFORDSHIRE AND THE DIOCESE OF HEREFORD

NORTH CHANCEL SECOND WINDOW (nIII) was noted by the Royal Commission, 'In tracery of second window on N. side, five quatrefoils with leaves, etc. fifteenth century.'[403] The window was reglazed by Morris & Co. in 1912.[404] In the quatrefoils are two foliage designs; in the uppermost lights vine leaves and in the lower quatrefoils are oak leaves. In the mouchettes are borders reminiscent of those in the east window. These details, and the rather stilted tracery with quatrefoils at the heads of the main tracery lights, could be of a similar date to the east window, 1371.

More problematic are the angels in the larger tracery lights. The borders are wholly convincing as late fourteenth-century work, and there is a fragment of drawing of medieval tracery from another window. The overall impression of the panels is that they look like old glass repaired without the restoration of missing elements such as one of the heads, arms, hands and other parts. In 1826–27 wire guards were fitted on the north and south chancel windows;[405] was the damage to the tracery lights the reason? However, the faces and much of the drawing of wings, and the dark, charcoal impression of the combination of line and silver stain look modern. These figures have a style which is distinctive, and no similar images have been found which might suggest they are medieval or that they are the work of Morris & Co.

Fig. 89 Ledbury: angels with thurifers (I)

The angel at the centre of the tracery is modern, but there are two other medieval angels in the outermost lights, both of which are thurifers (Fig. 89). The thurifer to the left wears an alb with apparelled amice and cuffs. It is nimbed, and the rim of the nimbus is cusped. The other is dressed and nimbed in the same way, but has a cincture and stole (which are the work of Kempe & Co.). In the four largest tracery lights are saints. To the left is St Peter, bearded and tonsured with a book in his right hand and keys in his left.[402] He wears dark robes and stands on a ground of clover leaves. As with the donor figures, the robes probably contain Kempe's work. He is the only medieval figure in this row; St Paul, St John the Evangelist and St Andrew are Kempe's work.

In the NORTH CHAPEL NORTH WINDOW (nV) the Royal Commission noted the three shields which still exist: '(a) a chained swan on a field parted sable and gules, (b) France and England quarterly with a label argent, (c) Tracy, late fifteenth or early 16th century.'[406] Thomas Dingley made a detailed record of brasses and arms in the church c.1684 but these three shields are not included in his record.[407] The Tracy baronetcy (*or, an escallop in the dexter between two bandlets gules*), of Stanway was created in 1611 for Paul Tracy. The title became extinct on the death of the fifth baronet in 1678. The Tracy connection with Ledbury may be through the marriage of Robert, 2nd Viscount Tracy (d.1662) to Dorothy Cocks who was related to the Eltons (see monument to Ambrose and Ann Elton in the south aisle). The chained Bohun swan is associated with the earls of Hereford.[408] The Royal Arms with a label are those of Arthur, Prince of Wales. This shield probably dates the three shields to Arthur's short life, 1486–1502.

The OUTER NORTH CHAPEL EAST WINDOW (nVII) holds the head of a king high up in the tracery. The chapel was built in the late 1330s,[409] at which date the tracery lights were often filled with heraldry. This head is much later in date, possibly *c*.1500.

The OUTER NORTH CHAPEL WEST WINDOW (nX) has four panels of fragments. The Royal Commission noted, 'jumble of fragments of various dates including parts of two 13th century figure subjects, (a) the Flight into Egypt, (b) the Massacre of the Innocents, also fifteenth century kneeling figure of a king, crucifix, foliage, tabernacle work, fragment of inscription. etc.'[410]

The two narrative scenes (Figs 90a & 90b, overleaf) were in their present position by 1892.[411] They must have been part of a series of Nativity medallions. The tight curves of the plain red border, visible around the Massacre and partly seen in the Flight, suggest quatrefoils rather than discs. Certainly, if the late thirteenth-century date for the glass is right, it must have been introduced into the chapel from another part of the church. The north chapel underwent a thorough restoration in 1850 at a cost of £500,[412] and this might well be when the glass was collected in one place. It comes at the end of a period of about 50 years when expenditure on glazing was relatively high, and perhaps the exceptional sum of £86 7s 1d paid to Joseph Nicholas in 1812–13 relates to reglazing of the west end of the church and the removal of the narrative glass from its original position.

The two scenes are found together on the same page in illuminated books of the thirteenth and fourteenth centuries,[413] but it is difficult to find a parallel of the same date in glass in a parish church. Ashbourne has quatrefoils containing scenes from a Nativity cycle, including the Massacre, but the scale is smaller and the drawing cruder. A medallion showing the Massacre in the Jerusalem Chamber at Westminster Abbey has a quite different composition, but the mail of the soldiers is like that found at Ledbury. If the mail suit is looked for as a dating feature, the Westminster glass is *c*.1250, but the mail suit complete with mail coif is also reminiscent of the St George at Brinsop (Fig. 37), which, with its lattice background, must be of fourteenth-century date. Herod's face and those of the Virgin and child are the most clearly discernible. They are executed in black line on white glass with little or no shading distinguishable from the weathering of the glass. The three faces above share common characteristic: large eyes, crumpled mouths and strong noses, all of which would seem to be consistent with a late thirteenth-century or early fourteenth-century date.

The composition of the Flight is not unusual: the wrapped baby lies across the lap of the Virgin, and Joseph (with a staff in hand) leads the ass. The Virgin and child are nimbed, the child's nimbus bearing a Cross. The virgin wears a long kerchief.

There can be no more arresting scene in glass in this survey than the Slaughter of the Innocents. It is rare in glass but occurs twice in this survey: here and at Wormbridge (Fig. 149). The Ledbury image, with an impaled child held

Figs 90a–90b Ledbury (nX): the Flight into Egypt (ABOVE); the Slaughter of the Innocents (RIGHT)

up on a sword for Herod to see, is particularly grim. On the left of the scene is the bearded King Herod, bearing a sceptre in his left hand and wearing a blue tunic and gold cloak. His right hand is slightly raised, and the index finger points towards the child. Herod's crown has been replaced by a fragment of yellow drapery.

To the right of the Flight is the Crucifixion. The green Cross, once thought to be unusual, is the more typical rendering, and the figure, with its slight S-curve and arms making a Y, are seen in every other image from the two or three decades either side of 1300.

To the left of the Slaughter is a kneeling king with a label in Lombardic script 'CANCT', construed as CANUT (King Canute). There is only one other known representation of the king in medieval stained glass: in the west window of Canterbury Cathedral. The figure is well drawn with skilful use of silver stain and smear shading, which suggest a date in the fifteenth century. The Canterbury Canute is of similar date, but the figure is bearded and stands sternly. That bearded, regal stance is the one most often adopted in images of the king in other media.

If the figure is fifteenth-century, then the use of Lombardics for the label appears unusual. In this survey there seems to be a cut-off date for Lombardics of *c*.1350, after which black letter is used. There is nothing to link the label and the figure; indeed, the label would never have truncated the kneeling figure as it does now. The label is probably incomplete, and it would be no more tendentious to read it as part of the word *SCANCTA* (a medieval misspelling) than it is to turn the second 'C' into a 'U'. Unusually for a king, the figure is un-bearded and it is distinctly female in appearance. A saintly, crowned female in this context might be Catherine of Alexandria, the saint to whom the medieval Hospital in the town was dedicated, and an obvious companion to the local St Katherine Audley to whom the outer north chapel of the church was dedicated.

The NORTH AISLE WEST WINDOW (nXVII) has two panels of old glass from other windows, placed here after 1988, including a sundial (Fig. 91). The sundial was originally in the south aisle and was removed *c*.1895 when the south aisle windows were reglazed. It was made into a panel and stood on a window sill, upside down(!) until at least 1987, when it was illustrated in *Country Life*.[414] The oldest stained glass sundial is German and dated 1529.[415] They were in fashion in seventeenth-century country houses, and about 40 examples have been found from before 1700, many made by John Oliver; however, they are rarely found in church windows.[416]

Fig. 91 Ledbury: sundial (nXVII)

124 THE MEDIEVAL STAINED GLASS OF HEREFORDSHIRE & SHROPSHIRE

LEDBURY

The Hospital of St Katherine
(SO 7107 3764, HR8 1EA)

Joe Hillaby suggests that the introduction of the glass was part of a reconstruction programme of c.1335–40, and identifies the patron as Bishop John Grandison, who intended it as a memorial to his parents.[417] The arms of his father, William Grandison, are in the central panel of the east window (I.1b). The window has reticulated tracery which was in fashion at that time.

James Hill (1697–1727) visited and described the east window:

> In the East window of the Hospital Chappel is the effigies of St Catherine, also the arms of Grandison Lord of Markley being paly of six argent and azure on a bend gules 3 spread Eagles or.[418]

In 2015, the Dean and Chapter of Hereford Cathedral commissioned Jim Budd to reglaze the window.[419]

The contents of the EAST WINDOW, if not their arrangement, are broadly as seen by James Hill. The window is meant as a reredos, but the original composition can only be guessed at. A Crucifix in the centre, with saints and donors (probably in niches, as suggested in the glazing now) either side and below would be a good guess. Joe Hillaby suggests St Peter was among them because reused fragments of the bits and wards of two keys can be found in the borders below the Grandison shield, and low down on the left-hand vine border of the left-hand panel.

The left panel in Fig. 92b is an arrangement of fragments to form a human silhouette. The 'head' comprises part of a pair of clasped hands with the decorative cuffs of a vestment. The upper

Figs 92a–92b Ledbury, composite figures in St Katherine's Hospital Chapel (I)

torso looks like a chest clothed in a yellow tunic with a white robe over one 'shoulder'. The hem of the robe is represented by a patch of deeply-folded material. The borders on the white robe in both fragments suggest they belong together. The drapery is expertly folded with smear shading, and it is significant that there is no pot metal in the clothing of the figure. There are two borders forming the niche. The outer is a finely-drawn vine in white and silver-stained glass on a deep red ground; the inner is a thin band of mainly plain, yellow-coloured glass. The top of the panel has, in common with the other panels, a border with a narrow white hem enclosing black lozenges, with pointed white quatrefoils between bands of cross-hatched silver stain (the 'Ledbury border').

In the centre, the arms of Grandison in a plain roundel, sit on a section of lozenge border containing the bit (the part of the key inserted in the lock) of St Peter's key. When Hill visited, he drew the shield with the bend running down from top left to bottom right. At some later date this was reversed to show the bend in the manner associated with bastardy.

The right panel (Fig. 92a) contains a composite image of a female saint. She carries the cross staff associated with St Margaret but, unlike the usual images of Margaret, she is not crowned. Her drapery is clearly by the same hand as that in the left panel, and she is an exercise in grisaille with yellow stain and smear shading. This has resulted in an almost classical appearance, yet still retaining the sway of the Decorated style.

Joe Hillaby makes a convincing comparison with figures in Christ Church Cathedral, Oxford – and especially with the figure of the Virgin in the Latin Chapel, and with the nimbus of the Archangel Gabriel there.[420] However, dating is difficult. Oxford and Eaton Bishop are generally considered to be of 1330–50, but the Ledbury church Archangel Michael, which bears a striking resemblance to the St Catherine, is in the tracery lights of a window in the Perpendicular style, which may be as late in date as 1370. That affinity, across two architectural periods, is emphasised by the fact that the two Ledbury windows have similar borders. The Ledbury church glass is confidently dated to *c.*1371 by the representation of donors who were portionists at the same time. It is, of course, possible that the St Catherine's glass was installed some time after the stone window was made.

The SOUTH WINDOW contains a fragment of drapery, distinctly different from the garments in the east window. The bare feet suggest a saint, and the figure was seated on a plinth (rather like the Apostles in the Creed window at Ludlow).

LEINTWARDINE
St Mary Magdalene (SO 4046 7409, SY7 0LB)

The scale of the church, furnished with a noble roof, a magnificent reredos, stalls and misericords, suggests there should be treasures in the glass here, but there is nothing. In 1934, the Royal Commission found, 'Glass: In N. aisle-chapel – in N. window, fragments of borders, foliage, roses, etc., fourteenth and fifteenth century, made up with modern work.'[421]

Thanks to a former church warden, Mr Edward Pease Watkins, these fragments were discovered in the tower, collected and leaded into a frame. They may well have come from the tracery of the north window in the Crawshay Chapel.[422] The panel was displayed in the Crawshay Chapel for a while but, as it was no longer wanted by the church, it was given to the Leintwardine History Society. It has been returned to the church but is not on display.

LLANWARNE

Christ Church (SO 5055 2813, HR2 8JE)

The new church at Llanwarne, by architects Elmslie, Franey & Haddon, was consecrated at a service in August 1864.[423] The roundels were brought to Llanwarne by Walter Baskerville Mynors (1826–99), the long-serving rector, after they were removed from the east window of the church of St Weonards in 1884 by Walter's younger brother Robert (b.1819), to make way for a memorial window to their mother, Mary Elizabeth, who died in 1882. The chancel of St Weonards was extended eastwards at that time, but the east window tracery was reset.[424]

The roundels were brought to Herefordshire by Elizabeth (née Halliday) after she married Peter Mynors in 1817, and came from her family's Somerset estate at Chapel Cleeve in Somerset. They were not installed in St Weonards church until 1848. The roundels were installed at Llanwarne in 1901 as a memorial to Walter and, while they could not have seemed either appropriate or pleasing crammed together in the east window at St Weonards, they are now presented in a form and setting which allows them to be appreciated.

The roundels are in two NAVE SOUTH WINDOWS. They were recorded by William Cole, who dates them to the first half of the sixteenth century.[425] In the easternmost window, there are three panels depicting two scenes from the life of Sorghelosse, a mythical figure in the folklore of the Netherlands, whose life parallels that of the Prodigal Son (who is also found in the tracery) but whose end was far from happy. This type of story stemmed from Morality Plays, which were sponsored by trade and professional guilds in towns throughout medieval Europe.[426]

Figs 93a–93b Llanwarne: two scenes from the story of Sorghelosse, a version of the parable of the Prodigal Son. **Fig. 93a** (TOP): Sorghelosse sitting in poverty before a fire. **Fig. 93b** (BOTTOM): Sorghelosse returns home, carrying Aermoede, the personification of want, on his back. Copies of both scenes are in the collection of the Victoria & Albert Museum, catalogued as c.1520.

Window sVI

1a: Armorial, c.1550
1b: Joseph's dream, c.1550
1c: Tobias and the fish, c.1550
2a: Allegory of Justice, c.1515
2b: The Samaritan tending the Jew, c.1550
2c: Sorghelosse returns home, c.1525
3a: Sorghelosse returns home, c.1525
3b: Unidentified subject of a woman brought before a judge, c.1525
3c: Sorghelosse seated by the fire, c.1525
4a: The Crucifixion, sixteenth-century
4b: The Trial of Susannah, c.1515
4c: Armorial, c.1550
A2: The Prodigal Son received by his father, c.1540

Window sVII

1a: The Nativity, c.1510
1b: The Nativity, c.1540
1c: Saint Jerome, c.1525
2a: Saint George, c.1500
2b: Saint Martin, c.1525
2c: Saint Roch, c.1525
3a: Armorial. c.1550
3b: Pontius Pilate washing his hands, c.1540
3c: Armorial, dated 1548
4a: St Giles, c.1550
4b: Saint Lawrence with donor, c.1550
4c: Saint Matthias, c.1550
B2: A Messenger telling Abraham of the capture of Lot, c.1515
B3: Saint Andrew with donor, c.1525

LOWER HARPTON

Dunfield House, Christian Retreat Centre

There are two panels of medieval glass in a staircase window (Figs 94a & 94b). They were seen by the Royal Commission c.1934. The house is about halfway between Old Radnor and Kington, and either of those churches could have been the source of the glass. Several of the Miles family, who owned the house from 1830 until the end of the century, were ordained but not appointed to the local livings.

The panels are mostly made from architectural fragments, but a few subjects stand out. In the LEFT PANEL (Fig. 94a), a nimbed and crowned head, finely drawn in black line on white glass without stain or shading. Also, a hand holding a bundle of reeds from a Passion series and, at lower right, an eagle from the emblems of the Evangelists. Above the eagle is a distinctive piece of border with a leaf curling round a stem, of a type found in Shropshire – notably at Munslow where David Evans copied it and subsequently used it in other projects (see Bromfield).

In the RIGHT PANEL (Fig. 94b), the head of a female with a rayed nimbus and simple coronet, probably drawn by the same hand as the head in the left panel but using yellow stain for the hair. There are further pieces of the leaf and stem border noted in the left panel.

Figs. 94a–94b Dunfield House, Lower Harpton: details from the staircase window

LUDLOW
St Laurence (SO 5115 7470, SY8 1AN)

The windows of Ludlow church hold fourteenth- and fifteenth-century glass of exceptional quality and quantity. What we see now is veiled by iconoclasm, centuries of decay and restoration, but the distinctiveness and beauty of the windows, which present several unique subjects, has not been lost.

The most important strand in the story of the glass was spun by the Ludlow Palmers, the town guild dedicated to the Virgin Mary and St John the Evangelist. It was one of only a handful of town guilds in England with more than 100 members[428] who, corporately or individually, were probably responsible for most of the glass in the church. Although not documented, they must have commissioned the Jesse window in the Lady Chapel (the Virgin being one of their dedication saints) and the important windows in the Guild Chapel on the north side of the chancel, which was dedicated to St John the Evangelist, including the east window which depicts the guild's foundation story. The guild probably played an important part in protecting the glass before 1551 when it was dissolved and its assets given to the Corporation.[429] The guild's continuing influence in church and town after that date may well account for the remarkable extent to which the glass survives.

Ludlow is an interesting place about which to consider iconoclasm because of this exceptional survival of medieval glass (compared, for example, to Leominster, Ledbury and Hereford Cathedral); and at Ludlow, the churchwardens' accounts and the notes of antiquaries illuminate the story. The destruction of statuary, wall paintings and books, was inexpensive – and even profitable, as a well-known page in the churchwardens' accounts for 1548–49 (the year after the first Edwardian injunctions against idolatry) shows. It sets down receipts from the sale of images, and their tabernacles. including seven pence for the dragon 'saynt George stode upon'.[430] However, the destruction of images in glass is an expensive matter, which only the wealthiest and most reforming churches could afford to embrace with enthusiasm.

There was deliberate breaking of glass, which is evinced by the absence of images of the Crucifixion and of any medieval glass, other than heraldry, in the nave. The accounts also suggest the breaking of windows in 1547 when a relatively large sum of 'xxs viiijd' was spent on 'mendynge the wyndowys about the church.'[431] In 1550, the windows in the chapels of both St Catherine and St Margaret were mended; the sums representing, perhaps, the repair of defacement. However, the guild and its successor, the corporation, must have felt strongly proprietorial towards the windows they had endowed, and were apparently powerful enough to subvert the injunctions against idolatry.

The windows in the church constitute a carefully-composed illustration of the elements of the Catechism (Creed, Commandments, Salutation, Lord's Prayer) for the edification of the congregation. Emma Woolfrey, developing the analysis of the Catechism by Ganderton and Laford,[432] has suggested that,

> The development in the literacy of the laity in the fifteenth century led to new modes of devotion in which the interplay between text and image became a significant aspect of religious practices. Through their contribution to the beautification of their parish church the laity can be seen to have shaped the contours of local piety by

providing the new requirements for their devotion to the fabric of St Laurence.[433]

We should not be surprised if they were unwilling to destroy what they had made.

Only a few miles away, in 1641, at Leintwardine and Wigmore, Robert Harley, who headed the Parliamentary committee for the destruction of superstitious images, gave his personal attention to the work. Ludlow's glass would have been a fine prize and yet, again, destruction was avoided. Ludlow was a 'Cavalier stronghold' in the Civil War,[434] which also seems to have kept the tide of Puritan iconoclasm, away.

Iconoclasm was a complex and continuous process. Although not confined to the two periods of authorised iconoclasm at the Reformation and during the Civil War, these are convenient points of reference. There are no detailed descriptions of the church between the two dates (c.1540–c.1640), but on the brink of the Reformation it was impressive, as Leland noted, 'There is but one paroche churche in the towne, but that is very faire, and large, and richely adornyd, and taken for the fayrest in all those quartars.'[435]

In the seventeenth and eighteenth centuries the church attracted antiquaries. Weyman illustrated part of a copy of the College of Arms visitation of 1663, which recorded several shields in the south aisle and two kneeling figures, one of which was in armour.[436] This also recorded five shields in the east window.[437] About 20 years later, Thomas Dingley wrote, 'Ludlow Church is very fair, famous for painted ancient glass windows.'[438]

> ... The east window beyond the ancient choir has in it the whole history of Saint Lawrence to whom this church was dedicated. The uppermost south window in the high chancel of the choir hath the singers in a choir describ'd with each their verse before them and this subscribed; Orate pro bono statu ... Hanc fenest. Fieri fecit AD 1445.
>
> A north window very fair with figures of saints and patriarchs is thought to be the gift of the clothier's or as I rather take it the Shearsman of this town and this is subscribed ... 1422.
>
> A window in the north part of the church ... Is adorned with curiously wrought figures of the twelve apostles each reading his article of the creed.

A copy of this appears in one of James Hill's (d.1727) notebooks[439] but not in his hand.

In 1722, William Stukeley described the church thus: 'Here is a very good church and handsome tower, with a pleasant ring of six bells in the cross thereof: the windows are full of painted glass pretty entire ...'.[440]

Not long after, William Mytton sketched several subjects in the chancel windows, which contribute to an understanding of the restoration carried out roughly 100 years later,[441] and towards the end of the eighteenth century, Francis Grose referred to 'curious painted glass'[442] which Thomas Wright described as having, 'been so barbarously mutilated by modern repairs as to present a strange mixture of patchwork.'[443] The corporation played a significant role in the later maintenance of the glass, despite its clumsiness. For example, in 1720 their wealth was probably the source of the largest single sum (£101) spent on the repair of windows in any church in this survey during the eighteenth century. It was noted above that the post-Reformation churchwardens' accounts for Ludlow record exceptionally large and regular expenditure on glazing, which must also have been a significant factor in the survival of so much ancient glass.

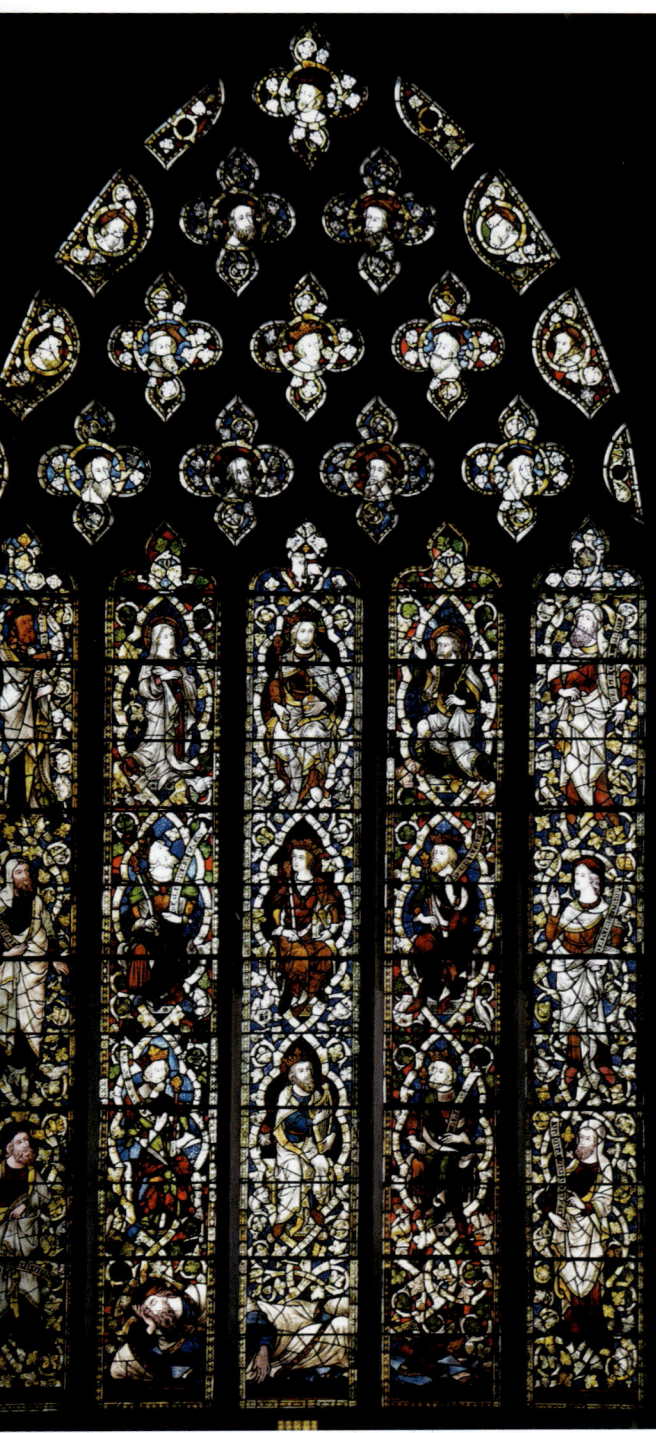

Fig. 95 Ludlow: the Jesse window (sV)

THE TREE OF JESSE IN THE LADY CHAPEL (sV)

The provenance of this window (Fig. 95) is considered with other fourteenth-century Jesse windows in Part One. It is an impressive sight, thanks to the work of Hardman & Co. in 1890,[444] but the rich, vibrant work of the Madley Master, remains discernible as the guiding inspiration.

Hardman's Jesse reclines at the base of the window and over him in the central light are his son David (1c), David's son Solomon (2c) and Christ with orb and sceptre (3c). Christ is flanked by Mary (3b) and Joseph (3d): all these figures are Hardman's. Mary and Joseph's place in the genealogy of Christ presented problems which the Jesse Tree painters tried to address. It was known that Joseph was of David's line, but he was not the biological father of Jesus, and it became a matter of great importance to demonstrate the nobility of the lineage of Mary who was undoubtedly Christ's mother. The image of the tree is based on a prophecy of Isaiah: 'And there shall come forth a rod out of the stem of Jesse, and a branch shall grow out of his roots', which, in the Latin Vulgate Bible, includes the phrase, 'virga de radice Iesse et flos'. M.D. Anderson suggests, 'As early as the third century Tertullian had expounded the association of this virga de radice Iesse with the Virgin Mary (virgo).'[445] To emphasise this, Joseph is rarely included in medieval Jesse Trees, and they are most often found in Lady Chapels, as at Ludlow and Madley.

The lineage from David, based on Matthew's Gospel (rather than the genealogy in Luke's) is represented in the two lights flanking the centre, but it is greatly compressed, with 25 generations represented by four seated figures, and it is not in chronological order. After Solomon comes Asa who sits to the right of David (1d) and Joram who sits on David's left (1b). Only the head of Asa is

Fig. 95a Ludlow: the Jesse window (sV), Micah

Fig. 95b Ludlow: the Jesse window (sV), King Joram

Figs 96a–96b (TOP), **96c–96d** Ludlow (BELOW): details from St Katherine's Chapel east window (sIX)

old but all of Joram is old, apart from a patch on his neck and the left side of his crown (Fig. 95b).[446] From Joram the line jumps to the right to the modern figure of Hezekiah (2d) and back to the medieval figure of Manessah (2b), whose crown, left hand and right knee are modern.[447]

The outer main lights hold six standing prophets who foretold the coming of Christ, all of which are modern except for Micah (3a). In the lower tier are Isaiah (1a), opposite is Ezekiel (1e), and in the next tier, Jeremiah (2a) and Daniel (2e). Level with Christ are Micah (3a) (Fig. 95a) and Malachi (3e). Micah's left hand, green tunic and cloak are modern.[448]

In the tracery lights are 14 heads of kings and prophets decked with foliage. The heads in A1, A3, A4, C3, C3, D1 and D3 are medieval. It is likely that more fragments of old glass, in the form of vines, foliage and diapering, are scattered throughout the window, including the birds and animals which give great delight.

South transept east window (sIX)

In 1876, James Irvine saw 'the remains of a fragment of a stained glass figure' in the east window.[449] The present window was assembled in 1904 by Miss M. Neville of Birmingham, from fragments of glass from several windows and periods.[450]

In the left light are architectural fragments and, at the top, black letter bands and a bearded face in the International Style. Halfway up the centre light, in a narrow band, are two devils and two angel faces with pointed chins and golden locks, reminiscent of the angels at Alveley and Claverley. There are delightful fish and an enigmatic nimbed grotesque with a long nose, above which is an almost complete bearded figure with a beret (Fig. 96a). In the top two panels are finely-drawn heads: a bearded man in profile, which seems like the bearded men in John Thornton's work at York (Fig. 96c), with five other fragments of heads. At the top of the central light are two characterful heads: one elegantly androgynous, wearing a cowl and amice, and the other with impossibly straight moustaches (Fig. 96d). In the right panel, is a chained white dog on a chequerboard floor, which may have been at the bottom of panel 1b of the Palmers' window.

In panel A2 of the tracery is the twin of the seated figure in Fig. 96a, and several more fifteenth-century heads including, at the top, a trio of kerchief, liripipe and coif cap. In A3 are a nimbed and bearded saint, and the head of a monk and several small heads hiding among the bits of black letter and buildings. At the top of the window (panel B2) is an elegant and demure fourteenth-century head which may be from an Annunciation (Fig. 96b), but the glazier has given her an ill-fitting crown so that this panel has been called the Coronation of the Virgin.

Nave north windows (nXII–nXIV)

There are seventeenth-century records of armorial glass and kneeling donors in the windows on the south side of the nave, all of which have disappeared.[451] On the north side, four shields remained in the seventeenth century, three of which can still be seen in the tracery. From the east, these shields represent Mortimer, de Verdon and de Clare, and have been dated to 1316–17.

Chapel of St John:
The Golden Window (nVIII)

This beautiful window was restored by Hardman & Co. in 1876. At first sight, the upper and lower parts of the window seem quite different; the upper part has a good deal of white glass and deep red drapery, while in the lower part the golden glow of silver stain and white robes predominates. Comparison of the drawing and lettering suggest that the same hands are at work throughout.

At the bottom of the window are the named donor, Catherine, with her husband and two children.[452] The man is John Parys,[453] warden of the Palmers, who died in 1449.[454] At this time, English glaziers were beginning to think of their pictures extending over complete windows rather than accepting the boundaries imposed by their mullions,[455] and in the upper scene a damask hanging provides a common backdrop, while a golden landscape spreads out below. The windows by John Prudde in the Beauchamp Chapel, Warwick (1447–64) display several similarities. The two Virgins have similar poses (Figs 97a & 97b, overleaf) and in both images decorative jewels encrusted with pearls are liberally applied.

The window has an unusual mixture of characters which look like the shopping list of the donors (Fig. 98). That may be true for the

Figs 97a–97b Ludlow: comparison of the Virgin in the Golden Window (nVII) (LEFT) with the Virgin in the east window of the Beauchamp Chapel, Warwick (RIGHT)

lower part, with their name saints, Catherine and John, but the upper part is a sophisticated essay on the Godhead and Incarnation. This is probably a unique picture in glass, combining the Annunciation with the risen Christ carrying a sceptre and a Resurrection Cross. It must have been the intention of the artist to show the 'Quinity' – Father, Son divine, Son human, Mary and the Holy Spirit – in one image.[456] This also provides a graphic illustration of the crucial tenets of the Creed that is the subject of the next window. Reading clockwise from the top:

GOD (*I believe in God the Father*), CHRIST (*... and in Jesus Christ*), HOLY SPIRIT (*... who was conceived by the Holy Spirit*), MARY (*... born of the Virgin Mary*). CHRIST RISEN (*... on the third day he rose*), FATHER AND SON (*... and sitteth on the right hand of the Father*)

The catechetical text of the Pater Noster is at the base of the upper window and the meaning of 'Pater' is set out above it in arresting detail. At the top, the Father holds a fully-formed and bearded Son (both restored by Hardman) ready to launch Him down a light beam to follow the Holy Spirit (in the form of a dove) towards the

Fig. 98 Ludlow: the Golden Window (nVIII)

seated Virgin (her head probably by Hardman). The archangel delivers another catechetical text, the Salutation, Ave Maria, the words of which are written out on a banderol. The risen, divine Christ sits opposite and looks on. And by this clever trick, two of the core elements of the catechism[457] are combined to sit beside the third, the Creed, in the next window.

The lower part of the window presents a luscious golden landscape as a backdrop to the three saints chosen by the donors. St Catherine, with her three attributes – crown, wheel and sword – impales the head of her tormentor, Maxentius. John the Baptist (with a head by Hardman) is unusually sumptuously dressed with a lamb and flag, while behind him is the hermit from the story of St Christopher in the next light. St Christopher bearing the infant Christ was traditionally placed on the north side of churches, where sight of him could bless travellers stopping to pray at the south door. Here, the pilgrim Palmers could be blessed by sight of him in their own chapel. Delightful details are found in Christopher's great staff, which has been made to blossom by the Christ Child, and the windmill on the far-off hill.

The Chapel of St John: The Creed Windows (nVI & nVII)

The Golden Window reveals a designer of unusual vision and originality; the Creed windows also display those qualities. The windows were seen by Thomas Dingley in 1684 and were sufficiently intact for him to identify their subject matter.[458] In 1856 the two windows had a quite different appearance:

> In the [west] window, St. James, St. Thomas, St. Andrew, St. Matthew, St. Peter, and a St, who is not clearly identified. The north eastern, a bishop with a procession of clergy, a funeral procession, probably the burial of St. Stephen, the Saviour, St. Thaddeus, a bishop attended by harpers, and a figure of St. George. The apex of one contains angels, and the other modern glass.[459]

Restoration was undertaken by Hardman & Co in 1876, and a good deal of the glass, including the upper part of the eastern widow (nVI), except for part of St Philip, is new.

The window must be of similar date to the Golden Window because both form essential parts of the Palmers' rebuilding of the east end of the church and the display of the Catechism in several windows. They are probably by the same workshop. Jean Lafonde makes a strong case for the same hand but rejects any connection with Prudde and the Beauchamp Chapel.[460] The faces do not seem to be closely related, but they include a significant number by Hardman. However, the vision and technique, the colours, the opulence of the drapery decorated with pearl-encrusted jewels, the lettering and the damask curtain background, are all shared with Warwick.

In the Hampton Court Creed window, and every other surviving example, the Apostles stand in panels or canopy-work with their Creed phrase forming part of the frame. This window, designed as a single scene with convincing perspective, has them sitting together in a grand architectural setting, recreating the moment when the Creed was first formulated (Figs 99a & 99b). It has been suggested that this was at the Council of Jerusalem in c.50AD,[461] but the account of the Council in Acts 15 makes no mention of it. Above each window, the dove of the Holy Spirit hovers, and rays of Her inspiration penetrate the room (another John Prudde detail – see Fig. 97a).

Fig. 99a Ludlow: the Creed Window (nVII)

Fig. 99b Ludlow: the Creed Window (nVII)

Fig. 100 Ludlow: the Palmers' Window (nV), & **Fig. 100a**: the right-hand light (the Guild Feast) (nV.1d)

The attributes carried by the figures of Apostles in medieval art are of great help in identifying them, although some Apostles have more than one. Here, they are named at the start of their Creed sentence and this reveals some unusual breaks with tradition – possibly by the restorer rather than the artist. The attachment of the Apostles to Creed phrases is not consistent, but Peter, Andrew, James the Great and John come first in almost every example.[462] The two windows are to be read together, starting at the top-left with Peter, and reading across both windows:

- Peter holds the keys of heaven, *Credo in Deum* …
- Andrew holds the saltire cross of martyrdom, *Et in Jesum Christum Filium* …
- James the Great holds a staff and wears a pilgrim's hat with a scallop shell, *Qui conceptus est de Spirito Sancto* …
- John holds a palm and a poisoned chalice containing a devil, *Passus sub Pontio Pilato* …
- Phillip holds a staff with a cross head, *Descendit ad inferno* …
- Bartholomew holds the flaying knife of his martyrdom, *Ascendit ad coleus* …
- Thomas holds a spear, *Inde venturus est* …
- Matthew holds the fulling club more usually associated with James the Less, *Credo in Spirito Sanctum* …
- James the Less holds an axe or possibly a halberd which are usually attributes of Thomas and Matthias respectively, *Sanctum, Ecclesiam* …
- Matthias holds a pole or lance which is normally described as a halberd, but which lacks a blade, *Remissionem peccatorum* …
- Jude (Thaddeus) holds a boat which is often thought to be a scimitar, *Carnis resurrectionem* …
- Simon holds the saw of his grim martyrdom, *Et vitam aeternam* …

THE CHAPEL OF ST JOHN:
THE PALMERS' WINDOWS (nV)

Windows representing religious guilds are rare, and usually depict patron saints in a single narrative scene, or simply with their attributes to identify them.

The Palmers' Window (Figs 100 & 100a) is without parallel in the way it lavishly sets out the foundation myth of the guild[463] with consummate artistry. Guild windows are normally a celebration of the saint, while this is a celebration of the guild and its members. It is also one of only two narratives of the life of St Edward in glass, and suggests a connection with the cult of St Edward around the time of the foundation of the Palmers.[464] The window must be of similar date to the windows on the north side of the Guild Chapel and shares some characteristics, but it is difficult to see the same hands at work. Some of the figures in both windows have the square eyes with curlicues from the outer corners and Fusilli hair and beards typical of the International Style.

The arms of Ludlow and the Palmers at the head of the window are by Hardman. So too is all but the very top of the first panel in the cycle at top-left (2a), which romantically portrays two pilgrim members of the guild, setting out for Jerusalem. Fortunately, Hardman adopted the colours of the whole window but did not copy the International Style in drawing faces and hair. In the next scene (2b) the story shifts to Jerusalem, and we see the kingly St Edward giving his ring to a beggar as alms. The beggar is St John the

Evangelist (patron of the Palmers' Guild and the Chapel) in disguise. In the third scene (2c), the pilgrims are in Jerusalem where they meet St John, also dressed as a pilgrim, who bids them return the ring to King Edward with the message that John and Edward would meet soon in heaven. In the fourth scene (2d) the pilgrims are in the court of King Edward, returning the ring to him.

On the lower tier, the first scene (1a) comprises a procession with the two pilgrims following the clergy (one of whom carries the brush-like holy water aspergillum). Next (1b) the pilgrims receive the charter of the guild from King Edward, and in the third panel (1c) they return to Ludlow where they are greeted by the town's Warden dressed in red. Christian Liddy suggests that the restorers arranged these three panels in the wrong order, and that the presentation of the charter should be first followed by a procession to Ludlow and the greeting at the gate.[465] The final panel (Fig. 100a) shows the Palmers at the guild feast, dressed in their regalia and listening to a harpist retelling the story of their foundation.

The chancel east window (I)

Further superlatives are required here for the largest surviving hagiographical window in an English parish church. It tells the story of St Laurence in 27 panels, and was a milestone project in the history of conservation. David Evans of Shrewsbury signed the bottom right pictorial panel with the year 1832.[466] His work is characterised by strong colours, well represented by the purple and yellow glass used in the St Laurence windows, and by the highly skilled copying of historical styles of drawing. Earlier writers concur that there is a great deal of Evans in what we see today and, where there are records from before 1836, they show that much was lost or changed. The comparison of panel 2d with Mytton's drawing in Figs 102a & 102b is probably typical in showing the loss of one complete figure and changes of detail. The forthcoming repair project to be carried out by the York Glaziers Trust, will result in a full account. Sarah Brown, speaking at the conference held in the church in 2016, identified the panel (2c) in Fig. 101c as one where the work of Evans could be seen beside the original.

At the top of the window is the 'Throne of Mercy' with the father holding the crucified Christ and the Spirit hovering in the form of a dove. Immediately below are the figures of Bishop Spofford and his adopted saint, Anne, teaching her daughter, the Virgin, to read (Fig. 101a). Spofford's image can be seen at Ross (Fig. 130) and David O'Connor, writing about the Ross glass, said about the Ludlow image of Spofford,

Fig. 101a Ludlow: detail of east window (I). The figures of St Anne teaching the Virgin, and Bishop Spofford

Figs 101b & 101c Ludlow east window (I): the Throne of Mercy, and a detail of panel 2c with a medieval figure to the left beside a modern figure by Evans to the right.

Figs 102a–102b Ludlow: comparison of Evans's work (TOP) and Mytton's record of the medieval glass in the east window (I) (BOTTOM) (by permission of the Cadbury Library, University of Birmingham)

The Story of St Laurence (I)

Laurence was born in Aragon, Spain in 226AD. The hagiography begins (**4a**) with the saint presented to Pope Sixtus II, who was martyred four days before him, in 258AD. He was ordained (**4b**) as one of the six deacons of Rome and the Emperor's heir gave him rich presents (**4c**) which he gave to the poor (**4d**). Laurence was taken (**4e**) and brought before the Emperor (**4f**) who tried to convert him to idolatry only to find that the idols collapsed in pieces (**4g**). He was imprisoned (**4h**) and while there performed several miracles, including restoring the sight of Lucillus (**4j**), which resulted in the gaoler Hippolytus, who witnessed the miracle, being converted (**3a**). The Emperor demanded that Laurence hand over the wealth of the Church and he presented the poor of his congregation as its greatest treasure (**3b**), whereupon the Emperor beat them (**3c**). Laurence was threatened with torture (**3d**) but refused to abandon his calling and was stoned (**3e**), beaten with reeds (**3f**), sticks (**3g**) and scourges (**3h**), torn with hooks (**3j**), burned with hot metal (**2a**) and finally roasted on a grid and regularly turned with iron forks until God received his soul (**2b**). He was buried (**3c**) (**Fig. 101c**) but continued to perform miracles. A deacon broke a chalice but his prayers to Laurence restored it (**3d**) (**Fig. 102a**) and when the Church of St Laurence was being repaired, a beam, which was found to be too short, grew again when help was sought from the saint (**3e**). The next four panels are out of order[470] and tell the story of builders working on the church dedicated to the saint. The priest engaged skilled men to rebuild the church which had been burned (**2j**) in a war with the Lombards. It was a time of scarcity and the builders prayed for food (**2h**). The priest, looking into the village oven to see if anything was left, found an unusually large loaf, and asked the villagers if it was theirs (**2g**). They said it was not and so he took it and shared it with the men (**2f**). A similar large loaf appeared in the oven every day until the famine ended.

The window was drastically restored in 1832, and only Spofford's armorial, held by a modern angel in another light [A5], the hands, and a few fragments of Saint Anne's jewelled hem are original. The inscription to Spofford, and the scroll: 'Ann[a] faciet media preco manna' are modern, but the latter, with its echo of glass at Catterick, suggests that the restorers reproduced what was once there. The window formed part of an extension to the choir built in the years after 1433, when the parishioners of Ludlow, exasperated by the inactivity of their rector, appealed to the Pope on account of the ruinous condition of the chancel. Spofford's role in sorting out the problem may have been publicly acknowledged by the figures and the shield.[467]

To the left are the Virgin and Child and St John the Baptist which, with the Trinity above, are Evans's work using cartoons he drew for the restoration of Winchester College Chapel.[468] To the right are Christ in Glory[469] and St Laurence holding the grid iron, his attribute in medieval art.

The chancel south side east: The Commandments Window (sII)

This window forms part of the Catechism with the windows in St John's Chapel, described above, and is the only representation of the Decalogue in glass in England.[471] Six commandment panels survive, which may originally have been in another window, perhaps in the nave where they would have been more visible to the congregation. In the late seventeenth century, Thomas Dingley saw this 'upper window on the south side' displaying 'a choir with verses written out.'[472] The window was restored by David Evans in 1854, but with the lighter touch of 20 years of experience since he restored the east window. He mimics more and his palette is less jarring, so that the International Style of the mid fifteenth century still shines out in scenes of pleasing complexity and iconographic richness.

The Commandments Window (sII)

2a (**Fig. 103c**): Commandment 5. *Non occides*: 'Thou shalt do no murder'. God (by Evans) with orb and sceptre and flanked by medieval feathered angels, looks down on Moses, still 'horned' with rays of heavenly light[473] as he presents the tablets to a motley gathering, including a figure with a laurel crown. The picture below, however, is from the Fourth Commandment, 'Honour thy Father and Mother ...', with a child kneeling before an adult.

2c: Commandment 6. *Non moechaberis*: 'Thou shalt not commit adultery'. God (by Evans) is seen in profile against a backdrop of celestial bodies above Moses showing the crowd the tablets. Below, a couple embrace while her husband grasps her by the shoulders. A priest looks on with a shocked (but resigned) expression.

2e: Commandment 7. *Non furtum facies*: 'Thou shalt not steal'. God (by Evans, and like his God in panel 2a) holds a sceptre and Resurrection flag. While Moses displays the tablets, a thief is stealing the purse of a sumptuously-dressed onlooker.

1a (**Fig. 103a**): Commandment 8. *Non loqueris contra proximum tuum falsum testimonium*: 'Thou shalt not bear false witness against thy neighbour'. God, probably with an original face and body, raises eight digits (the number of the command). The scene is of a kneeling king, which does not seem to fit the command in any obvious way. He could be from the first command about worshipping God before all others; he is demonstrating that even kings must kneel before that authority.

1c: Commandment 9. *Non desiderabis uxorum proximi tui*: 'Though shalt not covet thy neighbour's wife'. A conspicuously David Evans Virgin looks down on a scene wherein a wealthy merchant admires a well-dressed woman.

1e (**Fig. 103b**): Commandment 10. *Non concupisceris domum proximi tui*: 'Thou shalt not covet thy neighbour's house'. A David Evans angel presides over the presentation of the tablets to wealthy burghers, and covetousness illustrated by the siege of a fortified house.

  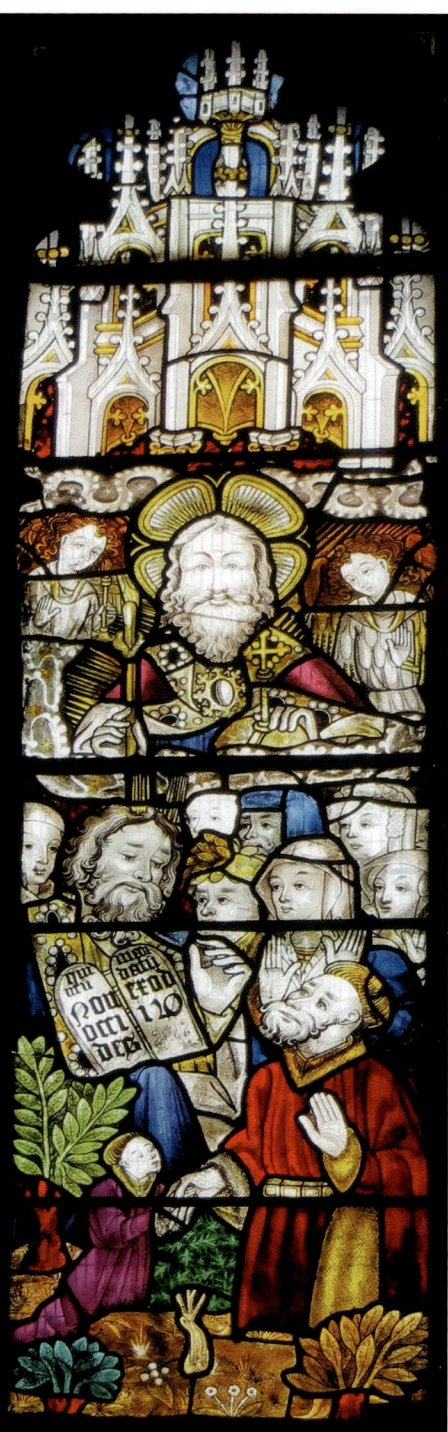

Figs 103a–103c Ludlow: panels from the Commandments Window (sII):
Fig. 103a (False Witness, 1a); Fig. 103b (Covetousness, 1e); Fig. 103c (Murder, 2a)

Each panel follows a pattern, with a celestial figure in a cloud window at the top, Moses displaying the inscribed tablets to a group of people and, at the bottom, a scene illustrating the command. The pre-Reformation numbering of the commands is used and the first four are missing, so the series starts in panel 2a with Commandment 5.

In the window above the six Commandment panels are three large figures which were heavily restored by Evans. The Archangel Michael weighing souls (panel 3a) is an appropriate companion to the Commandments. In the centre (3c) is the figure of a bishop, and on the right the Virgin of the Annunciation receiving the Holy Spirit dove. In the tracery are angels, saints, the Virgin and Child and the Risen Christ. Seen from the ground, these have the look of Evans's work.

Chancel south: middle window (sIII)

The window was restored by Clayton and Bell in 1859.[474] The glass has come from several windows, but there are some common themes in the strong colours and prominent jewelled bosses.[475]

In the tracery, Christ at the apex (D1) is modern. In the centre of the lower tiers are six figures (C1–4 & A3–4) painted with yellow stain and bearing books. Some have attributes – pens, palms, a flower – which might represent saints. The outer lights in row B represent the Annunciation, with Mary to the left and the archangel opposite. The left outer pair in the lower row (A1 & 2) are St Jerome, clad in red and holding a church, and another father of the church, Augustine. To the right is an angel and a kneeling female saint in a habit.

There are 15 figures in the main lights. The predominantly modern figures are in panels 2b: Elizabeth; 2d: Etheldreda; 3a: Paul, and 3d: Joseph of Arimathea. The three Magi belong together, but the perspective of their plinths suggests the two outer Magi were at a higher level than the central Magus. Panel 1d has the guiding star. The heads in 1c & 1d are beautifully drawn and have a strong affinity with Thornton's Apocalypse at York. The head in 1b is a modern replacement. Thomas, who is seen receiving the Virgin's girdle (1e), has been associated with the Magi, because he is thought to have met and baptised them. Certainly, most of his face, at least, is by the same hand as the adjacent Magi.

In the second tier are three female saints – Helen, Catherine and Margaret – drawn by the same hand which is not the hand that made the Magi. Their faces are simpler, almost unshaded and have eyes with acute outer corners. They do, however, follow the same fashion in dress.

There are four further figures with old glass, all of which have replacement heads. Based on the lettering styles 1a: Edward (modern head) and 3e: James the Less (incongruous old head) go together. The head of 3b: Luke is a fifteenth-century head of Christ with a rayed nimbus, but lettering links the figure to the adjacent 3c: James the Great with his pilgrim staff and scallop.

Chancel south: west window (sIV)

The window is the work of David Evans[476] and seems to be devoid of ancient glass. The suggestion, that one of the representations of St John is old glass from the firm's restoration of Winchester College Chapel (1821–28), is obviously wrong. Both figures are Evans at his most strident.

> **Chancel south: west window (sIV)**
> **1a**: Mary Magdalene with a jar; **1c**: St Peter with a key; **1e**: St John with the poisoned cup; **2a**: A pope/ saint holding ?; **2c**: St John with poisoned cup; **2e**: St Clement with anchor; **3a**: Archangel Gabriel with greeting; **3b**: St George and the dragon. **3c**: a queen holding a Cross of Lorraine; **Tracery**: Apostles with Mary at the centre.

Chancel north: east window (nII)

William Mytton drew three bishops and St Leonard in this window *c.*1735.[477] Leonard and one of the bishops have gone, possibly moved to the next window, nIII. The window is the work of David Evans in 1854 and seems to be devoid of ancient glass. The subjects are labelled and need no further explanation here. The panels of patterned quarries in all three north windows have a strident and unsatisfactory appearance.

> **Chancel north: east window (nII)**
> **1a**: Thomas Becket; **1c**: St Edward the Confessor; **1e**: St Augustine; **2a**: St Margaret with a dragon; **2c**: St Catherine with the wheel and sword; **2e**: St Helen with a Cross; **3a**: St Stephen with stones; **3c**: St Lawrence with gridiron; **3e**: St Vincent with a palm; **Tracery**: a heavenly orchestra with female saints.

Chancel north: middle window (nIII)

The window is the work of David Evans in 1854 and seems to be devoid of ancient glass except, possibly, in the tracery lights.

> **Chancel north: middle window (nIII)**
> **1a**: St Dunstan with tongs gripping the Devil's nose; **1c**: the Virgin and Child; **1e**: St George and the dragon; **2a**: St Barbara with the tower; **2c**: St Joseph; **2e**: St Apollonia with tooth tongs; **3a**: St Leonard with fetters; **3c**: King David; **3e**: St John of Bridlington; **Tracery**: winged figures in different guises, suggesting the nine orders of angels.

Chancel north: west window (nIV)

This window was restored by David Evans in 1859. Weyman and Lafond could not agree on the survival of medieval glass, and between them suggested remains in panels 1a, 2c, 2e, 3c and 3e. It is difficult to be certain from the ground. This may have been, according to Dingley (but he is not specific), the Shearmen's window of 1425 with figures of saints and patriarchs.

> **Chancel north: west window (nIV)**
> **1a**: Joseph in the stable; **1c**: the Virgin and Child; **1e**: the Magi; **2a**: St George and the dragon; **2c**: Christ rising from the tomb; **2e**: Mary Magdalene; **3a & 3e**: angels censing; **3c**: Virgin Mary throned; **Tracery**: the heavenly choir.

MADELEY

The former Church of St Michael

William Mytton drew several figures in glass in the north windows. There was a donor wearing vestments kneeling at a prie dieu, the Coronation of the Virgin and saints Catherine, Margaret and Peter. There was also an armed figure enmeshed in a vine, perhaps part of a Tree of Jesse.

MADLEY

The Nativity of the Blessed Virgin Mary
(SO 4198 3872, HR2 9DP)

Madley church is one of the grandest village churches in Herefordshire. The chancel and Chilstone Chapel of the fourteenth century, are especially important, and so too is the surviving stained glass. It was a possession of the Dean and Chapter of Hereford Cathedral from the early thirteenth century, and the scale and quality of the work, particularly in the first half of the fourteenth century, reflect that connection. The chancel, north aisle and south chapel are especially noteworthy. The unusual sumptuousness and rare dedication of the church, to the Nativity of the Virgin, can be explained by its possession of a miraculous statue of the Virgin which attracted pilgrims, and hence gifts and patronage.

In the early fourteenth century, the famed healing powers of the tomb of Thomas Cantilupe, in Hereford Cathedral, was attracting pilgrims. Many of those pilgrims would also have made a visit to the Virgin's statue at Madley. A document of 1318[478] in the cathedral archives, refers to the shrine at Madley and helps to fix the time of the work there. It set down a principle that offerings made before the statue of the Virgin were to be devoted to the fabric of the 'new chancel'.[479]

The apse and the eastern chancel windows that now hold the stained glass, were the work of a local mason and were probably begun soon after 1316.[480] The Chilstone Chapel, which was the Lady Chapel, and the north aisle were begun in the early 1330s and took about 10 years to complete.[481]

Sarah Brown[482] has described the demise of the medieval glass through iconoclasm and decay until its collection and re-leading in the apse windows. There is a documented instance of vandalism, or collateral damage (rather than iconoclasm) in the register of Bishop Spofford.[483] In September 1432, the Commissary General was instructed to inquire into bloodshed which involved fighting in the chancel and arrows being fired through windows. Later, in the dangerous periods of iconoclasm of the next two centuries, it seems, from the descriptions of antiquaries and from the extent and subject matter of the glass seen today, that there was no systematic destruction of superstitious imagery. James Malcolm c.1803[484] found figures whose faces had been destroyed, but many others remained that might have been regarded as superstitious.

In the churchwardens' accounts for the late sixteenth and seventeenth centuries there are only a few items for window repairs.[485] This is typical of the situation at the Reformation when the demand for religious imagery disappeared and the art of stained glass was almost lost. The only reference found in the cathedral archives is to work on the chancel by the glazier Morgan in 1727.[486] However, throughout the eighteenth century, relatively large sums were spent on the repair of the windows by both the wardens and the Dean and Chapter. In 1720, for example, £1 15s 9d was spent by the parish, 'to the glazier at several times', and 14s was spent on 'wiring the church windows'.[487]

Documents in the cathedral archives[488] referring to the chancel, show that in July 1754 William Reece gave an estimate for repairs of £7 15s 4d. This included 113 feet of painted glass that was in urgent need of re-leading and supporting with iron saddle bars, and 'pieces of paint'd glass to cut and make good the Deficiencies.' This was probably a conservative repair because the amount of new material in the form of 'paint'd glass' and 'New quarres' only amounted to £1 4s 10d. In 1793 an estimate of £8 10s was given by Mathew Seaborne for 'ten windows [the number of windows in the chancel] of nearly 300 feet of Glass and new leading exclusive of the painted Glass which must remain with repairs without Leading as it stands'.

The repairs were particularly costly in 1797: in March, 18s 8d was spent on window bars in the chancel and this was followed by a payment to Richard Powell for glaziers' work of £18 10s 0d, for 'wire lattices, painting, glazing & repairing Madley Chancel windows as estimate.' Then in May an estimate was given by Richard Powell for lattice work for eight windows, of £9 12s 0d, with an additional estimate from William Lane for frames.

At the same time, the parish was continually undertaking repairs to the aisle windows. The churchwardens' accounts for 1738–1815 show significant sums (in relation to the total expenditure) in almost every year.[489] These accounts give an unusually detailed picture of the efforts of churchwardens to keep their windows weatherproof, and reveal some interesting practices. The craftsmen involved were described as 'glaziers', especially in relation to larger sums, but clearly had wider plumbing skills, for in 1799 a relatively large sum of more than £13 was paid to the 'Glaziers as per bill for gutters and windows'. It seems to have been customary, when glaziers were employed, for the parish to provide charcoal, presumably for leadwork. Such sums of about one shilling are recorded in 1754 and 1780 (when they were also provided with coal). In 1793 the glazier's bill is associated with 'three bags of moss', which may have been used as packaging or protection for the glass.[490]

The larger sums in the accounts went to more skilled glaziers, and there are entries for payments to the wardens for expenses for travelling to Hereford to see a glazier. However, much of the work, represented in the accounts by more modest sums, was probably undertaken by unskilled local men. From 1804, payments to John Rogers, of three guineas annually, are described as 'salary'.[491] These payments to Rogers, and later to George Jennings, carried on until 1833.[492]

The maintenance of the glass was accepted and allowed for necessity, but the declining condition of the windows suggests that the efforts were never enough. In his description of the east end of the north aisle in 1810, Duncumb wrote, 'the colours remain very good, but the glass is much over-run with ivy and has been often broken and repaired.'

In 1791, a sum of more than £4 was paid to, 'the Glazier for the new windows and mending the others.' This is the only specific reference to new work in the eighteenth century, and may refer to panels which were inserted into the east window of the Chilstone Chapel, but were so disliked that they lasted but a short time (see below).

In 1675[493] Blount noted, 'The windows have been curiously painted of which there is a fair remainder.' Much later Duncumb, in the eighteenth century,[494] found that, 'Most of the windows of the church have remains of painted glass.' Those remains can be sketched from the notes of antiquaries:

NORTH AISLE WEST OF THE PORCH
Duncumb described the window immediately west of the north door as having 'a male figure over which is inscribed a word like Marbeus'. Sarah Brown suggests it is a misreading of 'Matheus' written in black letter script.

NORTH AISLE (nX)
Malcolm reported that all four windows of the aisle had 'large and beautiful figures of painted glass.' This window had a Crucifix under a Cross in a niche within a grand canopy. This was accompanied, on the right side, by the blessed Virgin with the infant on her left arm and the lily in the right; and on the left (see Fig. 1 & p. 76),

> Beata Milburgha with her crozier and mass book in a close garment of deep purple and blue mantle falling from her head be lined with ermine, in her attitude and meekness would not disgrace the pencil of Guido but the features are not quite true, those figures are under grand canopies, in the quatrefoils over them are angels kneeling.

In the eighteenth century, Duncumb also saw this with, 'A cross and female figure inscribed Sta. Milburga pray for [blank] and for the souls of all Christians.'

NORTH AISLE (nIX)
Malcolm found Christ in Glory showing his wounds, St Werburgh and a kneeling angel.

NORTH AISLE (nVIII)
Silas Taylor[495] found,

> In the middle partition is the effigy of a woman praying and before her an escutcheon paly of 4 O & B on a fesse G: 2 mullets A. On the next light is the portrait of one kneeling in his coat of armour of paly O & B and the fesse in the armour about his middle with the mullets upon it, a small buckler hanging by his two-handed sword with the same coat upon it.[496] and in the 3rd partition are many children, by the writing underneath of French in a very elderly character you may understand what they mean [paraphrased and translated]: 'Pray for John ap Rees and his wife Alice, for the souls of all children and for the souls of all Christians.'

Richard Symonds[497] offered a similar description together with a sketch, and James Hill[498] drew the arms in the window, which he described as, 'Thomas Clanvowe quartered by Barr.' Duncumb agreed with, 'In the third north window of 3 parts', and gave the same description and inscriptions as Taylor and Symonds; however, as noted above, found the windows to be in poor condition.[499]

NORTH AISLE (nVII)
Richard Symonds, the only antiquary to record this window, found other kneeling knights, one with the arms of Feld. George Marshall[500] recorded,

> It would not be improbable that this glass dates from 1394, or about that time, when John de la Feld, Richard de la Feld, clerk, and John ap Rees were associated with Sir Kynard Delabere of Tibberton in a grant of land to the Chantry of the Blessed Virgin Mary in this church.[501]

Chancel north side (nV)

Silas Taylor (c.1655)[502] described the first north window of chancel: '... the first north window exhibits the arms of the Dean & Chapter and the arms of England.'

North aisle (nVI) or chancel north (nIV or nIII)

Blount (1675) noted: 'In a north window St Ethelbert holding a Church in his Hand, and a Queen standing by Him, with the Arms of England.'

Chancel east window (I, nII, sII)
(Fig. 104, overleaf)

Malcolm was dismissive of the window's thirteenth-century medallions: 'The East window has imperfect painted glass badly done in circles Holy Family, Last Supper etc.' Duncumb (1810) gave a fuller description, confirming that the medallions were in place before the restoration projects later in the nineteenth century. George Marshall quotes from a publication of 1840:[503] 'In the upper half of the centre window, there remained in a state of good preservation, six compartments of painted glass, representing scriptural subjects, of very curious character ...'

Silas Taylor and James Hill (1717)[504] recorded the arms in this and another chancel window.

Chancel south side

Silas Taylor noted, 'On a south window of the chancel is the picture of a religious lifting up a shield G: a chief checky O & B over all a riband A.' Marshall thought these arms belong to the Cliffords, but Sarah Brown casts doubt on this and suggests Walter de Dunre, a prominent Madley parishioner.

Symonds and Duncumb noted other figures holding shields.

Other chancel windows

Several antiquaries identified the arms of Criketots in the chancel, but the locations are not certain. This ancient Norman family held land in the parish.[505]

Chilstone Chapel east window (sVIII)

Blount (1675) found, 'A very curious window representing the History of the Kings of Israel and the Genealogy of our Saviour.' Malcolm (1803) drew the window, noting, 'In the quatrefoils in the east over an old altar bearded busts of kings ...'.[506] Thomas Bird (1827) is more forthcoming:

> East window of south aisle has very fine stained glass – two kings crowned – several other figures but repaired without attention to the original design – a most incongruous addition by placing in the three centre divisions near the bottom Faith, Hope and Charity in squares with borders of modern design and execution but which might have been pretty ornaments in a modern chapel.

These 'incongruous' panels may well be the 'new windows' in the churchwardens' accounts of 1791. Sir Stephen Glynne (1876) recorded, '... and that at the east end a very beautiful one of five lights entirely full of brilliantly coloured glass.'

Chilstone Chapel south windows

In 1803 Malcolm noted,

> The 5 windows in the side ... in the quatrefoils those have beautiful golden ribbons, triangles and leaves of glass and each panel below them excellent portraits of Saints under highly finished canopies many of their figures are 3 feet in length with expressive faces and excellent

Fig. 104 Madley: east windows (nII, I, sII)

drapery disposed in folds very correct. In the window furthest East is a strange reproduction of a priest as I suppose by the cope lifting the chin of a female in order to kiss her but as the head has been purposely broken I cannot decide exactly whether Judas and Jesus Christ has been intended there is certainly no glory on the figure male or female.

Several other antiquaries found arms in these windows, including a shield of the Talbots.
THE CHANCEL EAST WINDOWS (I, nII & sII)
Sometime between the close of the account book referred to above in 1813 and the end of the century, the remaining glass was gathered into its existing position in the chancel east windows. George Marshall suggested that this task was finished by 1840.[507] In the *Picturesque Antiquities of the County of Hereford*, written about 1840, the writer says, speaking of the chancel:

> In the upper half of the centre window, there remained in a state of good preservation, six compartments of painted glass, representing scriptural subjects, of very curious character, and in the tracery of the head of the window the Royal Arms of England ... The lower part of this and the whole of the adjoining windows have been filled with fragments of the painted glass scattered throughout the church, and although was impossible to arrange these so as to delineate any particular subject, the pieces have been so disposed under the superintendence of the Dean [John Merewether, see below], as to produce at a distance, and especially at the western entrance to the church, a very striking effect.

The church was in appalling condition: it is said that children would slide up and down the nave on a thick film of green slime.[508] In 1867 and 1871 *The Builder* reported that, 'The roof is unsafe, the casements of the windows, which are large, and of which there are a great number, are decayed.' It was estimated that £335 was required for glazing.[509] In 1872, the vestry meeting was adjourned to the vicarage owing to the dilapidated state of the church.[510] The remedying of this situation began with the installation of Charles Underwood as vicar. He engaged the architect Frederick Kempson, whose name is associated with the heavy-handed restoration of several Herefordshire churches.

It is certain that, in 1878, the glass was as we see it today, when the *Hereford Journal* reported that the glass had 'just' been rearranged and re-leaded.[511] In a very fulsome article it was noted,

> This, perhaps the most interesting collection of old glass to be found in any parish church in the country, has just been re-arranged and re-leaded, the principle adopted being purely one of conservation, no attempt being made in any instance to restore missing portions of the painted work. The general design – when one existed – has been traced as far as possible, and missing pieces, whether of ornament or figure, made good with plain glass. Most of the glass was collected some years since, from various windows in the church. And placed in the apse, but unfortunately without any effort to preserve any design or connection that might have then been apparent, and this has rendered the present re-arrangement more difficult, and in some points not quite so complete as it otherwise might have been made.

Fig. 105 Madley: east window, the thirteenth-century medallions (I)

When Sir Stephen Glynn visited in 1876, two years before this report, he found that the east window of the Chilstone Chapel was still 'entirely filled with ancient glass of most brilliant colours.'[512] It is possible that Glynn confused the two east windows, but this report suggests that the pre-1840 gathering and reglazing of the glass was incomplete. Underwood and Kempson's ideas about conservation would have been rather different from those of Dean John Merewether,[513] and they must have had the east windows reglazed, finally gathering the remains of the Chilstone Chapel glass with the chancel glass in 1877–78.

When the glass was finally gathered up, it appears that a conscious effort was made to keep glass from each source more or less distinct, and it can be seen (in Fig 104) that each window has a distinctive character. The windows I and sII contain mostly the thirteenth-century and fourteenth-century material, probably from the chancel and east window of the Chilstone Chapel, while the material from the aisle windows, perhaps, is assembled in nII. The glazier responsible for the present arrangement has not been identified; the bills did not go through the parish or the Dean and Chapter accounts.

The EAST WINDOW (I) can be considered in four parts. In the tracery lights are shields of England (three lions), Bohun (diagonal stripe with lion heads on a blue background) and Warrene (gold and blue check). Marshall points out that John de Bohun was connected to the Warrenes by marriage to his first wife Alice in 1325[514] and that John died in 1335. These may be taken as the likely terminal dates for this glass. The arms are probably in situ, but Bohun and Warrene change places in a photograph taken by Alfred Watkins in 1927.[515]

At the top of the main light are six narrative medallions of what appears to be thirteenth-century glass (Fig. 105), which is generally thought to be not in situ, because the tracery seems to be later in date. It was in the church by 1650 when Silas Taylor recorded the panels without giving their location. He suggests that they came from a demolished monastic church at Moccas[516] and that they represented the story of King Pibianus of Irchenfield recounted in the Book of Llandaff. Some, if not all of it, was in its present position when Duncumb visited in 1810.[517]

It is not difficult to imagine that the Madley mason was required to accommodate them in his design because the medallions fit the lights so snugly; however, the apparent lack of a definite overall programme suggests otherwise. Also, as noted above, Duncumb's description could mean that in 1810 not all the medallions were in the same window, there specifically being 'a' circle of glass in each compartment. There is, of course, a further possibility that the glass and the tracery are contemporary, and the glass is simply old-fashioned. George Marshall (1924) thought that,

> the subjects are taken from three separate series, the two in the left-hand light being incidents in the life of St George, the vesica

East window (I)

3a: St John with Aristodemus: the Life of St John and the Golden Legend tells how the Ephesian high priest Aristodemus, annoyed by John's success as a missionary, challenged John to prove his holiness by taking poison. The brew was first tested, successfully, on two condemned men who are seen on the ground in the medallion. It was usual to show Disciples with bare feet, and to show John without a beard, and we see John thus in the panel raising the vessel of poison. He survived but, as if that were not enough proof of his saintliness, was further challenged to raise the dead men. He instructed that his cloak be laid over the men – as seen in the medallion – and they were raised.

3b: The Last Supper with John reclining against the breast of Christ.

3c: The Adoration of the Magi.

4a: The Death of St John. This subject is probably unique in English stained glass. George Marshall described this as the bringing back to life of St George by the Virgin Mary, but adds the word '(doubtful)'. Sarah Brown suggests, 'The Raising of Drusiana',[518] but the figure being raised appears to be bearded. The figure, apparently standing or sitting on the ground, is the only nimbed figure in the scene, and this supports the Royal Commission suggestion of the Death of St John. The nimbus allows the Raising of Lazarus to be discounted. The Acts of St John describes his death:

> when the young men had finished the trench as he desired, we knowing nothing

> of it, he took off his garments wherein he was clad and laid them as it were for a pallet in the bottom of the trench: and standing in his shift only he stretched his hands upward and prayed ... [519]
>
> **4b**: The Women at the Sepulchre: George Marshall thought that this was the Annunciation, with God the Father and the Christ Child looking on; but, again, the Royal Commission interpretation of the scene as the Women at the Sepulchre, appears more likely.[520] Among the fragments in this panel are the limbs of a feathered or mail suit and the eye of a grotesque which may be thirteenth-century work.
>
> **4c**: The Presentation in the Temple. There are some common characteristics in the thirteenth-century panels. They have similar rich blue backgrounds, thin red or white borders and spandrels with white trefoil and yellow/ green waterleaf decoration. The figures share a similar style characterised by large eyes, exaggerated expressions (which are almost all serious and unsmiling), heavy line-work, and acute 'V' drapery, and the rich blue, red, green and gold pot metal colours are also shared.

and the two in the right-hand light being incidents in the life of the Virgin, and the bottom central panel an incident in the life of our Lord.

The Royal Commission described them as scenes from the Life of Christ and scenes from the Life of St John the Evangelist, which seems more convincing.

The fourteenth-century glass at Madley has tended to take attention away from the earlier work which is, arguably, a more exceptional and significant survival. There is no other parish church[521] ensemble from the thirteenth century which so closely resembles the great programmes of medallions found in English and French cathedrals, as that surviving at Madley. The form and content of the glass, expressed in medallions, could perhaps be related to the appointment of a French bishop, Peter of Savoy, to the See of Hereford in 1240. Two buildings, Bourges and Chartres Cathedrals, both with extravagant thirteenth-century stained glass, stand on a line drawn between Savoy and Hereford. Both cathedrals express their theology through stories in windows full of medallions. It is unlikely that a bishop from France, who may have been involved in the commissioning of the Madley glass, did not bring knowledge of those French buildings to bear on the work, and maybe their artists were engaged too.

If it is accepted that the six panels come from two programmes which relate and possibly connect the lives of Christ and St John the Evangelist, then there is further reason to suspect French work. There is no surviving life of St John in glass in England, but both Bourges and Chartres depict the Saint's life in medallion windows, including versions of the scenes remaining at Madley. Furthermore, the Madley Last Supper, with its arresting image of St John leaning against Christ's breast, is a picture which is rare in Britain but not in Europe.[522] Again, both Bourges and Chartres have examples.

Richard Marks compares these panels, and especially the vesica panel (I.4b), with work at Westminster Abbey from the period 1246–59.[523] There are strong similarities in the scale of the medallions, their dark blue ground and in the acute V-folds of the drapery. The faces and drapery in the Westminster Stoning of St Stephen are very like that found in the Madley medallions. There are no comparable windows locally, and similar glass in parish churches is widely scattered. The tantalising question remains: if the medallions are older than the windows, where did they come from? The story that they came from Moccas seems unlikely, although there was a church there, larger than the existing chapel.[524] More probably, the medallions were part of a former chancel at Madley or perhaps cast-offs from the cathedral.

There is a fragment of V-drapery in sII.8a. More tantalising is the fragment of a Crucifixion showing the feet of Christ in sII.4b. This is of the right scale and resembles the heavy-lined drawing style of the thirteenth-century work, and could come from a lost panel in a Life of Christ series.

Below the medallions are three beautiful figures from the fourteenth-century Tree of Jesse that occupied the east window of the Chilstone Chapel (Figs 10 & 104). These were painted by an important master who also worked at Ludlow, Abbey Dore, Moccas and Clehonger.

The lower panels consist mainly of the decorative patterns of reticulated tracery lights, including the circular bosses from their centres. The reticulated tracery in both aisles of the church is very consistent in form and dimensions, but the south side of the Chilstone Chapel seems to have both reticulations and spandrel lights which would best fit the pieces now in the chancel east window. The unifying motif is the border band of black and yellow lines enclosing a broad, black band with a string of yellow shapes. This band may be cusped and often encloses a pale white/ grey rinceau or vine leaves on a black ground. The circular bosses are

Figs 106a–106b Madley: heads of two clerics in the chancel south window (sII)

particularly inventive and have been compared to work of similar date in the canopy gables in the chancel clerestorey of Tewkesbury Abbey.[525] In panel 1c there are several examples of the cup-and-cover and castle border decorations which are also found in I.1a and 1b.

The contents of sII have in common with I.1a–c the borders from the reticulated tracery, but only a few examples of the cup-and-cover decoration and none of the bosses that are a strong feature of I.1a–c. There is even less shared material with nII and this suggests that the material was deliberately segregated side-to-side in order to reflect where the glass was originally placed. The glass in sII is almost certainly from the chancel and the Chilstone Chapel. It can also be seen that the glass in the upper part of sII is more richly coloured, perhaps reflecting its source in the main lights of windows, while the lower panels are lighter and sourced from tracery lights.

Chancel south-east window (sII)

The two mitred heads in sII.8a & b (Figs 106a & 106b) differ from the Jesse figures in their stouter features, heavy jaw-line, cropped beards and deeper shading, but display the Madley Mouth. Sarah Brown thinks that these heads are by the same glass painters as the Jesse window, and,

> ... Their orientation (looking three quarters left) shows that they must have been made for a southern window. Neither figure is nimbed ... in all probability these are the remains of the main light glazing, of ecclesiastical saints beneath canopies, originally accompanied by donors with shields, similar to the near contemporary arrangement employed, albeit without shields, at nearby Eaton Bishop ...[526]

107a

107b

107c

107d

107e

Figs 107a–107e Madley: comparison with work at New College, Oxford by Thomas Glazier. **107a**: Oxford; **107b**, **107c** & **107d**: Madley; **107e**: Oxford

There are seven other heads or parts of heads in the window. In sII.6b an almost complete bearded head with all the hallmarks of the Madley painter, probably from one of the panels in the reticulated tracery of the Chilstone Chapel. There are similar heads at Ludlow, and more locally at Abbey Dore (Fig. 23) and Clehonger (Figs 45a & 45b). It is also possible that the two bearded, sketchy faces in sII.6a came from the same source.

There are two smaller and more simply-drawn naked figures in sII.6b. These recall the roughly contemporary naked donor figure in the east window of Tewkesbury Abbey.[527] In sII.6b there is a part of a face with quite different detailing of the mouth and nose, similar to some figures at Ludlow and Merevale.

Windows sII and nII both hold numerous fragments of distinctive architectural canopy-work characterised by flat white masonry with capitals and bases drawn in silver stain, and tracery thinly drawn in matt. This appears to be related to the canopy-work in glass at New College Chapel, Oxford (Figs 107a–107e). Some, if not all, will have come from the south side of the Chilstone Chapel where Malcolm found, 'each panel below them excellent portraits of Saints under highly finished canopies many of their figures are 3 feet in length with expressive faces and excellent drapery disposed in folds very correct.' At New College the saints are arranged one per light, and remain within their unusual canopies. These are from the workshop of Thomas Glazier and thought to date from 1380–86.[528]

There is a panel which may well be related to this 'Oxford' canopy-work at Pixley, and some fragments at Eaton Bishop, which are probably pieces from the stock of the restorer.

There are two fragments of Lombardic text, in sII.5a and sII.7b, which probably remain from the Jesse Tree in sVIII. One holds the word *S IOHANNES*, which may be related to the fragment of hair cape in sII.6a, and stands for John the Baptist (who is not normally a Jesse Tree character).[529]

In sII.4b is a bird held in a hand, which seems closely related to the birds populating the Jesse Tree at Merevale. At nearby and

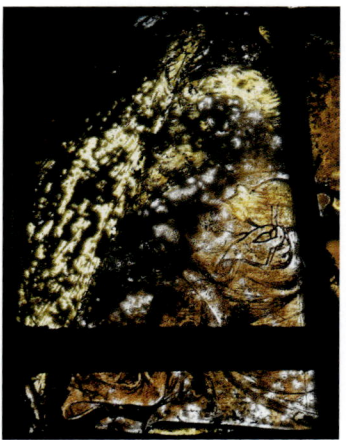

Figs 108a–108c Madley: details of window nII. Figs 108a & 108b angels (ABOVE LEFT & LEFT), Fig. 108c lion of St Mark & bull of St Luke (BELOW)

roughly contemporary Eaton Bishop, there is a depiction of the Virgin and Child. The Christ Child in Mary's arms holds a bird, which might suggest that the Madley fragment is from the same subject. It could also be the hand of Noah holding a dove, or of God cradling the Holy Spirit, possibly from the Jesse Tree in sVIII.

CHANCEL NORTH-EAST WINDOW (nII)
The white architecture in sII, attributed to the workshop of Thomas Glazier, is present, notably in the topmost panels of the main lights nII.9a & b and in panels nII.6b and nII.7a & b.[530]

There are three silver stain angel musicians obscured by corrosion. The figures in nII.6b and nII.9b clearly link these angels to the white architecture noted above (Figs 108a & 108b). These angels may be from the north aisle where Malcolm (see above) found, 'figures ... under grand canopies, in the quatrefoils over them are angels kneeling'.

There is a substantial collection of pieces of crocketed architecture in nII.5a, 6a & 7a which may be from the same workshop as the 'white architecture', but possibly from the north aisle.

Two well-drawn heads, later in date than the survivors from the Jesse Tree, are found in nII.4b and nII.5a (Figs 107d & 107e). If these are compared with the work at New College, there are striking similarities in their rather heavy modelling and shading. The details of mouths and eyes, and the techniques of modelling and shading, suggest the same workshop. In nII.4a there are parts of two winged tetramorphs (Fig. 108c); other fragments are scattered throughout the window. On the left of the panel is the head and part of the rear of a lion with smiling, moustached features.[531] The almost human face recalls the mythical manticore of medieval bestiaries. On the right of the panel is the body of a short-winged, stocky animal intended to be the bull of Luke.

An enigmatic blue-clad figure, perhaps the Virgin, is seen in nII.4b & 5b. She wears a three-quarter sleeve cotehardie with inverted pleats and one visible fichet or besom pocket.

North aisle windows
There are two small roundels of medieval glass. In nVIII, a much-corroded silver stain sun with flames radiating from its circumference. In nIX, a silver stain sun with long, narrow, straight rays.

The Madley Head
In 2011, the *Hereford Times* reported that the missing head from I.2c, said to have been removed during the nineteenth-century restoration and taken to America, had come up for sale.[532] However, the detached panel which was for sale is almost certainly a modern copy, with different colour and shading compared with figures in situ. The panel was withdrawn from the sale.

MANSEL LACY
St Mary (SO 4256 4556, HR4 7QH)

James Hill (d.1727) found, 'a few remains of religious paintings'.[533] In 1934, the Royal Commission reported, 'In S. aisle – in E. window, small shield of Burgh, probably fourteenth-century.'[534] The panel remains but is detached.

MATHON
John the Baptist

The Royal Commission found a small panel of fragments: 'In nave – in second N. window, sacred initials and foliated border; in third and fourth S. windows, Agnus Dei and foliated medallions, fourteenth or fifteenth century.'[535]

The windows have been reglazed in Georgian panes and this glass has been lost.

MICHAELCHURCH ESCLEY
St Michael (SO 3167 3419, HR2 0JS)

In the MIDDLE WINDOW ON THE SOUTH SIDE there is a panel with a rather crudely drawn depiction of the Instruments of the Passion (Fig. 109). This resonates strongly with the 'Sunday

Fig. 109 Michaelchurch Escley: Instruments of the Passion

Christ' or 'Christ of the Trades' wall painting on the north wall. It is combined with a fragment of sun and border originally from a different panel. There are two fragments concealed behind saddle bars, and two fragments of sun, again from a different scheme.

MOCCAS
St Michael (SO 5214 2552, HR2 9LH)

In the first half of the fourteenth century the fortunes of the de Frenes, a family associated with Sutton and Moccas, were rising. In common with other wealthy people at that time in Herefordshire, they improved their church, making it into a family shrine. The north and south side windows of the nave and chancel were inserted, probably with a magnificent scheme of stained glass. The chancel windows, with their trefoil tracery, may be earlier than the nave windows with their quatrefoils, but the glazing is of one campaign.

We can be sure that the patron of the fourteenth-century alterations and the glass was a John de Frene. The name John is first encountered in 1306 when Sir John de Frene presented Richard de Bockleton as priest.[536] In 1316 the manor and advowson were granted to John and his wife Sarah[537] in what may be the settling of a false claim (deforciant) by Thomas Talebot. In 1328, Sir John obtained a charter for a market in Moccas.[538]

A fine stone monument in the chancel has been firmly dated to the early fourteenth century.[539] If it is assumed that the glass and the monument are memorials to the same John de Frene, then a date for the glass of 1320–40 would be tenable.[540]

The Moccas de Frenes may have been relatively minor gentry, even in the milieu of Herefordshire, but they had good taste and engaged an eminent workshop for the stained glass. We can only imagine the beautiful images that have been lost from below the surviving canopy-work. That the de Frenes commissioned the glass is confirmed by their arms in the tracery and their banners raised among the pinnacles. Silas Taylor found the arms in the mid seventeenth century, with a now-lost 'coate' of the Longespees of Salisbury, another powerful Norman family.[541] Other arms mentioned by Taylor remain in situ, and a reminder of the singlemindedness of the old antiquaries is the omission from Taylor's description of the beautiful green birds attending the shields, which have no strict heraldic purpose. Marshall photographed the windows in 1918.[542] Isothermal glazing was fitted to the north windows by Jim Budd in 2010.

Fig. 110 Moccas: canopy-work in the north nave windows (nIII)

Fig. 111 Moccas: the arms of de Frenes (nIII)

The Moccas canopy-work is among the finest to be found in any English parish church. It seems to be related to contemporary work at Tewkesbury where the canopies are also elegant, drawn as viewed from above, three-dimensional and richly-coloured. The canopy-work at Moccas has been compared with that found in the east window at Gloucester Cathedral and in the Jesse window at Wells Cathedral, but neither match the refinement and colourful elegance of the Moccas work. It is suggested in Part One above that Moccas is the work of the master who made the gorgeous Jesse Trees at Ludlow and Madley.

CHANCEL NORTH WINDOW (nIII)
The two-light window (Fig. 110) holds two octagonal lanterns on broached square bases with crocketed ogee arches. The architecture is white with blue and silver stain dressings and window tracery drawn in blue. The standard bearers, dressed in silver stain togas, hold up the red, blue and white banners of the de Frenes, and the spire is set against brilliant red and green diapering.

In the trefoil light are reset fragments. There is an almost complete figure of a bearded man holding a stick and wearing a gambeson. This is parti-coloured, or more accurately parti-patterned (perhaps by quilted padding). These garments have a long history, but the drawing and silver stain suggest late fourteenth-century or early fifteenth-century. The other fragments include a winged beast, architectural pieces, part of a blue swastika border and a Lombardic T.

NAVE NORTH WINDOW (nIV)
As nIII but the tracery light is a quatrefoil with the arms of de Frene surmounted by a visored sugarloaf helmet, typical of the early fourteenth century, with a white contoise and a crest of holly (Fig. 111). The red border is cusped, and the ground is of amber vine diapering. The shield is surrounded by four emerald green birds. This must be the handsomest armorial in the county.

CHANCEL SOUTH WINDOW (sIII)
In the tracery, the same shield as nIV but there is less space so the crest of the helmet and two of the birds are lost.

NAVE SOUTH WINDOW (sIV)
In the tracery, the same splendid shield as nIV.

MONKHOPTON
ST PETER (SO 6257 9342, WV16 6SB)

William Mytton found a Crucifixion with St Mary and St John in the east window. In the WEST WINDOW are four rectangular Netherlandish grisaille panels which were previously in Upton Cressett church. William Cole identified the artist as Martinus Heemskerk who signed the Resurrection panel and based all four panels on his own series of prints of the Ministry of Christ. The panels are drawn in black paint. The date 1548 can be seen on the tomb of the resurrected Christ.[543]

West window (wI)
1: The Road to Calvary with St Veronica in the bottom left holding the vernicle with the image of Christ's face imprinted on it (back cover).
2: The Crucifixion with St John and the Virgin at the base of the Cross and soldiers dividing Christ's raiment at bottom left.
3: The Descent from the Cross.
4: The Resurrection with Christ bursting out of the tomb.

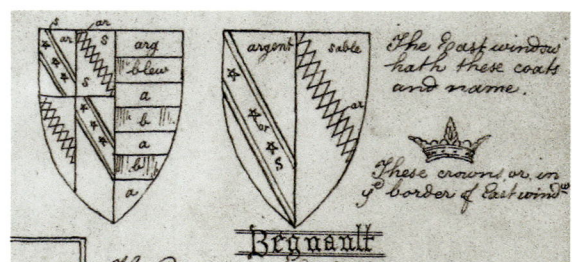

Monkland: **Fig. 112a** Dingley's drawing of arms in the east window (I) (TOP). **Fig. 112b** a royal head in the nave north window (nII) (BELOW)

162 THE MEDIEVAL STAINED GLASS OF HEREFORDSHIRE & SHROPSHIRE

MONKLAND
All Saints (SO 4604 5766, HR6 9DB)

Thomas Dingley (d.1695) recorded the arms of Hastings and St George, and two shields of Lenthall impaling Lanton (see Hampton Court Chapel) (Fig. 112a) and 'About this (east) window are several of these crowns or (gold) in ye glass border.'[544]

The church underwent a comprehensive restoration at the hands of G.E. Street under the direction of Henry Williams Baker, the incumbent (of *Hymns Ancient and Modern* fame). Apart from the tower, the walls were rebuilt, but it seems that some windows were reused.[545]

In 1934, the Royal Commission found the glass which survives today. In the tracery of the north-east window, vine-foliage and a crowned man's head of the fourteenth century (Fig. 112b); in the nave south-east window, a roundel with vine foliage of similar date. In the tower west window of the second storey, fragments including of leaves, drapery and crowns, of the fifteenth century.

MONNINGTON
St Mary (SO 3736 4333, HR4 7NL)

In the nave south-east window is an achievement-of-arms of Tomkins impaling Capell. When the Royal Commission visited in 1934 the panel was reversed, but has since been set the right way round. The arms must record the marriage of Uvedale Tomkins (d.1692) and Mary Capel (d.1728). Their initials appear on furnishings in the church they rebuilt and refurbished from 1679.

MORVILLE
St Gregory (SO 6696 9390, WV16 5NB)

There is a single panel of fourteenth-century glass in the CHANCEL NORTH WINDOW (nII). The glass is probably collected from more than one window, but the central figure of the crucified Christ stands out powerfully (Fig. 113). The Cross itself has wave decoration, and Christ's body describes the Y- and S-curves typical of other Crucifixes in this survey. Behind Christ's head is the original background of scratched squares each holding five circles. There are seven pieces of border with vine leaves curling round a stem, which is a Shropshire motif not encountered in Herefordshire. The strongly crocketed and cusped canopy-work in white and yellow on a black ground, is probably the original setting for the Crucifix.

Fig. 113 Morville: Crucifixion (nII)

MUCH MARCLE
St Bartholomew (so 6571 3276, hr8 2nf)

The glass of interest here is the Royal Arms of Charles I in the NORTH CHANCEL CHAPEL WINDOW (nII) (Fig. 114).

The chapel was built in the late 1200s as a chantry chapel but was adopted by Sir John Kyrle of Homme House in 1628. He was made a Baronet in 1627, and it is thought that he commissioned a grand tomb for himself between this date and his wife's death in 1635. The glass was commissioned at about that time too.

The arms were in place in c.1675 when Thomas Blount recorded them (but got the wording of the verse slightly wrong).[546] In a survey of Royal Arms in the county in 1958 the glass was described:

MUCH MARCLE. Inserted in the bottom of the east window in the Kyrle chapel there is a panel with the Stuart royal arms in stained glass, 1 ft. 8 in. square. The shield is encircled by the garter, with crest, crown, helmet, mantling, supporters and the motto 'DIEU ET MON DROIT '. Beneath the arms are these curious doggerel verses:

> *The Flewer de Luces lead the ring*
> *France shews the armes but we the king*
> *The Lyons next in order thre*
> *Present the ground of harmony.*

They ... represent Charles I.[547]

The verse is based on lines in Shakespeare's Henry VI Part 1, Scene 1:

> Cropp'd are the flower-de-luces in your arms;
> Of England's coat one half is cut away

Fig. 114 Much Marcle: the Royal Arms of Charles I (nII)

The panel is shown in Fig. 114. The arms are those adopted by Charles after 1625. If it is assumed that the glass dates from between 1628 and 1635, the only contemporary glass is that at Sellack (1630) and Abbey Dore (1634) both commissioned by John Scudamore. Sybil, the wife of John Kyrle, was a cousin and contemporary of John Scudamore, and the Scudamore arms are on the tomb in the chapel. John Kyrle was a business associate of John Scudamore in the iron trade located around the Woolhope Dome. It is not surprising that the Much Marcle panel appears to be by the same hand as the Abbey Dore and Sellack glass.

MUNSLEY

St Bartholomew (SO 6625 4093, HR8 2SQ)

There are a few fragments here, which the Royal Commission recorded. In the north nave middle window, fifteenth-century fragments of borders, leaves and leopards' heads (Fig. 115). In the south windows of the nave, are roundels and borders.[548]

Fig. 115 Munsley: a leopard mask (nV)

MUNSLOW

St Michael (SO 5212 8772, SY7 9ET)

A significant amount of medieval glass remains at Munslow, some of which was donated by John Lloyd, rector 1506–28, who endowed a chantry for St Mary's service with land in Hungerford.[549]

Glass from this period is scarce (see Alveley) and its importance at Munslow is enhanced by the survival of detailed records from the early eighteenth century, which help to unravel the extent of the restoration work carried out by David Evans of Shrewsbury. In 1833, just before the restoration of the church, the *Gentleman's Magazine* carried a description of the glass:

> In the north and east windows of the north aisle, are considerable remains of stained glass. In the second window, The Virgin and infant Christ; St John, in rich colours; an ecclesiastic, under the figure Joh's Lloyd. In the east window of the north aisle, is the Crucifixion, much mutilated. In this window are two Shields of arms; the first, argent, a chevron between three escallops sable, impaling argent, and lion rampant sable, debruised with a fess counter componee azure and or. The other shield is much mutilated.[550]

EAST WINDOW (I)

In 1733 four subjects were recorded by William Mytton, including a nimbed and robed figure standing with hands raised and palms facing out. Possibly from an Annunciation. The window now has striking images of three Apostles by David Evans of Shrewsbury, installed in 1835.[551]

Fig. 116 Munslow: the donor John Lloyd, from William Mytton's notes (by permission of the Cadbury Library, University of Birmingham)

The former CHANCEL SOUTH WINDOW had an image of John Lloyd at a prie-dieu (Fig. 116) which has been lost.

CHANCEL NORTH WINDOWS (nII & nIII)

The 1733 drawing of the north-east window shows an incomplete Virgin and Child and a kneeling priest with a black letter inscription, apparently and unusually referring to the repair or maintenance of windows at an early time – *bono statu fenestium* – 'the good state of the windows'. Neither of these subjects has survived.

The window to the west had a small roundel with St John holding a palm and a chalice with a beast emerging from it, which has also been lost.

NORTH AISLE EAST WINDOW (nIV) (Fig. 117)

This window can be dated to between 1526 and 1540 by the arms of the fifteenth earl of Oxford, John de Vere in panel 3a. There is no indication on the 1733 drawing of the borders and quarries, but they appear to be by the restorer, David Evans.

Fig. 117 Munslow: restored north aisle window (nIV)

> **North aisle east window (nIV)**
>
> **1a**: St Thomas – Becket or Cantilupe: Some medieval glass remains in the figure's left hand and the lower part of the crozier. Parts of the robes, notably the borders, also old.
>
> **1b**: Virgin and Child: This panel previously held St Kenelm and is now all Evans's work.
>
> **1c**: St Anthony: Little old glass survives despite the relative completeness of the figure in 1733. The top of the staff and the hand appear to be original.
>
> **Inscription band**: The inscription is partly restored and records the gift of the window by 'Richard Schepard'. The registers record that Richard Shappard was buried in 1542, and his wife Joan in 1553. This fits with the dating of the window by the de Vere arms (see panel 3a below) to 1528–40.
>
> [Of : your : charitye] : pray : for : the : [soul] : and : state : of : Richard : Schepard : and : Joane : his : wyff : yt : which : glazing : was : done : at : his : cost
>
> **2a**: The Virgin Mary at the Crucifixion: The figure is substantially as per Mytton's drawing. The head of Mary is very lightly drawn, relying on smear shading for effect.

2b: The Crucifix: The figure and its skull-scattered ground are original except for the head and upper torso of Christ. The upper part of the Cross is also new.

2c: St John the Evangelist: The figure is broadly original except for the large piece of glass with John's face, hair and collar.

3a: The arms of the earl of Oxford: the arms are those of the John, fifteenth earl of Oxford, who held the title 1528–40. He acquired his interest in Munslow through marriage to Elizabeth Trussell, the sister of Joan Burley (see panel 3c). This shield dates the window to the very brink of the Reformation, but whereas the Blount glass at Alveley is a hymn to Henry, this glass is a last shout of Popery.

3c: The arms of Sir Thomas de Lyttleton, (Lyttleton impaling Burley). The Manor belonged to William Burley, on whose death in 1458 Munslow passed to his daughters: one, Joan, became wife of Sir Thomas Lyttelton. The Lyttleton share was retained by the family through the sixteenth century.

Tracery lights: Only one of the three roundels – St Margaret (B1) – is shown in the 1733 drawing. That roundel is of 1500 and the other two are from a series of Apostles and probably of a rather later date. There are several churches in Shropshire with imported roundels, and the market in glass from Germany and the Low Countries was strong. Evans almost certainly acquired these roundels of St Philip (B2) and St Matthias (D1). All three are exercises in line and silver stain, but St Margaret is clearly earlier, a medieval figure, while the drapery of the Apostles is purely Classical.

NORTH AISLE WINDOW (nV)

This has been substantially rearranged. The inscription band has been raised to the top of panels 1a–1c and the inscription 'restored'. The Archangel Michael has been removed from panel 2a, and the Virgin and Child moved from 2b into Michael's place to make way for an entirely new Christ by David Evans of Shrewsbury.

The other panels have elements of the pre-1733 scheme, except for roundels in B2 and D1, which are new. As with window nIV, the borders and quarries are probably Evans's work. However, some of the borders in nV have a darker, more weathered appearance and are probably the original work.

North aisle window (nV)

1a–1c: The *Scutum Fidei* in 1a appears to be old. The 1733 drawing suggests that only half of the shield survived, but that is probably draughtsman's shorthand in that the form of the whole shield would be known. The border round this roundel has been used as the pattern for the whole restoration scheme. The kneeling figure of John Lloyd in 1b is mostly old but his head and collar are new. The banderol is entirely new. The Five Wounds shield in 1c is the work of Evans, but the border is probably old.

2a: The Virgin and Child: The figures are intact apart from the head of the Virgin. The lower part of her long hair is old. Evans was a clever copier of style and has based the new head on that of St John in panel 2c.

2b: Christ in Majesty: This panel, including the roundel with the dove, is entirely new.

2c: St John: this figure was complete in 1733. The drawing is quite stark and cartoon-like with little modelling and large features. The robes are also little more than blocks of colour. The hem of the mantle has a text in crude Lombardics. The left side can be discerned: *iste est johes qui su[p]ra pectus ...*[552]

Tracery Lights: the arms in B1 existed in 1733; the other two roundels are modern. The arms *argent a two-headed eagle displayed sable* are normally ascribed to the Empire. It was noted that these windows may be a counterblast to the pro-Tudor glazing at Alveley. But the suggestion that they were a tribute to the newly-crowned (1519) Charles V and supported the Spanish queen, with the mistress Blount not ten miles away in Alveley, is surely too bold?[553] In D1 are the arms of Thomas Musgrave, bishop of Hereford 1837–48.

NORTH AISLE WINDOW (nVI)

The figures in the main lights of this window correspond closely with the drawing of 1733.

Panel 1a St John and 1b St Anthony and the pig: the inscription, in black letter, asks for prayers for Robert Woode and his wife. The registers record the marriage of Robert Wood and Elizabeth Whetell in 1542, which is the earliest date for the glass if the glass and registers refer to the same man. This date, set alongside the dates for nIV and nV, suggests that the north aisle was glazed by the rector and local families between about 1528 and 1550. St Anthony (1b), depicted with the pig, seems to have been a local favourite: he was represented twice in the church and is also found at Alveley; Mytton also drew him at Aston Botterell.

Windows nV and nVI are by the same workshop. They share a similar design of plinth, and the drawing of the two heads with yellow stain hair is comparable. The pearl clasps are common to all three windows, as are some of the colours. Window nIV has no plinths and the drawing of Mary's head is by a different hand to the two heads of St John. So too is the head of Anthony, but not obviously by the same hand as Mary. All three windows share the same composition found in contemporary glass at, for example, the Withcote Chapel, Leicestershire (1536–37),[554] with large panels housing a single figure over small panels separated by an inscription, and with heraldry at the tops of the lights. However, the painting shares little with that contemporary, top-of-the-range glass by Henry VIII's glazier, other than the bold colours of garments.

At the top of the window, God in a roundel. This is of the same form as the other yellow stain roundels but not obviously by the same hand.

NORTH AISLE WEST WINDOW (nVIII)

The drawing of 1733 shows a nimbed female and six roundels. The arms of Lyttleton were at the centre, with arms recording other manorial interests, for example, Talbot (lion) and Hertwell (stag). None of this glass survives.

SOUTH AISLE WINDOW (sIV)

The 1733 drawing shows the Virgin and Child and St Michael weighing souls: all now lost. At the top is a shield with 'IHS', which survives.

SOUTH AISLE WINDOW (sVI) (Figs 118 & 119)

This contains numerous medieval fragments including the original border and quarry designs which Evans copied in other projects.

Fig. 118 Munslow: Virgin in the south aisle window (sVI)

Fig. 119 Munslow: kneeling donor and four daughters in the south aisle window (sVI)

South aisle window (sVI)

Panel 4: (top panel) Modern.

Panel 3: The arms of Beysin in silvery grey grisaille, sit above a seated Virgin and Child in much faded silver stain.

Panel 2: The Virgin, crowned and nimbed, wears a deep-blue cloak and a tunic with floral decoration. The infant wears dark red. They sit in a grand throne of gold, decorated with scallop shells and pearls.

Panel 1: The panel depicts a kneeling donor and four daughters, all robed in deep purple. They carry rosaries, except the smallest, and the daughters are all wearing kerchiefs. There is a banderol in black letter asking for the prayers of Mary. The figures have all suffered from erosion of the painted surfaces. The head of the smallest is incomplete. There are fragments of the three-flowered quarry and the original pole-and-leaf border on which Evans based his extensive restoration. A similar border can be seen in fragments at the top of the east window at Atcham.

OLD RADNOR

St Stephen (SO 2499 5909, LD8 2RH)

In the NORTH VESTRY EAST WINDOW (nIII) is St Catherine standing crowned and nimbed (Fig. 120). She holds a toothed wheel in her left hand and the hilt of a sword in her right. She wears a pearl-encrusted cloak over a deep-red pot metal robe. She is drawn in black line and silver stain, with the mannered features and gestures of the later fifteenth century. She is named in black letter and there are some fragments of crocketed canopy-work beside her name.

Catherine is surrounded by old quarries with the white rose en soleil which combines two Yorkist symbols. This theme is echoed in the beautiful (almost Classical) black bull of the Clarences found at the top of the window (Fig. 121). H. Mostyn Lewis suggested in relation to a Crucifixion at Llanwrin:[555]

> Of the same period as the York-type glass, but differing from it considerably, is some glass, including a Crucifixion, at Llanwrin near Machynlleth. This may be dated between 1461 and 1483 since it includes quarries with the rose ensoleilée, a white rose

Fig. 120 Old Radnor: St Catherine (nII)

Fig. 121 Old Radnor: the Bull of Clarence (nII)

with rays, the badge of Edward IV. The faces have a wild look which is rather reminiscent of German Rococo. The only similar glass that I know is the wild-looking St Catherine at Old Radnor, which also has rose ensoleilée quarries.

ORLETON
St George (SO 4945 6717, SY8 4JW)

Near the top of the east light of the NAVE NORTH-EAST WINDOW (nIII) are two beautiful heads, which were noted by Stephen Glynne in 1846.[556] A nimbed female wearing a kerchief shows a strikingly lovely face of the fourteenth century. She is drawn in line and smear shading with a small amount of yellow stain for her hair (Fig. 122a). Above and to the left is the tonsured head of a cleric (Fig. 122b). He is sepia-tinted and drawn in sepia line. The window also has a roundel, red-bordered and decorated with pellets, enclosing a vine leaf design on a black background with an inner border of yellow stain and some architectural and grisaille pieces.

The nave north-west window (nIV) and the east window on the south side (sV) have fragments and borders of the fourteenth century.

Figs 122a–122b Orleton, nave north window (nIII): head of a lady (ABOVE), and head of a cleric (LEFT)

Figs 123a–123b Pembridge: an angel (nVIII) (TOP) and St Christopher (sX) (ABOVE)

PEMBRIDGE
St Mary the Virgin (SO 3911 5808, HR6 9DT)

Antiquaries described and sketched shields in several windows[557] but Thomas Blount's account of the late seventeenth century, is the only one to note the survival of any religious glass:

GAZETTEER OF CHURCHES IN HEREFORDSHIRE AND THE DIOCESE OF HEREFORD 171

> In the church which is dedicated to the Assumption of the Blessed Virgin, two Windows of curious painted Glasse with some Saxon Letters escaped the fury of the late Wars ... [558]

In the upper lights of the NORTH AISLE MIDDLE WINDOW (nVII) are an abstract white vine scroll with vine leaves and acorns springing from a roundel holding a four-petalled flower, all on a hatched black and yellow ground. The lower lights have a five-petalled yellow flower in a white roundel from which toothed leaves reach into the corners. This glass appears original and in situ.

In the NORTH AISLE WEST WINDOW (nVIII), is a censing angel with green and bronze wings, wearing a gold fringed alb and standing on a trefoil-studded green ground. The background is a strong vermillion with paterae, and the border is of Ledbury type. The border and ground are strongly reminiscent of figures at Stanford-on-Avon, Dilwyn and Ledbury (Fig. 123a). In 1934 only the upper half of this figure was in place.[559]

In the SOUTH AISLE WEST WINDOW (sX), an image of St Christopher (Fig. 123b) drawn in line and yellow stain. The saint stands in fish-infested water against a ground of deep-blue diapering with bronze paterae with five-petalled flowers. The saint bears a hefty staff, and the child an inverted *Orbis Terrarum*. The child has a cruciform nimbus and holds his right hand in blessing. This panel is mostly original and in situ.

There are also images of St Stephen and St Lawrence, the first two martyrs of the Church. In common with the censing angel, they have the combination of alb, tunicle and apparelled amice, and all three panels have the 'Ledbury borders' and red background. In both panels, the green, trefoiled ground and the 'Ledbury borders' are original, but the figures seem to be renewed.

Fig. 124 Pitchford (sV): head of Christ, fourteenth century

PITCHFORD
ST MICHAEL (SJ 5270 0430, SY5 7DN)

In the quatrefoil of the tracery of a fourteenth-century window (sV) there is a small, bearded face of Christ drawn in matt and silver stain (Fig. 124). His nimbus is red and divided by a green Cross. The two side lobes have wavy borders and oak leaves. The upper lobe has an acorn, and the lower lobe is incomplete and made up with a piece of a different border in matt on white glass. This simple but arresting image appears to be in situ but was not recorded until Nelson's survey of 1911. Mytton visited in the eighteenth century but his attention was drawn to the colourful arms of *c*.1700 in sIV, which record the union of Ottley and Edwards.

PIXLEY
ST ANDREW (SO 6609 3880, HR8 2QA)

Pixley is better-known for its Annunciation, designed by William Morris. There is a small panel of medieval canopy-work in a NAVE SOUTH WINDOW (Fig. 125). This was almost illegible

Fig. 125 Pixley: fragment in a south nave window (sIV)

until recently cleaned and reset by Jim Budd. The Royal Commission made no report of the glass, which suggests that the panel is a later acquisition or that the inspectors thought it was post-medieval. However, this canopy-work is found at Madley, and is related to New College, Oxford. There are similar fragments at nearby Tarrington.

PRESTEIGNE
St Andrew and St Michael
(SO 3158 6456, LD8 2AF)

In 1684. Thomas Dingley visited the church and found,

> Here are seen in ye windows the ruines of good painted glass. In the north window, opposite to the south entrance, is discernible a Saviour and Cross of St. Andrew, between St. Peter and St. Paul.[560]

Numerous fragments have been assembled in three panels in the SOUTH AISLE CHAPEL UPPER EAST WINDOW (sIII) (Fig. 126). The drawing is of high quality and the several detached heads have the dipping, extended, slightly bulbous noses of the International Style. There are black letter inscriptions and the eight-pointed quarries which are associated with the York School elsewhere in this survey, and in North Wales.[561]

Window sIII
Panel 1a:
- The head of a large-eyed grotesque wearing a coif, possibly sleeping (**Fig. 126a**).
- A shield, possibly quartered, with a tower and three axes.
- A piece of a lion with black letter inscription – possibly a tetramorphic symbol.
- A fragment of two faces. The drawing here using line and modelling with grey shading is excellent.
- Several pieces of a grassy ground with steps and dovetail cut-outs. The ground is scattered with bones. This could be the base of a Crucifixion scene.[562]

Panel 1b:
- The calf and foot of an armed man. The sabaton appears to be of c.1500.[563]
- The head and shoulder of an eagle, possibly a tetramorphic symbol.
- Fragments of angelic feathers.
- Fragments of crocketed canopy-work.
- A shield with three black birds (jackdaws).
- Several heads showing different artists' hands. These reinforce the impression of a relationship with the late fourteenth- and early fifteenth-century work at York and Malvern.
- The fine head at centre is probably St Andrew holding his cross in front.

Fig. 126 Presteigne: collection of fifteenth-century glass in the south transept (sIII)

Panel 1c:
- Several heads in various styles. The head in the centre is beautifully drawn (**Fig. 126b**). Two small heads have oversized eyes in perhaps a later, semi-grotesque style. The small face at bottom right may be a donor figure.
- Several hands including one grasping a handle.
- Finely-drawn feathers.
- Further pieces of armour – perhaps a shoulder and a pike shaft.
- An open book. In several Welsh images of the Annunciation, the open book is a prominent element.[564]

Figs 126a–126b Presteigne: details of faces in south transept window (sIII)

174 THE MEDIEVAL STAINED GLASS OF HEREFORDSHIRE & SHROPSHIRE

QUATT
St Andrew

William Mytton found ten kneeling donors in several windows and St Catherine, with a huge sword and toothed wheel, St Margaret and Mary Magdalene. There were also several incomplete figures and numerous inscriptions, but no old glass has survived.

RICHARDS CASTLE
St Bartholomew (SO 4843 7027, SY8 4ET)

Silas Taylor visited the church and found arms in the west window.[565] Thomas Blount, visiting in the seventeenth century, made a detailed record of some of the iconography of the glass:

> In the West window of the church there are the ruynes [ruins] of the Story of our Saviour's Life and Passion in painted glass – the three Kings and Star that conducted them still visible, and at the top the arms of Say, and Arg 3 Bars az- tis like the donors of it –
> In the South window of the Chancel there is yet remaining a crucifix painted, and one kneeling at the foot of it with a Shaven Crown and …
> In the North side [of] the church is Saint Johns Chappel and in one of its windows St Elizabeth is curiously painted, with Her son, and the Paschal Lamb, and under that in Saxon Characters:
> > *Elizabet Mater beati*
> > *Johannis Baptistae*
>
> In another pane of the Window, the executioner taking St John out of Prison, the portcullis, and other ensignes, in order to his decollation, and in the third pane one holding his Head in a Platter, after execution was don, – over all a King and Queen with Crowns of Gold on their Heads – perhaps the founders of this Chappel or Donors of the Window.[566]

The narrative glass had probably been lost by 1852 when Stephen Glynne found:

> There are several fine pieces of stained glass in the windows, though mutilated. One in the South aisle has a fine green and yellow border – that at the east of the same head of Edw. I, and a fine border in the north chapel are heads of a king and queen; there is also some in the chancel.[567]

The tracery panels and heads of the main lights in the chancel south-west window have plain borders and fragments of diapering. The Crucifixion described by Blount, was probably in the other south window.

The top of the SOUTH AISLE EAST WINDOW (sIV) is an extravagant display of ballflower tracery. The following are of particular interest:

> #### South aisle east window (sIV)
> • In the uppermost quatrefoil, the head of a king in sepia tones and lines. The drawing is reminiscent of the head of a cleric at Orleton.
> • In the lower quatrefoils, grisaille.
> • In the heads of the main lights, borders with fleurs-de-lis and towers and vine and oak grisaille.
> • Roundels with rose paterae and quatrefoils with toothed leaves.
> • Rich red and blue border pieces and backgrounds.

Fig. 127a Richards Castle: Coronation of the Virgin (nIII)

Fig. 127b Richards Castle: Coronation of the Virgin (nIII)

In the next window (sVI), the quatrefoil has a crown drawn as though made of foliage. The blue lattice diapering, if ancient, has no parallel in this survey. This is dated 1300 in the church guide, but on what grounds?[568] In the heads of the main lights are borders of alternate plain green pieces and leaf quatrefoils enclosing fragments of leaf grisaille.

Blount found the Death of John the Baptist in the NORTH TRANSEPT EAST WINDOW (nIII) with, 'over all', figures of a king and queen. These two figures remain and are set in crocketed ogee canopies against deep-blue diapering (Figs 127a & 127b). They probably represent the Coronation of the Virgin. The figures sit in quatrefoils with vine-leaf designs and deep red paterae. There is also a roundel of seventeenth-century date, part of a garter arms.

The tracery lights of the NORTH TRANSEPT WEST WINDOW (nV) have 'Ledbury borders' and are divided into squares each with a yellow rose reminiscent of some small flowers at Eardisland.

ROSS-ON-WYE
St Mary (SO 5979 2405, HR9 5HZ)

The important glass at Ross was taken from the chapel in the Bishop's Palace at Sugwas in around 1792 when the palace was partly demolished.[569] There must have been glass of high quality in quantity in this important town church, but little survived into the seventeenth century when Silas Taylor[570] and Thomas Blount[571] recorded the arms of the diocese and local families in several windows. What remains of the medieval glass is in panels of fragments in tracery at the WEST END OF THE SOUTH AISLE (sX). The smaller panels are a jumble of fifteenth-century and nineteenth-century pieces, but the larger quatrefoil (Fig. 128) was described by David O'Connor,[572]

Fig. 128 Ross-on-Wye: collection of fifteenth-century glass in the south aisle (sX)

> ... mainly fifteenth century fragments in white and yellow stain ... In the centre ... is a female head with plucked forehead, templers and veil; probably part of a donor figure from the second quarter of the fifteenth century ... large scale ermine and patterned drapery, a hand holding a sceptre or staff, a hand protruding from a sleeve, an inside out mitred S ...'

The mitred S is a (reversed) fragment of the border described by Thomas Blount in the Sugwas Palace chapel.

East window (I)
This window is one of the most important in this survey. For a long time, it was held that the glass from the demolished palace at Stretton Sugwas had been transferred to the nearby church of Eaton Bishop (in the same parish). However, George Marshall,[573] using the accounts of James Hill[574] and Thomas Blount,[575] showed that their descriptions fitted the glass now at Ross. The Palace – in scale more a manor house – was one of several owned by the bishops, but rarely occupied by them.[576] Sugwas had become a farmhouse by 1784 and was in a poor state, with the glass defaced and some windows blocked-up.[577] It was partly demolished in 1792[578] during the bishopric of John Butler. The chapel had a four-light east window forming a reredos with a low sill (as at Eaton Bishop), and at least three two-light windows. Thomas Spofford was bishop 1421–48 and his register records documents issued from Sugwas, and ordination services held there after 1431 until the year before he resigned.

A guidebook to Ross church says,

> According to Ross accounts, the tracery in the East window of St Mary's had decayed so badly by that time that the churchwardens placed iron rods as mullions in the window, and sent to Stretton for the glass, which they heard was to be purchased cheaply. It came

to Ross in wooden boxes, and is said to have been fitted in between the iron rods just as it came out ...[579]

There is a connection between Ross and Sugwas in that the bishops of Hereford had palaces in both. The Ross palace was adjacent to the church and Bishop Butler or one of his successors might well have been instrumental in the transfer of the glass from Sugwas. This would perhaps account for there being no specific items in the churchwardens' accounts for the purchase or installation of the glass.

Most writers suggest that the installation of the glass occurred soon after the Sugwas Palace was demolished but this cannot be confirmed. The churchwardens' accounts[580] suggest the usual pattern of regular annual spending on glazing. From 1775 to 1810, Edward Hill, who was described as 'glazier', carried out the work. However, a relatively large sum of over £7, in 1780, seems insufficient for the installation of the Sugwas glass. There was a peak in the progress of Mr Hill's work in 1792, which could suggest that the glass was salvaged from Sugwas, as it was being demolished and installed immediately. If the panels were intact and were simply fitted into an ironwork lattice, the sum of £12 13s 7d spent that year, would probably be adequate. A considerably larger sum of £20 was spent in 1809, and it is possible that the installation of the glass was delayed until then.

The window was reglazed in 1873 in memory of Charles Ogilvie, a prominent theologian and former rector. The glaziers were Thomas Baillie & Co. Thomas established his firm in 1838, but also worked with his brother Edward Baillie (1812–56). After Edward's death, Thomas Baillie became head of the family firm, which was joined by George Mayer (from 1854) and then William Lutwyche (1840–1908).[581] The cartoons for Baillie's work survive and help to establish the extent of new work. David O'Connor wrote about the glass in 1995[582] following a detailed inspection:

> The Ross restoration was extremely skilful, producing a window which was not only aesthetically pleasing but looked authentic. So good is the copying, reinforced by a certain amount of antiquating with paint to suggest corrosion, that careful examination of both sides is needed to establish the authenticity of every piece.

The four main panels of the window depict Bishop Spofford and the saints who were most important to him. There can be no doubt that he was the donor of the glass. As O'Connor has pointed out, the reredos formed by the glass, when it was in his chapel at Sugwas, placed Spofford among the Holy Family of the Virgin Mary and her parents, Anne and Joachim. They were flanked by Ethelbert and Thomas Cantilupe, two saints of great significance in Hereford. The juxtaposition of Mary and Ethelbert also resonates as they are the dedication saints of Spofford's cathedral, and the abbey at York where Spofford had previously been abbot was also dedicated to St Mary.

There are no other surviving examples of this group of saints. Catterick – the church dedicated to Anne, and of which Spofford was rector – had an image of him kneeling with Anne and an 'orate' inscription of c.1415.[583] At Ludlow, in tracery lights of the east window, he appears with Anne, teaching the Virgin to read. This panel dates from c.1445 but is very heavily restored (Fig. 101a). St Anne was probably present in glass in the cathedral, as David O'Connor points out,[584]

Fig. 129 Ross-on-Wye: east window (I)

East window (I)

2a: St Ethelbert. Ethelbert was an East Anglian king who was martyred in Herefordshire on the orders of King Offa in 794. The king, dressed in ermine and a blue mantle, is crowned and nimbed. He holds a sceptre in his right hand and a church in his left. The inscription is modern and misnames him.

2b: The Virgin and St Anne with Bishop Spofford offering his heart (**Fig. 130**).

St Anne is teaching the Virgin, who sits on her knee, to read. At her feet kneels a bishop, dressed in a red chasuble, and an alb. He is offering his heart, which he holds between his hands, to St Anne. On the second finger of his right hand is a ring, and resting against his right shoulder is a white crosier. On a label is 'Hoc precor oblatum cor suscipe terge reatum' ('I pray you support this offered heart – cleanse its accursed state').[588] David O'Connor noted that, 'Restorations include the cope (except top right piece, crozier staff, cushion, lower part of Virgin's robe, canopy and borders).'

2c: Joachim. A figure of Joachim, the Virgin's father, with the right hand raised and fully extended. On his head is a curious form of green cap, and in his left hand he holds up cloak and a book. On a label is the inscription: 'Joachim virgini dans esse et hoc p miraculum de radice Jesse.' David O'Connor noted that all the borders and canopy-work are new. The upper section of robe, a piece of the mantle below the sleeve, a shoe and the background to the left of the saint are also modern.

The story of Joachim and Anne first appears in the apocryphal Gospel of James. They are a necessary part of the theology of the immaculate conception of the Virgin herself, and of her invented lineage. Images of Joachim are rare, and normally part of the fanciful legend of Mary's virgin birth, which includes the familiar themes of barrenness and annunciation.

2d: St Thomas of Hereford. The figure of a bishop in a jewelled mitre, with a white and yellow nimbus. In his left hand he holds a crosier, and the right is raised in the act of blessing. Over his head is a scroll, on which is inscribed: 'Scs Thomas Herefordensis'. The blue background, much of the vestments and most of the canopy are modern.

Much of the rest of the window is modern. The two angels in the central lower panels are of the same date as the principal figures, but almost all the canopy-work and background are by Baillie & Co.

Fig. 130 Ross-on-Wye: Bishop Spofford and St Anne teaching the Virgin in the east window (I.2b)

In about 1440 the bishop founded another altar to St Anne, this time in the south transept of his cathedral. He inserted a large window at the south end of the west wall to light the altar and was almost certainly represented in it with the saint.

The Holy Family, and especially Anne teaching Mary to read, were popular topics in England in the Middle Ages. The principal local example is that of Great Malvern Priory[585] where three versions of the Virgin and Anne survive. There was also a representation of the scene at Hampton Court,[586] in glass of similar date to that at Ross.[587] The pairing of Saints Ethelbert and Thomas is seen on the tomb of Bishop Mayhew in the cathedral c.1516, and Thomas Cantilupe is found in Credenhill in much earlier glass of the thirteenth century.

David O'Connor has considered the question of which workshop produced the glass. Other glass associated with Spofford, or the themes in his window, can be associated with John Thornton who had interests in both York and Coventry, and who may also have been involved at Great Malvern.

ST MICHAELS
St Michael (so 5830 6571, wr15 8ph)

The church is a High Gothic fantasy of 1854–57 with fine windows by Hardman of Birmingham. The four lancets in the north-east corridor have fragments of old glass probably from Hardman's stock. The easternmost has the head of a sheep and some black letter.

ST WEONARDS
St Weonard (so 4960 2433, hr2 8nu)

There is an important medieval record of the glass here, discovered by Christopher Woodforde,

> In 1356 three windows were made for St. Weonard's church at a cost of 13s. 4d. 4d. was paid for carrying them from Hereford and 2d. to hire a horse to carry William the Glazier there.[589]

William Hereford was working at St Stephen's Chapel in Westminster Abbey in 1351, where he was one of 11 glass painters.[590]

The surviving medieval glass, some of which was dated 1521, is related to the Mynors family who have occupied the nearby Treago Castle since the fifteenth century. Silas Taylor, visiting the church in the mid seventeenth century, made one of his longest church accounts.[591] He was followed by Thomas Blount (c.1765) who helpfully described some of the iconography in addition to the heraldry.[592]

In the east window of the chancel, no old glass remains but Blount saw 'Jesus and the Blessed Virgin, and underneath IHS in old characters.' He also saw, 'The Armes of Baskervyle, Myners and Pye in their proper colors –'. Taylor saw a figure holding the arms of the Mynors, 's: a displayed eagle O: under a fesse A.' He added, 'This I judge to be the most ancient piece of glass in armory in the church'. In the first light (probably the north light) were the arms of Baskervyle, 'A: cheveron G int' 3 Huerts proper' ('proper' in this case being blue). In the third light he saw the arms of Plukenet (lords of Kilpeck), 'ermine a bend lozengy G.' This is the shield attributed to Pye by Blount.[593]

ABOVE: **Fig. 131** St Weonards: east window of north aisle (nIII)

LEFT: **Fig. 132** St Weonards: east window of north aisle (nIII) before restoration

In the chancel north window, both antiquaries saw and recorded,

> In ye chancel in a north window is the picture of an old man in hermit's aray the remaynes of writing is onely Wenardus Heremita. The neighbours assure me that before the repair of the window lately there was the year of our Lord set there also viz 1000.

Blount added a, 'long beard, holding a Book in one Hand and an axe in the other, and under written in old characters – S. Wenadrus Heremyta.' There is no trace of this now.

In the north chapel east window, there are some remains of old glass. Silas Taylor found 'On the Toppe of the east window in that chapel', arms of Baskerville and Devereux. Blount also found here 'a Crucifix and other pictures.' Part of the body of Christ and a picture of St Catherine survived, and were retained in the nineteenth-century restoration. Taylor described inscriptions in the lower part of the window, seeking prayers for Richard Mynors and Johanna, and recording the foundation of the chapel by the said Richard and William ap Thomas in M: XXI, which Blount recorded as 1521. Somewhere between were two shields, of Vaughan and Clifford, associated with a praying woman and an attendant child.

In the north chapel north window, no original glass remains, but Taylor found:

> On the North side of ye church in a North window are the pictures of Richard miners and his wife [Catherine] the daughter of [Sir Richard] Vaughan of Porthamell in the County of Brecon both kneeling in their gowns, before the picture of the man is a shield with *a coat S: an eagle displayed O:*

fesse in chiefe A: by ye name of Minors and over him fairly written this in Welsh:

'Gobethe onye Bay Gallion a doney otto Gobethe otto Gobethe. Anno 1595'

Robinson suggests, *Gobeithiwn nietto gobeithiwn Pe calon a dori etto gobeithiw* translated as, 'Let us hope still, let us hope tho' the Heart break, still let us hope.'[594]

Taylor also found part of the motto of the Vaughans: *Heb Duw heb ddiw* – 'Without God without anything.'

In the north aisle there are some fragments of old glass in the upper lights. Taylor found a good deal to report here. There was the memorial of one Sir Roger Minors, knight of the Rhodes:

lower in the church on a North window fairly painted with the portraits of diverse saints and underneath them was the picture of a woman painted kneeling and in another pane a man in his coat armour wch is of ye Minors kneeling alsoe and under them both this writing remaining: '----------uxoris ejus felie Willm Mill militis qui hanc fenestram vitriari fecerunt.'

There was also:

In the middle paine of the window is empaled S: an eagle displayed O: on a chiefe B: a cheveron int two [crescents] and a rose O: bordured A impaled with ... A: guttee de salle a Brandicon or a mil thus expressed as in the margent S: by ye name of Mill: both these coates are expressed single on the Toppe of ye window the one over the man the other over the woman.

Blount saw this window and found, in addition to the arms, the figure of 'St Michael killing the Dragon'.

The glass must have gone through a steady decline of running repairs and patching in the eighteenth century. In the churchwardens' accounts there is a payment of £1 5s 2d for the 'glaziers bill' in 1794–95, and numerous payments over the whole account to a Mr Jones who might have been the glazier there.[595]

NORTH CHAPEL EAST WINDOW (nIII)
(Figs 131 & 132)
At some date before 1875, when Baillie and Mayer reglazed the east window of the north chapel as a memorial to Peter Rickards Mynors, the main lights must have been re-leaded. Before they started, Baillie and Mayer found figures of old glass set in a background of diamond quarries (Fig. 132).[596]

In 1912, John Matthews noted in the sixth volume of Duncumb's *Collections*,

Thomas Blount ... has left interesting particulars concerning the ancient stained glass of this church. A considerable portion of the old glass had escaped Reformation and Revolution, but most of what then survived has since been swept away by the ravages of Restoration.[597]

The 'before and after' pictures (Figs 131 & 132) show this very clearly. Below the tracery lights, little old glass remains, but parts of the figures in the upper part of nIII can be dated to 1521. But 'ravages' is probably unfair; the restoration was heavy-handed but not ignorant. The heraldry of the Mynors, recorded by Silas Taylor, must have guided the work, but it is perhaps unfortunate that the two shields which survived intact were not left in situ (A7 moved to A6 and A6 to A3). The inscription bearing the date of 1521, was repeated and it is possible that many old pieces of the original borders and the made-up panels have been reused.

The window is a memorial erected by a family – the Mynors – who were devout Catholics, Royalists and recusants, and who remained so throughout the sixteenth century. 'Sir Robert Harley's aunt, Jane Mynors ... was described in

> **North chapel east window (nIII)**
> **1a–1d**: These panels seem to be entirely of 1875.
> **2a**: St Catherine: Catherine is crowned and nimbed and holds a wheel and a sword. Her head, which is simply drawn and could be a century older than 1521, together with the crown and the wheel are the only medieval fragments in the panel.
> **2b, 2c & 2d**: There is no medieval glass in these panels.
> **A1**: Entirely of 1875.
> **A2**: St Margaret: The figure of the saint and her surrounding columns and possibly the band of paterae that she stands on, are original. St Margaret is drawn in black line and silver stain. She drives the shaft of the Cross into the mouth of the beast.
> **A3**: St Catherine: The figure of the saint and her surrounding columns and possibly the band of paterae that she stands on, are original. So, too, is the Baskerville shield which was previously in A6. This St Catherine carries her other attribute, a book in addition to the sword and wheel which are present.
> **A4 & A5**: The Annunciation: The panels are medieval except for the charming dove of the Holy Spirit, the head and chest of the Virgin, the top of the prayer desk in panel A5 and the archangel's robe at the viewers'
>
> bottom-right. The figure of the archangel, drawn in the same way as Margaret and Catherine in black line and silver stain, is a handsome, youthful and romantic figure. He carries a sceptre: perhaps this is the courtly annunciation of King Henry and Catherine – why else would there be two Catherines in this window?
> Panel **A6**: The crowned figure is all of 1875. However, the shield is older. The arms of Baskerville were moved from here to A3 and the Devereaux arms imported to panel A6 from A7.
> **A7**: St Helen: The figure of the saint and her surrounding columns and possibly the band of paterae that she stands on, are original. Helen holds the shaft of the True Cross. The three surviving women are probably based on the same cartoon.
> **A8**: St Leonard: The figure is medieval except for its head. A representation of St Leonard carrying a staff and the chains which are his attribute. The head is like the head of Gabriel in panel A4.
> **B3**: Christ, The Man of Sorrows (**Fig. 18**): A striking image of the Face of Christ, with a red robe and gushing blood. This grim-faced depiction has deep roots at Eaton Bishop (I.2e) and Sellack (nIII). The picture combines the two traditional images of 'Sorrow' and 'Glory'.

1609 as one of the principal women recusants in Herefordshire.'[598] They managed to preserve their memorials through both periods of iconoclasm, which speaks much of the power of out-of-the-way magnates, to ignore the ordinances which destroyed much elsewhere.

North chapel north window (nIV)

A faculty was granted in 1952 for the 'erection of a panel of stained glass inside the lower half of the first small window in the south wall.'[599] A note was added to the file: 'In 1971 this panel incorporated in the new glazing of the N E window in the N aisle without further formal Authority.'

The panel was formerly at Goodrich Court, which was demolished in 1949.[600] The Court, designed by G.F. Bodley, had housed the magnificent collections of Sir Samuel Rush Meyrick. There is another connection between glass in the church and Bodley: he was instrumental in the founding of the firm of glaziers, Baillie and Mayer, which was responsible for restoring the east window of the chapel. The glass is probably Netherlandish. The background of towers and walls is reminiscent of sixteenth-century paintings of the walls and gates of Amsterdam, and the dark, rich colouring of the robes is typical of Netherlandish painting of the sixteenth century. So too the cusped framework at the head of the panel. There is an escutcheon with a symbol which seems to combine the three Crosses of the three figures in the image – Jesus, Peter and Andrew. They are arranged around the initials 'M R'.

The **north aisle window** (nV) is part of the sixteenth-century alterations. In the tracery lights are heraldic crests of the Mynors repeated eight times. In each, a hand reaches out of a black and white torse (wreath).

SARNESFIELD
St Mary (so 3746 5090, hr4 8re)

The east end of the church, including the window that holds the medieval glass, was re-ordered in 1906–07 to the design of Roland Paul.[601] *The Builder* reported,

> In 1870 parts of the chancel and Chapel walls were rebuilt and new windows inserted, quite out of harmony with the old work. The floors were raised, destroying the good proportions of the interior, and the roofs were covered with Broseley tiles.[602] The work now done has included the total removal of all the work done in 1870. New windows have been inserted in the chancel and Chapel, and one in the nave aisle, and an arcade of two bays separating the chancel and Chapel. The windows have been re-glazed throughout; the few fragments of old glass having been inserted in the East window of the Chapel.[603]

There are 16 pieces of glass in a variety of styles, which are displayed in a ground of alternating columns of plain diamond and narrow rectangular quarries. A photograph in the Marshall papers,[604] taken before the Roland Paul project, shows much of the glass now in place, in a different arrangement, but the four small, elegant, full-length figures and the angel roundel (Figs 133a & 134, overleaf) were not there. Could they have come from the excavations at Abbey Dore, which Roland Paul supervised at about the same time? They are small quarries measuring only 185mm x 65mm, which were probably cut down from larger pictures because the leading now obscures details of the drawing, and the censing angel has lost its thurible.

Figs 133a–133b Sarnesfield: angel figures in the south chapel east window (sII)

Figs 133c–133d Sarnesfield: figures of an Apostle and a musician in the south chapel east window (sII)

The full-length figures and the archangel roundel are of the fourteenth century, in a highly distinctive style with figures on a dark background.[605] The two angels (Figs 133a & 133b) wear apparelled albs and amices. The alb is further embellished with a decorative band at knee-level. Both are nimbed and both have a plain headband, and they have similar hair and wings. In the north panel is a harpist playing a harp with a distinctive shoulder and sound board consistent with a fourteenth-century date.[606] In the south panel the angel swings a censer: the composition of the original setting demanded that the burner of the thurible be at the highest point of swing.[607]

The two other standing figures are an Apostle and a musician (Figs 133c & 133b). In the south light, a bearded male, robed and nimbed and carrying a book. These attributes suggest that this is an Apostle, maybe one of the Evangelists. The subtly sinuous pose and the simply-drawn expression of awe or adoration are very engaging. In the north light is a standing youth playing a six-stringed psaltery. He wears a trumpet-sleeved cote with a hood. The psaltery is quite crudely drawn, with only six strings which do not cross the sound hole.

In the upper tracery light is a monogram of the letters 'I' and 'U' in Lombardic style.

This delightful collection was assembled by people with clear knowledge of medieval stained glass, with a predilection for the fresh, flowing forms of the fourteenth century. That exercising of artistic confidence can also be seen in the modern east window which is a fine First World War memorial by Christopher Whall, installed in 1922.

South chapel east window, north panel
The rose: the rose in yellow stain could be taken, with the sun in the south panel, to represent the 'sun in splendour' and white rose associated with Edward IV, the Yorkists and the Battle of Mortimer's Cross (which took place 14 miles north of Sarnesfield in 1461). There are other Yorkist symbols in this window, in the lions *rampant guardant* and the fleur-de-lis, which are elements of the Yorkist Royal Arms.
The hand and the blue patera: two quite different objects set together. The upper part, which was inverted in the pre-1901 window, has a hand and sleeve in two pieces; the lower part has a blue patera with a five-petalled flower.
The crowned head: part of a fourteenth-century crowned, bearded figure set in part of a cusped trefoil arch or roundel.
The lion: the lion *passant guardant* is simply drawn with yellow stain against a dark background. This possibly comes from a border.
The arabesque: an eight-pointed star formed by two interlaced, concave-sided squares, the centre of which is occupied by a grotesque mask with ivy fronds issuing from its mouth.
The angels, a saint and a musician – see above.

South chapel east window, south panel
The 'sun in splendour'.
Fleur-de-lis: A deep-amber fleur-de-lis on a dark ground, probably from a border.
Crowned Figure: This is an exercise in yellow stain and fine black line, depicting a crowned head. The face is rather androgynous. The crown (a crest coronet) might also be called a Plantagenet crown.[608] There are puzzling details. Above the crown is a sloping, thatched roof, and piercing one of the rafters is a very deliberately drawn object; and, to the left of the crown is what may be a bird's beak.
Part of a lion: The almost illegible head of a lion *passant guardant*, vigorously drawn with a shaggy outline and wide leer. Again, this probably comes from a border.

Fig. 134 Sarnesfield: Archangel Gabriel (sII)

Angel of Annunciation (**Fig. 134**): this roundel is drawn in yellow stain on a dark ground. It depicts a kneeling angel with a scroll, presumably the Archangel Gabriel meeting the (missing) Virgin. The figure is nimbed, but bare-headed, and wears a white cloak (almost a toga), open at the front, over its feathered body. The spaces in the background are filled by a vine with curled tendrils.

SELLACK

St Tysilio (so 5654 2766, hr9 6lt)

The east window of the late fourteenth century, contains some medieval glass. The window was reglazed as a memorial to Roland Scudamore and bears the date 1630 with the initials 'RS'. The window is by the same hand as the east window at Abbey Dore, which is dated 1634.

East window (I) (Fig. 58)
John, 1st Viscount, Scudamore was responsible for the Sellack east window which commemorates his great uncle Rowland who occupied Caradoc Court, the big house to the west of the church. John Scudamore inherited his bachelor great uncle's estate on his death in 1630 (by the old calendar, not 1631, his death year as reckoned now) and is known to have held him in high regard.[609]

At Abbey Dore, John Scudamore had a clean canvas to work with, and the experience of the Sellack window to build on. At Sellack, the young aristocrat of 29 years, harbouring a growing disquiet about the source of his wealth in the Dissolution and in the thrall of Archbishop Laud, was guided by his own fervour and confidence. He was also constrained by an existing late fourteenth-century window, and the presence of a medieval figure that he considered worthy of preservation (an act of conservation remarkable in itself at that time). The Sellack window has many figures which had been regarded as idolatrous or superstitious, and would be again little more than a decade later.

In the catalogue of 'superstitious' and 'idolatrous' images that were broken in the Reformation, Christ crucified and Mary were priorities, and yet John Scudamore had them displayed twice in his window which tells of the birth and death of Christ. In the upper part of the window the rood, which dominated the top of countless medieval screens destroyed in the Reformation, is recreated in light and colour. This surely is the window of a man of great passion who, despite having been at Oxford when the van Linge brothers were starting their career in college chapels, seems to have cared little for art, preferring instead to make the window himself (as suggested at Abbey Dore) or use a local glazier of limited artistic ability.

At about the time the Sellack window was being made, Abraham van Linge was installing windows at Lincoln College, which look utterly unlike the Sellack window. The Lincoln College east window is a great collage of various scenes from the Bible. The Crucifixion is there and the Nativity, but they sprawl across the window rather than being placed in compartments

Perhaps what John Scudamore saw in his local churches was more influential. In the Crucifixion he adopted the green Cross, the *arbor vitea*, which is seen in most of the surviving Crucifixes in this county survey. It is interesting to see Sellack as a prototype of Dore, and it is possible that the figures of Mary (A2 and 2c), John (A5) and Mary Magdalene (1a) represent attempts at chiaroscuro, which were ultimately abandoned for the black line on white glass of the bearded Magi, which is the style throughout the Dore window. The form of the Sellack window, as a series of niches, is carried through at Dore with the same borders, but Dore develops the canopy-work into something much more complex.

The window has a uniform appearance imposed by the very strong border and canopy designs also used at Abbey Dore. The figures in the bottom row have white glass grounds while all the others have the grey diapering seen at Dore. The canopy-work is also quite different from stage to stage. The bottom row has arabesque ogee arches while the upper canopies are all composed from straight lines.

In the NAVE SOUTH WINDOW (sV) (Fig. 135), an incomplete panel of the Throne of Mercy. The head of God is missing and the Holy Spirit, in the form of a dove, might normally be expected. This panel of exceptional beauty, is probably early fifteenth-century. In the top-right corner, a crown from a border and the corner of a timber-framed building.

East window (I)

1a: Mary Magdalene nimbed and holding a stone jar. She stands on a white tile floor.
1b: A puzzling drawing of a Magus. He is crowned and holds a sceptre, and kneels above a gold jug and four gold objects. The face in profile is unique among the figures in John Scudamore's windows and seems of a different quality to the body.

The initials 'RS' are at the base of the panel in florid caps with looped rope decoration.
1c: The ox and ass of the Nativity under a sloping stable roof. At the base of the panel the date 1630 in a diapered rectangle. The numbers are by the same hand as the Abbey Dore date.
1d: A nimbed figure with a black, gabled hood of c.1500 or later. She piously holds a book and wears a deep-red cloak over a white robe edged in gold pellet borders. She was probably originally intended to be St Catherine of Alexandria, although her attributes of a sword and barbed wheel may be additions of 1630. Catherine is usually crowned but not always. This is a fine figure, perhaps a donor now cast in the role of Catherine. In the Royal Commission survey published in 1931, St Catherine faces towards the ox and ass.
2a: One of the Magi holding a cup. He is crowned and wears blue hose over which he has a belted, sleeveless tunic and a gold cape.
2b: Probably Joseph. Bearded and balding, he points towards his neighbour in 2a.
2c: Mary holding the infant Jesus. In case the onlooker did not get that this is a representation of the Nativity, the Star of Bethlehem with a downward beam, shines in the top-left of the panel.
2d: Bearded and crowned, the third Magi bears a cup and a gold box, and looks towards Mary and the Child. He wears a full-length robe and amber cloak.
A2, A5 & B1: The Rood: the head of Mary is unlike any other. It is almost entirely drawn in yellow stain with some ochre line. This looks like an instance of the artist wrestling with the medium, part of the learning process, or a failure of the darker materials in weathering. John is far more competently drawn, with expression and modelling. The figures are on a dark, diapered ground with wave and pellet decoration in thin white line.

The Crucifix on a green Cross is almost abstract with its vivid red and blue diapering and gold, restless borders. The left side of Christ's cloth is a replacement piece.

Fig. 135 Sellack: the Throne of Mercy (sV)

The inscription in black letter reads as follows (but the first word may be unconnected fragments): *Ele - - sine me fecit.*

The panel is almost certainly not in situ and may have been acquired by John Scudamore as part of his reordering project. It is significantly positioned by the 'new' three-decker pulpit.

In the NORTH CHAPEL WINDOW (nIII), the face of Christ, probably of the later fourteenth century, with a crossed nimbus within a black and yellow pellet border.

SOLLERS HOPE
ST MICHAEL (SO 6125 3312, HR1 4RW)

The north and south chancel windows have a few yellow stain crowns from borders which may be in situ. The west window has a collection of crowns and other fragments in the tracery.

STOKE EDITH
ST MARY (SO 6040 4066, HR1 4HG)

There is a single panel of fragments in the west tower window. The west tower was built in the fourteenth century, and the spire added probably in the sixteenth century. The rest of the church was rebuilt in 1740–42.

James Hill (d.1727) visited and recorded several images.[610] In a north window were Thomas and Margaret Walwyn in the roles of donors. Thomas inherited the Stoke Edith manor in 1362 and died in 1444.[611] The window showed the Virgin attended by angels, and St Michael weighing a soul beset by devils trying to tip the balance.

ANTICLOCKWISE FROM TOP-LEFT: **Figs 136a, 136b & 136c**
Stoke Edith: details from the tower west window

There was an 'Our Lady' chantry to which this window may have been related.⁶¹² The arms of Walwyn (*gules a bend ermine*) and (probably) Chandos (*argent a queued lion purple crowned or*) were also present. Margaret brought the Chandos connection.

In 1932, the Royal Commission reported, 'In W. window of tower – jumble of fragments, including a shield-of-arms, argent a lion with a forked tail gules(?) crowned or, angel-head, figure playing lute; fifteenth-century and later.' ⁶¹³

The shield of arms and most of the angel-head have disappeared since 1932.

The principal subjects are:

- At the centre, a bearded figure holding a tromba marina (a triangular, bowed instrument popular in the fifteenth century) [**Fig. 136c**]. The grim mouth and countenance is emphasised by the drawing and shading in black, with yellow stain being used sparingly for the instrument and apparel.
- A quarter of a nimbed head – possibly Archangel Michael.
- A line drawing of a lutenist [**Fig. 136b**].
- A small bird.
- The bound hands of the soul and the wing of Archangel Michael, from the Judgement scene noted by James Hill [**Fig. 136a**]. There are further fragments of wing in the window.
- The Virgin's blue mantle and triple-crown noted by James Hill.

STOTTESDON
St Mary (so 6724 8288, dy14 8uh)

The medieval glass is in the west windows of the aisles.

South aisle south-west window (sVII)
(Fig. 137)

William Mytton recorded several coats of arms in the 1730s.⁶¹⁴ As noted in the inscription at the base of the main panels, the glass was originally in the east window, and Peter Newton established that it was in the tracery lights.⁶¹⁵ In

Fig. 137 Stottesdon: heraldic glass in the south aisle (sVII)

the eighteenth century, there were more shields than the four existing now, and two of the missing shields belonged to the Segraves who acquired the manor in 1270. This is the earliest possible date for the glass, and the latest is defined by the presence of the king's arms with three lions, which went out of use in 1340. In 1325 the Segrave heir, Stephen, was a minor and wardship of his lands was granted to the earl of Norfolk. Peter Newton argues that the absence of Norfolk arms in the antiquarian record suggests that the window was made before 1325, the date when Norfolk's wardship would have required his arms to be placed in the window.

The tracery quatrefoil has the head of a knight in a coif-de-mailles banded with yellow stain set on modern white glass. The head is framed by a green mandorla bearing a rough foliage design and dotted border, and is between two yellow pot metal rosettes. The border of the quatrefoil comprises plain ruby plaques alternating with yellow pot metal leaf quatrefoils.

The east light has shields on a ground of vine grisaille with patterned borders, originally forming a now lost geometrical pattern:

- A ruby rosette set in leaf grisaille, of palmate leaves from yellow stain stalks and a piece of vine decoration with leaf and grapes in yellow stain against a black ground.
- The arms of Zouche – *Gules bezanty or* – the bezants separately leaded.
- Crocketed canopy-work highlighted in yellow stain and smear shading.
- The arms of the King of England – *Gules three lions passant guardant in pale or*.
- A piece of cup-and-cover border.
- The west light has shields on a ground of vine grisaille with patterned borders, originally forming a now lost geometrical pattern:
- The arms of Zouche – *Azure bezanty or*.
- A shield – *Argent a lion rampant gules (crowned or), a bordure engrailed sable*. Peter Newton did not identify this shield but it is probably connected to the Cornwalls who had, and still have in the form of fine monuments, a presence at nearby Kinlet.

The SOUTH AISLE WEST WINDOW (sVIII) was assembled in 1910 from fragments. The most legible are sections of border, probably fourteenth-century.

The NORTH AISLE NORTH-WEST WINDOW (nVII) has two frontal images of heads in coif-de-mailles with yellow banding. These were originally set above the shields in the east window, with the similar head now in the south aisle.

STRETTON GRANDISON
St Lawrence (SO 6328 4407, HR8 2TS)

The Royal Commission found a small panel of fragments in the tower and, in the head of the west window, a quatrefoil with roundel and fragments, belonging to the fourteenth or fifteenth century.[616] This glass remains.

SUTTON ST MICHAEL
Freen's Court (demolished)

George Marshall wrote about the house in 1917, and described a large oriel window to a parlour with several armorial roundels which were photographed by Alfred Watkins.[617] The arms of Lingen, Russell, Breynton and Milwater were described by Marshall who thought that the glass dated between 1550 and 1650. The glass had been removed by 1932.[618]

TARRINGTON
St Philip and St James (SO 5262 4582, HR1 3AY)

James Hill (d.1727) made a cursory note. He saw the complete figure of St Catherine in a north window. The surviving glass had been moved to its present location by 1903, when the Woolhope Club visited.[619]

Chancel south window (sII)
Angel musicians (Figs 138a & 138b): Four panels have very darkened and pitted images of angel musicians. The angels are drawn in black line and yellow silver stain and all wear tiaras with crosses at the front. They are robed, rather than vested, with loose outer robes hemmed with decorative borders. In 1a, the angel is playing small cymbals both of which are seen in front of the feathered wing. In 1b the hands and forearms seem to be raised and one hand is held flat against a board, but the instrument cannot be identified. The robe has a gold panel which is an inverted garment from another scene. A foot can be seen under (over) the hem. In 3a a long, straight pipe comes from the angel's mouth, probably the long trumpet seen for example in stone at Gloucester.[620] In 3b the angel plays a psaltery. There seem to be two hands at work here. The angels in 1a and 1b have flowing, curly locks and Classical features while those in 3a and 3b have darker, more combed hair and almost grotesque faces.

St Catherine (Fig. 139): James Hill saw a complete figure of Catherine. This remnant

TOP: **Figs 138a–138b** Tarrington: angels in south chancel window (sII). ABOVE: **Fig. 139** Tarrington: St Catherine (sII)

GAZETTEER OF CHURCHES IN HEREFORDSHIRE AND THE DIOCESE OF HEREFORD

is crowned and nimbed (as is typical of representations of the saint) and, even without her other attributes, can be identified. The RCHM suggested this is the Virgin, but she looks up rather than down towards a child. This is one of the loveliest images in this survey. She bears hallmarks of the International Style with the bulbous end to her nose, the small mouth and the rolled hairline.

There is tabernacle-work in panels 5a and 5b, with battlements and round turrets reminiscent of the work at New College, Oxford, and also found at Madley and Pixley. In A1 there are two starkly different heads. Other subjects include an eagle in a roundel, probably from the four tetramorphic symbols.

The glass is now set in a separate panel inside the external glazing.

THRUXTON

St Bartholomew (SO 4372 3464, HR2 9AX)

The church has a simple, aisleless outline and is mostly of fourteenth-century date – that is of similar date to the glass. In 1866 William Chick, architect, guided the repair of the church, which had fallen into poor condition. In an article about the work of Chick, Philip Anderson wrote,

> The church's greatest treasure, which was installed at the restoration, is an exquisite fragment of fourteenth-century stained glass found by the Revd Jacson and depicting Christ on the Cross. This was restored by Hardman's and inserted in the tracery of the chancel south window.[621]

A year later, the Cambrian Archaeological Association visited the church. As usual, the *Hereford Journal* devoted a whole page to reporting the various site visits,

LEFT: **Fig. 140** Thruxton: cup-and-cover decoration (sII).

BELOW: **Fig. 141** Thruxton: Crucifixion (sII)

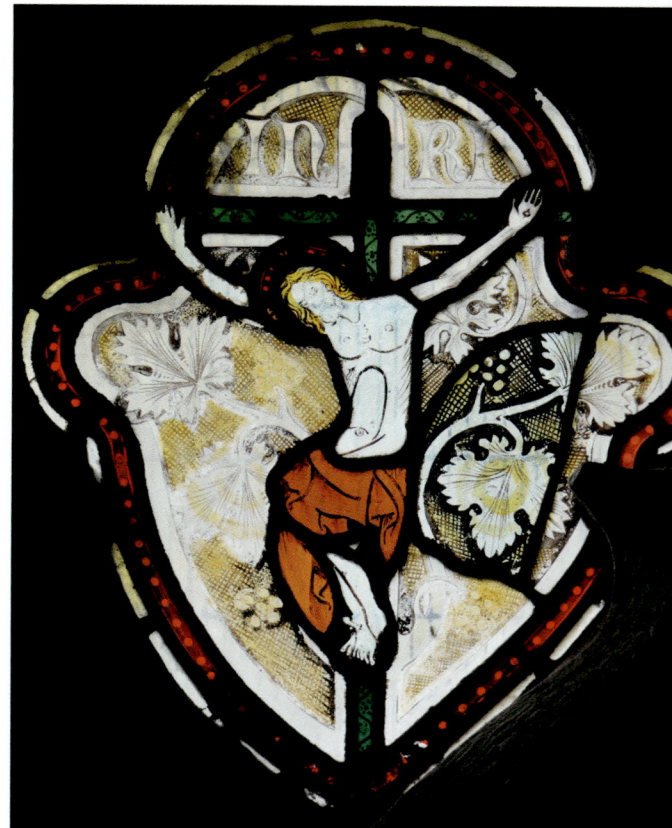

The archaeologists made a short visit to Thruxton Church, which is an exceedingly neat and small specimen of the restored perpendicular style. It is dedicated to Saint Bartholomew, and is in the gift of Merton College, Oxford. It contains an interesting stained glass window made up from some ancient specimens brought from Merton College at the time of its restoration.[622]

Much fourteenth-century glass remains at Merton College, in the chapel and, to a lesser extent, the Old Library. There is one characteristic shared with the Thruxton glass, which is the broad borders. At Merton they are mostly filled with alternating castles and fleurs-de-lis, while at Thruxton it is lions, crowns and castles (of similar colour to the Merton castles but different form).

The borders are broad and formed of crowns alternating with red quarries which have white borders with strings of black pellets. The crowns vary in detail and Hardman's workshop almost certainly drew some of them. In the bottom corners of both lights are white *lions rampant* separated by border-work with a lozenge at the mid-point of the light. At the top of the east light are covered cups. These are not found at Merton College, but match the Madley examples exactly (Fig. 140). At the top of the west light are castles.

In the tracery quatrefoil is the Crucifixion (Fig. 141). The several Crucifixes in the survey share key characteristics: the reversed S-curve of Christ's body, the Y of his arms and the green Cross. The latter is treated very differently at Thruxton in that it is combined with the vine diapering to be part of the vine itself – a reference to one of Christ's 'I am' statements.[623] This device singles Thruxton out and, perhaps, suggests a more rarefied theological client – an Oxford College? The panel appears to be substantially medieval. The dark patch of vine must be by Hardman; the lighter areas appear aged and pitted. That new piece stands out too strongly, as does the heavy, impenetrable lattice-work of the greater part of the two larger lights.

ULLINGSWICK
St Luke (SO 5965 4991, HR1 3JQ)

The EAST WINDOW is by Clayton and Bell and was installed in 1860. Alan Brooks[624] suggests that the Virgin and Child (Fig. 142) may be earlier, and the panel is included in Painton Cowan's inventory as fifteenth-century.[625]

Fig. 142 Ullingswick: Virgin and Child (I)

The window is not mentioned by Duncumb and is omitted from George Marshall's list of medieval glass.[626] It is not counted in the list of fittings in the Royal Commission inventory.[627] The panel looks quite fresh and little weathered. It is, however, a very convincing drawing in the International Style with the curlicues from the corners of the eyes, the nose with its bulbous end and the slightly oval nimbus. The heads of the Virgin and Child are one piece, and the Virgin's hair changes colour where it continues down to her collar. The Child's left hand, a piece with the heads, also seems to be drawn differently from the other hands in the panel. The eight-point quarries are also remarkably like quarries produced by the York School.

UPTON BISHOP
St John the Baptist (SO 6503 2723, HR9 7UL)

The glass is as found by the Royal Commission c.1930:

> In S. aisle – in tracery of S.E. window (sVI), foliage, etc., in situ, also a round quarry with geometrical figure and foliage, fourteenth-century; in tracery of S.W. window (sVII), foliage and borders, in situ, fourteenth-century.[628]

The glass remains in situ, with some making good with fragments from elsewhere and with crowns, or bulls' eyes from the manufacture of blown crown glass.

WALTERSTONE
St Mary (SO 34072498, HR2 0DX)

The cartouche in the CHANCEL SOUTH WINDOW (Fig. 74b) was originally one of two at the Cecil seat at Allt yr Ynys, in a room off the hall (see Hereford Museum on p. 109 for the history of the glass). The cartouches left Allt yr Ynys some time before 1872, and the one in the church was installed about that time.

The arms were formed by the time of William Cecil, 1st Baron Burghley (d.1598). His heir, Thomas, used the straightforward Barry of *ten argent and azure, six escutcheons sable, each charged with a lion rampant of the first, 3, 2, 1 seen in the 1st and 6th quarters*.[629] His second son, Robert, used the arms but with a crescent cadence mark (as befits a second son) and so it would be safe to presume the two Herefordshire cartouches are pre-1598 in date.

WELLINGTON
St Margaret (SO 4971 4821, HR4 8AZ)

In 1882, the Woolhope Club visited (in carriages) and found,

> The east window is of late construction. It is large, with three lights, containing fragments of old glass and ornamental quarries.[630]

In 1932, the Royal Commission reported:

> Glass: In chancel – in tracery of E. window, quarries with flowers, fifteenth century; in S.E. window, quarries with roses, a crown, nimbed head of an abbot holding crozier, fragment of inscription –' [ec]clesie qū . . . propi[etur]' etc., fifteenth century.

Fig. 143 Wellington: head of an abbot (sII)

The glass in the east window has been lost, but the glass in the chancel south window remains.

The glass is all from one scheme. It is executed in black line and yellow stain. There are quarries with a rose/ star motif and a stylised flower with long sepals, but the nimbed head of a tonsured (Cistercian?) abbot with a crozier in B1 (Fig. 143) stands out. The drawing is in the International Style, possibly representing one of the monastic saints with local connections – Owen or Guthlac.

WEOBLEY

S<small>T</small> P<small>ETER</small> & S<small>T</small> P<small>AUL</small> (SO 4017 5185, HR4 8SF)

The church is large and dates from the twelfth to the late fifteenth century. It is, however, the fourteenth century that stands out. The aisles were added, and a transept chapel was built on the north side. In this chapel was an altar dedicated to the Virgin. The north aisle was further extended in the later fourteenth century to form another, more spacious chantry chapel. The tracery pattern is like that found in the chapel windows at New College, Oxford of *c*.1380, which are the work of William Wynford.

Silas Taylor (*c*.1650) referred to the founding of chapels to the Virgin (east end of north aisle) and St Nicholas (east end of south aisle) and recorded one shield of Verdon on the north side. Thomas Blount (*c*.1675) also noted these arms. Neither Taylor nor Blount took much notice of devotional imagery; their interest was genealogy. Sir Stephen Glynn (prior to 1840) noted: 'In the north aisle are two rectilinear windows, one a large one of four lights containing some stained glass of rich colouring. In the north transept [see window nIII] ... some stained glass.'

N<small>ORTH AISLE MIDDLE WINDOW</small> (nV) (Fig. 144)
The window is broad with a relatively low sill, which would suggest it was intended as an altar reredos. A chantry of the Holy Rode was founded in Weobley sometime before 1400[631] and this may well be the reason for the enlargement of the north aisle and the commissioning of a window of significant quality. The stained glass angels hold Instruments of the Passion which would have appealed to the sentiments of a Holy Rode guild. Guilds dedicated to the Holy Rood or Holy Cross are relatively uncommon, but in the Midlands they are associated with wealthy and powerful townsmen.[632] All Saints in Hereford had a Rood chantry, and the well-documented guild in Birmingham, founded about the same time as the Weobley guild, played an important role in civic matters. So too, the famous guild in Stratford-upon-Avon, whose fine guild chapel can still be seen. Although the guild was less richly-endowed at its winding-up in 1547 compared to the other chantries in the church dedicated to Our Lady and St Nicholas,[633] the Weobley angel window was an expensive statement about the status of the members of the Holy Rode guild in the town, in the same

Fig. 144 Weobley: angels in the north aisle (nV)

way that the Palmers commissioned beautiful windows in Ludlow.

Rushforth referred to an altar to Archangel Michael as the reason for the window's existence, but the source of his assertion is not given. The archangel did have some significance locally, as can be seen in the sixteenth-century timber door lintel in Hereford Museum. On this, the mark of the merchant frames the scene of Michael weighing souls, while the Virgin intercedes by tipping the scales, though there is no record of a Michael altar in the church. If potential donors were being looked for among the tombs in the church, Agnes, the Lady of the Manor of Weobley, and Sir John Marbury (or Merbury) of nearby Lyonshall, can be found on the south side of the chancel. Marbury was probably living at Weobley Castle when he made his will in 1437.

The angels are the fortunate survivors from a scheme for the whole window, that has probably been the subject of iconoclasm. In the chancel of the church is a monument to John Birch, a high Puritan and a prominent military leader in the Civil War, who took Hereford in 1645. Not 15 miles away is the home of Sir Robert Harley who headed the Committee for the Demolition of Monuments of Superstition and Idolatry. What sumptuous saints or images of Christ could have survived those times and those leaders of men in Weobley?[634]

In 1692 and 1696, relatively large sums of £1 2s and £1 3s 1½d were spent by the churchwardens 'for Glasing and pointing ye church windows.'[635] In 1698, the parish book records an agreement to make annual payments of 13s 4d to Walter Sheaperd (Shepheard, Shepherd). In 1700 additional amounts were spent:

> Walter Sheaperd for glasing 13s 4d
> Paid him more for mending
>   ye chappel window 6s 6d
> For iron curbs and braces for
> ye chappel window weighing
>   86 pounds £1 8s 8d
> For Watts to fasten ye pillar
>   in ye window 1s 0d

The annual payment of 13s 4d for glazing continued, with occasional additional payments until 1729 when Shepherd was paid 8s 'by agreement'.

The arrangement, whereby a local man was paid regularly for 'maintenance' of the windows, is found in many churchwardens' accounts. At Weobley, Madley and Ross, the 'glazier' was a clerk or other prominent parishioner. They might also be paid for other work about the church such as cleaning or helping with 'mending the leads'. This may be partly explained by the encouragement to carry out regular maintenance found in the form accompanying the annual Visitation, which included a question about the condition of the glazing.

Fortunately, George Marshall photographed the window not long before the re-leading in 1928–29. He thought that the tracery had been replaced in about 1830 and the window re-leaded then.[636] In 1928–29 Messrs Kempe & Co. re-leaded the window; Messrs William Powell & Sons of Hereford were the contractors. George Rushforth, a leading authority on stained glass in his day, wrote an article for the *Kington Times*, 27 July 1929, after the dedication of the window in memory of Ella Mary Leather.

Figs 144a–144b Weobley: angels bearing symbols of the Passion (nV)

The theme of the tracery lights is angels holding Instruments of the Passion. In medieval art, the identity of different orders of angels is ambiguous,[637] but the presence of multiple eyes suggests that the intention is to portray cherubim[638] rather than seraphim.[639]

Window nV

C1 & C2: these present two substantially complete cherubim which have been renewed from the knees down.

C1 (**Fig. 144a**): this is nimbed, but much of the gold annulus, with its multiple pie-crust cusps on the inner edge and much of the hair, is new. It wears a feathered suit with a gold-edged collar. The feathered trousers stop at the ankles and bare feet are planted on flower-decked ground. It appears to have three pairs of wings, each partly made of peacock feathers with large eyes. The palm of the right hand is presented in greeting, while the left hand carries a scourge. The large, eyed feather below the scourge is modern. At the neck, with its distinctive annular folds of flesh, are an amice and a collar. The feet and flower-spangled ground in C1 were found at the head of 5c (see below).

C2: this is less complete than C1. It is similarly dressed and nimbed, and clearly drawn by the same hand. The right hand is held, palm in, across the left breast, and the left hand bears a bundle of reeds. This figure wears a tiara, with a trefoiled cross over centre-parted, curly hair.

C3 & C4 (**Fig. 144b**): Panel C3 shares some details with C1 and C2. The feathered suit, the peacock eyes on some feathers, the flower-decked ground are obvious. Much of this panel is the result of careful rearrangement, and the top and bottom parts of the ladder are new.

The figure in C4 is relatively complete and shares many details with C1 and C2. The cusping of the nimbus is treated slightly differently. This figure wears a tiara with a trefoiled cross over parted hair. In the right hand is a Crown of Thorns and in the left a spear. The right shoulder and feet have been replaced with plain glass.

E1 & E2: these panels are wholly rearranged, but the Passion symbol (hammer), upper body and head survive of E1. The upper wings are a modern introduction. E2 is even more heavily restored, with little more than the head surviving; however, the upper wings are possibly original.

Canopies to the main lights: these were a jumble of small pieces before the 1928 re-leading. The feet and flower-spangled ground in C1 were found at the head of 5c. There were fragments of canopy-work in some of the minor lights, some of which have been incorporated into the canopies above: for example, the double-gable in 5c was previously in A1.

It was suggested above that the window formed the reredos to an altar of the Holy Rode. The evidence of the founding of the chantry, and the similarity of the window tracery to that at New College, Oxford, suggest a date of *c*.1400. Rushforth thought that the four main lights might have held the four archangels. He did not know of a local example, but there is an important one only eight miles away at Kingsland; and, to the south at Eaton Bishop, two beautiful archangel figures remain. It would, however, seem more likely that a chapel of the Rode would have images of the Passion. A four-light window is not ideal for a representation of the Crucifixion because it does not allow a central position for the Cross with supporters in a symmetrical arrangement either side. It is more likely that the window was filled with square panels depicting consecutive scenes from the Passion. This narrative approach to the Passion, and other stories, can be seen in the great east window of Great Malvern Priory,[640] which is thought to be the work of John Thornton of Coventry *c*.1420. A more distant, and probably later, example which might closely resemble the approach at Weobley is found at St Kew in Cornwall.

Devotion to the *Arma Christi* is deep-rooted in Christian imagery. Locally, there is a pretty representation (probably repainted) on the shields forming a crest over a fourteenth-century tomb recess in the chancel of Eardisland church. Jenny Judova, writing about the Bohun Hours, noted,

> The Arma Christi poem first appears in Middle English before the end of the fourteenth century. It is written as meditation on the Instruments of Passion. It is loosely based on the gospel Passion narrative: the main premise of torture and crucifixion of Christ is kept; however, the poem greatly expands on it and does not take the reader through the Passion narrative; rather it concentrates on some of its instruments and introduces them to the reader but not in the same order as in the gospels.[641]

Evidence of that devotion is seen from 1387, when the 7th earl of Hereford (whose Bohun family arms appear in several Herefordshire windows), commissioned an image of the *Arma Christi* with emphasis on the wound in Christ's side. A century later, still prominent in the mind of a local bishop, a shield bearing the Instruments formed part of the decoration of the Stanbury Chapel of Hereford Cathedral (completed 1492).

Not far to the south of Weobley, at Michaelchurch Escley, there are two representations of the *Arma* from the fifteenth century. One is a surprising 'Sunday Christ'[642] wall painting and the other an armorial in the tracery light of a chancel window (Fig. 109). Always, in looking for fifteenth-century affinities we look at Great Malvern Priory, where so much survives. There are several groups of *Arma*, but all take the form of demi-angels holding shields which bear the images of the Instruments, while the Weobley angels are naturalistic and hold convincing representations of the *Arma* in hand.

All six angels have six wings, and they all wear feather tights with gold-edged collars and amices. Their tights end at wrists and ankles, mimicking the costumes worn by performers in Corpus Christi plays. Angels dressed in this way are a common sight in East Anglia, but rarer in the Welsh Marches. That is not a reflection of their popularity in medieval times but of their survival. Where substantial amounts of glass remain – for example at Great Malvern, Ludlow or Gresford – angels in feather tights are present.

There is no attempt to illustrate different orders of angels;[643] the Weobley figures are all dressed and winged in similar fashion. Two of the six wear tiaras, but these are not necessarily indicative of any particular order of angel. This suggests that the identity of the bearers was secondary to their role in displaying the *Arma Christi* – further confirmation of their association with the Holy Rode chantry.

All the heads of the angels were in place before the Kempe restoration of *c*.1928. At first sight, the drawings appear to fall into two groups of three. The angels in C3, E1 and E2 seem undersized for their bodies and show little variation in expression and hairstyle. None are crowned, but they may have been nimbed. They are also less well-made so that a good deal of drawing and shading has been lost. However, there are definite similarities in the drawing of eyes, mouths and hair to suggest that they are, if not by the same hand, by the same studio.

The similarity of tracery design with windows at New College, Oxford might suggest a connection with Thomas Glazier's Oxford workshop, but it is difficult to see any real similarity with the work there. More convincing is a comparison with the work of the workshops of John Thornton. The drawing of the eyes, noses and hair, and the quizzical looks, resonate. John Thornton's great commissions involved several craftsmen, one of whom specialised in angels and minor female figures; could this be the hand that drew the Weobley angels?

In the library of Hereford Cathedral is a collection of glass fragments, six of which come from a scheme of angels and Instruments of the Passion by the same artist as the Weobley angels. One of the pieces illustrates a hand with pieces of silver (Fig. 71a) and the others have the distinctive feathers of peacock wings. The library has no information about their provenance, but they could be from the Weobley window.

In the NORTH TRANSEPT EAST WINDOW and SOUTH AISLE SOUTH-EAST WINDOW are fragments of red glass, crosses and fleurs-de-lis worked into borders.

WESTHIDE
St Bartholomew (SO 5865 4422, HR1 3RQ)

The Royal Commission found a small panel of fragments in a chancel north window, including letters of the fourteenth or fifteenth century. This glass remains.

WORFIELD
St Peter (SO 7581 9581, WV15 5LF)

In the 1730s, Mytton saw the arms of England and another shield bearing a maunch in the east window of the north aisle, both of which have gone. In the SOUTH AISLE EAST WINDOW (sVI), he noted the inscription and Crucifixion, which remain, now much-restored. This was described not long before the restoration in 1843,[644]

> In one of its compartments are the representations of our Saviour upon the cross and several of the apostles, with an inscription underneath in the old church characters, but from some deficiency are rendered totally unintelligible. In another compartment is the representation of a King with a crown on his head, a bishop in full dress and several of the monastic clergy in full procession with books in their hands.[645]

This broadly describes the present arrangement (Fig. 145). In the centre, is Christ crucified on a green Cross flanked by the Virgin and St John. Christ's head, upper torso and right hand are original, but the heads of Mary and John are new (as is the canopy-work in this panel). The group of saints to the left (north) are all modern, but there is a good deal of old glass in the right-hand assembly, which consists of Saint Stephen holding a book and the stones of his martyrdom, an ecclesiastic and a king, another ecclesiastic, a bishop in benediction, a Cistercian monk holding a book and two laymen. Peter Newton thought that the figures were all fourteenth-century, but possibly not in their original arrangement.[646] The panels occupy less than half of the window.

Considering the whole composition, and assuming it is broadly original, this is an

Fig. 145 Worfield: east window of south aisle (sVI)

important and unusual image, and the work of a considerable talent. It takes the fourteenth-century predilection for niches with individuals or small groups (see Eaton Bishop) and creates a unified scheme across the whole window, which is richly coloured, elegantly drawn and ahead of its time. The head of the king (Fig. 146b) is clearly related to the work of the Madley Master, and the light, complex, colourful canopy-work, partly in perspective, is surely by the same hand as the Moccas canopies. The relationship with the Madley circle is further indicated by a head

Figs 146a–146b Worfield: head drawn by Charles Winston, and head of a king

GAZETTEER OF CHURCHES IN HEREFORDSHIRE AND THE DIOCESE OF HEREFORD

Fig. 147 Worfield: angel musician (sVII)

drawn by Charles Winston (Fig. 146a) which may be a lost fragment from the north aisle east window.⁶⁴⁷

In tracery lights of the NEXT WINDOW IN THE SOUTH AISLE (sVII) is an angel playing a psaltery (Fig. 147). This is a composite figure but clearly by the same hand as the king in the east window above. The SECOND WINDOW FROM THE EAST (sVIII) has a jumble of fragments in the tracery, which are mostly modern and probably from the workshop of Betton & Evans. The THIRD WINDOW FROM THE EAST (sIX) has part of the head of a woman wearing a kerchief.

WORMBRIDGE
St Peter (SO 4271 3066, HR2 9EA)

The church has a simple, early, aisleless outline but was 'violently restored' in 1858.⁶⁴⁸ The Royal Commission reported in 1931,

The church, consisting of Chancel and Nave, is of 12th-century origin but was lengthened, and the West Tower added, probably in the 13th century. The building was drastically restored in 1851–9 when all the windows were renewed and the tower practically re-built.

In 1867 Sir Stephen Glynne noted, 'In the chancel one of the north windows has some excellent coloured glass with figures well preserved.'⁶⁴⁹

This does not necessarily mean the glass in the south chancel window was not there when Glynne visited in 1867; he only noted the more eye-catching north window with its impressive Virgin and Child. In October of that year, the Cambrian Archaeological Association made a visit to the church,

> Wormbridge church was hastily visited, and only a brief glance was taken at the building, which is a plain structure. The edifice has been restored within the last 10 years by the Reverend Archer Clive, as shown by an inscription on a stained glass window in the tower. Two windows on the north and south of the chancel contain some very good specimens of stained glass.⁶⁵⁰

The local antiquaries took no note of the church, and the only record of the glass before the nineteenth-century restoration is in the churchwardens' accounts. They tell the same story as other eighteenth-century accounts, of modest sums spent year-on-year: in 1713–14, £2; in 1719, £2 and in 1722, £3.⁶⁵¹

The glass is from five or six different schemes from the early fourteenth century to the seventeenth century. None of it is in situ, and some of it may be from other buildings. The restoration was overseen by Revd Archer Clive

Fig. 148 Wormbridge: Madonna and Child (nII)

who was a well-connected local antiquary and who is famous for salvaging the columns of the old Hereford Market Hall in 1861.[652] Such magpies might find it hard to resist the glitter of glass and this ensemble has the air of a collector's collection (like Sarnesfield) rather than the random survivals from a modest parish church.

North chancel window (nII)

In 2017, thieves broke into the church through this window. They smashed and tore open the lower part of the leaded glass. Luckily, the breathtaking Madonna, possibly one of the most beautiful panels in this survey, had a narrow escape. The fifteenth-century Madonna and Child (Fig. 148) is drawn in fine black line and smear shading with silver stain for the hair, crowns and nimbi. The robes of the Virgin are in rich blue and red pot metal hemmed in silver stain. The setting, beneath an embellished, depressed arch, with fan vaulting to the niche, is highlighted in silver stain.

This is a regal, queenly Virgin, but the most striking detail is her hand, which is foreshortened and speaks of a Renaissance artist who understood the power of stance, gesture and nuance. The way her head inclines away from the child, the way she looks downwards, is enigmatic, sophisticated and wholly un-parish-church-like. The Child is naked and holds a pear, the symbol of His love for humanity.

The panel is broadly intact. The repairs to the Virgin's right side, and to the adjacent parts of the whole panel, are obvious. The drawing is faint in places and the glass much-pitted. The long-term conservation of this panel needs urgent consideration.

In the top of the west light is a depiction of the Slaughter of the Innocents in harrowing detail (Fig. 149). This appears to be of the fourteenth century, and probably not before 1330, although the mail armour with a hemispherical helmet is usually dated to the thirteenth century (see, for example, the Easter Sepulchre at Lincoln Cathedral). The large, heart-shaped pauldron decorated with a lion's head on the standing figure, is unusual. The drawing is in lively black line and smear shading on white glass, with yellow stain for details such as the crown, the spear of the standing soldier and the dressings of architectural details. The other and much earlier depiction of the subject at Ledbury (Fig. 90b) makes an interesting comparison. The Ledbury scene at first seems cumbersome, without the freedom of drawing allowed the later artist at Wormbridge, but that stillness gives a menacing quality missing from the Wormbridge picture.

Fig. 149 Wormbridge: Slaughter of the Innocents (nII)

In the jumble of fragments surrounding the two subjects is a dark-green vine diapering, and a later yellow stain vine with bunches of grapes. A border within this has Lombardic S decoration, part of which is used as the clasp for Mary's robe in the later repairs.

The upper part of the east light is filled with a jumble of fragments including dark-green vine diapering and two pieces of an elegant, light-blue leaf pattern. There are also fragments of light-brown drapery. In the top of the panel is the head of a female saint. The fluid drawing suggests she is related to the fourteenth-century work at Madley.

In the CHANCEL SOUTH WINDOW (sII) are eight fourteenth-century saints drawn in black line and silver stain against a black background (Figs 150a–150d). They are not in situ and look as if they were originally in the tracery lights of

Figs 150a–150d Wormbridge (sII):
Fig. 150a: St Peter, Fig. 150b: St Margaret,
Fig. 150c: a prophet, Fig. 150d: St Edmund

a larger window, perhaps in nearby Dore Abbey or Kilpeck Priory. Their legs, torsos and heads have been muddled, probably to make figures of similar height, resulting in a game of 'heads, bodies and legs'. In addition to these figures there are also fragments of silver stain hair and feathers.

St Peter (Fig. 150a) is readily identified by his attribute of keys. He is nimbed and carries a book in his right hand. His lower body and feet are from another figure. The latter are shod, which would be against convention for an Apostle, and seem to be walking in the wrong direction.

St Paul has been crudely repaired with a blob of putty, but his balding head, his sword and his book identify him.

St Margaret (Fig. 150b) seems to form a pair with St Paul (above) in terms of colour, drawing and weathering. She holds the cross staff which is her usual attribute and in her left hand a book.

St Edmund (Fig. 150d), an East Anglian king, is shown with the arrows which killed him. He is crowned but not nimbed. His legs have been given to the nearby male saint.

The figure is in three parts. The top is probably St Margaret with the sceptre. The lower parts depict the vestments of a high-ranking cleric. These probably belong with Thomas Becket, who has been given Edmund's legs.

Thomas is nimbed, clean-shaven and wears an apparelled amice. The top of his head is flattened.

St Catherine holds two of her common attributes, the wheel and the book. Her feet are from a lost figure – perhaps John the Baptist.

The final figure of a prophet, possibly Moses (Fig. 150c), is not nimbed and holds a scroll which trails upwards to heaven. This could be interpreted as the Commandments. He wears a *pileum cornutum* (horned cap) used to denote Jews in medieval art.

This is an important collection. It urgently needs the attention of a conservator, and possibly the installation of a protective system of glazing.

Fig. 151 The Tree of Jesse window in St Mary's, Shrewsbury

APPENDIX ONE

Gazetteer of Churches in North Shropshire[1]

The principal church in this survey of north Shropshire is St Mary's, Shrewsbury, but there is little there that engages with the other churches in this book unless they have Netherlandish or other Continental glass imported in the nineteenth century. It has an important fourteenth-century Jesse window (Fig. 151), but this will be shown to have probably come from a workshop in Cheshire, and which stands apart from the group of Jesse windows already considered in Part One. If this window were to be classified in the terms used in Part One, it is distinctly traditional. Other glass of the same period in the north of Shropshire, not included in Part Two, consists of fragments with little of substance to compare with the south.

The later fourteenth century and fifteenth century are represented in the collegiate churches of Battlefield (the glass now at Prees) and Tong and in the few pieces at Clungunford, Eyton on the Weald Moors and St Mary's, Shrewsbury. The glass of this period has, perhaps, been described too loosely here as 'the International Style' or 'the York/ Coventry Style' (associated with John Thornton) because it is by no means clear to what extent windows in this style were made by York/ Coventry craftsmen or by local workshops.[2] Battlefield and Tong were begun in the first decade of the fifteenth century, and both display characteristics of York glass, including the same eight-pointed quarries, but there are clearly several hands at work and the glazing almost certainly extended beyond the completion of the buildings.

Richard Marks delineates the evolution of the York style, comparing the formulaic drawing of later windows – with little coloured glass, line or smear shading – with Thornton's earlier, more vigorous images spread across the great east window at York Minster, which bears his name on the contract.[3] He suggests that, as the style spread across the country and was taken up by local artists, it changed, and it is possible to see that in the Tong glass. Peter Newton considered Tong to be the work of Coventry glaziers[4] who also made windows at Coventry, Wixford and Mancetter (Warwickshire), Thurcaston and Frolesworth (Leicestershire), Haddon Hall (Derbyshire) and Newark (Nottinghamshire). However, he described the difficulties in analysing the tenuous affinities between the glass in these places:

> It may be significant to point out that, despite the various affinities this glass displays, there is no remaining evidence of

identical cartoons being used in different places. There are a few examples of identical subjects, the cartoons used for them are quite different.

It has been suggested that the glass in the Midlands ... displays a number of stylistic affinities in common. The glass is perhaps too widely disposed geographically and covers too wide a period in date to suppose that a single workshop could have produced all of it. It seems reasonable to suppose, however, that the artists concerned have sufficient similarity in style and technique to suggest a common origin.[5]

Considering the body of glass from this time in the whole of this survey, and the important collections in the adjacent part of Worcestershire, the same frustrations apply. There are family resemblances in the many surviving images, but there seem to be no reused cartoons and too many quirks of drawing in too many combinations to allow proof of a common hand. Added to that are the uncertainties of date and source, and the impact of restoration which apply in many cases, so that a clear pattern cannot yet be seen.

There is no English glass of note after the mid fifteenth century and before 1700 in this part of the survey. In north Shropshire, perhaps more than elsewhere, focus shifts to the first half of the nineteenth century when conflicts of conservation and restoration are played out. The use of imported glass was seen in Part Two in several churches with roundels and, as is typical of imported glass in this survey, not one of the 65 recorded in Part Two has any provenance. In this part of the survey, there are two churches with significant amounts of imported glass. St Mary's Church in Shrewsbury is extensively glazed with imported glass that has little affinity with English traditions, and that is its great interest. Not only is it foreign in style, but the content, and especially the selection of saints that stand with the donors, is fascinating. Uffington has an important collection of Netherlandish and Swiss roundels, possession of which seems to have dictated the design of the church building. Again, the source of much of this glass is unknown.

The trade in imported glass is discussed in Part One (p. 22) and under the entries for St Mary's, Shrewsbury and Uffington. The roles of the collectors and dealers is becoming clearer, but discussion of the nineteenth-century trade is disjointed here and deserves a volume of its own, building on the research of P.L. Martin.[6] It is noted in the description of the Uffington roundels that Philip Corbet, local artist and associate of the glazier David Evans, advertised for sale '100 circular and square subjects, exquisitely finished.' It is perhaps too tidy a coincidence that 99 such subjects can be found in Shropshire.[7]

As with Part Two it was not possible to see domestic glass, but all the known church glass was seen with the help of local people. The help of staff of the Shrewsbury Museum and the Shropshire Archives reading room was also important.

ASHFORD CARBONELL
St Mary (SO 5251 7100, SY8 4BX)

In the quatrefoil of a SOUTH WINDOW (sV), a few strands of grisaille foliage have been arranged around a rosette.

BADGER
St Giles (SO 7682 9962, WV6 7JR)

William Mytton (d.1746) recorded three shields. In the east window *a fesse vair three eagles displayed* (Kinnersley of Badger).[8] In the WEST WINDOW OF THE NORTH WALL OF THE NAVE, he found the Five Wounds of Christ (Fig. 152b) and *argent a chevron gules between three hunting horns* (Focton, Wayt or Wayle).

The church was rebuilt in 1833–34. Alterations in 1886 included the insertion of an ogee arch in the tracery of the central light of the EAST WINDOW. The principal lights hold glass by David Evans, but the upper quatrefoil of the tracery has the shield with the Five Wounds recorded by Mytton in the old church (Fig. 152a). This is probably glass of the later fifteenth century. In the three lower lights are Netherlandish roundels, almost certainly supplied by David Evans. Cranage noted that the glass in the east window was brought from Belgium early in the nineteenth century.[9] William Cole recorded the roundels and the following dates are his:[10]

Fig. 152a Badger: The Five Wounds, fifteenth century

Fig. 152b Badger: The Five Wounds by William Mytton

Fig. 153a Badger: St John the Baptist, seventeenth century

Fig. 153b Badger: St Margaret c.1500

East window (I)
I.A1: St John the Baptist holding a lamb amidst trees and animals, seventeenth century. (**Fig. 153a**)

I.A2: Sorghelosse playing dice. Scenes from the life of Sorghelosse can also be found at, for example, Llanwarne. Cole suggests that this image is based on images found in the Kunstmuseum at Basle, and also in woodcuts published by Jan Ewoutz at Amsterdam in 1541.

> **I.A3**: St Margaret with a dragon. A rather faint and weathered roundel of c.1500. There is a scratched date in the border, 1834, and a scratched inscription, 'this window was made up from stained glass and presented by B…ngton Esq. 1834 Wm. The iiii / 4th reigning'.[11] (**Fig. 153b**)

The Boddingtons funded the rebuilding of the church, and Thomas Boddington became rector of the parish in 1838.

BATTLEFIELD
St Mary Magdalene (SJ 5126 1725, SY4 3DB)[12]

The body of the church was built between 1406 and 1409 for a college of priests dedicated to the celebration of masses for the souls of the multitude of men killed at the Battle of Shrewsbury in 1403.[13] It was a project supported by Henry IV, the victor.

A record of glass was made by Dugdale in 1662–63.[14] In the middle of the east window (I) Dugdale found part of a portrait of Henry IV (from the neck to the knees) in armour, with his coat of arms on the surcoat. He was holding a poleaxe in his left hand, but his head and legs were broken off.

> **Dugdale recorded that the south side of the nave displayed:**
>
> **sII**: a kneeling figure in armour with a surcoat of the arms of Strange and Mohun quarterly. Also, the arms of Richard Lord Strange of Knokyn (d.1448–9), together with his first wife.
>
> **sIII**: the arms of Arundel and Maltravers impaling Montacute and Monthermer. These are the arms of William Fitzalan, 11th earl of Arundel (d.1487), and his wife Joan Neville, daughter of Richard earl of Salisbury. At the bottom of the window was the Fitzalan badge with a white horse in front of an oak tree. In the centre of the window was the picture of St George and the Dragon. This is no surprise in a chapel associated with Henry IV, for in his reign the saint was 'employed officially, including during the Garter festivities and as the name of four royal ships. He was pictured on a new seal cut in 1408 and was even one of six saints depicted on windows in the King's study in his palace at Eltham.'[15]
>
> **sIV**: the Instruments of the Passion, and a bishop with his crozier.
>
> **sV**: the arms of Hussey.
>
> **sVI**: the kneeling figure of Roger Yve, the founder and first master, in white, above the image of his mother.
>
> **sVII**: St Nicholas and St Chad, also of a kneeling man in a red robe with an orate inscription.

The north side of the nave displayed (from the west):

nX: the beheading of St John the Baptist. Fletcher thought this may have been brought from the church of Albright Hussey, dedicated to that saint, which was replaced by Battlefield Church.

nIX: a shield of the Sandford arms, and the kneeling figure of Richard Sandford in armour. Richard Hussey also kneeling in armour with a surcoat and, in the right panel, a shield of the Englefield arms, and the kneeling figure of Robert Englefield (Fig. 154).[16]

nVIII: a shield red and white.

nVII: St Winifred, and a shield of arms. The relics of the Welsh Saint Winifred (Gwenfrewi) were enshrined in the abbey church of Shrewsbury.

nVI: further unidentified arms.

When the church was restored and classicized in 1749 the medieval glass was gathered in the east window, but much was destroyed. A further radical reordering of the church was undertaken between 1860 and 1862. Fletcher suggests that the glass was removed, but on 15 February 1862 the *Illustrated London News* reported on the reopening of the church after the restoration, and noted that '... the great east window remains untouched for the present.' Fletcher's date is therefore in doubt, but it is certain that sometime after 1862 fragments from several windows were taken to the Sandford Chapel in Prees Church (see below, p. 221) where they fill a three-light window.

WEST WINDOW OF THE VESTRY (nIV)
During the Victorian restoration,[17] a chapel was built on the north side of the chancel to house memorials to the Corbet family. This has become the vestry where medieval glass can be seen today. Fletcher says that 'the glass in the vestry is old and was brought from France in 1861; it had no connection originally with Battlefield Church.'[18] This is not true: some, if not all, of the glass is English.

The tracery holds a random collection of brightly-coloured ancient and modern glass with a modern representation of the Crown of Thorns in the quatrefoil. In the main lights there is a good deal of fifteenth-century canopy-work and deep-blue seaweed background. The main panels have three composite figures, the heads of which are shown in Figs 155a–155g. The head in the left panel (Fig. 155a) is imported, but not from France. It is the head of St Laurence and has travelled only 33 miles from Ludlow, where it was in the east window, and seen by Mytton in the eighteenth century (Fig. 155b) until replaced by David Evans with the copy shown in Fig. 155c.

Fig. 154 Battlefield: Sketch of glass formerly in a north window (by permission of Shropshire Archives)

 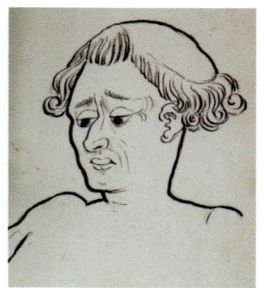 

Fig. 155c Ludlow, St Laurence, east window as existing. The probable source of the Battlefield head

ABOVE LEFT **Fig. 155a** Battlefield: detached head in vestry. ABOVE **Fig. 155b** Mytton's drawing of St Laurence seen in Ludlow. LEFT **Fig. 155d** St Laurence being stoned, formerly in library of Sundorne Castle

Fig. 155e St Laurence being stoned, Ludlow, St Laurence, east window

Fig. 155f Battlefield: Head of a king in vestry

Fig. 155g Battlefield: Unidentified head in vestry

One of the local men involved in the trade in old glass was Philip Corbet (see Uffington, p. 245). The Corbet seat, Sundorne Castle (now mostly demolished), is about one mile from Battlefield.[19] The library had a 'recess, twelve feet square, in the mullioned window of which (was) some very fine, ancient, stained glass',[20] and there were fragments of medieval glass in five other windows in the house in 1903.[21] Images of two windows survive and the hand of David Evans is clear in the multitude of workshop fragments.[22] In one window is the figure of a saint with stones on his head (Fig. 155d) which probably also came from Ludlow. The present stoning scene in the east window at Ludlow is different, except the saint is naked (Fig. 155e). However, the Sundorne figure is certainly of York type, with the tonsure used to distinguish Laurence across the whole east window at Ludlow.[23]

David Evans died in 1860, but the heads must have come from his studio's stock, which suggests that the Battlefield windows, and possibly those at Sundorne, are the work of his sons. They share characteristics of the York/ Coventry workshops with the glass now at Prees and the female figure in the adjacent window; however, the middle and right panels (Figs 155f & 155g) are strikingly different. The Old Testament king in the centre is in the International Style, but the drawing is emphatic, almost crude, and lacks the refinement of the York work. So too the other face, which is shown in profile, the face exaggerated and cartoon-like. These heads are almost certainly imported and probably from Germany rather than France. They may well have come from the Evans workshop stock – as did St Laurence's heads and, possibly, the drapery of the figures, characterized by jewel bosses, could have come from Ludlow.

Fig. 156 Battlefield: female figure in the vestry north window

NORTH WINDOW OF THE VESTRY (nIII)

The single female figure is in the mid fifteenth-century style of York/ Coventry (Fig. 156). She is one of the most strikingly female figures in this survey and probably represents, with her demure expression and rayed nimbus, the Virgin of the Annunciation. Her bejewelled drapery is strongly akin to work at Ludlow, notably in the Palmers' Chapel and the chancel.

BECKBURY

St Milburga (SJ 7651 0156, TF11 9DQ)

There are two panels of fragments of medieval glass in the south aisle (sV). This aisle was built between 1854 and 1856 so the glass is not in situ. Philip Nelson recorded the glass in 1913 as being in the east window,[24] but that is unlikely since the present east window by Burlison and Grylls was

Fig. 157 Beckbury: fourteenth-century glass in the south aisle

GAZETTEER OF CHURCHES IN NORTH SHROPSHIRE   215

installed in 1884.[25] Nelson was probably working on out-of-date information and the glass could have been in the east window before 1884.

SOUTH AISLE, SOUTH-EAST WINDOW (sV) (Fig. 157) Some of the glass is of the first half of the fourteenth century, with several depictions of windows with geometrical tracery, pinnacles from canopy-work and dark green vine-leaf foliage. A particularly strong motif comprises fragments of yellow vine wound around a white stem with a wave and dot decoration, which looks as if it could have been part of a later fourteenth-century Jesse window. The borders of the panels have oak leaves and acorns springing from a continuous stem which is modern but follows a strong tradition in Shropshire (see Munslow, for example) that was adopted by David Evans in several restoration projects. This window does not bear his hallmarks of vivid colours and flashy drawing and was probably the work of Burlison and Grylls when they replaced the east window.

CLUNGUNFORD
St Cuthbert (SO 3948 7874, SY7 0PS)

The CHANCEL EAST WINDOW is Hardman's work of 1885. In two of the tracery lights (A1 and A3) are fifteenth-century heads of angels (Figs 158a & 158b). A1 is a vigorous drawing with an interesting pose and an expressive face and not by the same hand or of the same date as the angel in A3. In A3 the angel has a still serenity, pale and unshaded, and bears a strong resemblance to the Weobley angels (Figs 144a & 144b).

Fig. 158a
Clungunford: fifteenth-century head in the York style in the east window (I.A2)

Fig. 158b
Clungunford: fifteenth-century head in the York style in the east window (I.A3)

DUDLESTON
St Mary the Virgin (SJ 3460 3843, SY12 9EF)

In the WINDOW BETWEEN THE NAVE AND THE TOWER, there is a collection of subjects set in modern bronzed-coloured glass (Fig. 159). In December 1877 the church re-opened after the first restoration,[26] which included rebuilding the chancel and glazing the windows with 'tinted cathedral glass by William Done', but there was still a west gallery in the nave, and the tower window must have been glazed later.[27] In 1887 the visiting archdeacon was able to praise the completion of the work.[28]

In windows nIII, sIII, sV and sVI there are shields of arms, some of which are clearly modern. Cranage says that the 'good deal of' heraldic glass dates from 1819,[29] but Done must have reset it and restored and added to it in the 1877 restoration. William Done was a pupil of David Evans and executed numerous commissions with his partner John Davies, until they separated in 1873. He occupied Evans' Wyle Cop studio, and it is almost certain that the NAVE WEST WINDOW (Fig. 159) is his work and contains glass from that studio's stock.

> **Nave west window (wI)**
> **1a**: the letter 'G' in a star-burst. This is an unusual subject in churches. The 'G' being significant in masonic symbolism.
> **1b**: hexagram.
> **2a**: Christ consecrating wine and bread, His eyes turned up to Heaven, drawn in matt and silver stain (probably seventeenth-century).
> **2b**: the Crucifixion, of dark and macabre character with a cockerel.
> **3a**: a star-burst with a crowned lion above.
> **3b**: the sacred monogram IHS (*Jesu Hominum Salvator*) and a sinister black-clad figure holding a chalice.

Fig. 159 Dudleston: west window of the nave

The several subjects in the window are unrelated in execution and in subject. They appear to be of Continental origin from the sixteenth century and later, and are possibly from houses as well as churches:

EDGMOND
St Peter (SJ 7202 1929, TF10 8JY)

Edgmond is a surprise with its fine Perpendicular south aisle. The chancel is distinctly fourteenth-century, and Eyton noted four fourteenth-century shields in the windows: of Mortimer (with inescutcheon), Warren, Verdon and Fitzalan.[30] Mytton recorded further shields in the nave, that may have been lost by Eyton's time.

The only old glass now is in the NAVE NORTH-WEST WINDOW (nVI) composed of eighteenth-century arms and five faces from the fifteenth century (Figs 160a–160e, overleaf).[31] All the medieval arms have gone. At the top of the window is a female face with an enigmatic expression drawn in black line and silver stain. Below are an angel, two praying donors and a composite monk in white habit with two faces.

Figs 160a–160e Edgmond: small fifteenth-century roundels in the north aisle (nVI)

Fig. 160a

Fig. 160b

Fig. 160c

Fig. 160d

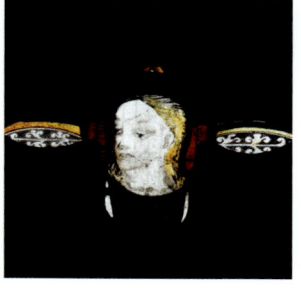

Fig. 160e

EDSTASTON

St Mary the Virgin (SJ5177 3197, SY4 5RF)

William Mytton recorded the arms of Mainwaring, *argent two bars gules,* in a south window. Now in the tracery of the SOUTH-WEST WINDOW OF THE NAVE (sV) are fragments of fifteenth-century glass drawn in matt and silver stain. There are pieces of canopy-work and the upper part of a representation of God holding an orb (Fig. 161). He is nimbed and wears rich vestments decorated with jewelled bosses. He resembles, in style, the angels at Claverley and Alveley.

Fig. 161 Edstaston: God the Father, late fifteenth century

Fig. 162 Eyton on the Weald Moors: St Catherine

Fig. 163 Eyton on the Weald Moors: St Christopher

EYTON ON THE WEALD MOORS
St Catherine (SJ 6509 1484, TF6 6ET)

The church is dated 1743. Mytton's (d.1746) record probably relates to the small medieval building it replaced because he only illustrates three shields, all of the Eyton family. The present nave windows have shields. Some were probably installed when the new church was built, although two correspond with Mytton's drawings, and the extravagant strapwork surrounds look older than the eighteenth-century date given by most authorities.

In the MIDDLE NORTH NAVE WINDOW are three very pleasing medieval subjects which appear to be by the same hand. They are drawn in black line with smear and hatched shading and silver stain hair and highlights. St Catherine is shown with her book, palm and wheel (Fig. 162). She wears the clinging kirtle and a surcoat with the sides cut away to display her hip belt. This was in fashion from the mid fourteenth century until about 1425.[32] Above her is a black letter inscription 'Je m'y oblige'. This was a motto of the Eytons and is said to have been first voiced by Catherine de Eyton who pledged to establish a church if her husband survived the Holy Land.

These figures might be classified as being in the International Style, but they don't bear the hallmarks of the York School.

Beside Catherine is St Christopher (Fig. 163). A quite restless picture with the saint bearing on his gnarled staff and looking up at the infant on his shoulder. The child carries an orb with a tall cross in his left hand while his right hand is raised in blessing.

Above is a representation of a grindstone in a covered trough with a turning handle.

These figures do not relate to any other glass in this survey and are probably imported. Had they been in the former church, Mytton would probably have noted them, given his interest in medieval imagery. David Evans installed a St Catherine in the east window in 1856 and might have supplied these panels.

HOPTON WAFERS
St Michael and All Angels
(SO 6373 7655, DY14 0NA)

In the eighteenth century, William Mytton drew the upper part of an angel brandishing a sword in a south window of the body of the church. This survives in a panel in an INTERNAL LIGHT between the nave and the tower (Fig. 164) but has been roughly treated and restored in the past, and is seen reversed when viewed from the nave. It is drawn in black paint and silver stain, and dates from the fifteenth century.

Fig. 164 Hopton Wafers: a fifteenth-century angel in the window between the tower and nave

LITTLE NESS
St Martin (SJ 4075 1989, SY4 2LG)

In the EAST WINDOW OF THE VESTRY (Fig. 165) on the north side of the chancel (nII) is a beautiful image of a bearded head, probably of Christ, from c.1400. It is not in situ; the vestry is part of the sumptuous restoration funded by the Darby family of Coalbrookdale fame, but it belongs to the church. In the eighteenth century, William Mytton sketched two figures, one of which resembles the head. He did not label them, but there were only three windows at that time, on the south side and at the east end of the chancel-less nave.[33] Cranage found the panel in the north window[34] and it must have been moved when the present glass was installed as a memorial to Maurice Darby who died in France in 1915.

Fig. 165 Little Ness: the face of Christ(?), fifteenth century

The head is an exceptionally moving image executed in matt and silver stain with smear shading scratched away to make highlights. It is quite badly weathered with a good deal of the line drawing eroded. It presents a three-quarter view of a pensive, downcast face.

MORETON CORBET
St Bartholomew (SJ 5611 2324, SY4 4DW)

There are two collections of fragments in the TOWER WEST WINDOW and the ENTRANCE SCREEN. These appear to be waste from the Evans workshop and entirely modern. Evans worked here in 1849 providing sacred emblems in the west window of the south aisle.[35]

PREES
St Chad (SJ 5569 3346, SY13 2EE)

In the NORTH AISLE NORTH-EAST WINDOW (nIII) (Figs 166 & 166a) is a collection of glass taken from Battlefield Church (see p. 212) which was built between 1406 and 1409. Most of the smaller heads bear the characteristics of the York School, and there are many of the eight-pointed quarries related to that workshop, which are also found at Tong.

Fig. 166a Prees: the kneeling figure from the central panel of the north-east window of the north aisle (nIII)

GAZETTEER OF CHURCHES IN NORTH SHROPSHIRE   221

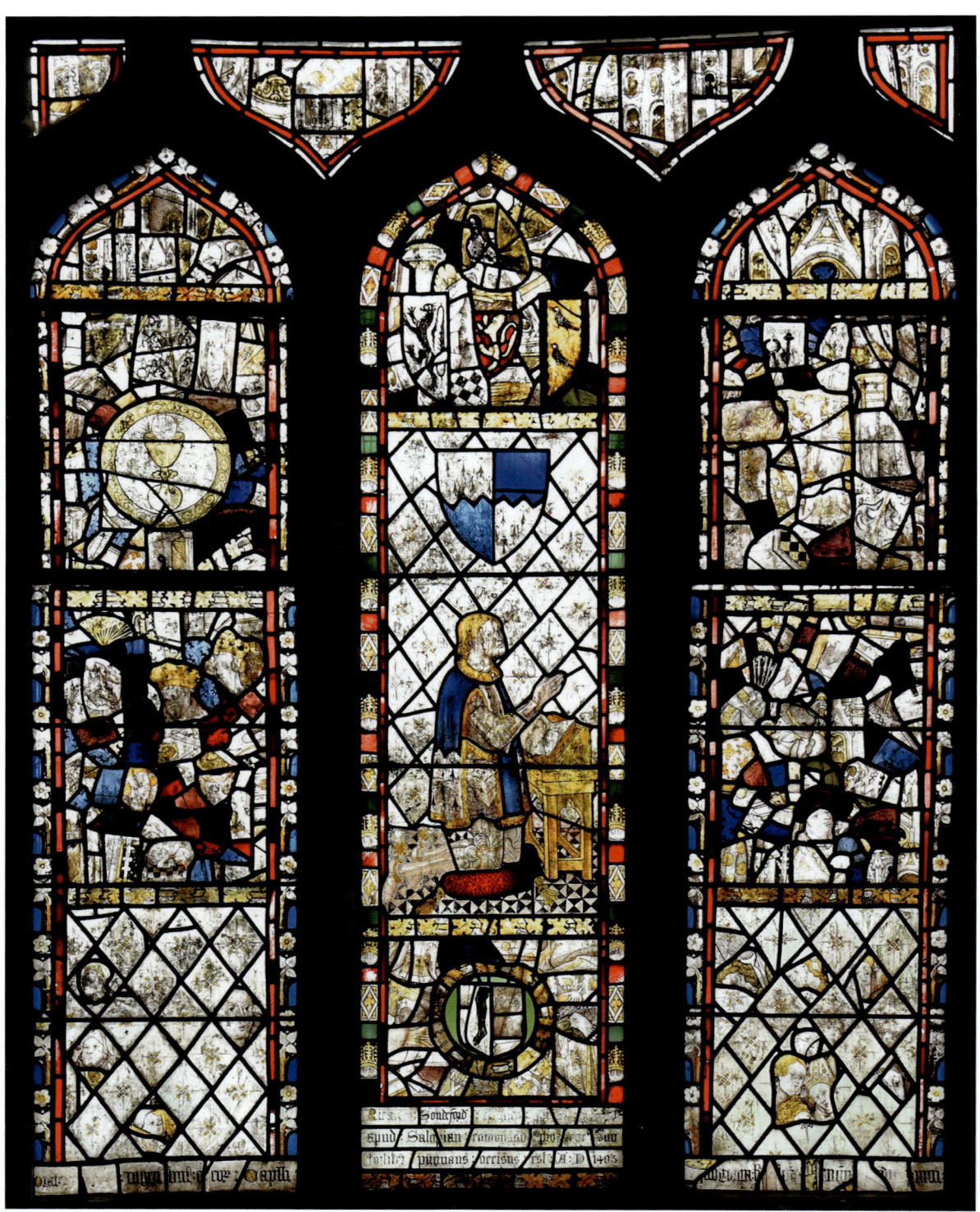

Fig. 166 Prees: north-east window of the north aisle (nIII), with glass removed from Battlefield Church

Figs 167a–167c Prees: details from the north aisle north-east window (nIII). **Fig. 167a** (TOP) panel 2a: heads of John the Baptist (on a plate), Herod and Herodias. **Fig. 167b** (ABOVE) panel 2c: a man leads a woman in a scold's bridal. **Fig. 167c** (RIGHT) panel 3c: the Throne of Mercy and Instruments of the Passion

Window nIII

1a: side borders with vine of white apple leaves and flowers on a sepia stem. Upper border: a stem with oak leaves familiar throughout Shropshire; lower border: a jumbled 'orate' black letter inscription. Numerous quarries of eight-pointed type typical of York School (among which are three heads, one bearded and wearing a liripipe hood, with left hand raised and right hand holding a scroll).

1b: side borders formed of crowns and lozenges. At the centre, the arms of Hussey (centre **Fig. 154**). Fragments of vestments, a feathered angel's foot, and a bare foot.

1c: borders and quarries as panel 1a, and six fragments of people. Clockwise from upper left: a head of an angel with spear and sponge, probably from window sV at Battlefield, where Dugdale found: Instruments of the Passion; a nimbed female; a bearded king; part of the face of a woman wearing a kerchief, all executed in matt. Also four faces from two different places. The larger piece includes a mitred bishop.

2a: the panel includes much red and blue glass from drapery and seaweed backgrounds. Near the top of the panel are pieces previously recorded at Battlefield nVII which depicted the beheading of John the Baptist. His head on the plate is at top left and beside him King Herod and the crowned Queen Herodias (**Fig. 167a**). There are several courtiers beside and below with their hair in netted side buns. At the bottom, a dog with a bone lies asleep on a chequerboard floor.

2b: borders as 1b. Richard Sandford (1342–1403) kneeling in prayer against a field of eight-pointed quarries. The late eighteenth-century drawing (**Fig. 154**) identifies him, but he has lost his 'orate' inscription. His shield, much restored, is at the top of the panel. The figure itself is also heavily restored, including the head which is distinctly unlike York work of the time. A list of the medieval fragments at Battlefield, prior to their removal, includes, 'among other designs two crowned heads, a human head in a dish, a chalice and wafer, the Crucifixion, some escutcheons of arms and an inscription – Orate pro animabus Rogeri … hujusce capellini.'[36] There is no mention of the figure of Sandford, which surely could not have been accidentally omitted, which suggests that this figure is probably entirely the work of the Evans brothers.

2c: borders as 1c. Fragments of canopy-work. In the top left, four studies of hands holding, inter alia, staves and a pommel. In the centre is an unusual subject in which a bearded figure with a brimmed hat leads a woman in a scold's bridle (**Fig. 167b**). Below is another face shown three-quarters.

3a: at the centre, a chalice and host in matt and silver stain, all surrounded by architectural fragments.

3b: borders as 2b. Fragments of arms including the crows of Englefield and the rampant lion of Arundel or Fitzalan from sIV at Battlefield.

3c: at the centre, the Seat of Mercy, with God holding the Crucified Christ (**Fig. 167c**). Around this are several Instruments of the Passion, including the shirt and dice, pincers and a nail, and a ladder.

A1–A4: various architectural fragments.

SHAWBURY
St Mary (sj 5592 2118, sy4 4nh)

Mytton only recorded an inscription here, but the glass in the CHANCEL SOUTH-WEST WINDOW (sIII) (Fig. 168) was in its present location in 1882 and was recorded by Cranage (c.1900). Nelson (1913) suggests that the glass was originally in the east window. The glass is characterised by its sparing use of colour and stain. The drawing is vigorous and strongly shaded. There are two figures: in the right panel probably the Virgin of the Annunciation, and in the left panel, a head of a male cleric with a hand raised in a gesture of blessing. The style of this glass suggests the later fifteenth century, but it is unlike any other glass in this survey.

Fig. 168 Shawbury: panel from window sIII, with fragmentary figure, possibly the Virgin of the Annunciation

SHERIFFHALES
St Mary (sj 7580 1201, tf11 8qy)

Peter Newton looked at the glass in this church[37] and identified two medieval coats of arms incorporated into modern glazing. In the tracery of the SOUTH NAVE MIDDLE WINDOW (sV) is a shield: *Argent fretty gules, on each joint a bezant or reserved* on a black enamel ground. These are the arms of the Trussells, who held the manor and living from the thirteenth to the fifteenth century.

Fig. 169 Sheriffhales: fragments in a south chancel window

This shield is probably from late in their tenure. In the SOUTH NAVE EAST WINDOW (sIV): *Argent fretty gules, on each joint a bezant or a bordure azure* (Trussell) impaling *Argent a lion rampant sable over a fess chequy or and azure* (Burley). This shield has been reversed. In the CHANCEL SOUTH WINDOWS are two square panels of fourteenth-century fragments (Fig. 169).

SHREWSBURY MUSEUM
The Square (sy1 1lh)

The museum collection holds six late fifteenth-century roundels from a house in Lower Pulley which was demolished in 1964, some of which are on display.[38] J.B. Blakeway (d.1826) sketched eight roundels, but not the 'August' roundel now in the Museum.[39] For many years, the roundels were in the porch of Rowley's House Museum in Shrewsbury, which is where the late Kerry Ayre recorded them in her survey of English roundels.[40]

Three Labours of the Months – June, August and September (Figs 170a–170c) – present substantially complete pictures. They have black enamel surrounds and yellow stain backgrounds on which the scenes are drawn in black paint. All of the panels share a similar border formed by two lines but there is little shading, and it is mostly hatched. Compared to the 'February' in the Burrell Collection, which is dated to 1450–60,[41] or the 'September' in the Victoria and Albert Museum, of 1480,[42] these roundels are quite crudely drawn, and it is tempting to think of them as earlier in date. The details of faces and the drawing technique suggest that the three roundels are not by the same hand. A fourth pictorial roundel, April, is very badly eroded and little of the subject can be distinguished.[43]

One of the other two roundels is a fragment of illegible black letter inscription which has doubtfully been construed as 'Lady'.[44] The other is a shield with a riband in the place of a fess.

Figs 170a–170c Shrewsbury Museum: roundels from Pulley Farmhouse, Meole Brace, depicting three Labours of the Months.
170a (TOP LEFT): June
170b (TOP RIGHT): September
170c (LEFT): August

SHREWSBURY

ST MARY (SJ 4934 1261, SY1 1DX)

This large and important church at the centre of a thriving town attracted the attention of iconoclasts, leaving little for later antiquaries, notably Dugdale, to record. The parishioners resisted in the case of a north window depicting the Assumption of the Virgin, and a complaint was lodged against the churchwardens for not removing it in 1595.[45] The effectiveness of those purges can be gauged by William Mytton's meagre haul of heraldry in the eighteenth century, and the records of the period immediately before the nineteenth-century interventions, which note the absence of any pictorial glass. Subsequently, the existing *collection* of glass (for it is that) was installed and is now among the most important in Britain. It also has significance in the European context because most of it was imported from Continental churches.

CHANCEL EAST WINDOW (I)

This was seen by William Mytton in the eighteenth century. He recorded two shields in the east window, neither of which remain in the church.[46] They were removed to accommodate the principal panels of English glass in the collection, a relatively large representation of the Tree of Jesse (Fig. 151), which was made for the Grey Friars church, moved to St Chads, possibly at the Dissolution, and moved again to its present location in 1792, when John Betton installed it.[47] The original inscription, in French, recorded its making for Sir John Charleton and sought prayers for himself and his wife Hawise. They were originally shown as donor figures along with their sons who were represented as knights. It is known that Sir John and Hawise were married in 1309 so their sons would have reached the age of

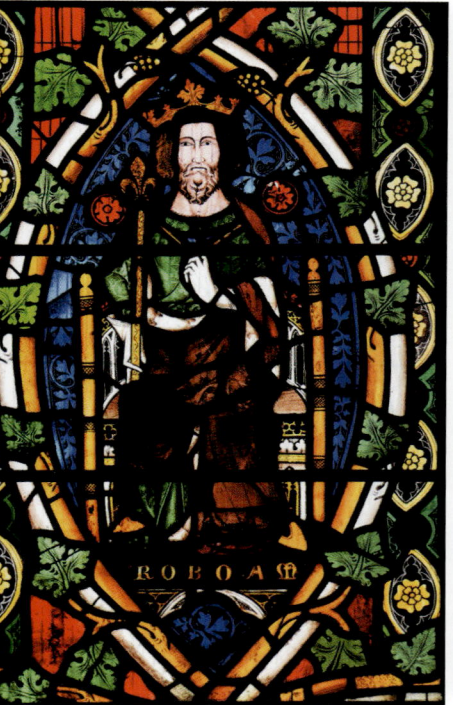  

Figs 171a–171c Shrewsbury St Mary: kings from the Jesse window (FROM LEFT TO RIGHT): Roboam, Ozias and Asa

knighthood around 1332, which can be assumed as the earliest date for the window. Sir John died in 1353, which can be taken as the latest date.[48] The window was restored, and the original scheme enlarged by David and Charles Evans in 1837.[49]

The window has seen two reconstructions and restoration and enlargement in the Evans fashion, a story that is reflected in the large amount of modern glass. The panels in the rectangle between 3b–f and 6b–f still contain a significant amount of medieval glass,[50] but even in that part, most of the vine scroll and many parts of the figures are modern. The glass in the tracery and the lowest two rows of panels, including the convincing mailed knight, is also modern.

This Jesse window shares characteristics with those at Madley and Ludlow in the way the vine makes the frames for the figures. The kings are at the centre, forming the lineage, sitting in frames formed by the stems, while the Prophets stand at the edges entangled in the vine. The Lombardic lettering is also a common feature. However, unlike the other examples in this survey, the Shrewsbury vine stems are not decorated with trefoils and there are no birds or animals set among the foliage, as at Ludlow. The faces of the Shrewsbury figures are characterized by glum mouths down-turned at the corners, and there is little of the verve seen in the painting and coloration of Madley and Ludlow. Only a few cartoons were used, and the overall picture is somewhat workaday.[51] There does not seem to be a strong affinity with the other Jesse windows in this survey, but there is a possible link with a workshop identified in Cheshire, possibly based in Chester, the principal surviving work of which is at Grappenhall.[52] In both places it is difficult to unpick modern interventions.

However, the colouration, shading and general character of figures and their faces are similar. More convincing is the way that both have similar hawthorn rinceau[53] and the drawing of eyes with a horizontal lower lid can be seen in several figures in both places (Figs 172a & 172b).

172a & 172b comparison of faces and rinceau at Grappenhall, Cheshire (ABOVE) and Shrewsbury St Mary (LEFT)

The Imported Glass

The circle of clergy in Shrewsbury in the early decades of the nineteenth century included the eminent antiquaries John Blakeway (1765–1826) and Hugh Owen (1761–1827). Owen was a collector of medieval glass, an enthusiasm well illustrated in the remarkable photograph of his summerhouse at 6 Swan Hill (Fig. 173, now demolished),[54] which was glazed with panels containing English medieval figures, borders and canopy-work. Their younger colleague William Rowland (1770–1851) also became an avid collector.

Fig. 173 The Revd Hugh Owen's summerhouse, now demolished (with the permission of Shropshire Archives)

They were successive vicars of St Mary's Church and must have seen in the Jesse window (a work of salvage) the possibilities of, and attractions of, using second-hand panels. Rowland was involved in moving the Jesse window to St Mary's while assistant curate at the Abbey Church[55] and in 1803 Rowland oversaw the installation of glass from Herkenrode Abbey (Limburg, Belgium)[56] in the Lady Chapel at Lichfield Cathedral.[57] He was rewarded with a gift of some of the Herkenrode panels[58] (see below), but perhaps his greater rewards were in establishing contacts with the trade in Continental glass and cementing a working relationship with the Shrewsbury glaziers Betton and, later, Evans, that was to continue throughout all his work at St Mary's. When appointed vicar of St Mary's in 1828 the Jesse was the only significant painted window; the church was a blank canvas for Rowland to paint.

Chancel north window (nII)

Sometime between 1822 and 1837, three medieval figures from Winchester College, by Thomas Oxford, were installed in this window by David

Evans. They were left over from his brutal remaking of the Winchester windows. Between 1837 and 1851, Evans sold this medieval glass to the Victoria and Albert Museum,[59] and it was replaced by the present German glass which tells the story of St Bernard of Clairvaux.[60]

The Bernard panels were made for the cloisters of Altenburg in the early sixteenth century.[61] The scenes are not placed in chronological order, and Evans cropped some of the panels to fit them into the window. Each scene is described by inscriptions and speech ribbons (Figs 174a & 174b).

Figs 174a–174b Shrewsbury St Mary: chancel north window. **Fig. 174a** Bernard's vision of angels checking on the brothers' devotions (1b) (TOP) **Fig. 174b** Bernard appeals for the release of a thief so he can serve the brothers (1c) (BELOW)

Window nII

1a: St Bernard and his brothers being sent out to Clairvaux by Abbot Stephen. Clairvaux is in the background under construction.
1b: Bernard saw angels during the night office, writing in black, silver or gold according to the devotion of the monks.
1c: Bernard saves a robber from execution by convincing the Count that he will deal with him so that he will have a lingering death. He makes a monk of the reprieved man.
2a: a religious, having been restored to health, seeks to join the order, but Bernard sends him away.
2b: Bernard restores the sight of blind men by making the sign of the Cross on them, and cures a lame man and a deaf woman.
2c: Bernard asks forgiveness of Abbot Stephen for failing to say the seven penitential Psalms.
3a: Bernard writing to Pope Eugenis III urging him to abolish simony.
3b: Bernard negotiating for the reinstatement of the bishop of Poitiers. The dean conspired against the bishop and Bernard, and was eventually consumed by the devils lurking in the background.
3c: Bernard heals a paralysed woman while entering Metz.
4a: Bernard entering Cistercian Order, 1113.
4b: Bernard challenges a peasant to recite the Lord's Prayer and promised him his mule if he can. The peasant recites, 'Our Father – that mule will soon be mine – who art in the heaven'.
4c: Bernard prays that he can keep up with his brothers in work.

5b: Bernard's married sister went to visit him at the Abbey but he turned her away because she was, in his view, a conduit for sin. She subsequently left her husband and joined a convent.

6b: Bernard was sent to persuade Henry I of England to accept Innocent II who had been constitutionally elected as Pope.

There are four more panels from this series in the south aisle (sVIII).

Pidgeon noted that, 'this glass was brought from the vaults of the Church of Saint Severin at Cologne, where it was hid, having been preserved from the desecration of the great (Cistercian) Abbey of Altenburg'.[62] Altenburg Abbey was suppressed in 1803 and its glass was removed and stored until it was auctioned in 1824. In 1828 it was acquired by an English dealer, Edward Spenser Curling, and taken to London. After many attempts at selling the glass, it was eventually acquired by Betton & Evans, perhaps in about 1840.[63]

In the FORMER VESTRY (now the café) is a collection of roundels. They are included in the inventory of William Cole, and the following dates and attributions are his. Figs 175a–175g show the roundels not illustrated by Cole.

Figs 175a–175g Shrewsbury St Mary: sixteenth-century roundels in the former vestry: **Fig. 175a** the Betrayal (nII & nIII.1b); **Fig. 175b** Esther appealing to Ahasuerus on behalf of her people (nII & nIII.2c); **Fig. 175c** Joseph's brethren showing his coat of many colours to Jacob (nII & nIII.2d); **Fig. 175d** an act of mercy in giving water to the thirsty (EI.3b); **Fig. 175e** the Jew falling among thieves (EI.1a); **Fig. 175f** Jonah gazing at Nineveh (EI.2a); **Fig. 175g** a Dominican monk is welcomed; God looks on (EII.3b)

Vestry eI (east wall of vestry, south side)
Ia: an act of mercy: giving water to the thirsty, seventeenth century (**Fig. 175d**) (COLE 2602).
Ib: Jonah cast upon land by the fish, seventeenth century.
2a: a Dominican monk being welcomed, with God looking down, seventeenth century (**Fig. 175g**) (COLE 2020).
2b: Shadrach, Meshach and Abednego in the furnace, dated 1639.
3a: Joseph in prison with the butler and baker, seventeenth century.
3b: Jonah under the gourd, gazing at Nineveh, seventeenth century (**Fig. 175f**) (COLE 2019).

Vestry EII (east wall vestry, north side)
Ia: Samaritan departing, after giving money to innkeeper, seventeenth century (Antwerp?).
Ib: Samaritan dressing Jew's wounds, c.1550.
2a: the Last Supper, seventeenth century (Antwerp?).
2b: the Harrowing of Hell with Adam and Eve released and the Serpent in retreat, seventeenth century.
3a: the Samaritan lifting the Jew onto his ass, c.1550.
3b: the Jew falling among thieves, c.1550 (**Fig. 175e**) (COLE 2018).

Vestry nII and nIII (north wall of vestry, numbered as if a single window)
Ia: St John on the island of Patmos with his symbol the eagle and the Virgin and child in the sky, c.1525.
Ib: the Betrayal of Christ, c.1550. (**Fig. 175a**) (COLE 2010).
Ic: Elisha with the robe of Elijah, seventeenth century.
Id: Joseph retelling his dreams of the sheaves, early seventeenth century.
2a: Job, naked and diseased, with his comforters, c.1550.
2b: Elisha warning Hazael, the Aramean king, of the misery he would one day bring upon Israel, c.1550
2c: Esther appealing to Ahasuerus on behalf of her people, seventeenth century (**Fig. 175b**) (COLE 2012).
2d: Joseph's brethren showing his coat of many colours to Jacob, c.1525 (**Fig. 175c**) (COLE 2015).
3a: Daniel in the lion's den with an angel bringing prophet Habakkuk, c.1525.
3b: the Ascension, seventeenth century.
3c: Jezebel thrown to the dogs, seventeenth century.
3d: Shimei throwing a stone at David, who is restraining the sons of Zeruiah, c.1600.

Between the vestry and the north transept was ST CATHERINE'S CHAPEL. In the east wall are two windows. The upper one (nIV) is a representation of the Last Judgement in which Christ is shown as judge, seated on a rainbow with his feet resting on a globe and displaying his wounds. To his right is an unusual symbol, a white lily, suggesting innocence and acquittal. Christ has a cruciform nimbus typical of German conventions and the glass is probably late sixteenth-century in date. The lower part of the trefoil contains a riot of odd figures and quirky details but follows the usual pattern of souls being dragged off to hell on the right and shepherded to heaven on the left. The base of a post-mill can be seen on the left.

A lancet below (nIII) shows the Assumption of the Virgin, of unknown provenance.

St Catherine's Chapel, north window (nV)
This window holds a collection of glass from several sources. The upper part has the Crucifixion under a striking blue sky (probably by David Evans) extending across three lights. It is generally considered to be German of *c*.1500, but shares much with two Crucifixions of the sixteenth century from Rouen,[64] notably the blue sky and the overall composition with mounted men contrasting with the vulnerability of the group of mourning women. One of the French windows also has story panels at the bottom of the window. Mounted figures were popular with Continental painters at the time and can also be seen in Barnard Flower's Netherlandish image at Fairford (Glos). However, there are some highly unusual aspects of this picture which, perhaps, betray its Germanness. At the foot of the cross is a red-winged angel and laddish men fighting, one cutting the top-knot from another. However, the possibly unique part of the scene is that the woman closest to the Cross is Mary Magdalene, and she is holding a hank of hair (?) between her praying hands.

> **St Catherine's Chapel, north window (nV)**
> Along the bottom of the window are three panels of later date and from a different source:
> Ia: A donor monk with Mary Magdalene.
> Ib: The betrayal of Christ at the moment of the kiss.
> Ic: A donor priest with St Lambert.

In the tracery there are three roundels in well-drawn black paint and shading with yellow highlights. The Evangelists adopt mannered classical poses, but the Christ is a fierce, stout, almost medieval figure. They are included in William Cole's inventory as sixteenth-century (**Figs 176a–176c**, below).
B1: St Luke with his emblem of an ox.[65]
B2: St Mark with his emblem of a winged lion.
C1: the risen wounded Christ holding an *Orbis Terrarum* and blessing. He stands on a paved terrace before a background of buildings and landscape.

Figs 176a–176b
St Catherine's Chapel: roundels (nV) (William Cole's numbering in brackets)

Fig. 176a
B1 (2030): St Luke and ox

Fig. 176b
B2 (2029): St Mark and lion

Fig. 176c
C1 (2031): the risen Christ

St Nicholas Chapel, north transept chapel, east window roundels (nVIII)

1a: Tobias and Archangel Raphael nearing Ecbantana, are met by Raguel, his wife Edna and daughter Sara, dated 1617.

1b: Tobias, having married Sara, exorcises the evil spirit Asmodeus by burning the heart and liver of the fish. Asmodeus is seen going up the chimney, c.1600.

1c: Tobias returning home to Nineveh, c.1600.

1d: Tobit's eyes are anointed with the fish gall and his sight is restored, probably nineteenth-century.

2a: Tobit sleeping outside his house, probably nineteenth-century.

2b: Tobit disputing with Anna over a kid, dated 1634.

2c: Tobias sets out for Rages in Media with Archangel Raphael on a quest to recover Tobit's money, probably nineteenth-century.

2d: Tobias and Archangel Raphael reach the Tigris and Tobit is told by the archangel to catch a fish and remove its liver, heart and gall, early seventeenth-century.

3a: The Adoration of the Magi, seventeenth-century.

3b: King Ahasuerus consulting with Haman, and Haman leading Mordecai through the city, c.1600.

3c: Bagoas the eunuch discovering the headless body of Holofernes, c.1600.

3d: St Michael triumphing over Satan, seventeenth-century (**Fig. 177**).

Fig. 177 Shrewsbury St Mary: roundel depicting St Michael triumphing over Satan in the St Nicholas Chapel (nVIII.3d) (William Cole's number 2050)

In the NORTH AISLE WEST WINDOW (nXIII) is a panel from Herkenrode Abbey[66] depicting St John the Evangelist, from a Crucifixion dated 1532. It was one of the panels given to William Rowland when he oversaw the installation of Herkenrode glass at Lichfield Cathedral. The canopy is English medieval glass removed from Winchester College Chapel by Betton & Evans.[67] The upper part of the figure is modern.

In the NORTH AISLE NORTH-WEST WINDOW (nXII) is Netherlandish glass of the sixteenth century given by William Rowland in 1848 (as recorded in an inscription in Dutch). The lack of provenance is regrettable. Two of the panels (1a and 1c) are dated 1551, and all present painting of the highest quality with enamelling of rich colour and fine detail.

North aisle, north-west window (nXII)

1a: a male donor kneeling at a prayer desk with Saint Gereon, armoured, mitred and holding a crozier and a ring, dated 1551.

1b: probably Christ washing Peter's feet with the table being laid for the Last Supper, seventeenth-century.

1c: a female donor kneeling at a prayer desk with St Catherine, dated 1551.

2a: Balaam the prophet and the angel.

2b: God calling the prophet Amos.

2c: unidentified scene of a man, possibly a bishop, distressed at the sight of a wedding.

3a: a male donor at his prayer desk with St John the Baptist holding a lamb.

3b: Mary of the Seven Sorrows, surrounded by Instruments of Christ's Passion and with her heart pierced by seven swords (**Fig. 178**).

3c: a female donor kneeling at her prayer desk, presented by her patron Mary, the sister of Lazarus.

At the top of each light is a roundel depicting:

4a: The Virgin and Child with St Anne, sixteenth-century.

4b: Adam tempted by Eve, c.1550.

4c: The Allegory of Justice, c.1540.

Fig. 178 Shrewsbury St Mary: north aisle, north-west window: Mary of the Seven Sorrows, surrounded by Instruments of Christ's Passion, and with her heart pierced by seven swords

different workshops. Much of the glass is in a rather poor condition with corrosion and paint loss. The style is distinctive, with the canons in their sugar-loaf-shaped caps and long, inscribed scrolls coiling around them.

The style is very different from the previous window's Netherlandish panels; the drawing is darkly elaborate against strikingly colourful robes and strong blue and vermillion rinceau backgrounds. The faces are exaggerated, with a hint of the grotesque, that can also be sensed in the Last Supper at Coalbrookdale (Fig. 46). The original window, from which window nXI is constructed, consisted of votive panels with the donors, probably canons of the cathedral, addressing their intercessing saints with speech

In the NORTH AISLE, NORTH CENTRE WINDOW (nXI) are late fifteenth-century panels from Trier Cathedral,[68] one of which is dated *147-*. The *Vidimus* article of 2019 notes here that:

All the Trier Cathedral glass at St Mary's came from two now demolished chapels dedicated to St Andrew and St Stephen. All the panels date from 1479 but are from

labels, which entwine with the canopy-work. Some of the donors and saints were separated in the assembly of the window by David Evans. In the centre is an inscription recording the donation of, *Everhardus de Hoenfels dominus in Rypoltskirchen archdiaconus*, an eminent cleric in Triers and Luxembourg who died in 1515.[69]

Figs 179a –179b Shrewsbury St Mary: north aisle north centre window (nXI). Donors praying with their patron saints: St Luke with his ox (ABOVE) and St Agatha (LEFT)

> **North aisle, north centre window (nXI)**
> 1a: A donor with St Luke, identified by his symbol of a bull and an inscription (**Fig. 179a**).
> 1b: Heraldry with wild men and beasts as supporters.
> 1c: A donor with St Peter.
> 2a: A donor praying to St Lambert.
> 2b: A wild man wearing a helm, and reading a document, perhaps a building plan.
> 2c: A donor praying to 'St Stephen ... Patron of this Chapel'.
> 3a: St Stephen clad as a bishop with a crozier.
> 3b: St Agatha with a donor praying '*Agatha Virgo sancta tua* [at the lower end of the label] *prece me deo conserva*' (**Fig. 179b**).
> In the canopy-work above are small figures of St Bartholomew with a flaying knife, St Peter with keys, and St James the Great with a scallop shell.
> 3c: St Lambert, patron saint of Liege, with a sword.

GAZETTEER OF CHURCHES IN NORTH SHROPSHIRE 235

In the NORTH AISLE, NORTH-EAST WINDOW (nX) are further panels from Trier Cathedral. The panels are by the same hand as the panels in the previous window except for panel 2a.

Figs 180a–180b Shrewsbury St Mary: panels from Trier Cathedral. LEFT: St Jerome in the north aisle, east window (nX). RIGHT: The Virgin and Child from the south aisle, east window (sX)

North aisle, north-east window (nX)

1a: a bishop holding the three nails of the Passion. Trier Cathedral boasted one of the Holy Nails among its relics.

1b: a composite panel with a shield bearing St Peter and supporters in the form of a wild man and a wild woman. Such supporters were not uncommon in Europe in the sixteenth century.

1c: a donor surrounded by an inscription asking for the prayers of St Helena. There is a connection with 1a in that St Helena is said to have travelled to the Holy Land and collected relics of the Crucifixion, including the nails.

2a: Saint Sebastian holding an arrow and towering over a kneeling donor who is asking for his prayers.

2b: Saint Lambert with a donor.

2c: a magnificent, red-robed St Jerome removing a thorn from a lion's paw while a donor asks for his prayers (**Fig. 180a**).

There is more German glass from Trier in the south aisle. In the SOUTH AISLE, EAST WINDOW (sX) are late fifteenth-century panels, two of which are dated 1479. The three lower panels (1a–1c) have heraldic devices, above which are the following splendid figures:

South aisle, east window (sX)

2a: St Helena with St Catherine and St Barbara in the canopy-work.

2b: Virgin and Child (**Fig. 180b**).

2c: Charlemagne wearing an imperial crown and holding a sword and a crossed globe of the Christian Empire, with St Peter and St Paul in the canopy-work. It is, perhaps, this image of a Continental emperor-saint, which symbolises the importance of this collection in an English context. The striking foreignness of the style and content, with saints such as Lambert, Helena, Gereon and Charlemagne, makes a deep impression.

In the SOUTH AISLE, CENTRE WINDOW (sXI) there is an interesting variety of panels from several sources. There are further images of the life of St Bernard from Altenburg Abbey (see the north chancel window nII) and two panels from the cloister of a convent in St Apern, Cologne, as well as some of unknown provenance:

> **South aisle, centre window (sXI)**
> **1a**: Presentation of Christ in the Temple. This panel and 1c are from unknown sources, and considered to be of early sixteenth-century date.[70] However, the Presentation looks as though it might be modern – perhaps an idle doodle by David Evans, the master faker.
> **1b**: St Bernard writing to a monk who had moved to the more liberal rule at Cluny. When it rained, he commanded the scribe to continue, and the letter remained dry.
> **1c**: The Crucifixion. The style and drawing seem more related to the roundels in the church rather than the larger panels.
> **2a**: Donors praying with St Peter, from St Apern Abbey. The two panels from Apern are considered to be earlier in date than those from Altenburg.
> **2b**: St Bernard and the flies, in which a troublesome swarm dies after Bernard excommunicates them.
> **2c**: St Bernard's Christmas dream from St Apern Abbey. The infant Jesus appears to Bernard who has fallen asleep during the Christmas office.

> **3a**: St Bernard's unwanted woman. The young Bernard suffered from migraine and was sent a woman to comfort him with lullabies. He drove her away from his bed and the Holy Spirit eased his pain.
> **3c**: St Bernard preaching to the Pope and Emperor about the second Crusade in 1146.

In the SOUTH AISLE, SOUTH-WEST WINDOW (sXII) is an incomplete image of the Adoration of the Kings (one is missing) with an image of St Martin, robed as a bishop and holding one of the churches he founded. He can be identified by his commonly used attribute, the geese at his feet. The style of painting, with much plain white glass, is quite unlike other glass in the church, but no provenance has been found.

In the SOUTH AISLE, WEST WINDOW (sXIII) is another image from Trier, of St Andrew and a praying canon. The drawing and especially the canopy-work is very like that in sX.

Figs 181a–181b Shrewsbury St Mary: English roundels in the south porch

The only English glass which is probably in its original location is in the tracery of the LOWER WINDOWS OF THE SOUTH PORCH. There are two small roundels of the 1490s depicting mythical beasts (Figs 181a & 181b).[71] In the east window an elephant with hoofs carrying a howdah, drawn in black paint and silver stain. In the west window a fascinating if fanciful crab inscribed 'sol in cancro'. Kerry Ayres, in her catalogue of English roundels, calls it an extraordinary Sign of the Zodiac and says,

> Set in original tracery glass. It is rare to find Zodiac signs in stained glass. The only other [known] representation of Cancer is in the Liverpool Museum, and is also a fantastic creation.[72]

William Cole recorded imported roundels in the SOUTH PORCH SOUTH WINDOW:

- Adam tempted by Eve, sixteenth-century.
- Judith beheading Holofernes, c.1600.
- A man in bed arguing with three others, c.1600.
- A bishop saint, c.1600.
- Esther accusing Hamaan, c.1600.
- Judith brought to Holofernes, c.1600.
- St Eligius with his anvil, c.1600.

There is more medieval glass in the south transept and south chancel chapel, but it is mostly incorporated into new work by David Evans.

The SOUTH CHANCEL CHAPEL EAST WINDOW (sII) was previously two separate windows glazed by David Evans in 1847. In 1897 the masonry between the windows was removed and the space filled with glass by Powell & Co.[73]

In the tracery above the original windows are several shields. The suggestion that they came from the chancel or chapel is not supported by Mytton's notes. He sketched four shields, only one of which – *argent a lion rampant gules* – bears any resemblance to shields in the present window.[74]

In panels 1b and 1f there are fragments of medieval glass, but most of the fragments in both panels are waste from the Evans workshop.

The four SOUTH CHANCEL CHAPEL SOUTH WINDOWS are the work of David Evans but include some glass from Liege and Trier:

> **South chancel chapel, east window**
>
> **sIII**: by David Evans, based on illustrations of the glass in St Jacques Church in Liege.
>
> **sIV**: there are three figures from Liege[75] enclosed in their original canopy-work encrusted with shields. The donor, a priest, John de Hornes,[76] kneels with a prayer book. To the left is St Hubert, who became the first bishop of Liege in 708, or St Lambert.[77] To the right, St John the Evangelist holding a chalice.
>
> The bottom row of three panels contains late fifteenth-century saints and a donor from Trier Cathedral. The columns and speech ribbons are instantly recognisable if the north aisle windows have been seen.
>
> **sV**: at the centre is the crucified Christ in the arms of Joseph of Arimathea and the inscription *VENIT ERGO ET TULIT CORPUS* ('He came and took away the body'). The Passion theme is emphasised by two angels in the backgrounds of the outer lights, bearing Instruments of the Passion. To the left is St Luke holding his book, on which sits an ox with the donor, a knight of the Juliers[78] family. To the right, St Anne with the Virgin and Child accompany a finely-dressed lady reading from a prayer book.
>
> **sVI**: by David Evans based on illustrations of the glass in St Jacques Church in Liege.

The SOUTH TRANSEPT SOUTH WINDOW (sVII) was glazed in 1851, after the death of William Rowland as a memorial to him. His brother found the residue of his collection and David Evans and his son Charles glazed the three lancets. The overall composition is the Virgin and Child between St Thomas (attribute: a lance) and St Matthias (attribute: an axe).

The NORTH PORCH comes as a surprise. Normally, panels of fragments dealt with by Evans are unrewarding, but here there are pearls among the swine. There are several pieces recognisable as York School glass. These pieces are probably not from St Mary's but rather from Ludlow, Battlefield or another Evans project (Figs 182a–182e).

In the NORTH PORCH EAST WINDOW is a jumble of fragments, mostly waste from the Evans workshop. There are, however, four roundels which are listed by William Cole, although not all illustrated by him:

182a

183a

182b

183b

182c

183c

182d

North porch east window

2a: Adam and the animals with Eve offering the apple, seventeenth-century.
2b: the allegory of blind faith, c.1550.
2c: the birth of a saint (?), c.1560.
2d: a family at prayer. Seventeenth-century (**Fig. 183a**).

North porch west window

2a: the Holy Family with a donor, seventeenth-century.
2b: St John the Evangelist and St Gertrude bearing a ?, seventeenth-century (**Fig. 183b**).
2c: the Virgin Mary, seventeenth-century (**Fig. 183c**).

182e

Figs 182a–182e (LEFT) Shrewsbury St Mary: fragments of medieval English glass, north porch

Figs 183a–183c (ABOVE) Shrewsbury St Mary: north porch roundels not illustrated by William Cole. **Fig. 183a**: a family at Prayer (2054); **Fig. 183b**: St John the Evangelist and St Gertrude (2056); **Fig. 183c**: the Virgin Mary (2057)

GAZETTEER OF CHURCHES IN NORTH SHROPSHIRE 239

The medieval fragments include part of an angel holding reeds from a Passion scene (a1 and a2) and the head of an albed angel (3d and 4d).

The NORTH PORCH WEST WINDOW has similar panels of fragments and roundels (Figs 183b & 183c). The medieval pieces here include a fine head in the York style (3a and 4a), St Catherine's wheel (b3) and pieces of the eight-point quarry associated with York (1c and 2d) (Fig. 182c). These pieces probably didn't come from St Mary's but from Ludlow, Battlefield or another church where Evans replaced old glass with new.

There are several more panels of fragments in the CHANCEL CLERESTORY and the upper part of the north transept. They are, however, entirely workshop waste from the Evans studio.

TONG

St Bartholomew (SJ 7956 0739, TF11 8PW)

The church was founded as a chantry college by Isabella de Pembrugge. Peter Newton established that it was described as 'raised and built' in the ordinances of the college of 1410, and suggested that the glass had been installed by then.[79] Tong is a contemporary of Battlefield but was the development of an existing church purchased from Shrewsbury Abbey, whereas Battlefield was an entirely new foundation. The building of Tong employed masons with court connections,[80] and the monuments and the fittings – for example, the collegiate stalls – are of high quality. The glass, in the style associated with workshops at York and Coventry, is also of importance; the more so because, unlike many local churches, it has not been restored by David Evans, and what looks old probably is.

In the seventeenth century, there remained numerous shields of arms[81] of Pembrugge, Fitzalan, Vernon, Ludlow, Lingen and Trussell. In the west window were three kneeling donor figures of Sir Fulk de Pembrugge, his great-nephew Richard Vernon and his wife Benedicta, which had probably survived from a larger group.[82] They had disappeared by 1662, and by the mid eighteenth century the arms had been lost, so that Mytton recorded only a few fragmentary inscriptions and half of a shield.[83]

In the CHANCEL EAST WINDOW (I) there is a connection between Tong and Haddon Hall in Derbyshire, through the Vernon family. It has been suggested that some of the east window at Tong, installed by Kempe & Co. in 1900, has medieval glass from the chapel at Haddon Hall[84] or that some figures by Kempe & Co are based on figures at Haddon Hall,[85] but no clear evidence has been found for this. The medieval windows in both places bear a strong stylistic resemblance to each other; they share the same eight-pointed quarry, for example, but the medieval glass remaining in the tracery lights of the Tong east window is in situ.[86] The three figures now in the west window were there too, as Nelson recorded,

> East window contains the following fifteenth-century glass. In tracery: An angel, the emblem of St. Matthew, Hannah and Samuel, Salome with St. James and St. John, a lion St. Mark, Eunice, Dorcas, an ox St. Luke, St. Mary Magdalene, St. Elizabeth and St. John the Baptist, an eagle St. John. Above are: An angel, the Archangel Gabriel, the Blessed Virgin, an angel.
>
> Of the figures in lower lights three are ancient, viz. St. Edmund, St. Peter, and the Holy Mother crowned, bearing the Infant Christ. In west window are fragments of fifteenth-century glass, and in several other windows.[87]

Nelson's book was published after 1900, when Kempe & Co. remade the window, but he must have been using old notes because the presence of medieval glass was recorded in 1897 in a local newspaper.[88] Perhaps the confusion arises because Kempe & Co. copied the three saints now in the Tong west window (see below) and one of the other saints they drew is John the Baptist, who appears at Haddon Hall. However, the Baptists bear little relation to one another (Tong could not be described as a copy) and the fifth figure at Tong, the patronal saint, Bartholomew, is not found at Haddon Hall.

The east window has several figures which are original, although parts of their plinths and canopies are modern. They are drawn in black line with yellow stain for hair, wings and nimbi against a background of ruby-red seaweed rinceau. They bear hallmarks of the York style (Fig. 184).

> **Chancel east window (I)**
> **I.C3 & I.C4**: in the uppermost panels is the Annunciation.[89] The angel kneels, and Mary stands with her pot of lilies (**Fig. 184**).
> **A2**: the Virgin and Child.
> **A3**: St Mary Salome with her Apostle sons, James the Great and John. She wears a coverchief and expression similar to the Virgin's and may be from the same cartoon.
> **A1, 4, 7 & 10**: tetramorphic symbols of Matthew, Mark, Luke and John respectively. The trefoils and quatrefoils have original foliage with radiating serrated leaves.

The CHANCEL MIDDLE SOUTH WINDOW (sIII) has a panel of quarries (Fig. 185) which clearly speak of the influence or involvement of the York/ Coventry glaziers here. There are more in the north light of the west window (W.3d).

Fig. 184 Tong: Annunciation at the top of the east window (I)

Fig. 185 Tong: 'York' quarries in a chancel south window (sIII)

Fig. 186 Tong: a saint and angels at the top of the west window

NAVE WEST WINDOW (wI)

This window is of exceptional interest. At the top is the nimbed head of a saint (W1.C2) which seems to have the same DNA as John Thornton's work in the York Minster east window (Fig. 186). The green-robed saint displays the balance between white glass and pot metal, the sparing use of yellow (silver) stain, the great amount of fine line-drawing and shading on the face, the panelled nose with its bulbous end, and the round eyes and the rolled hair-line that are found in Thornton's work. He shares his compartment with three yellow-haired and albed angels, also familiar members of the York School.

Figs 187a–187b Tong: Two groups of figures in the tracery of the nave west window

Fig. 188 Tong: the main lights of the west window, with St Edmund king and martyr, St Peter and the Virgin and Child

In the tracery below are two panels with groups of figures (W.B2 and B5). Those in B2 display the solidity of shading and colour which contrasts with the pale figures in the main lights. This group of four kneeling saints (Fig. 187a) was assembled from originally separate figures. The drawing of these in matt and silver stain is quite crude and they don't seem to be by the same hand as the saint in C2 or the opposing group in B5 (Fig. 187b), composed of a mitred priest and four clerics. That group is drawn almost entirely in black line and silver stain, and the bishop's mitre has jewelled bosses which are found in much later work at Ludlow.

At the tops of the main lights (W.3a, 3b & 3c) are three figures (Fig. 188):

Nave west window (wl)

3a: St Edmund, King and Martyr drawn in black line and matt on white glass with yellow stain for crown and nimbus against a blue seaweed background. Edmund carries the arrows of his martyrdom. He is probably by the same artist as the saint in C2.

Edmund was an East Anglian king, martyred by the Danes in 869, but given wider importance through his veneration by royalty. One of the three saints with Richard II on the Wilton Diptych, there is a small image of him at Wormbridge (**Fig. 150d**).

3b: St Peter holding a key and a book. He is probably not by the same hand as 3a. The head has frizzy curls, paler shading and softer lines.

3c: the Virgin and Child. The Virgin has the elongated face and sharply-pointed chin which seem to suggest a different hand to the male saints. However, her eyes and panelled, bulbous nose betray her relation to them.

All three share drapery and canopies made from fragments.

3d: two shields with Instruments of the Passion supported by fragmentary angels.[90] In the lower half of the window there are three fragments:

1a: two small heads, one with a book.

2a: a face with fragments of vestments, a quarry and a nimbus.

2d: a saintly, nimbed bishop with a jewelled mitre and a piece of the eight-pointed quarry. The enriched vestments and mitre are reminiscent of later fifteenth-century work at, for example, Ludlow and Munslow.

There are fragments of foliage borders in windows on the south side (sIII, sIV and sV).

The south aisle windows have medieval glass in their tracery:

sIV: a face of Christ with a cruciform nimbus and the Mary monogram (the letters AMR combined and standing for *Ave Maria Regina*).

sV: two assemblages of pieces of vestment, architecture and foliage.

Peter Newton considered Tong to be the work of Coventry glaziers[91] who also made windows at Coventry, Wixford and Mancetter (Warwickshire), Thurcaston and Frolesworth (Leicestershire), Haddon Hall (Derbyshire) and Newark (Nottinghamshire); but, as he admits, there are only tenuous similarities and no clear evidence such as the re-use of cartoons or distinctive quirks of draughtsmanship. All the medieval glass at Tong has affinities with the York style, but that style evolved, and it is possible that not all the Tong windows were made before 1410, as Peter Newton suggests. The green-clad image at the top of the west window (Fig. 186) seems most like the images in the York east window made before 1410. The larger saints, in the main lights, are closely related to saints at Haddon Hall which was glazed *c*.1427, and both show the dominance of white glass and the lightness of shading that typify later York work.

TUGFORD

St Catherine (SO 5571 8706, SY7 9HS)

William Mytton found figures in four windows (Fig. 189). In the east window there was a rich array with the Virgin and Child, Christ in Glory, a mailed knight, St Margaret, a bishop and the Crucifixion with saints Mary and John.

In the CHANCEL EAST WINDOW are three small collections of medieval glass in the tracery lights. Mytton's sketches include two heads in trefoils. These probably survive in A2 and B1 in very darkened red fragments. The rest of this meagre survival is pieces of oak and other foliage. The Crucifixion may have survived as the fourteenth-century image that Nelson reported on the north side of nearby Delbury Hall.[92]

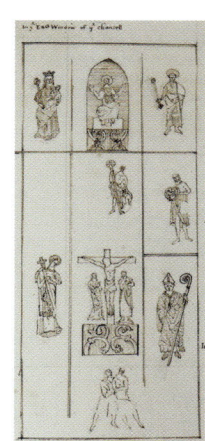

Fig. 189 Tugford: William Mytton's sketches of glass now lost (by permission of the Cadbury Library, University of Birmingham)

UFFINGTON
Holy Trinity (SJ 5280 1389, SY5 6RF)

The medieval church was demolished in 1854. William Mytton recorded arms and initials in the chancel and a south window. Window wI may contain fragments from the old church,[93] but these cannot be correlated with Mytton's record. The church was rebuilt on the old site, and consecrated in 1856. The architect was S. Pountney Smith of Shrewsbury. It could be argued that the design, with its multitude of lancets, had the display of the collection of glass in mind.

The incumbent at the time of the rebuilding was A.J. Pigott. The Pigotts were a dynasty of priests and must have circulated with Owen and Rowland, the glass collectors of St Mary's Shrewsbury. But a more important connection was with the Corbet family – one established by marriage and profession, as Dryden Corbet was patron of the church when Pigott was incumbent; and Sundorne, a Corbet seat, was in Uffington parish. A member of the Corbet family, Philip (listed as an 'artist' in a directory of 1851),[94] worked with David Evans on the south windows of the chancel chapel at St Mary's Shrewsbury. W.A. Leighton noted, 'Several of these figures are old, the rest are modern, executed by Mr. D. Evans, after designs by P. Corbet, Esq., of this town.'[95]

There is clear evidence of Philip Corbet's association with Evans and hence with imported glass, but that Corbet was a dealer or broker is confirmed by an advertisement placed by him in *Eddowes's Shrewsbury Journal* on 11 January 1854 advertising for sale the Winchester figures from the north chancel at St Mary's and '100 circular and square subjects, exquisitely finished.' These probably included the Uffington roundels, which were perhaps the most striking to look at, and probably those in the north chapels and vestry at St Mary's, Shrewsbury. Corbet was possibly acting for Evans or maybe this glass was the residue of Rowland's collection. It is also possible that he had purchased the glass and was trying to sell it on. The advert also refers to a Last Supper which could be the one at Coalbrookdale (Fig. 46), although it would have had to have been installed between January and July 1854 (see Endnote 176).

The more colourful panels are said to be from Einsiedeln Abbey in Switzerland[96] (Figs 190a & 190b). They certainly have the richly colourful character of Swiss glass that can be seen at Kentchurch Court (Fig. 79). Another infamous dealer in medieval glass, Maurice Drake (see Hampton Court, p. 84), was also an expert on Swiss glass and wrote, 60 years later,

Figs 190a–190b
Uffington: panels of Swiss glass.

Fig. 190a the Good Shepherd (from sII)

Fig. 190b
the Baptism of Christ (from sVIII)

Many thousands of Swiss panels must have disappeared during the eighteenth century ... The Napoleonic campaigns doubtless accounted for a great quantity of vanished windows: the panels were so gay in colour that they would catch the eye of the most uncultured soldier, and so tiny that they were easily carried away. ... Unbelievable as it may appear, it is on record that the Swiss eighteenth-century glaziers would not take these painted panels in exchange for plain panes of sheet glass of the same size, and even if they consented to do so ... Cartloads of Swiss panels, some of them of most exquisite workmanship, were destroyed in this way from the beginning of the eighteenth century till about the year 1820.[97]

The other roundels, mostly in the north and east windows, are Netherlandish, and some form parts of known series of images based on published prints. The dates and attributions of the Netherlandish roundels given below are from William Cole's inventory of roundels, with his reference numbers.[98] Figs 191a–191e show the roundels Cole did not illustrate.

191a

191b

191c

191d

191e

Figs 191a–191e sixteenth-century roundels not illustrated by William Cole: **Fig. 191a** Christ washing the Disciples' feet (sII.3); **Fig. 191b** The Last Supper (nIII.2a); **Fig. 191c** Christ before Pilate (nIII.2b); **Fig. 191d** Unidentified subject (sII.1); **Fig. 191e** Tobias burns the liver of the fish (sXII.1)

Window nIII

1a: Christ on the Mount of Olives. Based on a series of prints by Heemskerk depicting Christ's ministry. c.1600.

1b: the Scourging, from same series as 1a.

2a: the Last Supper, from same series as 1a (COLE 2309) (**Fig. 191b**).

2b: Christ before Pilate, from same series as 1a (COLE 2310) (**Fig. 191c**).

Window nIV

1a: Cyrus showing Bel to Daniel, based on a series of prints by Heemskerk, depicting the History of Bel and the Dragon, c.1600.
1b: Daniel revealing the fraud of Bel's priests, from same series as 1a.

Window nV

1a: Bel's priests feasting, based on a series of prints by Heemskerk, depicting the History of Bel and the Dragon, c.1600.
1b: Margaret of Antioch and the dragon, c.1600.

Window nVI

The previous roundels were drawn in black paint only. The roundels in nVI use some black paint and shading but also yellow stain and red enamel.
1a: the execution of a saint, seventeenth century.
1b: a domestic scene with a man in bed being visited, c.1700.
2a: unidentified scene of soldiers stoning a man and looting his chest, c.1600
2b: the arrival of Tobias at Ecbatana, from a print by Heemskerk, c.1600.

Window nVII

1a: the fifth Beatitude: The Merciful – feeding the hungry, burying the dead and clothing the naked, c.1600.
1b: a merchant's mark with an unknown scene. A woman is seated at a table with a man either side and servants bringing platters, seventeenth century.
2a: Christ in gardener's garb and Mary Magdalene, German, dated 1707.
2b: Tobit sleeping, c.1600.

Window sII

1: An old man and a woman mourn over the body of a young man, c.1600 (cole 2323) (**Fig. 191d**).
2: The Good Shepherd (**Fig. 190a**).
3: Christ washing the Disciples' feet, c.1600 (cole 2324) (**Fig. 191a**).

Window sIV

1: The Annunciation, seventeenth century.
2: The Flight into Egypt, seventeenth century.
3: An unidentified subject, c.1600.

Window sVI

The martyrdom of seven sons from two Maccabees, dated 1688.

Window sVII

A scene of blessing, an armed man and a St Christopher with the arms of the donor and a clothier's trade mark.

Window sVIII

The Baptism of Christ, dated 1633 (**Fig. 190b**).

Window sIX

Saint Sebastian and a noble burgher and his wife praying.

Window sX

A composite panel with heraldry.

Window sXI

A composite panel, dated 1579.

Window sXII

A Netherlandish panel of Tobias burning the liver of the fish, c.1600 (cole 2328) (**Fig. 191e**).

WHITCHURCH

St Alkmund (SJ 5409 4172, SY13 1LB)

The church dates only from 1713 but there are two panels of fragments of glass in a NORTH WINDOW which are thought to be medieval.[99] The two cruciform panels are almost entirely made of fragments from the David Evans workshop. A few small medieval pieces, notably parts of black letter inscriptions, are the only reward for a dispiriting search through Evans's debris.

WROXETER

St Andrew (SJ 5632 0825, SY5 6PH)

The EAST WINDOW was reglazed by E. Baillie in 1860. In the centre of the tracery are arms, *argent, a chevron gules, between three leopard's heads sable*, which are for the earl of Bradford.[100] The title was first created in 1694 for Francis Newport, and this panel was probably painted within a few years of that.

In the NORTH AISLE nV, a lozenge in black paint and yellow stain with the winged lion of Mark.

In the NORTH AISLE nVI are a few fragments of the fifteenth century including foliage, parts of black letter inscriptions and a headless angel bearing a shield with the Five Wounds of Christ (Fig. 192).

Fig. 192 Wroxeter: an angel bearing the Five Wounds in the north aisle (nVI)

APPENDIX TWO

Other important Stained Glass in the region of the Welsh Marches

TO THE NORTH
Gresford (Clwydd) rewards with the finest ancient glass in North Wales, mostly dating from the fifteenth century.[101]
Llanrhaeadr-yng-Nghinmeirch (Denbighshire) holds, in the east window, a complete medieval Jesse Tree of *c*.1533. There is another Jesse Tree of similar date not far away at Dyserth (Clwydd).
Grappenhall (Cheshire) has an exceptional fourteenth-century window.

TO THE EAST
Great Malvern Priory (Worcestershire) has one of the finest assemblages of fifteenth-century glass in England. Here, the Nine Orders of Angels can be found, and the Incarnation and Life of Christ (east window), and the Life of the Virgin (north transept) are laid out in glorious York School images.
Little Malvern and nearby Birtsmorton (Worcestershire) have important fifteenth-century glass.
Kempsey and Fladbury (Worcestershire) have fourteenth-century glass with affinities to glass in the gazetteer.
Merevale (Warwickshire) also has fourteenth-century glass possibly connected with Herefordshire glaziers.
Warwick, St Mary (Warwickshire) has outstanding glass of *c*.1440–62 by John Prudde.

TO THE SOUTH
Gloucester Cathedral must be seen for its great east window under a vault of angels.
Tewkesbury Abbey (Gloucestershire) is important for its fourteenth-century choir clerestory.
Bledington (Gloucestershire) has a fine collection of fifteenth-century glass displaying an exceptional variety of subjects.
Buckland (Gloucestershire) displays the Seven Sacraments in glass of *c*.1490.
Fairford (Gloucestershire) holds one of the finest assemblages of late fifteenth-century glass in Britain.

TO THE WEST
There are few collections of medieval glass of note other than those included above. Martin Crampin's *Survey of Wales* is an excellent guide to ancient and modern glass in Wales.[102]

APPENDIX THREE

Notes on Conservators & Restorers[103]

Thomas Baillie & Co. (also Baillie and Mayer)

Alexander Baillie (1787–1864), a Scot, moved his glass painting business to London in c.1815. His son Edward (1812–56) worked in the London studio and was joined by his brother Thomas (1815–83) shortly before Edward's death. The brothers worked with George Mayer who became Thomas's business partner, and the firm was sometimes known as Baillie and Mayer. William Lutwyche (1840–1908) joined the firm, which continued to work until the end of the nineteenth century.[104]

In the gazetteer: Ross-on-Wye (1873), St Weonards (1875), Kingsland (1866).
New windows: Pitchford (1853), Wroxeter (1860), Brampton Abbots (1861), Thruxton (1865), Titley (1869).

Betton & Evans: John Betton (1765–1849) and David Evans (1793–1861)

John Betton worked in his father's glazing workshop in Shrewsbury and became its master in 1806. In 1808 he took David Evans on as apprentice, and the younger man proved so precocious and able that he became Betton's partner in 1815. Betton was prominent in local affairs, he was mayor of Shrewsbury and was knighted in 1817. From then until he retired in 1825 he probably played little part in the work of the studio, but his standing brought in much of the important work of the firm, which allowed Evans to developed into a consummate draftsman, copyist and restorer.

Evans carried on the firm until his death in 1861. His sons William (1826–85) and Charles (1828–64) worked in the studio and succeeded him (see Hereford Cathedral p. 92 above). They were associated with William Done and John Davies, pupils of the studio, who were the last to occupy the Wyle Cop workshop in 1873.

Betton and Evans were working at the beginning of the revival of church building and restoration in the nineteenth century. They used the modern glass available to them, with its strong purples and oranges, and they always erred on the side of restoration not conservation as found. It is known that they replaced medieval glass with new glass and used the medieval images in other contracts. The work they carried out in Winchester College Chapel between 1821 and 1823 became infamous as conservation philosophy and practice developed. In 1823 the Hampshire press lauded the work at Winchester College, but in 1913 it was described in its pages as 'crude in colour and grotesque in design.'[105] This is discussed in Part One (p. 1) and particularly in the description of the chancel windows at Ludlow (p. 129).

In the gazetteer: BACTON AND ATCHAM, CHURCH STRETTON, HEREFORD CATHEDRAL, KINLET, LUDLOW.

New windows: LONGNER HALL (John Betton) (1808), CHURCH STRETTON (1819), BERRINGTON, SHROPSHIRE (1820), ST GEORGE, SHREWSBURY (1833), MUNSLOW (1835), BISHOP'S FROME (1848), WIGMORE (1849), STANTON LACY (1850) (Fig. 193), WELSH BICKNOR (1853). David and Charles Evans installed windows at CLEOBURY NORTH in 1861 (see Gazetteer entry, p. 60).

Fig. 193 Stanton Lacy: chancel east window by David Evans c.1850

BUDD, JIM

See: HEREFORD CATHEDRAL, KINGSLAND, MADLEY, WORMBRIDGE.

Jim Budd is a local craftsman specialising in conservation and new commissions. www.jimbudd.co.uk

BURLISON AND GRYLLS

Burlison and Grylls produced stained glass from 1868 with the encouragement of the architects George Frederick Bodley and Thomas Garner. Both John Burlison (1843–91) and Thomas Grylls (1845–1913) trained in the studios of Clayton and Bell. In the last quarter of the nineteenth century the firm was among the most successful stained glass firms in England, and collaborated with the great ecclesiastical architects of the day, including George Gilbert Scott. The firm was carried on by Thomas Henry Grylls (1873–1953) who was a founder of the British Society of Master Glass Painters. The firm closed when he died. The rose window above Poets' Corner in Westminster Abbey is one of the company's most highly regarded works.

In the gazetteer: EARDISLAND, GOODRICH.

New windows: There are more than 40 new windows by Burlison and Grylls in Herefordshire and Shropshire, including at: MICHAELCHURCH ESCLEY (1879), HOPE UNDER DINMORE (1882), TITLEY (1880), WORMBRIDGE (1880), GOODRICH (1883), STOTTESDON (1900).

CLAYTON AND BELL

The firm of Clayton and Bell was founded in 1855 and continued until 1993. It was one of the most prolific and proficient English stained glass workshops, building its reputation on high production standards which included the revival of the manufacture of pot metal glass by medieval methods. The workshop had as many as 300 employees in its Regent Street studio in the heyday of church building and restoration in the latter part of the nineteenth century. This is reflected in the exceptionally large number of their windows (more than 80) in the two counties in this book. The founding partners were John Richard Clayton (1827–1913) and Alfred Bell (1832–95), both of whom were highly regarded by, and collaborated with, their peers and the leading gothic architects of their time. Their glass is found throughout the United Kingdom, most famously in the east window of Kings College Chapel and in the windows depicting the history of the Christian Church in Truro Cathedral.

In the gazetteer: LUDLOW AND ULLINGSWICK.
New windows: OSWESTRY (1861), WITHINGTON (1871), STOKE PRIOR (1876), WIGMORE (1879), EYE (1884), MONKLAND (1878) (Fig. 194).

HARDMAN & CO. OF BIRMINGHAM

Hardman & Co., founded in 1838 by John Hardman (1766–1844), began making stained glass windows in 1844, and became a world-leading manufacturer of stained glass and ecclesiastical fittings. John's son, also John (1812–67), worked with the architect, Augustus Welby Pugin (1812–52), who was instrumental in Hardman's entry into the craft. They collaborated on glazing projects, for example at Pudleston (1850) (Fig. 195). Hardman was joined by his nephew, John Hardman Powell (1827–95) who married Pugin's daughter Anne in 1850. Powell became the principal designer from about 1849, always working in Gothic but creating his own masterly interpretation of that style. The successors to both John Hardman and A.W. Pugin collaborated for many decades. The company continued to work from Birmingham's Jewellery Quarter until 2008.

Fig. 194 Monkland: chancel east window by Clayton and Bell c.1878

Fig. 195 Pudleston: part of the series of Apostles in the nave by Hardman & Co., to designs by A.W. Pugin c.1850

NOTES ON CONSERVATORS & RESTORERS

In the gazetteer: Foy, Ludlow, Thruxton.
New windows: There are more than 100 Hardman windows and other works in the counties of Herefordshire and Shropshire. They range from the modest scale of the Pudleston nave and east windows (1850) to the impressive north transept window of Hereford Cathedral (1864).

Heaton, Butler & Bayne

The studio was founded in 1852 by Clement Heaton (1824–82). Prior to establishing his own firm in London, he had worked for William Holland. James Butler (1830–1913) became a partner in 1855, and in 1862 Robert Bayne (1837–1915), who had worked with John Richard Clayton at Clayton and Bell, entered the partnership. The firm continued to be run by their sons, and closed in 1953, after the death of Basil Richmond Bayne.
In the gazetteer: Dilwyn (1867) (Fig. 50)
New windows: Weobley (1867), Hereford Cathedral, north-east transept (1878) and north aisle (1888), Brilley (1888), Church Aston (1888), Holy Trinity, Coalbrookdale (1900), Bodenham (1892).

Kempe & Co.

Charles Eamer Kempe (1837–1907) began to make windows in 1868. His studio produced over 4,000 windows as well as designs for church furniture, furnishings, lichgates and memorials. The earlier Victorian glass painters took their inspiration from the fourteenth century, but Kempe's glass looks to the later period in which white glass, yellow stain, dark seaweed backgrounds and line predominate. His figures are sumptuously dressed and beautifully drawn. He often signed his work with a wheatsheaf or a shield with three sheafs.

When Kempe died, his distant cousin, Walter Earnest Tower (1873–1955) took over. It was Tower who undertook the repair of the Eaton Bishop east window. His work is distinguished by the rebus of a tower which may be combined with a wheatsheaf.
In the gazetteer: Eaton Bishop (1928), Weobley (1929).
New windows: There are many Kempe windows in the diocese.[106] The small church at Hamnish has several windows of 1924, contrasting with earlier and grander work of 1895 in Hereford Cathedral south transept and of 1898, 1903 and 1922 at Leominster Priory (Fig. 196).

Fig. 196 Leominster Priory: Part of the Nativity window in the south aisle by Kempe & Co. (1903)

King & Co. of Norwich

George King and his son Dennis started the Norwich studio in 1927. G. King and Son (Lead Glaziers) Ltd became the most important conservators of medieval stained glass in the twentieth century, and Dennis played an important part in the setting up of the Ely Stained Glass Museum and the York Glaziers Trust. Their catalogue of projects is impressive, including King's College Chapel, Cambridge. The studio records of their commissions, including several in the Hereford Diocese, are held in the Norfolk Records Office in Norwich.
In the gazetteer: Abbey Dore, Eaton Bishop, Wormbridge.

Morris & Co.

William Morris (1834–96) founded the studio of Morris, Marshall, Faulkner & Co. in 1861, to commercialise the design work of the Pre-Raphaelites. It became Morris & Co. in 1875 and worked until 1940. Morris was extremely influential, not only in his creative enterprises, but in his impact regarding the treatment of medieval windows. His clarion call, 'Repair not Restoration' amplified the earlier appeal of Charles Winston to preserve ancient glass. His early glass has a breathtaking simplicity, while the later work, in which he and designers such as Edward Burne-Jones collaborated, displays fiery angels and rich landscapes.[107]
In the gazetteer: CREDENHILL, LEDBURY.
New windows: PIXLEY (1864) (Fig. 197), MEOLE BRACE (1870).

William Warrington (1796–1869)

Warrington was the son of a painter of armorial shields. He worked in the studio of Thomas Willement (1786–1871) who was called 'the Father of Victorian Stained Glass' in his working life from 1811 to 1865. Warrington opened his own studio in 1832. He studied the history of English stained glass and published one of the first historical surveys.[108] His work was of such high quality and so in tune with the expectations of the Gothic Revival that he worked at many cathedrals and for important architects, notably A.W. Pugin.
In the gazetteer: Warrington's work at HEREFORD CATHEDRAL is considered in Part One (pp. 100–102).
New windows: There are few new windows by the company. The east windows at BISHOPSTONE (1843) and KINNERSLEY (1851) are important. Warrington's son succeeded him, and the firm worked on until 1905. There is an example of his work at NORTON IN HALES (1886).

Fig. 197 Pixley: the Annunciation by William Morris in the east window (1864)

NOTES ON CONSERVATORS & RESTORERS

NOTES & REFERENCES

FRONT MATTER
1. See gazetteer entry for Eaton Bishop, starting on p. 70.
2. Woodforde, C., (1935).
3. Newton, P., (1961).
4. Whitehead, D., (1995).
5. Marks, R., (1993).
6. Copies of the whole survey have been deposited with CVMA, the Society of Antiquaries of London, the Herefordshire and Shropshire records offices and the Hereford Cathedral Library.

PART ONE
7. Brown, S., (1994), 13.
8. https://www.bbc.co.uk/news/science-environment-57768815?fbclid=IwAR1QER-FLxeiFL2Fx90M-9Gy1klYWImb7V4B09R9cMgEjz4rhRN3tCsUPk0
9. Marks, R., (1993), 105.
10. Willmott, H., & Welham, K., 'Late Seventh-Century Glassmaking at Glastonbury Abbey.' *Journal of Glass Studies,* 55, (2013), 71–83.
11. It is interesting that two monastic sites in this survey, Moccas and Abbey Dore, are associated with field-names which might indicate glassworks.
12. Hicks, C., *The King's Glass,* London (2007), 46.
13. Marks, R., (1993), 30, quoting Dugdale, W., *Antiquities of Warwickshire,* London (1730), Vol I, 446–7
14. Salzman, L.F., (1952), 183.
15. Armitage, E.L., *Stained Glass: History, Technology and Practice,* London (1959), 79.
16. Jones, L., 'Churchwardens' Accounts of the Town of Ludlow.' in *Transactions of the Shropshire Archaeological and Historical Society,* Vol 12 part 2, (1889), 268.
17. Marks, R., (1993), 33.
18. Armitage, E.L., *Stained Glass: History, Technology and Practice,* London (1959), Plate 72.
19. Salzman, L.F., (1952), 182.
20. These sites are listed in the Shropshire Historic Environment Record. https://shropshire.gov.uk/environment/historic-environment/historic-environment-record.
21. https://htt.herefordshire.gov.uk/herefordshires-past: SMR Number: 447 & 7298
    Marmont, B., 'A Huguenot Glass Works near St Weonards, Herefordshire.' in *TRANS.,* (1922), 69–72.
    Bridgewater, N P., 'Glasshouse Farm, St Weonards: A Small Glassworking Site' in *TRANS.,* (1963), 300–315.
22. The Gloucestershire HER has an admirable and accessible file on this site. The possibility that Newent was the source of the glass associated with Viscount Scudamore at Abbey Dore, Sellack and Much Marcle was considered, but the glass fragments in Gloucester Museum (A. 24520 & 24521: 1968) are very thin and have a distinct green cast which is also found in the much more numerous fragments of goblets. It is also probable that the Newent works was in decline in the 1630s when Scudamore was active.
    Vince, A., *Newent Glasshouse,* Committee for Rescure Archaeology in Avon, Gloucestershire and Somerset (1968), 15.
23. Woodforde, C., (1931), 62.
24. Woodforde, C., (1935-7)A, 62.
25. Suggested by David Thomson.
26. Marks, R., (1993), 41.
27. Marks, R., (1993), 6.
28. Hillaby, J., (2003), 87–94.
29. Marks, R., 'Wills and Windows' in *Studies in the Art and Imagery of the Middle Ages*, Pindar (2007).
30. Badham, S, *Seeking Salvation,* Shaun Tyas, 2015, 80–88.
31. Marks, R., (1993), 139 and Fig. 110.
32. Marks, R., (1993), 141.
33. Saul, N., (2020).
34. Saul, N., (2020), 113–25.
35. Saul, N., (2020), 114.
36. Woodforde, C., (1935-7)B.
37. Marks, R., (1993), 164.

38 A Northamptonshire example included here because it is firmly dated and illustrates developments in form in the early fourteenth century.
39 Brown, S., (1995), 129.
40 Frederica Law-Turner, 'The Ormesby Psalter and a Lost Midlands Jesse Window', *Vidimus* 52 (2011).
41 Brown, S., (1995), 127 relying on R.K. Morris, 'The Mason of Madley, Allensmore and Eaton Bishop' in *TRANS* (1974), 194.
42 Woodforde, C., (1935-7)B, 184-90.
Newton, P., (1961), 62-71. The seven windows Woodforde associated with Madley are: Ludlow, Merevale, Tewkesbury Abbey (vestry), Mancetter, Shrewsbury St Mary, Bristol Cathedral and Lowick.
43 Based on the likely date of the building of the Chilstone Chapel, see: R.K. Morris, 'The Mason of Madley, Allensmore and Eaton Bishop' in *TRANS*, (1974), 194.
44 Brown, S., (1995), 128.
45 Green, M.A., 'Old Painted Glass in Worcestershire: Part XI' in *Transactions of the Worcestershire Archaeological Society*, Vol. XXIV, (1947), 8.
46 Tim Ayres spoke of these last two possibilities in the church of St Laurence, Ludlow on 25 June 2016. The lecture is available from the church shop on DVD.
47 Morris, R.K., 'Late Decorated Architecture in Northern Herefordshire', *TRANS* (1982), 36-52.
R.K. Morris, 'The Mason of Madley, Allensmore and Eaton Bishop' in *TRANS*, (1974), 180-9.
48 Marshall, G., 'Some Remarks on the Ancient Stained Glass in Eaton Bishop Church' in *TRANS*, (1922), 108-14.
49 Brown, S., (1995), 126.
50 Hillaby, J., (2003), 92. Joe Hillaby also draws attention to similarities in the cross head of the saint's staff and border designs with similar details at Christ Church Oxford.
51 Read, H., *English Stained Glass*, Putnam's, London (1926), 41-2.
52 Rosewell, R., *Stained Glass*, Oxford (2012), 55.
53 Lorna Roberts points out that in 1808 Evans was apprenticed to John Betton, a Shrewsbury glazier, eventually becoming his partner in 1815. https://www.buildingconservation.com/articles/david-evans/david-evans.htm
54 Martin. P.L., 'The European Trade in Stained Glass, with Special Reference to the Trade between the Rhineland and the United Kingdom, 1794-1835', MPhil Thesis, the University of York (2012).
55 Cole, W., (1993) is the authority on roundels but omits Coalbrookdale, Monkhopton and Bishopstone completely and some of the Bromfield panels.
56 There are more Magi in window nIV but they are David Evans.
57 Morgan, F.C., (1979), 11.
58 Seraphim, Cherubim, Thrones / Dominions, Virtues, Powers / Principalities, Archangels, Angels.
The hierarchies are described in *The Golden Legend* and the writings of Dionysius the Areopagite.
59 Grandison arms were also recorded in the nave south aisle and Peter de Grandison's early Perp. tomb is on the north side of the Lady Chapel.
60 Price, J., *An Historical & Topographical Account of Leominster and its Vicinity*, (1795), 93.

61 Whiting, R., *The Reformation of the English Parish Church*, Cambridge (2010).
62 Cooper, T., Ed. *The Journal of William Dowsing*, Boydell, Woodbridge (2001), 337-44 for a useful summary.
63 Wright, T., (1869).
64 Spraggon, J., *Puritan Iconoclasm During the English Civil War*, Boydell, (2004), 84-5.
65 Wright, T., (1869), 37 for a catalogue of sales including the '*dragon that the image of saynt George stood upon.*'
66 Barratt, J., *Cavalier Stronghold: Ludlow in the English Civil Wars*, Logaston, (2013).
67 Thomas Season and his son Richard continue in the accounts down to 1634.
68 Llewellyn Jones published the accounts in the *Transactions of the Shropshire Archaeological and Historical Society* as follows: Vol. 12.1 (1889) down to 1606, Vol. 13.1 (1890) down to 1628, Vol. 15.1 (1892) down to 1652, Vol. 15.2 (1892) down to 1691, Vol. 16.1 (1893) down to 1749.
69 HRO AC16/27.
70 HRO AC16/28.
71 Lloyd, D., Clark, M., & Potter, C., *St Laurence's Church Ludlow*, Logaston, (2010), 181.
72 Brown, S., 'Medieval Stained Glass and the Victorian Restorer', *Interdisciplinary Studies in the Long Nineteenth Century* (2020), 7-8. The consideration of repair and restoration draws much from this paper. <https://doi.org/10.16995/ntn.2901>
73 Ibid.
74 *Illustrated London News*, 1 April 1950.
75 Op. cit. Brown, S., (2020), 10.
76 Winston, C., 'Painted Glass', *Archaeological Journal*, (1844), 14-23.
77 Warrington was a pupil of Thomas Willement who was a friend of Winston.
78 *A Concise Account of Some of the Ecclesiastic and Domestic Stained Glass Windows ...* by Thomas Baillie & Co, London 1875. A copy of this volume annotated by Baillie is in the Patent Office Library of the British Library.
79 Duncumb 6, 70.
80 O'Connor, D., (1995), 138-49 and plates B, XXIV-XXVIII.
81 HRO HD10/283.

PART TWO
82 BoE H, 71.
83 Marks, R., (1986), 211-12.
84 Williams, D., 'The Dissolution', in Shoesmith, R. & Richardson, R. (eds.), *The Definitive History of Abbey Dore*, Logaston (1997), 149.
85 HRO AC/27.
86 HRO AC/28.
87 *The Builder*, 19 April 1902, 387.
88 Hillaby, J., 'The Paul Restoration', in Shoesmith, R. & Richardson, R. (eds.), *The Definitive History of Abbey Dore*, Logaston (1997), 202-3.
89 Marks, R., (1993), 128. Marks illustrated the pattern at Fig. 100.
90 Marks, R., (1986), 214.

91 The work was undertaken by John Hall & Sons of Bristol. It is difficult to understand how a wholly unacceptable scheme could have happened in a church subject to the Faculty jurisdiction.
92 Marks, R., (1986), 215.
93 Ibid. 223.
94 Hillaby, J., 'Cults, Patrons and Sepulture' in Shoesmith, R. & Richardson, R. (eds.), *The Definitive History of Abbey Dore*, Logaston (1997), 188–9.
95 Otherwise known as T-O globe, thought to symbolise the Cross at the centre of the world.
96 The T-O globe expresses the medieval idea of the world in three domains – Europe, Asia and Africa – which were repopulated by three sons of Noah – Japheth, Shem and Ham respectively. The globe is the underlying structure of Hereford's *Mappa Mundi*.
Arrowsmith, A., *Mappa Mundi: Hereford's Curious Map*, Logaston (2017), 12.
97 The inscriptions below the plinths are as follows:
Peeter 44 yares after the death ᵒᶠ our saviour // went to Rome to confu[?] simon magus and liv // ed there 25 yeares he was condemned by N // ero to be crucified which peeter desired to be done // with his head downwarde;
Andrew brother to peeter he lived at patris in // Achaia where he at last was crucified joyfully // embracing the crosse i[n] his armes
98 The inscriptions at the foot of the panels are:
James brother to Joh[n] he was beheaded b[y] // Herod his accuser likewise confessing Chri[st] // suffered matyrdome with him
16 34
John the beloved desipell was banished by do // mition to the Ile of Pathmas where he write // the Revellation he died 60 yeares after Christ // and was buried neere to Ephesus
99 Matthew's book: Liber generation This Mathew – that Angell Doth imply // Chriestes Royall ligne in his humanitie // Man like him-selfe deriving downe the same // to Joseph's Tribe faithful Abraham
Mark's book: Marke's Lion as his Gospel doth beginne // a criers voice the Wilderness within // make straight His paths the same is only Hee // of Judah's Tribe – who was fortould to bee
100 John's book: Looke, How the quick sight Eagle Mounts on High Beholds the Sunne with her all piercing eie // so unto Christes Divinity I soar // beyond the Straine of those that are before
101 This is an unusual pairing in English art but can be seen in the portals of French cathedrals – for example Reims. It probably represents the unveiling of the old and new covenants. Moses revealed the tablets while the Baptist revealed the Christ in the Jordan river.
102 Hillaby, J., (1997), 185–94.
103 Atherton, I, 'Viscount Scudamore's 'Laudianism': the religious practices of the first Viscount Scudamore' *Historical Journal* 34, issue 3, (1991), 567–96. Tries to understand Scudamore's theology but notes, 'It is no longer possible to construct a system of divinity for the Viscount, if he did ever work out his theological position comprehensively; perhaps like his friend William Laud he preferred to leave off the deeper points of divinity.'
104 Gibson, M., *A View of the Ancient and Present State of the Churches of Door, Home-Lacy and Hempstead ...*, London (1727), 41.
105 Although not without parallel in modern times, as I remember one of the Manners of Haddon Hall telling a group of students from the Leicester Polytechnic conservation course how the distinctive glazing was remade by the family using the billiard table as a bench.
106 Several reorganisations, austerity and moving some records to HARC have left their mark on the archives in the city library, and it is difficult to give an accurate reference here. I am grateful to Lauren Price for her assistance.
107 Jim Budd has established that the window design is for the church of Edington Priory. There is a grand memorial in Edington Priory to Sir Edward Lewis of Van who is named on the window drawing in the Scudamore papers.
108 Heather Hurley, who has studied the Scudamores recently, was of great assistance here.
Hurley, H., *The Scudamores of Kentchurch and Holme Lacy*, Logaston (2019).
109 Trevor Cooper is of the view that prints were a significant source for artisans in the seventeenth century.
110 Marks, R., (1993), 58.
111 Litzenberger, C., *Tewkesbury Churchwardens' Accounts, 1563–1624*, Bristol & Gloucester Archaeological Society (1994), 113. Paynter was paid for glazing between 1611 and 1622. He also built a gallery in 1609.
112 Although Ian Atherton points out that Scudamore was antipathetic to Huguenots and their churchmanship. Op. cit. Atherton (1991), 588.
The Gloucestershire HER has an admirable and accessible file on this site. The possibility that Newent was the source of the glass associated with Viscount Scudamore at Abbey Dore, Sellack and Much Marcle was considered, but the glass fragments in Gloucester Museum (A. 24520 & 24521: 1968) are very thin and have a distinct green cast which is also found in the much more numerous fragments of goblets. It is also probable that the Newent works was in decline in the 1630's when Scudamore was active.
Vince, A., *Newent Glasshouse*, Committee for Rescue Archaeology in Avon, Gloucestershire and Somerset (1968), 15.
113 Hillaby, J., (1997), 191.
114 It will be shown that the Ascension is copied from an engraving by Egbert van Panderen. He published two versions, one with the Virgin and one without. If Scudamore had seen both, he made a choice, and we can wonder whether his High Church aspirations acted on that choice. It is more likely that he only saw the one engraving and the decision had no bearing on his attitude to the Virgin.
115 Cooper, T., 'A comely partition betwixt the chancel and the church: English Chancel Screens from Elizabeth I to the Civil War.' In Kirby, M., Ed., *Chancel Screens Since the Reformation*, Ecclesiological Society, (2020), 62–4.
116 For example: https://nds.museum-digital.de/index.php?t=objekt&oges=53149

117 Thanks to Trevor Cooper for leading me from the Evangelists by pointing out Peake's relation to Laud.
118 Henderson, G., 'Bible Illustration in the Age of Laud', *Transactions of the Cambridge Bibliographical Society*, Vol. 8, No. 2, (1982), Plate 14.
119 Private collection.
120 RCHM 1, 9.
121 The Heraldry Society website.
122 Hillaby, C. & Hillaby, J., 'Aconbury Priory Church: a national monument?', *TRANS*, (2018), 61.
123 Scott's plan can be viewed online at the Lambeth Palace Library website.
124 Marks, R., (1993), Fig. 114.
125 BoE S, 101.
126 HRO X8 photocopy f.68.
127 HRO CF50/116 f.98.
128 HRO CF50/241 f.32
129 Nelson, P., (1913), 98.
130 Morgan, F., (1979), 21.
131 BoE H, 83.
132 IHS are the first three letters of the Greek name of Jesus, ΙΗΣΟΥΣ. IHS may also represent the Latin, *Jesus Hominum Salvator* = Jesus Saviour of Mankind.
133 Symonds, R., (1859), 247–8. The notebook of Symonds in the British Library includes a crude drawing of the shields: BL Harley MS 944.
134 Mytton f. 73 & 778.
135 BoE S, 113.
136 Gray, Madeleine, *Politics, Power and Piety: The Cult of St Armel in Early Tudor England and Wales*. Accessed at https://core.ac.uk/download/pdf/289635721.pdf
137 ibid.
138 Mytton f. 96.
139 William Mytton drew them at Coton: Mytton f. 80.
140 These are not included in the survey of *Medieval English Figurative Roundels* by Kerry Ayre, but appear to have some affinity with English silver stain roundels of the fifteenth century which she illustrates.
141 Cranage, D., Part 4, (1900), 268.
142 Marks, R., (1993), 139–40.
143 Mytton f. 96.
144 Rushforth, G. McNeil, 'The Bacton Glass at Atcham in Shropshire', *TRANS* (1935), 157–62.
145 Eginton, William Raphael, *Some account of the works executed in stained glass, by William Raphael Eginton, F.A.S.E., glass painter, Birmingham,* Lichfield [1820?].
146 Ganderton, E., (1961), 29 describes numerous iconographical errors in Ludlow sIV.
147 Johanes Rosse is a mystery in that he is not found in the registers of either diocese.
148 Rushforth, G., (1936), 140.
149 HRo CF50/114 f. 274–5.
150 RCHM 3, 16. and https://historicengland.org.uk/images-books/photos/englands-places/
151 MacLean, D., 'The Royal Arms in Herefordshire Churches', *TRANS* (1956), 110.
152 Masters, Rachel, 'A Didactic Legend in Glass: Netherlandish Silver-Stained Roundels Depicting Scenes from the Book of Tobit', *Vidimus* 94, 2015.
153 Green, M., 'Old Painted Glass in Worcestershire: Part I', *Transactions of the Worcestershire Archaeological Society*, (1933), 51.
154 Symonds, R., (1859), 196. and BL Harley MS 944, f. 40–2.
155 Mytton f. 186.
156 The report of a field meeting in *TRANS* (1908), 165.
157 A picture of the window before the present reordering is in the Bustin Collection: https://herefordshirehistory.org.uk/archive/bustin-image-collection/bustin-churches/1154020-g36-347-01-brinsop-church-interior-jpg.
158 HRO CF50/114.
159 Symonds, R., (1859), 196. Symonds made a sketch of the window – BL Harley MS 944.
160 Good, J., *The Cult of St George in Medieval England*, Woodbridge (2009), 165–6.
161 Mytton f. 96. There are images at Ludlow notably in nIV but probably the work of David Evans. William Mytton also recorded the lower half of the George with a dragon at Cheswardine in north Shropshire.
162 There is a tradition of a Dragons Well in Brinsop which marks the spot where the dragon was slain.
Fletcher, H.L.V., *Herefordshire,* London (1949), 147.
163 Alexander, J. & Binski (eds), *The Age of Chivalry: Art in Plantagenet England 1200–1400*, RA (1987), 213.
164 ibid. 214.
165 BoE S, 172.
166 Cole, W., (1993), 37–8.
167 HRO CF50/116 f. 362.
168 Grounds, D., *A History of the Church of St Laurence, Church Stretton,* Logaston (2002), 172 & 218.
169 Cole, W., (1993), 60–2.
170 Mytton f. 289.
171 HRO X8.
172 https://churchmonumentssociety.org/monument-of-the-month/hawise-de-la-barre-d-1385-heiress-of-the-Pembridge-family-of-clehonger-herefordshire.
173 HRO K38/Cd/5/8.
174 RCHM 1, 35.
175 BoE S. 217.
176 The *Shrewsbury Chronicle* of 28 July 1854 reported the consecration of the church and noted that 'one of the windows in the south aisle is filled with some foreign glass the gift of a gentleman resident in the neighbourhood.' However, the *Manchester Courier* of 5 August 1854 reported, 'A side window, too, the gift of Mrs H Whitmore (ne'e Adelaide Darby), is also of stained glass, beautifully painted, the subject being The Last Supper.' Adelaide Darby gave the land on which the church is built and was present when the foundation stone was laid on 11 December 1851.
177 BoE S, 634. Surely, Pevsner can be given the benefit of the doubt here!

178 https://www.clevelandart.org/art/1940.340. The 'fireplace' surround is seen in a panel from St Apern, Cologne of c.1525, formerly in the church of St Peter Hungate, Norwich. See – King, D., 'A Panel of German Stained Glass in St Peter Hungate Church, Norwich', *Transactions of the Norfolk and Norwich Archaeological Society* (1981), 1–4.
179 V&A number C.211-1928.
180 See if you can find the six-fingered Apostle.
181 V&A number C.213-1928.
182 Martin. L., 'The European Trade in Stained Glass, with Special Reference to the Trade between the Rhineland and the United Kingdom 1794–1835', MPhil Thesis, the University of York (2012).
183 Labouchere, R. & Thomas, E., (eds) *The Private Journal of Adelaide Darby of Coalbrookdale*, Ironbridge (2004).
184 RCHM 2, 52.
185 Mytton f. 372.
186 Newton, P., (1961), 324.
187 HRO X8 a photocopy, f. 141.
188 HRO CF50/114 f. 133.
189 Weaver, P., (2015), 75–6.
190 Havergal, F., *Description of the Ancient Glass in Credenhill Church Herefordshire*, Hereford (1884).
191 Alexander, J. & Binski, P. (eds), *The Age of Chivalry: Art in Plantaginet England 1200–1400*, RA (1987), 212.
192 Marks, R., (1993), 77.
193 Saul, N., (2020), 71.
194 Bishop Swinfield's Register shows that Richard Talbot of Eccleswell and Richards Castle (d.1306) and subsequently his son, Gilbert (d.1346) had the advowson and appointed a series of relatives to the church. Philip Talbot was presented in 1277 and was made Archdeacon of Salop in January 1301 and Prebend of the cathedral in August the same year. He must have died soon after because in October of 1301 John Talbot is described as Archdeacon of Salop, and the church at Credenhill was annexed to the archdeaconry for as long as he remained in position.
195 Faraday, M., (2012), 34.
196 Cranage, D., *Part 1*, (1901), 69.
197 Symonds, R., (1859): 264–6 & BL Harley MS 944 f. 108–11.
198 *Hereford Times* 7 December 1867 accessed at British Newspaper Archive online.
199 '... the windows painted and chequerly bordured with lyons passant as in ye Kings armmes 4 colours and B: with flowers de lis o:'
200 Mytton f. 395B.
201 Newton, P., (1961), 529–35.
202 Dingley, T., (1867), ccxlvii.
203 HRO CF50/114 f. 302–3.
204 'The East Window in the Parish Church of St Mary the Virgin Eardisland', unsigned and undated paper on the village website: http://www.eardisland.org.uk/downloads/history/church/East%20Window.pdf
205 Alternatively: *Azure, crusily botonnee and a lion rampant or*.
206 Leominster Museum accession 0345.
207 HRO AJ32/44.
208 This brief sketch of the man is taken from Wikipedia, George Marshall's 'Some Remarks on the Ancient Stained Glass in Eaton Bishop Church' in *TRANS* (1922), and Heather Gilderdale, 'St Michael Weighing a Soul: chancel east window, St Michael's church, Eaton Bishop (Herefs.)' *Vidimus*, Issue 4, 2006.
209 Marshall, G., (1922), 108–14.
210 Marshall G., (1922) and notes on the church at HRO AG4/14.
211 HRO: HRO X8 f. 146 & 238.
212 HRO AG4/22, HRO N25/8 & 9.
213 HRO CF50/241.
214 HRO CF50/98.
215 Marshall, G., *TRANS* (1922) 101–14.
216 HRO Watkins Collection 313–16. There are further pictures by Watkins showing the previous arrangement of the glass among the papers of George Marshall: HRO K38/Cd/5 Box 2.
217 Walter Tower was the successor to the firm of Kempe & Co. 'Studio established in 1866 by Charles Eamer Kempe (1837–1907) in London to make windows under his direction. Kempe insisted that the members of the studio should remain anonymous, and that only the firm's name should be credited. The firm perfected the use of silver stain on clear glass which leaves a yellow tint. Kempe left the firm to his nephew Walter Tower, after which the firm was known as C.E. Kempe & Co. Ltd. The emblem used by the firm, the wheatsheaf, had a tower added to it.'
218 HRO BM81/1/5.
219 HRO BM81/1/5.
220 *TRANS* (1927), 179, reports the successful appeal.
221 RCHM 1, 59.
222 HRO HD10/283.
223 There is a further example in the same church but with the Crucifixion surrounded by scenes of the Joys of the Virgin. This panel has the lattice background, the green Cross and the cup-and-cover borders also found at Eaton Bishop.
224 Read, H., *English Stained Glass*, Putnams, London (1926) 92. 'At first (as at Eaton Bishop, one of the earliest examples of the use of silver-yellow stain in England) the stain was merely employed as a substitute for yellow pot metal; but it gradually assumed all manner of subtleties, and eventually dominated the whole technique of glass-painting, reaching a final height of meretriciousness in the fifteenth century window at Winscombe, Somerset, which is executed entirely in yellow stain.'
225 Gilderdale, H., 'St Michael Weighing a Soul' in *Vidimus*, Issue 04 (2007). Available online at the CVMA website.
226 Window nX: James Malcolm gives a detailed account: '*The four windows of the N aisle have had large and beautiful figures of painted glass, one is a crucifix under a cross in a niche within a grand canopy, on the right side is the blessed Virgin with the infant on her left arm and the lily in the right, the colours and drapery of this figure are rich and graceful*'. HRO CF50/61.
227 Gilderdale, H., 'St Michael Weighing a Soul' in *Vidimus*, Issue 04, 2007.
228 Brown, S., *Stained Glass: An Illustrated History*, London (1992), 75.

229 Williamson, P., *Medieval and Renaissance Stained Glass in the Victoria and Albert Museum,* London (2003), Plate 20.
230 Drake, M., *A History of English Glass Painting,* London (1912) Plate VI and Fig.2.
231 Accessed at http://ica.themorgan.org/manuscript/page/20/77322
232 Marshall, G., 'The Church of Eaton Bishop' in *TRANS* (1922), 95–100.
233 HRO CF50/98.
234 Brown, S., (1995), 122–31.
235 Read, H., *English Stained Glass,* London (1926), 41–2.
236 Glynne, 41.
237 RCHM 2, 80.
238 George Marshall, Notes on Gillow Manor, and the Churches of Llandinabo, Foy, Ross-On-Wye, and Brampton Abbotts, Herefordshire, *TRANS* (1938), 162.
239 Powell, H.J., 'Renaissance Churches of Herefordshire', *TRANS*, (1975), 321.
240 ibid.
241 BoE H, 240.
242 The jar is theological 'fake news'. Pope Gregory I declared that Mary Magdalene, Mary of Bethany who anointed Jesus and the unnamed 'sinful woman' who anointed Jesus's feet in Luke 7:36–50 were the same person. Mary Magdalene did not anoint Jesus and was a good woman who supported His ministry. The jar is a symbol of the misogyny of the Catholic Church, calculated to deny women their rightful place in the Apostolic succession.
243 Lowe, R., 'The Monumental Mysteries of Goodrich Church', *TRANS. EXTRA*, (2000), 10. The source of the image is given as: *College of Arms MS King, Heraldic Miscellanies vol 16, 492.*
244 *Monmouthshire Beacon,* Sat. 4 February 1860: accessed at British Newspaper Archive online.
245 *Abergavenny Chronicle,* 19 October 1883: accessed at British Newspaper Archive online.
246 Caviness, M., (1970), 35–60.
Beavan, Marilyn M., 'Grosvenor Thomas and the Making of the American Market for Medieval Stained Glass' in *The Four Modes of Seeing,* Lane, E.S., Pastan, E.C. & Shortell, E.M. (eds), Routledge, London (2016), 481–96. Sets out how Thomas was supplying glass to major US collectors, including George D. Pratt, Edsel Ford and the Metropolitan Museum. Thomas was associated with glazier and stained glass restorer Wilfred Drake (1879–1948). Thomas and Drake formed a business partnership that was continued after Thomas's death by his son, Roy Grosvenor Thomas.
247 Catherine Beale provided this picture. She has written extensively about Hampton Court and its occupants. http://www.cbeale.co.uk/.
248 Dingley, T., (1867), ccxxxviii. The date is given by Caviness (1970), 42 but not corroborated.
249 HRO CF50/114 f. 339–40. Dating is difficult but vol. 5 of Hill is 'made about 1716', so vol. 2 can be assumed to be earlier.
250 Caviness, M., 'Gothic Glass Paintings: The Struggle for Survival' in *Gothic Art and Thought in the Later Medieval Period,* (ed. Colum Hourihane), Penn State University Press (2011), 176–204.
251 Symonds, R., (1859), 264–6 & BL Harley MS 944 f. 108–11.
252 Hillaby, J. & C., *Leominster Minster, Priory and Borough c.660–1539,* Logaston Press (2006), 234.
Atherton, I., 'Viscount Scudamore's 'Laudianism': the religious practices of the first Viscount Scudamore' in *Historical Journal* 34, issue 3, (1991), 578, describes the incumbent at Leominster, John Tombes as, 'an increasingly radical baptist and an opponent of episcopacy who refused to observe the established rites and ceremonies of the pre-civil war church.'
253 Dingley, T., (1867), cxxiii.
254 Price, J., *An Historical & Topographical Account of Leominster and its Vicinity,* Ludlow (1795), 93.
255 Beale, C., *Champaign and Shambles,* Gloucester (2006).
256 Grosvenor Thomas Sales Book in the Society of Antiquaries of London Library.
257 ibid.
258 Hillaby, J., (1997), 187.
259 http://collections.vam.ac.uk/item/O7965/panel-linge-abraham-van/.
260 HRO X8.
261 Robinson, C., *Mansions and Manors of Herefordshire,* London & Hereford (1873), 136.
262 Register of Bishop Spofford accessed via a summary at www.melocki.org.uk/MelockiDiocese.html
263 Register of Bishop Stanbury accessed via a summary at www.melocki.org.uk/MelockiDiocese.html
264 Horn, J.M. (ed.), *Fasti Ecclesiae Anglicanae 1300–1541: Volume 9, Exeter Diocese*, 53 – accessed at British History Online.
265 Fisher, A.H., *The Cathedral Church of Hereford: A Description of Its Fabric and a Brief History of the Episcopal See,* London, George Bell and Sons (1898).
266 Cathedral Archives 7101/1.
267 Siddons, M., *The Visitation of Herefordshire, 1634,* The Harleian Society (2002), 1–7.
268 Symonds, R., (1859), 197–202.
269 HRO: HRO X8.
270 Rawlinson, R., *The History and Antiquities of the City and Cathedral Church of Hereford,* London, (1717).
271 Malcolm, J., *Excursions in The Counties of Kent, Gloucester, Hereford, and Somerset,* London, (1814), 73–82.
Duncumb, J., *Volume 1,* 542–5.
272 Iles, P., (2000), 314–21.
273 Whitehead, D., 'A Goth among the Greeks', in *Annual Report of the Friends of Hereford Cathedral,* Vol 57 (1991), 30–1.
274 Dingley, T., (1867), cxxviii.
275 Caviness, M., (1970), 35–60.
Caviness, M., 'Gothic Glass Paintings: The Struggle for Survival' in Ed. Hourihane, C., *Gothic Art and Thought in the Later Medieval Period,* Penn State University Press (2011), 176–204.
276 HRO CF50/118 f. 100–1.
277 Rawlinson, R., *The History and Antiquities of the City and Cathedral Church of Hereford,* London, (1717), 52.
278 Duncumb, 1, 588.
279 Dingley, T., (1867), cc.
280 ibid. 537.
281 Whitehead, D., (2000), 242–3.

282 ibid.
283 For example, in 1779 Thomas Symonds, Surveyor of the Fabric, received an allowance of £3.6s while the plumber received and allowance of £8.8s.
284 HRO CF50/118 f. 62.
285 Cathedral Archives R610.
286 *Hereford Journal* on microfilm in HRO.
287 British Newspaper Archive.
288 Powell died in 1796. *Hereford Journal*, Wednesday 7 September 1796, British Newspaper Archive.
289 ibid.
290 *Hereford Journal*, 9 October 1822, British Newspaper Archive.
291 British Newspaper Archive.
292 ibid.
293 Cathedral Archives, 7101/3.
294 Cathedral Archives, 7101/3 85.
295 *Hereford Journal* 28 July 1838, National Newspaper Archive online.
296 Cathedral Archives, 7101/3 195.
297 Cathedral Archives, 7031/4 164.
298 Cathedral Archives, 7031/10.
299 Cathedral Archives, 7101/1 1734 items 15 & 16.
300 Cathedral Archives, 3982. There is another bill from Reece in 3983 for leadwork showing that he was also, and perhaps primarily, a plumber.
301 Whitehead, D., 'A Goth among the Greeks', *Annual Report of the Friends of Hereford Cathedral*, Vol 57 (1991), 30–1.
302 Iles P., (2000), 315.
303 Cathedral Archives, 7101/1 1736 items 14 & 15.
304 Cathedral Archives, 7031/24 152.
305 Morgan, F. C., (1979), 21.
306 Caviness, (1970), 35–60.
307 Beavan, M., 'Grosvenor Thomas and the Making of the American Market for Medieval Stained Glass' in Eds. Lane, E., Pastan, C., & Shortell, E., *The Four Modes of Seeing*, Routledge, London (2016), 481–96. Sets out how Thomas was supplying glass to major US collectors, including George D. Pratt, Edsel Ford and the Metropolitan Museum. Thomas was associated with glazier and stained glass restorer Wilfred Drake (1879–1948). Thomas and Drake formed a business partnership that was continued after Thomas's death by his son, Roy Grosvenor Thomas.
308 Cathedral Archives, 7031/24 152.
309 Op. cit. Caviness, (1970), 40.
310 The story of the remaking of the west window can be read in the Cathedral Archives, notably at 7020/2/2, 7031 and 3982 and in Whitehead, D., 'A Goth among the Greeks', *Annual Report of the Friends of Hereford Cathedral*, Vol 57 (1991), 30–1.
311 Eden, S., 'Ancient Painted Glass Recently Restored to Hereford Cathedral' in *Burlington Magazine*, 47, (1925), plate 1C. In this illustration the panels in nXIX were at the bottom, with the panels now in nXVIII arranged 2-3-1 in ascending order.
312 ibid. Plate I.A.
313 ibid. 121.
314 ibid. 116.
315 The scene is depicted at Clavering in Essex (CVMA picture archive).
316 Quoted in Eden, S., (1925), 116.
317 Nichols, A.E., *The Early Art of Norfolk*, Michigan (2002), 107.
318 Caviness, (1970), 38.
319 Ursula is more often seen ascending with the virgins nestling for protection in her robes, as at Morley, Derbyshire (nII) (CVMA image).
320 Symonds, R., (1859), 197.
321 Duncumb, J., *Volume 1*, part 2, 558.
322 https://sussexparishchurches.org/architectsandartistswxyz/
323 Cathedral Archives, 7031/21.
324 https://www.buildingconservation.com/articles/david-evans/david-evans.htm
325 Cathedral Archives, 7101/3, 135.
326 Cathedral Archives, 7031/21, 194.
327 Sawyer, William, *Cathedral Church of St. Ethelbert briefly described*, privately printed, c.1830–40. Havergal, F., *Fasti Herefordenses*, Edinburgh (1869), 210 says of the Sawyer book, 'This work is very rare. The only known copies at Hereford are in the Permanent Library, and in the possession of Miss A. Parry of Warham Court.' The Cathedral Archives copy has Thomas Bird's signature on the flyleaf.
328 Friends of Hereford Cathedral. *Third Annual Report* (1935), 23 and *Fifth Annual Report* (1937), 15.
329 The Malvern scene is in the mainstream of representations of this subject which can be traced back to Chartres.
330 Duncumb, J., *Volume 1*, part 2, 599.
331 BoE H, 312.
332 Iles, P., (2000), 316.
http://stainedglass.llgc.org.uk/person/502 gives the following summary,
'A partnership of John Betton of Shrewsbury (1765–1849), who began making stained glass in 1806, and his apprentice, David Evans, in 1815. John Betton retired in 1825, but Evans continued to work under the name of the firm, assisted by his sons Charles and William, until his death in 1861.'
BoE S, 72–3:
There are no other examples of their work in Herefordshire, but they did extensive 'restoration' work at Ludlow and new windows at Church Stretton, Munslow, Ironbridge, Cressage, Harley, and St Chads, St Julian and St George in Shrewsbury. Weaver, P., (2015), 24.
333 Cathedral Archives, 7101/3, 135.
334 *Handbook to the Cathedrals of England: Western Division*. John Murray, London, 1864, pl. VIII
335 Marks, R., (1993), 141.
336 Friends of Hereford Cathedral. *Fifth Annual Report*: (1937), 22.
337 I am grateful to Jim Budd, who re-leaded the windows, for confirmation of this.
338 http://www.medievalart.org.uk/PoitiersWindows/100_Crucifixion/Poitiers_Bay100_Panel_e2.htm
The upper panel is described as the 'Assumption' but that is not correct. The central figure with flaming angels is like the Hereford Majesty.
339 Information provided by Jim Budd who re-leaded the glass.
340 It is interesting that Pevsner did not suggest that the glass is German. At Coalbrookdale the Germanness of the glass drew his attention.

341 Friends of Hereford Cathedral. *Fifth Annual Report: 1937,* 22.
342 Oakes, C., 'In Pursuit of Heaven: The Two Chantry Chapels of Bishop Edmund Audley at Hereford and Salisbury Cathedrals', *Journal of the British Archaeological Association*: Volume 164, (2011).
343 Dingley, T., (1867), clxi.
344 RCHM 1, 110.
345 Cathedral Archives 2006/41 Box 8 & Box 9.
346 HRO CF50/118.
347 Dingley, T., (1867), ccv.
348 I am grateful to Judith Stevenson for her help with this collection.
349 http://craswallpriory.org/craswall-new-pages/c-j-lilwall-excavations-1904-8/.
350 Robinson, C., *The Mansions and Manors of Herefordshire and their Memories,* London, (1872), 283.
351 http://cadwpublic-api.azurewebsites.net/reports/listedbuilding/FullReport?lang=en&id=1931
352 *TRANS,* (1918), 183.
353 http://www.ewyaslacy.org.uk/Trewyn-Walterstone/Press-Cutting-Obituary-Notice-of-Mrs-Lucia-Rosher/1927/gc_ewy_3068.
354 Strong, G., *The Heraldry of Herefordshire,* London, (1848).
355 HRO CF50/115 f. 284.
356 Glynne, 86.
357 *TRANS* (1918), XX.
358 Ayre, K., *Medieval English Figurative Roundels,* Corpus Vitrearum Medii Aevi and The British Academy (2002), 33. The only entry for Herefordshire in this important national survey.
359 Cole, W., (1993), 351.
360 ibid.
361 Newton, P, (1961), 536–7.
362 Eyton, R., *The Antiquities of Shropshire, Vol. 6,* London (1857), 306.
363 Mytton f. 767c.
364 RCHM 1, 153–155.
365 Hurley, H., *The Scudamores of Kentchurch and Holme Lacy,* Logaston (2019), 96.
     Heather Hurley was immensely helpful in checking the likely date of the installation of the glass.
366 Drake, M., *A History of English Glass-Painting with some remarks upon Swiss Glass Miniatures of the sixteenth and seventeenth Centuries,* London (1912).
367 HRO CF50/116 f. 21.
368 Matthews, J. H., *Collections Towards the History and Antiquities of the County of Hereford: in continuation of Duncumb's History: Hundred of Wormelow.* Hereford: Jakeman & Carver, (1915), 60–1.
369 BoE H, 388.
370 Morris, R.K., 'Late Decorated Architecture in Northern Herefordshire', *TRANS* (1982) 53–6.
371 *The Gentleman's Magazine* (1826) Pt. IL 583.
372 Baillie, T., *A Concise Account of Some of the Ecclesiastic and Domestic Stained Glass Windows … by Thomas Baillie & Co.,* London (1875). A copy of this volume annotated by Baillie is in the British Library Patent Office archive.
373 Marshall, G., 'Notes on Kingsland Church', *TRANS* (1930), 21–8.
374 ibid. Marshall (1930).
375 ibid. Marshall (1930).
376 BoE S, 315. David Evans went into partnership with Betton in the following year.
377 Blakeway, J. B., 'Notes on Kinlet'. *Transactions of the Shropshire Archaeological and Natural History Society,* (1908) 105–6.
378 ibid.
379 BoE S, 314.
380 Marks, R., (1993), 169.
381 Capwell, C, Undated typescript text on exhibition in the church when visited on 13 March 2018. Signed as Curator of Armour at the Wallace Collection.
382 Ayre, K., *Medieval English Figurative Roundels,* Corpus Vitrearum Medii Aevi and The British Academy (2002), 113.
383 RCHM 3, 100.
384 HRO BO92/54a.
385 Payments to plumbers/ glaziers for moss are not uncommon in churchwardens' accounts. Moss was placed under lead sheets, but its use in connection with glazing is not certain. There are account entries where its use is almost certainly in connection with glazing, but others where the plumber is engaged in roofing and glazing and where its use must relate to the former. See for example Madley and: C.J. Litzenberger (ed.) *Tewkesbury Churchwardens' Accounts 1563–1634,* Bristol and Gloucestershire Archaeological Society, 1994, 7, 8 & 12. Also: Salzman, (1952), 266.
386 HRO BO92/55.
387 HRO BO92/56.
388 Collins, P., (ed.), *Corpus of Kempe Stained Glass,* Kempe Trust (2000), 104. The Kempe signature of sheaves is in I.3e.
389 HRO Ref, Li13040. Can be viewed online at: https://www.herefordshirehistory.org.uk/archive/herefordshire-images/ledbury-images/st-michael-all-saints-parish-church-ledbury/166517-st-michael-and-all-angels-parish-church-interior-view-ledbury?
390 Bishop David Thompson helped in identifying these inscriptions and priests.
391 http://www.melocki.org.uk/MelockiDiocese.html and Parry, J., (ed.), *The Register of John Trellick 1344–1361,* Hereford (1910), 391.
392 Parry, J., (ed.), *The Register of John Gilbert 1375–89,* Hereford (1913), 120.
393 Capes, W., (ed.), *The Register of John Trefnant 1389–1404,* Hereford (1914), 174.
394 Capes, W., (ed.), *The Register of William de Courtenay 1370–1375,* Hereford (1913), 13.
395 This style of cassock can be seen in the brass of Roger Parkers c.1370 at North Stoke, illustrated in Clayton, H., *The Ornaments of the Ministers as shown on English Monumental Brasses,* Alcuin Club, (1919), 171.
396 Hart, S., *Medieval Church Window Tracery,* Boydell Woodbridge (2010), 120 classifies this type of tracery as 'alternate supermullioned' and finds early examples thirteenth century.

397 Hillaby, J., (2003), 87–93.
398 This might mean a later dating for much of the Decorated work in this survey.
399 Ledbury had several relatively wealthy guilds, but the high altar remained the focus of donors down to the Reformation. The will of Giles Keyes, d.1521, for example, 'Item: I leave to the high altar of the aforesaid church 10s. Item: I leave to the fabric of the Hereford cathedral 3s. 4d.', accessed at https://www.victoriacountyhistory.ac.uk/explore/items/ledbury-wills-and-inventories-pre-1541.
400 Watkins, M., *Collections towards the History and Antiquities of the County of Hereford in Continuation of Duncumb's History: Hundred of Radlow,* Hereford, Jakeman & Carver, 1902, 87.
401 Hillaby, J., *Ledbury: A Medieval Borough,* Logaston (1997), 53.
402 A similar figure can be found at Stanford-on-Avon.
403 RCHM 2, 101.
404 BoE H, 418.
405 HRO BO92/56.
406 Op. cit. RCHM 2.
407 Dingley, T., (1867), ccxlvii–ccxlix.
408 Sally Badham, writing about examples of correspondence between windows and monuments suggests, 'Finally at Ledbury, the mid 14th century monument probably commemorating lady Carew is set below a window in a former chantry Chapel. Although most of the glazing is lost, several shields remain, including one with arms which also feature on the heraldic screen on the monument surrounding three sides of the figure.' The Carew shield with three lions on the monument might not be related to the three lions on the arms in the window which are probably the arms of Prince Arthur and much later in date. The Carews claimed common lineage with the Tudors but the different dates of the shields in monument and glass might rule out any intentional connection. Badham, S., *Seeking Salvation,* Shaun Tyas, (2015), 87.
409 Op. cit. Hillaby, J., (1997), 55.
410 RCHM 2, 55.
411 Freeman, E., *A Guide to Ledbury, Herefordshire,* Ledbury (1892), 34.
412 HRO F96.
413 Flight into Egypt and Massacre of the Innocents from *Psalter of St. Louis and Blanche of Castille,* French (Paris), ca. 1225 Paris, Bibliotheque Nationale de France MS Arsenal 1186. fol. 19v. Flight into Egypt and Massacre of the Innocents from *Winchester Psalter,* Anglo-Norman, mid C12–2nd half of C13, London, British Library MS Cotton Nero C IV, fol. 14r. Flight into Egypt and Massacre of the Innocents from Manuscript Miniatures: BL Arundel MS 157 Psalter with calendar. There is an example in wall painting of *c.*1310 at Croughton, Northampton.
414 Daniel, D., 'Shedding a Glorious Light', *Country Life,* 26 Feb, (1987), 72–4.
415 http://www.advanceassociates.com/Sundials/Stained_Glass/sundials_SGS1.html
416 There are examples at Merton, Widdington and Elmdon.
417 Hillaby, J., (2003), 87–96.
418 HRO CF50/116, 178 and detached, unnumbered folio. The illustration is from the detached folio.
419 *The Ledbury Letter,* Number 101 Spring 2016, Ledbury & District Civic Society.
420 Hillaby, J., (2003), 92. Joe Hillaby also draws attention to similarities in the cross head of the saint's staff and border designs with similar details at Christ Church Oxford.
421 RCHM 3, 5.
422 Williams, J., *Leintwardine Church: An Illustrated History* (2019), 60.
423 *Hereford Times,* 3 September (1864).
424 BoE H, 590.
425 Cole, W., (1993), 131–4.
426 http://collections.vam.ac.uk/item/O11223/the-story-of-sorgheloos-roundel-unknown/
427 ibid.
428 Liddy, C., speaking at the conference in the church on 25 June 2016. The conference is available on a DVD which can be purchased in the church shop.
429 Lloyd, D., Clark, M. & Potter, C., *St Laurence's Church Ludlow,* Logaston (2010), 69–70.
430 Wright, T., (1869), 36.
431 Ibid. 29.
432 Ganderton, E., (1961), 32.
433 Woolfrey, E., 'Liturgy and Liturgy: The Fifteenth-century Catechism Windows of St Laurence, Ludlow', *Vidimus,* Issue 90 (2015).
434 Barratt, J., *Cavalier Stronghold: Ludlow in the English Civil Wars, 1642–1660,* Logaston, (2013).
435 Leland, J., *Itinerary, (c.*1535–43), Vol. 2 Pt. 5, 76.
436 Weyman, H., (1905), 24–5. All this glass has gone. The lower parts of the aisle windows were blocked with stone when galleries were inserted.
437 Newton, P., (1961) gives the source reference as College of Arms, MS. c.35. Weyman was using a copy in the Bodleian: MS. 1663, Ashmole, dated 1663.
438 Dingley, T., (1864), 19–24.
439 HRO CF50/115. 297.
440 Stukeley, W., *Itinerarium Curiosum: Iter IV,* (1722), 73.
441 The Mytton Papers, Cadbury Library, Birmingham University, MYT3.
442 Grose, F., *The Antiquities of England and Wales,* (1774), Pt. 5, 15.
443 Wright, T., (1856), 74.
444 Ganderton, E., (1961), 4. The work cost £670 which was paid from a legacy of Miss Nightingale. The authors refer to a cartoon by Hardman which recorded the old glass he re-used. There is a chance it survives in the uncatalogued collection of Hardman & Co. papers in Birmingham Museum.
445 Anderson, M. D., *The Imagery of British Churches,* London (1955), 98.
446 Newton, P., (1961), Vol. III, 19–44.
447 ibid.
448 ibid.
449 Op. cit Irvine (1878), 4.
450 Ganderton, E., (1961), 9.
451 Newton, P., (1961) gives the most complete account. There are illustrations in Ganderton, E., (1961) and Weyman (1905).

452 Weyman (1905) casts doubt on the authenticity of these donor images.
453 Lloyd, D., Clark, M., & Potter, C., *St Laurence's Church Ludlow,* Logaston (2101), Plate 7.
454 Angold, M.J. et. al., 'Religious Guilds: Ludlow, Palmers' Guild', in *A History of the County of Shropshire: Volume 2,* ed., London (1973), 134–40.
455 Marks, R., (1993), 190.
456 There is a famous 'Quinity' from the late C12 in BL., Cotton Titus D XXVII, fol. 75v
457 Duffy, E., *The Stripping of the Altars,* Yale (1992), 53.
458 Dingley, T., (1864), 19–24.
459 Wright, T., (1856), 89.
460 Ganderton, E., (1961), 47.
461 Ganderton, E., (1961), 45.
462 Anderson, M.D., *The Imagery of the British Church,* London (1955), 189.
463 Liddy, C., speaking at the conference in the church on 25 June 2016 and Liddy, C., 'The Palmers' Guild Window, St Lawrence's Church, Ludlow: A Study of the Construction of Guild Identity in Medieval Stained Glass', *Transactions of the Shropshire Archaeological and Historical Society,* Vol LXXII (1997), 26–37.
464 Ibid. The other is at Fécamp in Normandy. Liddy suggests that the pilgrim spirit of the Palmers' may only have carried them to Westminster and Edward's shrine and that they brought back the story of Jerusalem to Ludlow and adapted it to make their own legend.
465 Liddy, C., speaking at the conference in the church on 25 June 2016.
466 From floor level, signature only partly visible with binoculars.
467 O'Connor, D., (1995), 141 & and plate XXVIID. See also: Lloyd, D., Clark, M., & Potter, C., *St Laurence's Church Ludlow,* Logaston (2101), 36–9.
468 Ganderton, E., (1961), 13.
469 Ward, S., *The Stained Glass of St Laurence, Ludlow: A Short Guide,* Ludlow (2014) describes this figure as a 'King' and points out that it had previously been wrongly identified as God the Father. He must however be Christ in Glory for He is surrounded by a glory of rays, wears a crossed nimbus, holds the O-T globe of the earth in the form of an orb and holds up His right hand in blessing.
470 Wright, T., (1856), 74: 'The legendary history of the life of Saint Lawrence, was particularly defaced and wantonly broken, so much so indeed that the various subjects displayed could with difficulty be traced. It appears from a date near the top of the window, to have been repaired in a bungling manner about a century ago, when the numerous fractures it then contained were filled with common painted glass, quite opaque.'
471 The Ten Commandments cycle at the Museum-Schnütgen of c.1440 is described in *Vidimus,* Vol. 68.
472 Dingley, T., (1684), 19.
473 'The depiction of a horned Moses stems from the description of Moses' face as '*cornuta*' ('horned') in the Latin Vulgate translation of the passage found at Exodus chapter 34, specifically verses 29, 30 and 35, in which Moses returns to the people after receiving the commandments for the second time.' https://en.wikipedia.org/wiki/Moses_(Michelangelo)#cite_note-12.
474 SRO 6683/4/150/3 is Clayton and Bells receipt for £145 date October 1860.
475 Weyman, H., (1905), 19. Weyman suggests that panels 1a, 1c, 1e, 2a, 2c, 2e, 3a, 3c, 3e had old glass before Clayton and Bell restored the window in 1859.
476 SRO LB15/1/215/1 is Evans' estimate for £200 and his recommendation that the masonry be renewed.
477 Mytton f. 534.
478 The statue was there in 1318: William Capes, *Charters and Records of Hereford Cathedral,* Hereford (1908), 183.
479 HRO BO11/31. Undated church guide. The document is referred to in the introduction.
480 Morris, R.K., 'The Mason of Madley, Allensmore and Eaton Bishop' in *TRANS* (1974), 180.
481 Ibid 194.
482 Sarah Brown, 'The fourteenth-Century Stained Glass at Madley' in, *Hereford: Medieval Art, Architecture and Archaeology,* ed. David Whitehead, London: British Archaeological Association, (1995), 122–131 and plates A, XIX and XX.
483 Arthur Thomas Bannister, 'The Register of Thomas Spofford (1422–48)' Hereford, Wilson & Phillips (1917), 139–42.
484 HRO CF50/61. *A Tour of Herefordshire.* The notebook appears to be part of Malcolm's preparation for the book of the tour, but Madley was not included in the final publication.
485 HRO BK52/34.
486 Cathedral Archives R603.
487 HRO BK52/36.
488 Anon, 'Madley Church repairs, etc. in the 17th and 18th Centuries', *TRANS* (1957), 308–10.
489 HRO BK52/39.
490 Moss was also used by plumbers in lead roofing as a bed for lead sheets.
491 This had increased to four guineas by 1812.
492 HRO BK52/45. This might mark the year in which the painted glass was gathered into the chancel and regular payments became unnecessary.
493 Botzum, R. & C., (1997), 30.
494 HRO CF50/241 f., 286–94
495 HRO X8 f., 146 & 238.
496 BL Harley MS 944 f17v.
497 Symonds, R., (1859), 232–3.
498 HRO CF50/140 f. 189–95.
499 Duncumb f. 287 quotes 'from Coningsby MS' and repeats the Johan Rees inscription.
500 Marshall, G., 'The Ancient Glass in Madley Church co. Hereford' in *TRANS,* (1924), 66.
501 That grant was not necessarily a founding grant and refers to a chantry of the Blessed Virgin Mary already in existence.
502 HRO X8 f. 146 & 238.
503 Op. cit. Marshall, G., (1924), 67 quoting from Charles Radclyffe, *The Picturesque Antiquities of the County of Hereford* of c.1840.
504 HRO CF50/140 f. 189–95.

505 Brown, S., 1995, 126.
506 HRO CF50/61.
507 Op. cit. Marshall, G., (1924), 67.
508 Hereford Cathedral Archives 5747.
509 Cutting at HRO AA51/1.
510 Hereford Cathedral Archives 5747.
511 *Hereford Journal* 27 April 1878 accessed at: www.britishnewspaperarchive.co.uk.
512 Glynne, 123. This entry is undated but 1876 is a fair assumption based on the dates of visits of nearby churches. It is unlikely that he made a special visit to Madley at a much earlier date.
513 Dean Merewether was a noted historian and Fellow of the Society of Antiquaries who published much on the restoration of Hereford Cathedral and undertook inexpert excavations of Silbury Hill and other important ancient sites. He was also vicar of Madley and Tibberton, and died at Madley Vicarage, in 1850.
514 She was the daughter of Edmund Fitzalan, earl of Arundel and Alice, who was a Warrene.
515 HRO AA17/55 among the papers of George Marshall.
516 Moccas was the site of a Dark Age abbey established by St Dubricius. At Domesday Book it was owned by St Guthlac's Priory in Hereford and Nigel the Physician. Silas Taylor, the seventeenth-century antiquarian, wrote 'in the churchyard at Moccas are to be seen the foundations of a very large church to which this standing was but a chapple'.
517 HRO CF50/241 f. 286–294.
518 Brown, S., (1995), 129 endnote 4. Giotto painted Drusiana in Santa Croce, Florence in 1320.
519 Acts of St John on http://gnosis.org/library/actjohn.htm accessed on 26/06/2018.
520 The scene can be found in other media, of course, and there are close parallels in French manuscript illustration, for example, The Three Women at the Tomb From *Livres d'Images de Madame Marie,* Belgium (Hainaut), 1285–1290, Paris, Bibliotheque Nationale de France, MS Nouvelle acquisition française 16251, f. 43v.
521 Round medallions at Aldermaston, Beverley, Dorchester (Oxon), Oxburgh Hall Chapel, Saxlingham, Upper Hardres and West Horsely. Vesica shapes at York Walmgate. Foiled shapes at Ashbourne.
There are 21 round and vesica twelfth- and thirteenth-century medallions at the Victorian church at Wilton, Wilts., but much restored and laid out in a very different way to Madley. The Wilton work is thought to be French glass.
522 Muir, C., *Saintly Brides and Bridegrooms,* Belgium, Harvey Miller, (2013).
523 Marks, R., (1993), 135, 139, 140, 150, 164, Plate IX.
524 HRO X8 f. 146 & 238.
525 ibid.
526 Brown, S. (1995), 125.
527 Brown, S., 'The Medieval Stained Glass' in, *Tewkesbury Abbey: History, Art and Architecture,* Morris, Richard K. & Shoesmith, R (eds), Logaston (2003), 187.
528 Cowan, P., (1985), 172; also Marks, R., (1993), 178.
529 Brown, S. (1995), 128.
530 The work in the antechapel at New College dates from 1380–86: Cowan, P., (1985), 172; also Marks, R., (1993), 178.
531 There are many examples of the smiling lion in glass, for example, at Warham in Norfolk.
532 *Hereford Times,* 7 July 2011
533 HRO CF50/114 f. 163.
534 RCHM 3, 145.
535 RCHM 2, 141.
536 Register of Bishop Swinfield, 3 November, 1306 accessed, with thanks, at: http://www.melocki.org.uk/MelockiDiocese.html.
537 http://www.medievalgenealogy.org.uk/fines/abstracts/CP_25_1_82_32.shtml.
538 https://archives.history.ac.uk/gazetteer/herefs.html.
539 RCHM 1, 203 also BoE H, 513.
540 The name John appears in the registers from time to time down to 1347. In 1362, John's wife, Margaret, died and she, being the subject of an inquisition post-mortem, probably survived him. We can, however, be sure he was dead by October 1369 when a priest was appointed to his chantry chapel in Sutton St Nicholas. It seems unlikely then that the monument is as late as 1347-62, which suggests that there are two generations of Johns represented in the record, one whose wife was called Sarah and one whose wife was Margaret. There are, of course many other possibilities. John could have married more than once and the monument may belong to another unknown de Frene or another family (the Talbots for example), but one plausible hypothesis is that the tomb is for John I and the glass was commissioned by John II in his memory. There are other examples of glass being commissioned by aristocrats as a memorial at St Katherine's Hospital, Ledbury in the fourteenth century and, much later, at Sellack.
541 HRO X8.
542 HRO K38/Cd/5 (in the box of negatives).
543 Cole, W., (1993), 151–2.
544 Dingley, T., (1867), cclxix.
545 *The Ecclesiologist* (1866), 210.
546 Botzum, R. & C., (1997), 32.
547 Maclean, D., 'The Royal Arms in Herefordshire Churches.' *TRANS,* (1956), 115.
548 RCHM 2, 148.
549 https://www.british-history.ac.uk/vch/salop/vol10/pp151-167#p98.
550 *Gentleman's Magazine,* Vol. 103, (1833), 9.
551 BoE S, 432.
552 John 13.23–25: 'itaque cum recubuisset ille supra pectus Iesu dicit ei Domine quis est'.
553 The double-headed eagle has local significance in the arms of Leofric and Mercia, and the *Dictionary of Arms* suggests Sygeston and Morris as likely family names, although no connection has been found with Munslow. The Mytton arms had a double-headed eagle, but not in argent and sable.
554 Also, closer, at Cilcain and Llanassa which has a dense quarry background and plinths like those at Munslow.
555 Mostyn Lewis, H., 'Stained Glass in North Wales', *Archaeologica Cambrensis,* Vol. 123, (1974), 3.
556 Glynne, 27.

557 Peter Klein, *Pembridge Parish Church: some seventeenth century visitors and its medieval heraldry*, TRANS, (2012), 68–82. The arms of England quartered with France, Mortimer quartered with St George, de Braose, de Geneville, Grandison and Monnington.
558 Botzum, R. & C., (1997), 44–6.
559 RCHM 3, 159.
560 Dingley, T., (1864), 99.
561 Mostyn Lewis, H., 'Stained Glass in North Wales', *Archaeologica Cambrensis*, Vol. 123, (1974), 3 & Pl X.
562 see the Crucifixion in the east window at Llanllugan.
563 https://en.wikipedia.org/wiki/Sabaton.
564 Crampin, M., *Stained Glass from Welsh Churches*, Talybont, (2014), 39.
– see Gresford Lady Chapel and Hope.
565 HRO CF/50 119. *G: 2 barres verry (vaire)* – Say of Richards Castle. *Barry of five A & B* – de Grey? The coats illustrated in a loose note dated 1663 in a volume of Hill's *Collections*.
566 Botzum, R. & C., (1997), 51.
567 Glynne, 64.
568 The Churches Conservation Trust, *Church of St Bartholomew Richard's Castle, Herefordshire*, London, (2009), 10.
569 Tonkin, J., 'The Palaces of the Bishop of Hereford' in *TRANS*, (1976), 58. See also Marshall, G., (1922).
570 HRO X8. I am grateful for help from Bishop David Thompson in deciphering Taylor's hand and understanding the heraldry.
571 Botzum, R. & C., (1997), 53.
572 O'Connor, D., (1995), 149.
573 Marshall, G., (1922), 108–14.
574 HRO C50/116 f., 249–54.
575 Botzum, R. & C., (1997), 63.
576 Tonkin, J., 'The Palaces of the Bishop of Hereford' in *TRANS*, (1976), 53–64.
577 Marshall, G., (1922) quoting Edward Kennion's 1784 work.
578 Marshall, G., (1922) quoting John Price, *A Historical Account of the City of Hereford*, 1796, 189.
579 John Tarrant et al., *A History of St Mary's Church, Ross-on-Wye*, 2018. Ring binder held in the church or accessed at www.rawchurch.org.uk/st-marys-ross-on-wye. This is an exemplary church guide which has been the foundation of well-designed interpretation boards in the church. Old photographs show the 'iron lattice' but, the 'accounts' cannot be found to check this statement.
580 HRO L78/3 is the account book for 1772–1814. It is relatively well presented, and most recorded payments give the craft of the person being paid – unlike the later volumes L78/4E 1814–1861 and AT25/1 1862-1924 which just give lists of people presenting bills without saying what the bills are for. Marshall refers to a booklet attached to the 1814 volume prior to records being deposited in HRO which cannot be accounted for.
581 http://stainedglass.llgc.org.uk/person/469.
The company also carried out restoration work at St Weonards, recorded in an inscription of 1875, and at Kingsland in 1866. Their new work in Herefordshire can be seen in churches at Brampton Abbots, Thruxton, Titley and Little Birch and at Michaelchurch Court. Alan Brooks and Nikolaus Pevsner, *Herefordshire*, The Buildings of England, Yale University Press, (2012) – from the invaluable index of craftsmen and designers.
582 O'Connor, D., (1995), 138–149 and plates B, XXIV–XXVIII.
583 ibid.
584 O'Connor, D., (1995), 142.
585 Rushforth, G., (1936) figs. 46, 154, 158.
586 Caviness, M., (1968), Pl. 38. Glass now in a private collection.
587 O'Connor, D., (1995), 143.
588 A more modern reading might be '*I pray you will take this offered heart and cleanse its guilt*'.
589 Woodforde, C., (1936), 243.
590 Marks, R., 'Window Glass' in John Blair and Nigel Ransay (eds.), *English Medieval Industries*, London, (1991), 280.
591 HRO X8.
592 Botzum, R. & C., (1997), 71.
593 George Strong gives the same shield for Pye and Plukenet. See: http://www.bosburyhistoryresource.org.uk/Heraldry-of-Herefordshire.html#p
594 Robinson, R., *Mansions and Manors of Herefordshire*, (1873), 295.
595 HRO AB73/34.
596 *A Concise Account of Some of the Ecclesiastic and Domestic Stained Glass Windows ... by Thomas Baillie & Co*, London, (1875). A copy of this volume annotated by Baillie is in the British Library.
597 Duncumb 6. 70.
598 Jacqueline Susan Levy, *Perceptions and Beliefs: The Harleys Of Brampton Bryan and The Origins and Outbreak of The First Civil War*. Thesis submitted for the Degree of Doctor of Philosophy in the Faculty of Arts, London University. Bedford College, (1983), 62.
599 HRO AB73/24.
600 BoE H, 590.
601 He was a sound antiquary and active as an architect in Herefordshire. He married Isabel, daughter of Revd Alfred Philipps, rector of Abbey Dore, and his wife, Isabella Bulmer of the Bulmer cider family. He undertook restoration work at Abbey Dore from 1900 to 1909 saving many of the medieval fittings, including glass, tiles, stones and wood. He published reports of his restoration work and his archaeological findings in *The Builder*. Roland and Isabel Paul donated the reredos to the Abbey. http://www.sanhs.org/Documents/RolandPaul.pdf. He was working at Pembridge at the same time.
602 A drawing survives from this time in the Lambeth Palace digital archive viewable online at: http://images.lambethpalacelibrary.org.uk
603 *The Builder*, 1 June (1907), 666.
604 HRO AA/17/194/11. The original is out of focus.
605 A surviving roundel at Stanton St John, Oxfordshire, employs the same technique.
606 See for example the harpist in the *Luttrell Psalter* in the British Library.
607 The spherical bells at the ends of the chains are typical of thuribles used in the Eastern Orthodox church. This detail combined with the rather too-good-to-be-true quality of the figures may suggest that the four figures and possibly the angel roundel are modern.

608 J.P. Brooke-Little, *Boutell's Heraldry*, Warne, (1973), 183.
609 Hillaby, J., (1997), 188–9.
610 HRO C50/114 f.55.
611 https://www.historyofparliamentonline.org/volume/1386-1421/member/walwyn-thomas-i-1444
612 Faraday, M. (2012), 22.
613 RCHM 2, 172.
614 Mytton f. 1243.
615 Newton, P., (1961), 582–97.
616 RCHM 2, 174.
617 TRANS, (1917), 221. Also, HRO K38/Cd/5 (in the additional box in the photo store). The Watkins image can be seen online at https://herefordshirehistory.org.uk/archive/alfred-watkins-collection/
618 RCHM 2, 180. See also the image of 1956 on the England's Places website which shows the parlour window without the roundels. https://historicengland.org.uk/images-books/photos/englands-places/card/196219/
619 TRANS, (1903), 111.
620 Montagu, J., *Minstrels and Angels*, Berkley, (1998), 77.
621 Anderson, P., *William Chick, Herefordshire Architect*, TRANS, (2010), 160.
622 *Hereford Journal*, 17 August 1867 (accessed online at British Newspaper Archive).
623 John 15.5: *I am the vine, you are the branches.* He who abides in Me, and I in him, bears much fruit; for without Me you can do nothing.
624 BoE H, 631.
625 Cowan, P., (1985), 116 (in table).
626 HRO K38/Cd/5/1.
627 RCHM 2, 191.
628 RCHM 2, 192.
629 Strong, G., *The Heraldry of Herefordshire: Being a Collection of the Armorial Bearings of Families Which Have Been Seated in the County at Various Periods Down to the Present Time*, London, (1848).
630 TRANS. (1882), 211.
631 Hair, P., 'Chaplains, Chantries and Chapels on North-West Herefordshire *c*.1400' (Second Part) in TRANS (1989), 262.
632 There were Holy Cross guilds in Birmingham, Stratford-upon-Avon and Northampton. Other important medieval towns had Holy Cross guilds: Ely, King's Lynn, Norwich and, probably best known, the Scottish examples at Edinburgh and Stirling which had royal connections.
633 Faraday, M., (2012), 66–7. The St Nicholas service was valued at £6.17s.1d, the Our Lady Service at £1.16s.8d and the Holy Rood at 2s.8d.
634 Civil War iconoclasm was often random or inefficiently executed. The Parliamentary Ordinance of 1644 added angels to the previous lists of images which were to be demolished: 'That all Representations of any of the Persons of the Trinity, or of any Angel or Saint, in or about any Cathedral, Collegiate or Parish Church, or Chappel, or in any open place within this Kingdome, shall be taken away, defaced, and utterly demolished; And that no such shall hereafter be set up, And that the Chancel – ground of every such Church or Chappel, raised for any Altar, or Communion Table to stand upon, shall be laid down and levelled; And that no Copes, Surplisses, superstitious Vestments, Roods, or Roodlons, or Holy-water Fonts, shall be, or be any more used in any Church or Chappel within this Realm; And that no Cross, Crucifix, Picture, or Representation of any of the Persons of the Trinity, or of any Angel or Saint shall be, or continue upon any Plate, or other thing used, or to be used in or about the worship of God …' See Cooper T., (ed.), *The Journal of William Dowsing*, Woodbridge, (2001), 337–44 for a summary.
635 HRO N/3.
636 HRO K38/Cd/5 (in the additional box in the photo store). There is a glass slide of this photograph in HRO K38/Cd/7 Box 2. The church records are unhelpful about when the glass was re-leaded. The churchwarden accounts end mid-C18 and the subsequent books, HRO N3/2 and HRO N3/3 are vestry books with little said about the fabric.
637 The closest surviving scheme of Nine Orders of Angels is at Great Malvern Priory. The feathered suits with bare hands and feet are there, but there are no figures that correspond closely with the Weobley images. See Rushford, G., (1936).
638 '… many eyed Cherubim of most subtle movement bless thee.' John Parker, 'The Works of Dionysius the Areopagite: Part I', (London, Parker (1897), 190.
639 Nelson, P., *Ancient Painted Glass in England*, London, Methuen (1913), 99.
640 … and in the north window of the north transept and in St Anne's Chapel.
641 Jenny Judova, 'Wound of Christ and Arma Christi in Bohun Hours MS Auct. D.4.4, f. 236v' at https://www.academia.edu/1645156/Wound_of_Christ_and_Arma_Christi_in_Bohun_Hours_MS_Auct._D.4.4_f._236v accessed on 1 July 2019.
642 The Sunday Christ or 'Christ of the Trades' is an extension of *Arma* devotion. In the devotion the Instruments of the Passion are considered, and their torment contemplated; in the Sunday Christ, the everyday tools of people failing to attend church are accorded the power of wounding Christ.
643 The so-called 9 Orders of Angels are represented at Gresford, Great Malvern in two schemes and in the tracery lights of the north choir clerestory at Ludlow (Fig. 19).
644 BoE S, 712.
645 Collections of E. Hardwick: BM Additional MS. 29245, 94. As quoted by Newton, P., (1961), Vol. III 617.
646 ibid.
647 Winston, C., *An Inquiry into the Difference of Style Observable in Ancient Glass Paintings, Especially in England; with Hints on Glass Painting, by an Amateur*, Vol. II, Oxford (1847), 19 & Plate 49. Winston says it is from the 'east window'.
648 BoE H, 685.
649 Glynne, 21.
650 *Hereford Journal*, Saturday 24 October 1863.
651 HRO L36/1.
652 Weaver, P., (2015), 91 says these were erected at Whitfield, the family home.

APPENDIX ONE: GAZETTEER OF CHURCHES IN NORTH SHROPSHIRE

1. As with Part Two, all original photographs have been deposited with CVMA, libraries and records offices.
2. Brown, S., *Stained Glass at York Minster*, London (2017), 74; Marks, R., (1993), 182; Newton, P., (1961), 98–134.
3. This window can be explored on the website: York Minster Stained Glass Navigator (yorkglazierstrust.org)
4. Newton, P., (1961), 98.
5. ibid, 113 and 116.
6. Martin, P.L., *The European Trade in Stained Glass, with Special Reference to the Trade between the Rhineland and the United Kingdom, 1794–1835*, MPhil Thesis, The University of York (2012). This exceptional study tells the fascinating story of the trade in religious glass from the Continent.
7. … and 133 in the two counties combined.
8. See monument to Elizabeth Kynnersley (d.1649) in the church.
9. Cranage, D., Part IX, (1908), 174.
10. Cole, W., (1993), 14. These roundels are not illustrated in his survey and he has reversed their order across the window.
11. The Arts Society inventory of the church.
12. Vested in the Churches Conservation Trust.
13. Cranage, D., 'Battlefield Church', *Transactions of the Shropshire Archaeological and Natural History Society* Vol. 3, pt. II (1903), 171–6. Cranage says the tower was not started until after 1444 and took more than fifty years to complete. Also, BoE S. 136.
14. Fletcher, W., 'The Stained Glass Formerly in Battlefield Church' in *Transactions of the Shropshire Archaeological and Natural History Society*, Vol. 3, pt. II (1903), xix–xxi.
15. Good, J., *The Cult of St George in Medieval England*, Woodbridge (2009), 81.
16. SRO XPR/2/27.
17. Under the direction of the architect Samuel Pountney Smith.
18. op. cit. Fletcher, xxi.
19. Phillip Corbet lived at Belmont, on the south side of Shrewsbury.
20. Neale, J.P., *Views of the Seats of Noblemen and Gentlemen in England, Scotland, Wales and Ireland*, Second Series Volume 3, (1826).
21. Shropshire Archives, *Collections relating to Battlefield*, Ref. 6001/225 has sketches of the fragments on a loose folio.
22. In the Uffington parish file on the England's Places website.
23. The Sundorne Laurence looks earlier than the Battlefield head. Could there have been an earlier or unfinished Laurence window in Ludlow?
24. Nelson, P., (1913), 174: 'The glass as now, … *with natural leaf work*'.
25. BoE S, 139.
26. *Oswestry Advertiser*, 12 December 1877, 4.
27. *Oswestry Advertiser*, 12 December 1887, 8.
28. *Wellington Journal*, 30 April 1887, 3.
29. Cranage, D., Part III (1905), 173; Gorton, A., *The Heraldry of Dudleston Church* (held at Oswestry Library, ref. XLS 16013).
30. Eyton, R.W., *The Antiquities of Shropshire*, Vol. 9 (1859), 127.
31. There are several good modern windows including work by Hardman and Kempe. In the chancel south window (sIII) are Mary Magdalene and Martha by William Morris.
32. Brooke, I., *English Costume in the Later Middle Ages*, London (1935), 14, 30, 38. See, for example, the image of Princess Joan (1326–1385) in BL MS Cotton Nero D VII.
33. Cox, D., *Sir Stephen Glynne's Church Notes for Shropshire*, Keele (1997), 59.
34. Cranage, D., Part IX, (1908), 772.
35. BoE S, 412.
36. Shropshire Archives, *Collections relating to Battlefield*, Ref. 6001/225, 18.
37. Newton, P., (1961), 565–9.
38. Shropshire Archives PH/P/28/39 is a photograph of the roundels in situ.
39. Ayre, K., *Medieval English Figurative Roundels*, Corpus Vitrearum Medii Aevi and The British Academy (2002), 114. *Transactions of the Shropshire Archaeological and Natural History Society*, Vol. 19, pt. 2 (1896), 157 quotes Blakeway's notes: 'The windows were filled with roundels of stained glass, descriptive of several months of the year – March, a man digging, with a flagon of liquor by his side; April, one frightening birds from the corn; June, a labourer weeding corn; September, threshing; November, killing a Pig, which is done not by our present mode of sticking, but, by felling with a hatchet; and December, an infant with crown and sceptre and covered cup, also a cypher.'
40. ibid.
41. *Vidimus* 111.
42. September | Unknown | V&A Explore The Collections (vam.ac.uk).
43. Ayre, K., (2002) has a copy of Blakeway's sketch of this eroded picture.
44. Moriarty, A., *Explanatory Note of Shrewsbury Museum Roundels*, unreferenced note attached to the Museum catalogue.
45. Owen, H., *Some Account of the Ancient and Present State of Shrewsbury*, Shrewsbury (1808), 247.
46. Lloyd, J., *Notes on St Mary's Church, Shrewsbury*, Shrewsbury (1900), 61, suggests that they are now in the west window of the Abbey Church which was another glazing project supervised by Rowland. However, neither of the shields could be found there now.
47. BoE S, 531. St Chad's was closed for worship because of its condition, and the parishioners were accommodated at St Mary's. When St Chad's was demolished the Jesse window was presented to St Mary's as a token of gratitude.
48. Newton, P., (1961), 580.
49. Pidgeon, H., *Memorials of Shrewsbury*, Shrewsbury (1851), 74.
50. ibid. diagram after 581.
51. ibid. 69.
52. Hebgin-Barnes, P., *The Medieval Stained Glass of Cheshire*, The British Academy for Corpus Vitrearum Medii Aevi (2010), cli–clv.
53. Blue behind the Shrewsbury kings and green at Grappenhall.
54. Shropshire Archives PH/S/13/S/39/75.
55. Lloyd, J., *Notes on St Mary's Church, Shrewsbury*, Shrewsbury (1900), 61.
56. The claustral buildings of Herkenrode Abbey still stand about 25km north west of Maastricht. The Abbey was destroyed by fire in 1828.

57 Martin, P.L., *The European Trade in Stained Glass, with Special Reference to the Trade between the Rhineland and the United Kingdom, 1794–1835*, MPhil Thesis, the University of York (2012).
58 Bartles-Smith, D., *A Royal Church in Shrewsbury*, Shrewsbury (2014), 24.
59 These beautiful figures can be seen on the V&A website: Prophet Ezekiel flanked by Saints John the Evangelist and James the Less | Thomas of Oxford | Thomas of Oxford | V&A Explore The Collections (vam.ac.uk).
60 Pidgeon, H., *Memorials of Shrewsbury*, Shrewsbury (1851), 77, reports the St Bernard panels. The earlier 1837 edition (p. 45) records the Winchester saints.
61 *Vidimus*, 128 (2019).
62 ibid. Pidgeon (1851). Altenburg is 25km south of Leipzig.
63 Op. cit. Martin, P. L., (2012), 166.
64 In glass from L'eglise Sainte-Jeanne-d'Arc formerly in L'eglise Saint-Vincent, Rouen and in the Crucifixion from Rouen now in York Minster.
65 Cole, W., (1993), 255. Gives them as Mark and John the Evangelist.
66 Herkenrode Abbey is south east of Antwerp near Hasselt. The glass at Shrewsbury, Lichfield and Ashtead (Surrey) is catalogued in: Vanden Bemden, Y., and Lecocq, I., *The Stained Glass of Herkenrode Abbey*, The British Academy, (2022).
67 *Vidimus*, 128 (2019).
68 Trier is a German city in the Moselle region, near the Luxembourg border.
69 Moriarty, A., 'Notes on the Glass: S. Mary's, Shrewsbury', *Transactions of the Shropshire Archaeological and Natural History Society*, Vol. 8, pt. I (1921), 133–41.
70 *Vidimus*, 128 (2019).
71 Ayre, K., *Medieval English Figurative Roundels*, British Academy (2002), 113.
72 ibid.
73 *Vidimus*, 128 (2019).
74 de Turberville, or perhaps a version of the Talbot shield.
75 ibid. suggests the glass is from Munsterbilzen Abbey, Limburg (Belgium).
76 ibid.
77 The bishop bears no attributes, neither the sword of Lambert nor the stag of Hubert.
78 *Vidimus*, 128 (2019).
79 Newton, P., (1961), 608.
80 BoE S, 659.
81 Eyton, R.W., *The Antiquities of Shropshire*, Vol. 2 (1855), 256–7.
82 Newton, P., (1961), 609.
83 His record of the tombs is unusually detailed with drawings and notes, and he recorded a few inscriptions in the windows. Had any arms or figures remained he would have noted them.
84 Collins, P., Ed. *Corpus of Kempe Stained Glass*, Kempe Trust (2000), 253.
85 The guidebook published in 2002 (reprint 2014) compiled by Robert Jeffery.
86 Newton, P., (1961), 603–5.
87 Nelson, P., (1913), 180.
88 *County Advertiser and Herald for Staffordshire and Worcestershire*, 3 July 1897. This article refers to 'patches of ancient glass of rare excellence … It would be tedious to recount the subjects depicted, and it may suffice to say that it contains, *inter alia*, representations of the articles … associated with the passion of our Saviour.' It also suggests that the glass had been buried to escape iconoclasm, and later dug up.
89 There is an important representation of the Annunciation on the misericord of the master's stall in which the pot of lilies bears the Crucified Christ.
90 It is worth noting that the wings of these ghostly angels are not much like those surviving at Haddon Hall.
91 Newton, P., (1961), 98.
92 Nelson, P., (1913), 174.
93 Church Guide, 8.
94 Bagshaw, S., *History, Gazetteer and Directory of Shropshire*, Sheffield (1851), 98.
95 Leighton, W.A., *A guide, descriptive and historical, through the Town of Shrewsbury*, John Davies (1855), 79.
96 Newman, J. & Pevsner, N., *The Buildings of England: Shropshire*, Yale University Press (2006), 666. This attribution is supported by a Swiss panel dated 1618 in the collection of the V&A. It bears the arms of Hofmann von Baden, Abbot of Einsiedeln. The panel, Ref. 9057-1863, was purchased by the V&A in 1863.
97 Maurice, D., *A History of English Glass-painting with some remarks upon the Swiss glass miniatures of the sixteenth and seventeenth centuries*, London, 1912.
98 With further reference to his notes on the CVMA website.
99 BoE S, 689.
100 The title of the peerage refers to the Shropshire hundred of Bradford.

APPENDIX TWO: OTHER IMPORTANT STAINED GLASS IN THE REGION OF THE WELSH MARCHES

101 Painton Cowan's national survey (Cowan, P., 1985) remains the best guide, if a second-hand copy can be found.
102 Crampin, M., *Stained Glass from Welsh Churches*, Talybont, (2014).

APPENDIX THREE: NOTES ON CONSERVATORS AND RESTORERS

103 The indexes of artists in BoE H and BoE S are the sources of many of the new works quoted here.
The principal studios are represented in Hereford Cathedral see Morgan, F. C. (1979) and Iles, P. (2000).
104 Chronology taken from the Sussex Churches website.
105 *Hampshire Observer* and *Basingstoke News* – 2 August 1913, 8.
106 Collins, P.N.H., *The Corpus of Kempe Stained Glass in the United Kingdom and Ireland*, The Kempe Trust, (2000).
107 Bellamy, R., Goodey, B., Thompson, D., & Wheeler, R., *William Morris at Middleton Cheney: The Stained Glass in All Saints Church*, Fircone Books, (2019).
108 Warrington, W., *The History of Stained Glass, from the Earliest Period of the Art to the Present Time*, London, (1848).

LIST OF FIGURES

Fig. 1	Eaton Bishop: Madonna and Child (I.2a) (C14)	ii
Fig. 2	Eaton Bishop: Archangel Gabriel (I.2b) (C14)	x

PART ONE

Fig. 3	Assembly of a leaded window over a cartoon	3
Fig. 4	Antiquarian sketches of lost glass at Dilwyn	5
Fig. 5	Credenhill: Bishops Thomas Becket and Thomas Cantilupe (sIV) (C14)	10
Fig. 6	Stanford-on-Avon, Northants: St Barnabas (nIII) (C14)	11
Fig. 7	Richard's Castle: Christ with a cruciform nimbus (sIV) (C14)	11
Fig. 8	Donington: Christ with a cruciform nimbus (nIII) (C14)	11
Figs 9a–c	Comparison of kings in C14 Jesse windows	12
Fig. 9a	Madley (I.2b)	
Fig. 9b	Ludlow (sV.2b)	
Fig. 9c	Merevale (I.3d)	
Fig. 10	King Ozias from Madley Jesse window (I.2a) (C14)	12
Figs 11a–c	Comparison of C14 faces	14
Fig. 11a	Kempsey: St Catherine (sIII.2a)	
Fig. 11b	Worcester Cathedral: Crowned saint in nave S aisle	
Fig. 11c	Hadzor: Annunciation now in Ely Stained Glass Museum	
Figs 12a–c	Comparison of C14 faces	14
Fig. 12a	Oxford, Christ Church Cathedral: Archangel Gabriel (nVII)	
Fig. 12b	Ledbury Church: Archangel Michael (I.C2)	
Fig. 12c	Ledbury St Katherine's Hospital: St Margaret (I)	

INSETS OF CHANGING FACES:		16–17
Inset 1	Astley Abbotts: the face of Christ (I) (C13)	
Inset 2	Madley: the Last Supper (I.3b) (C13)	
Inset 3	Hughley: fragments (nII.A3) (C13)	
Inset 4	Hereford Cathedral: the Crucified Christ (sV) (C13)	
Inset 5	Ledbury: King Herod (nX.1d) (c.1300)	
Inset 6	Donington: a king (nIII) (late C13)	
Inset 7	Madley: the head of a king (I.2a) (C14)	
Inset 8	Kempsey, Worcs.: a head (nII.2b) (C14)	
Inset 9	Abbey Dore: a head (sX) (C14)	
Inset 10	Madley: the Madley Master experimenting (sII.6a) (C14)	
Inset 11	A head from the Ludlow Tree of Jesse window (sV.A2) (C14)	
Inset 12	The Virgin in Latin Chapel, Oxford Cathedral (nVII) (C14)	
Inset 13	Eaton Bishop: Archangel Michael (I.1b) (C14)	
Inset 14	Fladbury: the Virgin (detached panel)	
Inset 15	Wormbridge): St Peter (sII) (later C14)	
Inset 16	Tarrington: female figure (sII) (c.1400)	
Inset 17	Madley: figure possibly by Thomas of Oxford (nII.4b) (C14)	
Inset 18	Weobley: an angel (nV.C2) (C15)	
Inset 19	Presteigne: a bearded face (sIII) (C15)	
Inset 20	Old Radnor: St Catherine (nII) (C15)	

Fig. 13	Deerhurst, Gloucestershire: St Catherine (s.IX.2b) (C14)	18
Figs 14a–b	Madonna and Child figures from the same cartoon (C14)	18
Fig. 14a	Madonna and Child, Warndon, Worcs	
Fig. 14b	Madonna and Child, Fladbury, Worcs	
Fig. 15	Chapel of Hampton Court: Assumption of Virgin (Burrell Collection) (C15)	20
Fig. 16	Chapel of Hampton Court: Annunciation (Burrell Collection) (C15)	20
Fig. 17	Hereford Cathedral Old Library: Dingley's sketch of the Virgin	24
Fig. 18	St Weonards: Man of Sorrows (nIII. B3) (C15)	25
Fig. 19	Ludlow: Nine Orders of Angels (nIII tracery) (C15)	26

PART TWO

Fig. 20	Abbey Dore: A Cistercian possibly Abbot Straddell (1305–46) (sVIII.7)	35
Fig. 21	Abbey Dore: coif-capped head of a woman (sVIII.5) (C15)	35
Fig. 22	Abbey Dore: S chapel (sIX)	36
Fig. 23	Abbey Dore, S chapel: Faces by the Madley Master (sIX.7) (C14)	36
Figs 24a–c	Abbey Dore: Viscount Scudamore's great E window of 1634 (I)	37–8
Fig. 24a	Abbey Dore: E window, central light	37
Figs 24b–c	Abbey Dore: E window, flanking lights	38
Fig. 25	Abbey Dore: St Mark (I.2b)	39
Fig. 26	Abbey Dore: vidimus for Viscount John Scudamore's great E window	40
Fig. 27a	Abbey Dore: the Ascension (I.1c)	41
Fig. 27b	The Ascension by Egbert van Panderen (1581–1637) published in Haarlem by Theodore Galle (1571–1633)	41
Fig. 28	Aconbury: quatrefoil using glass of c.1270 (nIII)	42
Figs 29a–b	Alberbury: panels from SE window of Loton Chapel	43
Fig. 29a	A censing angel (sV.C3) (C14)	
Fig. 29b	The Coronation of the Virgin (sV.C2) (C14)	
Fig. 30	Allensmore: Crucifixion in E window (I) (C14)	44
Fig. 31	Alveley: St Armel and St Anthony (SII) (C16)	46
Fig. 31a	Alveley: St Armel (SII) (C16)	47
Fig. 32	Alveley: the Virgin Annunciate (SII) (C16)	48
Fig. 33	Astley Abbotts: Apostle in E window (I) (C13)	49
Fig. 34	Atcham: glass from Bacton, restored by Betton & Evans (I) (C15)	51
Fig. 35	Atcham: memorial to Blanche Parry of Bacton (nV) (C15)	51
Figs 36a–b	Bishopstone: Netherlandish roundels (sII) (C16)	52
Fig. 36a	Crucifixion	
Fig. 36b	Marriage of Tobit	
Fig. 37	Brinsop: St George (I) (C14)	54
Fig. 38	Brinsop: Christ in Majesty (nV) (C14)	55
Fig. 39	Brockhampton by Ross: angel (sV) (C15)	56
Figs 40a–b	Bromfield: Netherlandish roundels (vestry) (C16)	56
Fig. 40a	Nativity	
Fig. 40b	Crucifixion	
Fig. 41	Castle Frome: donor's head (sIV) (C15)	57
Fig. 42	Church Stretton: Netherlandish roundels of Circumcision (nII.2b) and Crucifixion (nii.1b) (c.1540)	58
Fig. 43	Claverley: an angel in N aisle (nIV)	59
Fig. 44	Clehonger: fragments (nVI) (C14)	59
Figs 45a–b	Clehonger: two heads (nVI) (C14)	59
Fig. 46	Coalbrookdale: The Last Supper and Christ washing Peter's feet (sII) (C16)	61
Fig. 47	Cound: St John the Evangelist (sV) (C14)	63
Fig. 48	Credenhill: detail of nave NE window (nIII) (C14)	64
Fig. 49	Diddlebury: Crucifixion (nII) (C14)	65
Fig. 50	Dilwyn: angel thurifers (sIII) (C14)	66
Fig. 51	Donington: fragments (nIII) (C14)	67
Fig. 52	Donington: Doom figures (nII) (C15)	68
Fig. 53	Eardisland: antiquarian records of heraldry	69
Fig. 54	Eaton Bishop: Alfred Watkins's photograph of E window	72
Fig. 55	Eaton Bishop: east window (I)	73
Fig. 56	Eaton Bishop: Crucifixion and donors (sII)	79
Fig. 57	Foy: E window (I) (C17)	81
Fig. 58	Sellack: E window (I) (C17)	81
Fig. 59	Goodrich: the Lisle arms (nII) (C15)	83
Fig. 60	Hampton Court Chapel: before sale of glass in 1924	84
Fig. 61	Hampton Court Chapel: Deposition by Abraham van Linge	85
Figs 62a–c	Hentland: figures in E window (I) (C15)	90–1
Fig. 62a	Donor Richard Rotheram	90
Fig. 62b	Unidentified figure	90
Fig. 62c	Unidentified figure	91
Fig. 63	Hereford Cathedral: Dingley's drawing of the Virgin in old library	93
Fig. 64	Hereford Cathedral Audley Chapel: quarry signed by glazier in 1822	96

Fig. 65	Hereford Cathedral: glass from Hampton Court (nXVIII) (C15)	98
Fig. 66	Hereford Cathedral: glass from Hampton Court (nXIX) (C15)	98
Fig. 67	Hereford Cathedral: saints (nVIII) (C14)	101
Fig. 68	Hereford Cathedral: Mary Magdalene (sX) (C15)	102
Fig. 69	Hereford Cathedral: Joseph lowered into the dry well (sXIV) (C15)	102
Figs 70a–b	Hereford Cathedral Lady Chapel windows	104
Fig. 70a	Christ in Majesty and medallions (sV) (C13)	
Fig. 70b	Grisaille glass (sVI) (C13)	
Figs 71a–d	Hereford Cathedral: fragments in cathedral archives (C15)	107
Fig. 72	Hereford, Coningsby Hospital: Coningsby heraldry (nII) (1614)	108
Fig. 73	Hereford Museum: fragment from Craswall Priory	109
Figs 74a–b	Hereford Museum and Walterstone	109
Fig. 74a	arms of William Cecil in museum store (C16)	
Fig. 74b	arms of William Cecil, Walterstone Church (sII) (C16)	
Figs 75a–c	Holme Lacy: N side of chancel (nIII) (C15)	110
Fig. 75a	Head of Edward the Confessor(?)	
Fig. 75b	Woman wearing a horned headdress	
Fig. 75c	Bearded head with liripipe hood	
Fig. 76	Hopesay: Fitzalan coat of arms (sIX) (1390–97)	111
Fig. 77	Hughley: William Mytton's sketches of lost glass	112
Figs 78a–b	Hughley: fragments of faces (nII) (C13)	112
Fig. 79	Kentchurch Court: arms of Canton of Zurich (C16)	113
Fig. 80	King's Caple: head of Christ (nV.B2) (C15)	113
Figs 81a–d	Kingsland: tracery lights	114
Fig. 81a	Christ in Majesty, on rainbow (I.B2) (C14)	
Fig. 81b	Coronation of the Virgin (I.A2, I.A3) (C14)	
Fig. 81c	Coronation of the Virgin (I.A2, I.A3) (C14)	
Fig. 81d	Christ in Majesty (I.B2) and the Coronation of the Virgin in situ (I.A2, I.A3) (C14)	
Fig. 82	Kingsland: the four archangels (I) (C14 & C19)	115
Fig. 83	Kinlet: donor knight (I) (C15 & C19)	118
Fig. 84	Birtsmorton: donor knight (sII) (C15)	118
Fig. 85	Kinlet: the face of Christ (sIV) (C15)	118
Fig. 86	Ledbury: extract churchwardens' accounts	119
Fig. 87	Ledbury: two portioner donors (I.C4 & I.C6) (C14)	120
Fig. 88	Ledbury: Archangel Michael (I.C4 & I.C6) (C14)	121
Fig. 89	Ledbury: angle thurifers (I.B4 & I.B5) (C14)	122
Figs 90a–b	Ledbury: the Flight into Egypt and Slaughter of the Innocents (nX) (C13?)	124
Fig. 91	Ledbury: sundial (nXVII)	124
Figs 92a–b	Ledbury, St Katherine's Hospital chapel: composite figures (C14)	125
Figs 93a–b	LLanwarne: scenes from story of Sorghelosse (sVI.2c and sVI.3b) (C16)	127
Fig. 93a	Sorghelosse in poverty, before fire	
Fig. 93b	Sorghelosse returns home	
Figs 94a–b	Dunfield House, Lower Harpton: details from staircase window	128
Fig. 94a	A queen (C15)	
Fig. 94b	A king (C15)	
Fig. 95	Ludlow: Jesse window (sV) (C14 & C19)	131
Fig. 95a	Ludlow: Micah (sV.2b) (C14)	132
Fig. 95b	Ludlow: King Joram (sV.4a) (C14)	132
Figs 96a–d	Ludlow: figures from St Katherine's Chapel (sIX) (C15)	132
Figs 97a–b	Ludlow: comparison of the Virgin Annunciate (nVII) with the Virgin in the Beauchamp Chapel, Warwick (I) (C15)	134
Fig. 98	Ludlow: the Golden Window with saints Catherine, John the Baptist and Christopher, the Quinity and donors (nVIII) (C15)	134
Figs 99a–b	Ludlow: the Creed Window (nVII) (C15)	136
Fig. 100	Ludlow: the Palmers' Window (nV) (C15)	137
Fig. 100a	Ludlow: Guild Feast in the Palmers' Window (nV.1d) (C15)	137
Figs 101a–c	Ludlow: details of the east window (I)	139–40
Fig. 101a	Bishop Spofford and Anne teaching the Virgin (I.A6, A7) (C15)	139
Fig. 101b	The Throne of Mercy (I.D6) (C15)	140
Fig. 101c	A medieval figure beside Evans's work (I.2c) (C15/ C19)	140
Figs 102a–b	Ludlow: Evans's work and Mytton's record (I.2d) (C15/ C19)	140
Figs 103a–c	Ludlow: panels from Commandments Window	143
Fig. 103a	False Witness (sII.1a) (C15)	
Fig. 103b	Covetousness (sII.1e) (C15)	
Fig. 103c	Murder (sII.2a) (C15)	
Fig. 104	Madley: E windows (I, nII & sII) (C14 & C15)	150
Fig. 105	Madley: scenes of life of St John and the Passion (I) (C13)	152
Figs 106a–b	Madley: heads of clerics in the chancel S window (sII.5a & 5b)	155
Figs 107a–e	Madley: comparison with work at New College, Oxford by Thomas Glazier	156

Figs 107a & e	Oxford	
Figs 107b–d	Madley	
Figs 108a–c	Madley: details of window nII (C14 & C15)	157
Figs 108a–b	Hidden angel figures	
Fig. 108c	Lion of St Mark & Bull of St Luke	
Fig. 109	Michaelchurch Escley: Instruments of the Passion (sIV) (C15)	159
Fig. 110	Moccas: canopy-work in N nave windows (nIII) (C14)	160
Fig. 111	Moccas: arms of de Frenes (sIII)	161
Fig. 112a	Dingley's drawing of arms in E window	162
Fig. 112b	Royal head in nave N window (nII) (C14)	162
Fig. 113	Morville: Crucifixion (nII) (C14)	163
Fig. 114	Much Marcle: Royal Arms of Charles I (nII) (C17)	164
Fig. 115	Munsley: a leopard mask (nV) (C15?)	165
Fig. 116	Munslow: donor John Lloyd from William Mytton's notes	165
Fig. 117	Munslow: Crucifixion and donors (nIV) (C15/ C19)	166
Fig. 118	Munslow: Virgin and Child (sVI.2a) (C15/ C19)	169
Fig. 119	Munslow: donors (sVI.1a) (C15/ C19)	169
Fig. 120	Old Radnor: St Catherine (nII) (C15)	170
Fig. 121	Old Radnor: Bull of Clarence (nII) (C15)	170
Figs 122a–b	Orleton: nave N window (nIII) (C14)	171
Fig. 122a	Head of a lady	
Fig. 122b	Head of a prelate	
Figs 123a–b	Pembridge: aisle W windows	171
Fig. 123a	An angel (nIX.A3) (C14)	
Fig. 123b	St Christopher (sX.B2) (C14)	
Fig. 124	Pitchford: head of Christ (sV) (C14)	172
Fig. 125	Pixley: fragment in S nave window (sIV) (C15)	173
Fig. 126	Presteigne: collection of fragments (sIII) (C15)	174
Figs 126a–b	Presteigne: Faces (sIII) (C15)	174
Figs 127a–b	Richards Castle: Coronation of the Virgin (nIII.A2 & A3) (C14)	176
Fig. 128	Ross-on-Wye: collection of fragments (sX) (C15)	177
Fig. 129	Ross-on-Wye: E window (I) (C15)	179
Fig. 130	Ross-on-Wye: Bishop Spofford, the Virgin and St Anne (I.2b) (C15)	180
Fig. 131	St Weonards: E window of N aisle (nIII) (C15/ C16)	182
Fig. 132	St Weonards: E window of N aisle (nIII) before restoration	182
Figs 133a–d	Sarnesfield: various figures (sII) (C14 & C15)	186
Figs 133a & b	Angel figures	
Fig. 133c	Figure of an Apostle	
Fig. 133d	Figure of a musician	
Fig. 134	Sarnesfield: Archangel Gabriel (sII) (C14)	187
Fig. 135	Sellack: the Throne of Mercy (sV) (C15)	190
Figs 136a–c	Stoke Edith: details from the tower W window (C15)	190
Fig. 137	Stottesdon: heraldic glass in S aisle (sVII) (C15)	191
Figs 138a–b	Tarrington: details from S chancel window (sII) (C15)	193
Fig. 139	Tarrington: St Catherine (sII) (C15)	193
Fig. 140	Thruxton: cup-and-cover decoration (sII)	194
Fig. 141	Thruxton: Crucifixion (sII) (C15)	194
Fig. 142	Ullingswick: Virgin and Child (I) (C15/ C19)	195
Fig. 143	Wellington: head of an abbot (sII.A2) (C15)	197
Fig. 144	Weobley: angels (nV) (c.1400)	198
Figs 144a–b	Weobley: angels bearing symbols of the Passion (nV) (c.1400)	199
Fig. 145	Worfield: Crucifixion (sVI) (C14/ C19)	203
Figs 146a–b	Worfield: head of a king and Winston's drawing of a woman	203
Fig. 147	Worfield: angel musician (sVII) (C14)	204
Fig. 148	Wormbridge: Madonna and Child (nII) (C15)	205
Fig. 149	Wormbridge: Slaughter of the Innocents (nII) (C15)	206
Figs 150a–d	Wormbridge: saints and prophets (sII) (C14)	206
Fig. 150a	St Peter	
Fig. 150b	St Margaret	
Fig. 150c	A prophet	
Fig. 150d	St Edmund	

APPENDIX I: NORTH SHROPSHIRE

Fig. 151	Shrewsbury, St Mary: Tree of Jesse (I)	208
Fig. 152a	Badger: The five wounds (I.B2) (C15)	211
Fig. 152b	Badger: The five wounds drawn by William Mytton	211
Fig. 153a	Badger: St John the Baptist (I.A1) (C17)	211
Fig. 153b	Badger: St Margaret (I.A3) (c.1500)	211
Fig. 154	Battlefield: Sketch of glass formerly in a N window	213
Figs 155a–g	Battlefield: comparative heads	214
Fig. 155a	A detached head of St Laurence in vestry (C15)	
Fig. 155b	Mytton's drawing of the head of St Laurence in Ludlow Church	

Fig. 155c	Ludlow, St Laurence, east window: David Evans's head of St Laurence	
Fig. 155d	St Laurence being stoned, formerly in library of Sundorne Castle	
Fig. 155e	St Laurence being stoned, Ludlow, St Laurence, east window	
Fig. 155f	Head of a king in vestry (C15)	
Fig. 155g	Unidentified head in the vestry at Battlefield (C15)	
Fig. 156	Battlefield: Female figure in the vestry N window (C15)	215
Fig. 157	Beckbury: fragments (sV) (C14)	215
Figs 158a–b	Clungunford: heads in the York style	216
Fig. 158a	(I.A2) (C15)	
Fig. 158b	(I.A3) (C15)	
Fig. 159	Dudleston: W window including a Crucifixion (C16/ C17)	217
Figs 160a–e	Edgmond: Small roundels with heads (nVI) (C15)	218
Fig. 161	Edstaston: God the Father (sV.A3) (C15)	218
Fig. 162	Eyton on the Weald Moors: St Catherine (nII.1a) (C15)	219
Fig. 163	Eyton on the Weald Moors: St Christopher (nII.1b) (C15)	219
Fig. 164	Hopton Wafers: an angel (W) (C15)	220
Fig. 165	Little Ness: face of Christ (vestry east) (C15)	221
Fig. 166a	Prees: Kneeling knight (nIII) (C15)	221
Fig. 166	Prees: glass removed from Battlefield	222
Figs 167a–c	Prees: N aisle NE window (nIII)	223
Fig. 167a	Heads of the Baptist, Herod and Herodias (nIII.2a) (C14)	
Fig. 167b	A man leading a scold (nIII.2c) (C15)	
Fig. 167c	The Throne of Mercy and Instruments of the Passion (nIII.3c) (C15)	
Fig. 168	Shawbury: Fragmentary figure, possibly the Virgin of the Annunciation (sIII)	225
Fig. 169	Sheriffhales: a panel of fragments (sIII)	225
Figs 170a–c	Shrewsbury Museum: Roundels from Pulley Farmhouse, showing the Labours of the Month	226
Fig. 170a	June	
Fig. 170b	September	
Fig. 170c	August	
Figs 171a–c	Shrewsbury St Mary: Jesse window kings (I) (C14/ C19)	227
Fig. 171a	King Roboam	
Fig. 171b	King Ozias	
Fig. 171c	King Aza	
Figs 172a–b	Shrewsbury St Mary: comparison with faces and rinceau at Grappenhall	228
Fig. 173	The Revd Hugh Owen's summerhouse (now demolished)	228
Figs 174a–b	Shrewsbury St Mary: panels from N chancel window (nII)	229
Fig. 174a	Angels checking the brothers' devotions (nII.1b) (C15)	
Fig. 174b	Bernard appeals for release of a thief (nII.1c) (C15)	
Figs 175a–g	Shrewsbury St Mary: roundels in the former vestry (C16)	230
Fig. 175a	The Betrayal (vestry nII & nIII.1b)	
Fig. 175b	Esther appealing to Ahasuerus on behalf of her people (vestry nII & nIII.2c)	
Fig. 175c	Joseph's brethren showing coat of many colours to Jacob (vestry nII & nIII.2d)	
Fig. 175d	An act of mercy in giving water to the thirsty (vestry EI.3b)	
Fig. 175e	The Jew falling among thieves (vestry EI.1a)	
Fig. 175f	Jonah gazing at Nineveh (vestry EI.2a)	
Fig. 175g	A Dominican monk being welcomed, with God looking down (vestry EII.3b)	
Figs 176a–c	Shrewsbury St Mary: Roundels in the Catherine Chapel (C16)	232
Fig. 176a	St Luke with his ox (nV.B1)	
Fig. 176b	St Mark with his lion (nV.B2)	
Fig. 176c	The Risen Christ (nV.C1)	
Fig. 177	Shrewsbury St Mary: St Nicholas Chapel: St Michael triumphing over Satan (nVII.3d) (C16)	233
Fig. 178	Shrewsbury St Mary: Mary of the Seven Sorrows (nXII.3b) (C16)	234
Figs 179a–b	Shrewsbury St Mary: donors with their patron saints St Luke and St Agatha (nXI.1a and 3b) (C16)	235
Figs 180a–b	Shrewsbury St Mary: panels from Trier Cathedral	236
Fig. 180a	St Jerome (nX) (C16)	
Fig. 180b	The Virgin and Child (sX) (C16)	
Figs 181a–b	Shrewsbury St Mary: English roundels in S porch (C15)	237
Figs 182a–e	Shrewsbury St Mary: fragments in N porch (C15)	239
Figs 183a–c	Shrewsbury St Mary: Roundels in N porch	239
Fig. 183a	A family at Prayer (C16)	
Fig. 183b	St John the Evangelist & St Gertrude (C16)	
Fig. 183c	The Virgin Mary (C16)	
Fig. 184	Tong: the Annunciation (I.C3 & C4) (C15)	241
Fig. 185	Tong: 'York' quarries (sIII) (C15)	241
Fig. 186	Tong: a saint and angels (W.B2) (C15)	242
Figs 187a–b	Tong: two groups of figures (W.A2 & A5) (C15)	242

LIST OF FIGURES

Fig. 188	Tong: St Edmund, St Peter and the Virgin and Child (W)	243
Fig. 189	Tugford: William Mytton's sketches of glass now lost	244
Figs 190a–b	Uffington: Swiss panels	245
Fig. 190a	The Good Shepherd (sII) (C16)	
Fig. 190b	The Baptism of Christ (VIII) (C16)	
Figs 191a–e	Uffington: Roundels not illustrated by William Cole	246
Fig. 191a	Christ washing the disciples' feet (sII.3) (c16)	
Fig. 191b	The Last Supper (nIII.2a) (C16)	
Fig. 191c	Christ before Pilate (nIII.2b) (C16)	
Fig. 191d	Unidentified subject (sII.1) (C16)	
Fig. 191e	Tobias burns the liver of the fish (sXII.1) (C16)	
Fig. 192	Wroxeter: Angel bearing the Five Wounds (nV.A2) (C15)	248

APPENDIX THREE: NOTES ON RESTORERS

Fig. 193	Stanton Lacy: E window by David Evans	252
Fig. 194	Monkland: E window by Clayton and Bell	253
Fig. 195	Pudleston: Apostles by Hardman & Co.	253
Fig. 196	Leominster: Nativity by Kempe & Co.	254
Fig. 197	Pixley: Annunciation by Morris & Co.	255

FRONT COVER

The east window at Eaton Bishop with the Archangel Michael at the centre.

BACK COVER

MAIN PICTURE:
The chancel of Abbey Dore looking east.

SMALL PICTURES CLOCKWISE FROM BOTTOM LEFT:
Ludlow, Jesse Window, King Joram.
Donington, Doom figures.
Hampton Court, The Deposition.
Ullingswick, Virgin and Child.
Brinsop, Christ in Glory.
Hope Bowdler, St Martin and the beggar.
Monkhopton, The Road to Golgotha.

INDEX OF PLACES

Main entries are shown in **bold**; illustrations in ***bold italic***

Abbey Dore vii, viii, ix, *xvi*, 6–7, 12, 14, **16**, 19, 22, 24–5, 29, **32–42**, 88, 155–6, 164, 188–9, 254
Aconbury *xvi*, 6, 8, **42–3**
Alberbury *xvi*, 11, **43**
Albright Hussey Manor 213
Allensmore *xvi*, 11, 15, 19, 23, 28, **44–5**, 97
Alveley *xvi*, 21, 23, **45–9**, 57, 59, 133, 165, 167–8, 218
Ashford Carbonell **210**
Astley Abbotts *xvi*, 7, *16*, **49**
Aston Botterell *xvi*, 25, 48, **50**, 168
Atcham see Bacton

Bacton *xvi*, 7, 21, 25, **50–2**, 252
Badger *xvi*, **211–2**
Battlefield *xvi*, 21, 30, 60, 209, **212–5**, 221, ***222***, 224, 239–40
Beckbury *xvi*, **215–6**
Birley *xvi*, 31, **52**
Birtsmorton 21, 118, *118*, 249
Bishopstone *xvi*, 22, **52–3**, 255
Bledington 249
Bockleton *xvi*, **53**
Bosbury *xvi*, **53**
Bridgnorth *xvi*, **53–4**
Brinsop *xvi*, 8, 11, 25–6, **54–5**, 76, 87, 101, 123
Bristol Cathedral 9, 13
Brockhampton, All Saints *xvi*, 21, **55–6**
Bromfield *xvi*, 3, 22, **56–7**, 128
Buckland 249
Byford *xvi*, **57**

Canterbury Cathedral 1, 48–9, 105, 124
Castle Frome *xvi*, **57**
Church Stretton *xvi*, 22, **57–8**, 252
Claverley *xvi*, 49, **58–9**, 133, 218
Clehonger *xvi*, 12–3, 15, **59–60**, 155–6
Cleobury North *xvi*, **60**, 224, 252
Clungunford *xvi*, 209, **216**
Coalbrookdale *xvi*, 21–2, **60–2**, 220, 234, 245, 254
Coddington *xvi*, **62**
Colwall *xvi*, **62**
Cound *xvi*, 11, 25, **62–3**
Craswall Priory 6, **109**, 109
Credenhill *xvi*, **10**, 11, 26, 54, **63–4**, 76, 101, 117, 181, 255
Croft *xvi*, 48, **64**

Deerhurst *18*, 18
Diddlebury *xvi*, **65**
Dilwyn *xvi*, 3, 5, 7, 18, 25, 27, **65–7**, 86, 172, 254
Donington *xvi*, 11, *11*, *16*, 18, 25, **67–9**
Dudleston *xvi*, **216–7**

Eardisland *xvi*, **69–70**, 176, 201, 252
Eaton Bishop *ii*, viii, x, *xvi*, 6, 9, 11, 15, ***17***, 18, 24, 26, 28, 31, 41, 44, 60, 67, **70–80**, 102, 110, 120–1, 126, 156–7, 177, 200, 203, 254
Eaton-under-Heywood *xvi*, **80**
Edgmond *xvi*, **217–8**
Edstaston *xvi*, **218**
Eyton on the Weald Moors *xvi*, 209, **219–20**
Exeter Cathedral 70, 106

Fairford 21, 94, 232, 249
Fladbury ***17–8***, 18, 75, 249
Fownhope *xvi*, **80**
Foy *xvi*, 23–4, **80–2**, 254

Gloucester Cathedral 9, 13, 54, 86, 92, 120, 161, 193, 249
Goodrich *xvi*, **82–3**, 185, 252
Grappenhall 227, *228*, 249
Greete **84**
Gresford 201, 249

Hampton Court Chapel viii, ix, 5, 19, **20**, 22–3, 25, 36, 39, 65,
 84–9, 92–3, 97–9, **98**, 107–8, 135, 163, 181, 245
Hentland *xvi*, 6, 21, **90–1**
Hereford Cathedral ix, *xvi*, 3–5, 8, 15, **16**, 19, 23–30, **24**, 33, 36, 40,
 44, 50, 54–6, 60, 64, 86–91, **92–107**, 108, 116, 119–20, 125, 129,
 146, 155, 178, 181, 201–2, 224, 234, 251–5
Hereford Museum 21, **109–10**, 196, 198
Hereford, All Saints *xvi*, 23, **108**, 197
Hereford, Coningsby Hospital Chapel **108**
Hereford, St Nicholas **108**
Hereford, St Peter's 8, 95, 100, 103, 105, **108**
Holme Lacy *xvi*, 33, 80, **110**
Hope Bowdler *xvi*, **110–1**
Hope under Dinmore *see also* Hampton Court Chapel *xvi*,
 111, 252
Hopesay *xvi*, **111**
Hopton Wafers *xvi*, **220**
How Caple *xvi*, **111**
Hughley *xvi*, 8, **16**, **111–2**

Kempsey 12–4, *14*, **16**, 249
Kentchurch Court Chapel *xvi*, 22, **112–3**, 245
King's Caple *xvi*, **113–4**
Kingsland *xvi*, 7, 11, 23–6, 76–7, **114–7**, 121, 200, 251–2
Kinlet *xvi*, 7, **117–8**, 192, 252
Kinnersley 255
Kinsham *xvi*, **119**

Ledbury *xvi*, 6, 8, *14*, 15, **16**, 19, 23, 26–7, 67, 76–7, 101, **119–24**,
 129, 172, 205, 255
Ledbury, St Katherine's Hospital viii, 7, *14*, 15, 27, 120, 124,
 125–6
Leintwardine *xvi*, 28, **126**, 130
Leominster 27, 69, 86–7, 89, 99, 129, **254**, 254
Little Malvern 21, 249
Little Ness *xvi*, **220–1**
Llanrhaeadr-Yng-Nghinmeirch 249
Llanwarne *xvi*, 22, 53, **127–8**, 211
Lower Harpton **128**
Ludlow *xvi*, 2, 4–6, 9, 12–3, *12*, *17*, 19, 21, 23, 25–30, **26**, 36, 60, 69,
 94–5, 104, 116, 126, **129–45**, 155–6, 161, 178, 198, 201, 213–5, *214*,
 227, 239–40, 243–4, 252–4

Madeley **146**
Madley xv, *xvi*, 4–9, 11–5, *12*, **16–7**, 18–9, 23–5, 27–8, 36, 40, 44,
 60, 69, 75–9, 92, 96, 102, 105, 107, 131, **146–58**, 161, 173, 194–5,
 199, 203, 206, 227, 252, **288**
Malvern Priory 5, 21, 23, 26, 94, 99, 102–3, 107, 116, 120, 173, 181,
 201, 249
Mancetter 209, 244
Mansel Lacy *xvi*, **158**

Mathon 31, **158**
Merevale **12**, 13–4, 35, 45, 48, 77, 157, 249
Michaelchurch Escley vii, *xvi*, **158–9**, 201, 252
Moccas *xvi*, 9, 13, 15, 18, 27, 60, 112, 153, 155, **159–62**, 203
Monkhopton *xvi*, **162**
Monkland *xvi*, **162–3**, *253*, 253
Monnington *xvi*, **163**
Moreton Corbet *xvi*, **221**
Mortimer's Cross 106, 187
Morville *xvi*, 24, **163**
Much Marcle *xvi*, 22, 39, **164**
Munsley *xvi*, **165**
Munslow *xvi*, 6–7, 21, 23, 24–6, 30, 48, 50–1, 112, 128, **165–9**, 216,
 244, 252

Old Radnor *xvi*, *17*, 21, 25, **169–70**
Orleton *xvi*, 7, 11, 18, **170–1**, 175
Oxford, Christ Church Cathedral 14–5, *14*, *17*, 126

Pembridge *xvi*, 7, 13, 27, **171–2**
Pitchford *xvi*, **172**, 251
Pixley *xvi*, 19, 157, **172–3**, 194, 255, *255*
Prees *xvi*, 209, 213–4, **221–5**
Presteigne *xvi*, 7, *17*, 21, 60, **173–4**, 224

Quatt **175**

Richards Castle *xvi*, *11*, 11, 25, 43, **175–6**
Ross-on-Wye viii, *xvi*, 5, 19, 23, 26, 31, 70, 83, 91, 96, 139, **177–81**,
 199, 251

St Michaels *xvi*, **181**
St Weonards *xvi*, 4, 21–5, **25**, 30, 40, 127, **181–5**, 251
Salisbury Cathedral 43, 106
Sarnesfield *xvi*, 19, 23, 25, **185–7**, 205
Sellack ix, *xvi*, 4, 7, 22–5, 33, 39–42, 51, 80–2, *81*, 88, 114, 164, 184,
 188–90
Shawbury *xvi*, **225**
Sheriffhales *xvi*, **225**
Shrewsbury Museum 210, **225–6**
Shrewsbury, St Mary *xvi*, 13, 22, 58, 61, 100, **208**, 209–10, **226–40**, 245, 252
Sollers Hope *xvi*, **190**
Stanford-on-Avon *11*, 11, 43, 172
Stanton Harcourt 43
Stanton Lacy **252**, 252
Stoke Edith *xvi*, **190–1**
Stottesdon *xvi*, 23, **191–2**, 252
Stretton Grandison *xvi*, **192**
Sundorne Castle 30, *214*, 214, 245
Sutton St Michael **192–3**

Tarrington *xvi*, *17*, 19, 25, 173, **193–4**
Tewkesbury Abbey 9, 13, 40, 54, 77–8, 92, 101, 156–7, 161, 249
Thruxton *xvi*, 11, 13, 28, 114, **194–5**, 251, 254
Tong *xvi*, 21, 209, 221, 223, **240–4**
Tugford **244**

Uffington *xvi*, 210, 214, **245–7**
Ullingswick *xvi*, 24, **195–6**, 253
Upton Bishop *xvi*, 104, **196**

Walterstone *xvi*, 21, *109*, 109, **196**
Warndon *18*, 18, 75
Warwick, St Mary 2, 21, 133, *134*, 135, 249
Wellington *xvi*, 6, **196–7**
Wells Cathedral 9, 54, 70, 161
Weobley *xvi*, 6, *17*, 19, 27, 78, 107, 120, **197–202**, 216, 254
Westhide *xvi*, **202**
Whitchurch *xvi*, **248**
Wigmore 28, 130, 252–3
Worcester Cathedral 13, *14*
Worfield *xvi*, 13, **202–4**
Wormbridge *xvi*, 8, *17*, 19, 23–4, 26, 123, **204–7**, 243, 252, 254
Wroxeter *xvi*, 4, **248**, 251

GENERAL INDEX

Main entries are shown in **bold**; illustrations in ***bold italic***

Abel, John 33
Abrahall family 80–2
Abraham 57, 128
Acts of mercy 58
Adam and Eve 116, 231, 234, 238–9
Ahasuerus, King *see kings*
alb *see garments & clothing*
allegory of blind faith 239
allegory of justice 128, 234
Amos, Prophet 234
angels *see also archangels* viii, 3, 6, 13, **17**, 18–9, 21, 25–8, 35, 37, 40, ***43***, 43, 45, 49–51, **56**, 56–60, **59**, 62, 65–7, **66**, 69, 82–4, ***83***, ***98***, 99, 104, 108, ***122***, 122, 133, 135, 141–2, 144–5, 148, ***157***, 158, 171–3, ***179***, 180, 185–7, ***186***, 190–1, ***193***, 193, 197–9, ***198–9***, 201–2, ***204***, 204, ***216***, 216–8, ***220***, 220, 224, ***229***, 229, 231–2, 234, 238, 240–2, ***241–2***, 244, ***248***, 248–9, 255, ***255***
Angels, Nine Orders of **26**, 116, 145, 249, 269, 274
animals 3, 39, 132, 158, 211, 239
  ass 123, 189, 231
  bull 118, ***157***, 158, 169, ***170***, 235
  lamb 39, 53, 62, 99, 104, 135, 175, ***211***, 211, 234
  leopard 116, ***165***, 165, 248
  lion 35, 37, **39**, 45, 50, 54, 59, 64–5, 69, 75, 84, 110–2, 117, 153, ***157***, 157–8, 165, 173, 187, 191–2, 195–6, 205, 217, 224–5, 231–2, ***232***, 236, 238, 240, 248
  mythical beasts 158, ***237***, 237
  ox 35, 58, 189, ***232***, 232, ***235***, 238, 240
  pig 48, 50, 168
  sheep 181
Annunciation (of the Virgin) 13–4, 19, **20**, 23, 44, **48**, 62, 87, 89, 91, 116, 133–4, 144, 154, 165, 172, 174, 180, 184, 187, 215, 225, ***241***, 241, 247, **255**
arbor vitae *see Cross, green*

archangels 15, ***17***, 18, 23, 26–7, 71, 74, 76, 99, 115–6, ***115***, 121, 135, 144, 184, 200
  Gabriel *see also Annunciation* x, 15, 23, 26–7, 44, 71, 74, 76, 91, 106, 116, 126, 144–5, 184, ***187***, 187, 240
  Michael ***17***, 26, 30, 55, 71, 74, 76–7, 116, ***121***, 121, 126, 144, 167–8, 183, 190–1, 198, ***233***, 233
  Raphael 26, 116, 233
  Uriel 26, 116
architectural styles
  Decorated **8–9**, 19, 44, 75, 121, 126
  Perpendicular vii, 6, 8, 19, 39, 80, 92, 110, 112, 126, 195, 217
armour 8, 45, 53–4, 65, 116–7, ***118***, 121, 130, 148, 174, 183, 205, 212–3, ***213***, **221**, ***222***, 234
arms & heraldry viii, 5–7, 21–2, **27**, 31, 39, 42, 44–5, 50, 52–5, 63, 67, 69–70, 80, 82–4, ***83***, 86–7, 92–3, 100–2, 106, 108–11, ***108–9***, ***111***, ***113***, 113–4, ***116***, 116–8, 120, 122–3, 125–6, 130, 138, 148–9, 151, 153, 159, ***161–2***, 162–9, ***164***, 172, 175–7, 181–5, 187, ***191***, 191–2, 196–7, 201–2, 212–3, ***213***, 216–8, 224–5, 236, 238, 240, 245, 247–8
  Dean & Chapter (Deanery) 6, 27, 45, 92, 102, 106, 149
  England 27, 54, 84, 92, 118, 122, 149, 151, 153, 192, 202
  family arms *listed under family name*
  France 54, 84, 92, 118, 122
  Royal Arms *see also England* 39, 52, 83, 118, 123, 151, ***164***, 164, 187
Ascension 24, ***37***, 37, 39–42, ***41***, 231
Assumption (of the Virgin) 19, **20**, 25, 69, 89, 172, 226, 232
Audley, Bishop Edmund (d.1524) 5, 106

Bagoas the eunuch 233
Baillie and Mayer *see glaziers & restorers*
Balaam the prophet 234
Baskerville family 54–5, 113, 182, 184
Beatitudes 58
Beauchamp family 2, 21, 83, 92, 133–5, ***134***
Betton & Evans *see glaziers & restorers*

282 THE MEDIEVAL STAINED GLASS OF HEREFORDSHIRE & SHROPSHIRE

Bird, Thomas (d.1836) 71, 76, 78, 149
birds 3, 13, 51, 53, 78, **98**, 117, 132, 157, 159, 162, 173, 187, 191
    dove 116, 134–5, 139, 144, 157, 167, 184, 189
    eagle 37, 118, 125, 128, 168, 173, 181–3, 194, 211, 231, 240
    owl 86
Blount family 45, 49, 167–8
Blount, Thomas (d.1679) 30, 70, 147, 149, 164, 171, 175–7, 181–3, 197
boat 138
Bockleton, Richard de 159
Bohun family 7, 27, 84, 92, 123, 153, 201
borders 9, 13, 15, 31, 36, 40–2, 44–5, 50–1, 54–7, 62, 64–5, 67, 69–71, 74–5, 79, 82, 101, 105–7, 110–2, 114, 117–9, 121–3, 125–6, 128, 149, 154–6, 158–9, 162–3, 165–70, 172, 175, 177, 180, 187–90, 192–3, 195–6, 202, 206, 212, 216, 224, 226, 228, 244
    castle 9, **98**, 119, 156, 195
    crowns 4, 9, 51, 110, 163, 189–90, 195, 224
    cup-and-cover 13, 15, 62, 75, 156, 192, **194**
    fleurs-de-lis 9, 65, 69–70, 119, 175, 195, 202
    foliage 9, 44, 55–6, 69, 106, 112, 125–6, 128, 158, 163, 169, 175–6, 216, 224, 244
    heraldic 54, **54**
    'Ledbury' *xiv*, 80, 112, 121, 126, 172, 176
    lion 65, 112, 195
    lozenge 50–1, 70, 110, 118, 126, 224
    quatrefoil 36, 62, 70, 118, 126, 192
    swastika 162
botanical *see plants & flowers*
de Braose 69, 102, 116
buildings & architecture (in glass) 9, 45, **57**, 57, 67, 78, 119, 133, **140**, 144, **156**, 156–8, 161, **173**, 189, 195, 232, 235, 244
bull *see animals*
Burgh family 158
Burley family 52, 167, 225
Burlison and Grylls *see glaziers & restorers*

canopy-work 9, 13, 19, 40, 45, 49, 62, 71, 74, 76–9, 99, 101–2, 112, 118, 135, 148, 157, 159, **160**, 161, 163, 169, 172–3, 180, 188–9, 192, 200, 202–3, **203**, 213, 216, 218, 224, 228, 233, 235–8
    crocketed 163, 169, 173, 192
    'Oxford' 79, 157
    with figures 40, 49, 71, 77, 99, 101, 148, 202, 235, 238
Capell family 163
Carwarden family 42
Caviness, Madeline *viii*, 86–7, 89, 92, 94, 99–100
Cecil family 21, **109**, 109–10, 196
chalice **35**, 37, **38**, **51**, 138, **140**, **194**, 217, **217**, 224, 238
Chandos family 54–5, 191
Charlemagne 236
Charlton, Bishop Thomas 63, 92
Christ & Saviour 1, 7–8, **11**, 11, **16**, 16, 24–5, 36–7, 39–40–2, 45, **49**, 49–51, **51**, 53, **55**, 55, 57–8, 60–1, **61**, 65, 67, 69, 75, 77–9, 88, 100, 104–5, 108, 110, 112–5, **113**, **114**, **118**, 118, 131–2, 134–5, 139, 141, 144–5, 148–9, 151, 153–5, 157, 159, 162–3, **166**, 167, **172**, 172–3, 175, 181–2, 184–5, 188–90, **194**, 194–5, 198, 201–2, 211, 217, 220, **221**, 224, 231–2, **232**, 234, 237–8, 240, 244, **245–6**, 246–9
    Baptism **246**
    betrayal **230**, 231–2

Christ & Saviour cont.
    Child *see also Virgin and Child* 100, 108, 135, 154, 157, 181, 189, 237
    Circumcision **58**, 58
    Crucifixion & Cross 13, 21, 24–5, 31, 40, **44**, 44–5, 49, 51, **52**, 53, 55, **56**, 57–8, **58**, 62, 64–5, **65**, 70–1, 74, 76, 78–9, 84, 88, 97, 103–5, **104**, 108, **112**, **113**, 114–5, 117, 121, 124, 128–9, **140**, 155, 162–3, **163**, 165–7, 169, 173, 175, **182**, 185, 188–9, **189**, **194**, 194–5, 200–2, **203**, 217, **223**, 224, 232–3, 236–7, 244
    Empty Tomb/ Resurrection 24, 104–5, 134, 142, 145, 162
    Five Wounds of Christ 40, 79, 167, **211**, 211, **248**, 248
    head of 37, 75, **113**, 114, **118**, 144, **172**
    in Glory 24, 79, 112, 141, 148, 244
    in Majesty 24, 49, **55**, 55, 69, **104**, 104–5, **114**, 167
    life of 7, 105, 154–5, 249
    Man of Sorrows 24, **25**, 77, 79, 184
    Nativity 23, **56**, 57, 62, 123, 128, 146, **152**, 153, 188, 189, 233, 237, **254**, 278
    Passion of *see also Instruments of the Passion* 8, 24, 175, 201
    washing feet 58, 60–1, **61**, 234, **246**, 247
Civil War *viii*, 86–7, 92–4, 130, 198
de Clare family 92, 133
Clarence family 169, **170**
Clayton and Bell *see glaziers & restorers*
clergy (in glass) 22, 135, 139, 202, 225
Clifford family 149, 182
Commandments 23, 129, 142–4, **143**, 207
Commonwealth 27, 86–7
Coningsby family 84, 86–8, 92, 94, 108, **108**
Corbet, Philip and family 210, 213, 214, 245
Cornewall family 7, 84, 92, **191**, 192
Creed 21, 25, 65, 86–7, 89, 126, 129–30, 134–5, **136**, 138
Cross *see Christ, Crucifixion*
    green cross 24, 41, **44**, 45, 78, 105, 112, **114**, 114, 124, 163, 172, 188–9, **194**, 195, 202, **203**
crown glass 2, 97, 99, 196
Crown of Thorns *see Instruments of the Passion*
crowns & tiaras 4, 9, 11, 21, 25, **43**, 43, 48–51, 56, 60, 64, 67, 69, 83, 99–100, 106, 110, **113**, **114**, 115, 117–8, 124, 128, 132–3, 135, 142, 149, 163–4, 169, 175–6, 180, 184, 187, 189–96, 200–2, 205, 207, 217, **223**, 224, 236, 240, 243
Crucifixion *see Christ & Saviour, also Cross*
cup-and-cover decoration *see borders*

Daniel 132, 231, 247
Darby, Abraham 60
David, King *see kings*
Delabere family 7, 148
Devereux family 57, 84, 182
diapering *xiv*, 9, 36, 48, 55, 57, 60, 64–5, 67, 75, 83, 112, 132, 161–2, 172, 175–6, 188–9, 195, 206
Dingley, Thomas (d.1695) **5**, 7, **24**, 24, **69**, 69–70, 86–7, 89, 92–3, **93**, 106, 108, 122, 130, 135, 142, 145, **162**, 163, 173
donors & patronage 4, **5–7**, 19, 21, 27, 30–1, 50, 53–4, **57**, 57–8, 62, 65, 70–1, 74–5, 78–9, 82, 90–2, 97, 108–9, 118, **120**, 120–2, 125–6, 128, 133, 135, 146, 156–7, 159, **165**, **169**, 169, 174–5, 177–8, 189–90, 198, 210, 217, 226, 232, 234–40, **235**, 245, 247

Doom 67, **68**, 74, 76–7
Duncumb, John (d.1839) 44–5, 71, 92–3, 97, 100, 103–4, 108, 113, 147–9, 153, 183, 196

Elisha 231
Englefield family 213, 224
Esther **230**, 231, 238
Evans, David & Charles *see glaziers & restorers*
Eyton family 219–20
Eyton, Robert (d.1881) 217

feathers 26–7, 35, 106–8, 111, 113, 116, 142, 154, 173–4, 187, 193, 200–2, 207, 224
Feld or Field family 148
fish 116, 128, 133, 172, 231, 233, **246**, 247
Fitzalan family 111, **111**, 212, 217, 224, 240
Fitzwilliam family 84, 108, **108**
fleurs-de-lis 12–3, 53, 65, 67, 69–70, 111, 119, 175, 187, 195, 202
Flight into Egypt 8, 23, 123, **124**
French glass 4, 8, 18, 22, 49, 80, 154, 213, 215, 232
de Frene family 27, 159, 161, **161**, 162

garments & clothing 35, 43, 45, 63, 77, 100, 103, **110**, 121–2, 124, 126, 132, 144, 148, 162, 168–9, 172, 186, 189, 193, 202
　vestments 35, 48, 110, 125, 133, 146, 180, 207, **218**, 218, 224, 244
　　alb 77, 122, 172, 186
　　amice 77, 83, **110**, 110, 122, 133, 172, 186, 200–1, 207
de Geneville 27
geometrical pattern & form 3, 36, 77, 80, 101, 105–6, 115–6, 119, 192, 196, 216
German glass 21, 60–1, 77, 105, 124, 167, 170, 215, 229, 231–2, 236, 247
glaziers & restorers
　Baillie & Co., Thomas 30, 114–7, 178, 180, 248, **251**
　Baillie and Mayer 178, 183, 185, **251**
　Betton & Evans 21–3, 29–30, 50–1, **51**, 58, 61, 100, 103, 117–8, **118**, 204, 230, 233, **251**
　Betton, John 22, 226, 228, **251**, 252
　Bond, Richard & Edward 29
　Bosworth, Mr 29, 34
　Bowers, James 96
　Budd, Jim 99, **114**, 114–5, 125, 159, 173, **252**
　Burlison and Grylls 69–70, 82–3, 215–6, **252**
　Childs, Charles 95, 106
　Clayton and Bell 144, 195, **252–4**, *253*
　Davies, John 217, 251
　Drake, Wilfred 22, 86, 97
　Dubberley, John 119
　Dubberley, William 95
　Evans, David & Charles *see also Betton & Evans* 22, 29–30, 50–1, 56–8, 60–1, 95, 100, 103–5, 117, 128, 139, **140**, 141–2, 144–5, 165–9, 210–1, 213–7, 220–1, 224, 227–9, 232, 235, 237–40, 245, 248, **251–2**, **252**
　Fisher, Samuel 79
　Glazier, William 107
　Goode, John and Samuel 96
　Gough, Thomas 79

glaziers & restorers cont.
　Griffiths, William 95
　Grosvenor Thomas, Roy 22, 86, 88–9, 97
　Hardman & Co. 82, 108, 131, 133–5, 138, 181, 194–5, 216, **253**, **253–4**
　Heaton, Butler & Bayne 65, **254**
　Hereford, William 181
　Hill, Edward 178
　Holman, William 29, 34
　Jaggard, James 40, 95
　Jennings, George 147
　Kempe & Co. 31, 71, 120–2, 199, 201, 240–1, **254**, 254
　King & Co. **254**
　Knill, Francis 95
　Madley Master 12–5, **16**, 18–9, 27, 131, 203
　Master of Archangels 15
　Mayer, George *see Baillie & Mayer*
　Merewether, Dean John 103, 151–2
　Morgan, Thomas 40, 95, 146
　Morris & Co. 64, 122, 172, **254–55**, *255*
　Nicholas, John 119
　Nott, Joseph 119
　Nott, Samuel 119
　Parry, James 79
　Pillinger, William 119
　Powall, Richard [sic] 29, 33, 95, 147
　Powell & Co. 238
　Price, Mrs Rachel 95
　Prudde, John 2, 5, 21, 133, 135, 249
　Reece (or Reese), Mr William 88, 95–7, 99, 147
　Rogers, John 71, 79, 147
　Rowberry, William 96
　Season, Thomas 28
　Shepherd, Walter 199
　Stephens & Sons 96
　Symonds, James 119
　Thornton, John 5, 19, 21, 91, 99, 107, 133, 144, 181, 201–2, 209, 242
　Tower, Walter *see also Kempe & Co.* 31, 71, 74–6
　Warrington, William 30, 55, 100–2, **255**
　Williams family 95
Glynne, Sir Stephen viii, 80, 110, 149, 170, 175, 204
God 23, 25, 36, 116, 134, 142, 154, 157, 168, 183, 189, **218**, 218, 224, **230**, 231, 234
Good Samaritan 128, 231
Grandison family 7, 27, 125–6
grisaille xiv, 3, 6, 7–9, 34, 43–4, 45, 53–4, 62, 64, 67, 71, 74, 77–80, 101–2, **104**, 105–6, 115–9, 126, 162, 169–70, 175–6, 192, 210
Grose, Francis 130
Grosvenor Thomas, Roy *see glaziers & restorers*
grotesque 21, 61, 110, 133, 154, 173–4, 187, 193, 234, 251

hands 12, **25**, 25, 35–6, **36**, **44**, 44–5, **47**, **48**, 48, 51, **55**, 55, 63, **67**, 67, 77, 79, **91**, 91, 99–100, 103–4, 107–8, **114**, 114, 119, 121–5, **125**, 128, 132, 141, 149, 157, 165–6, 169, 172, 174, 177, 180, 182, 185, 187, 191, 193, 196, 200–2, **205**, 205, 207, 212, 220, 224–5, 232
Hardman & Co. *see glaziers & restorers*

hats & headdresses 67, *110*, 110–1, 138, 180, 224
  mitre *10*, *36*, 36, 45, 49, 77, 99, 102, 121, *139*, *155*, 156, 180, ***203***, 224, 234, 243–4
Herod, King *see kings*
Herodias ***223***, 224
Hill, James (d.1727) 44, 52, 54, 57, 63, ***69***, 69–70, 86, 88–9, 92–3, 95, 108, 110, 113, 125–6, 130, 148–9, 158, 177, 190–1, 193
Holy Family, The 149, 178, 181, 239
Holy Spirit 134–5, 144, 184, 189, 237
Hussey family 212–3, 224

iconoclasm 5, 8, 23, ***27–8***, 70, 87, 93–4, 129–30, 146, 185, 198
Instruments of the Passion 6, 27, 53, 83, ***107***, 128, 158, ***159***, 197, ***199***, 199–202, 212, 224, ***223***, ***234***, 234, 236, 238, 240, ***243***, 244
  Crown of Thorns 37, 83, 114, 200, 213
  nails 53, 83, 224, 236
International Style 5, ***19–21***, 35–6, 56, 67, 83, 133, 138, 142, 173, 194, 196–7, 209, 214, 220

Jesse Tree viii, 6, 9, 11–3, ***12***, ***17***, 23, 60, 69, 129, ***131***, 131–2, ***132***, 146, 155–8, 161, ***208***, 209, 216, 226–9, ***227***
Jesus *see Christ & Saviour*
Jezebel 231
Joachim 23, 178, *179*, 180
Job 231
John the Baptist *see saints*
Jonah ***230***, 231
Joseph, husband of Mary 123, 131, 144–5, 189, 238
Joseph, son of Jacob 23, 57, 62, ***102***, 103, 128, ***230***, 231
Josiah 58
Judith 238

Kempe & Co. *see glaziers & restorers*
kings
  Ahasuerus ***230***, 231, 233
  Asa 28, 131, ***227***, 227
  Charles I 164, ***164***
  Charles II 93
  David, King 62, 145
  Edmund *see saints*
  Edward II 70
  Edward III 55, 110
  Edward IV 170, 187
  Edward the Confessor *see saints*
  Ethelbert *see saints*
  Henry I 230
  Henry IV 52, 92, 212
  Henry V 52, 92
  Henry VI 1, 92
  Henry VII 48, 106
  Henry VIII 45, 94, 168
  Herod 8, ***16***, 123–4, ***223***, 224
  Joram 131–2, ***132***
  Manessah 132
  Micah ***132***, 132
  Offa 180
  Ozias ***12***, ***227***, ***272***
  Richard II 92, 243
  Roboam ***227***
knights 7, 94, 117–8, ***118***, 148, 183, 192, 226–8, 244, 251
Kyrle, Sir John 164

Labours of the Month 58, 225–6, ***226***
lamb *see animals*
Last Supper 8, ***16***, 22, 24, 60, ***61***, 149, 153–4, 231, 234, 245–6, ***246***
Laud, Archbishop William 22, 33, 39–40, 42, 82, 88, 188
leopard *see animals*
lettering 9, 13, 45, 60, 63, 70, 93, 102, 106, 110, 117, 124, 133, 135, 144, 157, 162, 168, 172–3, 181, 186, 202, 206, 217, 220, 224, 226–7, 244, 248
  black letter 4, 7, 13, 50, 52, 57–9, 67, 84, 110, 117, 124, 133, 148, 166, 168–9, 173, 181, ***190***, 190, 220, 224, 226, 248
  Lombardic 9, 13, 45, 60, 63, 70, 102, 117, 124, 157, 162, 168, 186, 206, 227
Linge, Abraham van 39, ***85***, 88, 188
lion *see animals*
Lisle family 82–3, ***83***
Lloyd, John 6, 21, ***165***, 165, 167
Longespee family 159
Lyttleton family 167, 168

Madley Master *see glaziers & restorers*
Magi 23, 25, 62, 108, 144–5, ***151***, 153, 188–9, 233, 237
  Adoration of 62, 153, 233, 237
Mainwaring family 218
Mappa Mundi 24, 55, 78
Margaret of Antioch 247
Marks, Richard viii, 3, 5–9, 33–5, 39, 49, 63, 103, 109, 118, 154, 209
Marshall, George (d.1950) viii, 15, 31, 60, 70–1, 74, 77–80, 116–7, 148–9, 151, 153–4, 159, 177, 185, 192–3, 196, 199
Mary Magdalene *see saints*
Mary of the Seven Sorrows *see Virgin Mary*
Mary, sister of Lazarus 234
mills ***134***, 135, 220 (mill stone), 231
mitre *see hats & headdresses*
monk 34–5, 44, 133, 202, 217, 229, ***230***, 231–2, 237
monograms 45, 50, 53, 67, 80, 110, 168, 181, 186, 217, 244
  AMR (Mary) 53, 244
  IHS 45, 53, 168, 181, 217
Morris & Co. *see glaziers & restorers*
Mortimer family 7, 27, 69, 92, 111, 133, 217
Moses 37, ***37***, 39, 57, 142, 144, 207
Mountford family 92
Murimuth, Adam 6, 70, 75, 77
musical instruments 37, 62, 139, ***186***, 186, 191, 193, 204
  cymbals 193
  harp 37, 139, ***186***, 186
  lute ***190***, 191
  psaltery ***186***, 186, 193, 204
  tromba marina 191
  trumpet 193
  viola da gamba 62
Mynors family 127, 181–5

Mytton, William (d.1746) viii, 25, 30–1, 45, 48–50, 54, 58, 62, 67, 84, 111–2, *112*, 130, 139, *140*, 145–6, 162, *165*, 165–6, 168, 172, 175, 191, 202, *211*, 211, 213, *214*, 217–20, 225–6, 238, 240, *244*, 244–5

Netherlandish glass 1, 21–3, *56*, *58*, 116, 162, 167, 185, 209, 210–1, 232–4, 246–7
Newton, Peter viii, 62, 67, 111, 191–2, 202, 209, 225, 240, 244
nimbus ii, 7, *11*, *14*, 15, *16*–*18*, *20*, 37–9, 37, *41*, *44*, 45, *46*–*9*, 48–9, *51*, 51, *55*–*6*, 55, *61*, 61, *63*, *65*–*6*, 65, 69, 82, *90*–*1*, 91, *98*, 99–100, *110*, 110, 112, *114*, 114–5, 117–8, *118*, *121*–*2*, 121–3, *125*, 126, *128*, 128, *132*, 133, *134*, *136*, 139, *140*, *143*, 144, *152*, 153, 165, *166*, 167–70, *169*–*70*, 172, *176*, *179*–*80*, 180, *182*, 184, *186*–*7*, 186–7, 189, *190*, 191, *193*–*5*, 194, 196–7, *197*–*9*, 200, 202, *205*–*6*, 205–6, *214*–*6*, 215, *218*–*20*, 218, 224, *228*, 231, *234*–*5*, *241*–*3*, 241–4, *252*–*3*, *255*

Orbis Terrarum 25, *36*, 36, *55*, 55, 172, 232
Owen, Revd Hugh *228*, 228, 245

palm *see plants & flowers*
Palmers of Ludlow 25–6, 129, 133, 135, *137*, 138–9, 198, 215
Parry family 7, 50
   Blanche 21, 50, *51*, 52
patronage *see donors & patronage*
Paul, Roland 34, 36, 60, 185
Pembridge family 59–60
Pharaoh 57
Pietà 88–9
Pitchard 108
plants & flowers 3, 9, 12–3, 34, 43–5, 50, 53–6, 59, 62, 64–5, 67, 69–70, 75, 77, 79–80, 86, 100–1, 103, 105–7, 112–3, 115–9, 122, 125–6, 128, 132, 146, 155, 162–3, 165, 169–70, 172, 175–6, 183, 187, 192, 195–7, 206, 212, 216, 224, 227, 241, 244
   ivy 53, 65, 116, 187
   lily of the valley 75–6
   oak 43, 67, 106–7, 122, 172, 175, 212, 216, 224, 244
   palm 50, 117, 138, 144–5, 166, 192, 220
   rose 59, 67, 86, 106, 113, 117–8, 126, 169–70, 175, 183, 187, 196–7
   vine 9, 12–3, 44–5, 53–5, 59, 62, 64, 67, 69, 77, 79–80, 101, 105–6, 115–6, 118, 122, 125–6, 132, 146, 155, 162–3, 170, 172, 175–6, 187, 192, 195, 206, 216, 224, 227
Pontius Pilate 128
Presentation in the Temple 24, 154
Price, John 27, 87
Prodigal Son 53, 127–8
Prudde, John *see glaziers & restorers*

Queens
   Elizabeth I 21, 50, *51*
   Mary I 118
Quinity *134*

Reece (or Reese), Mr *see glaziers & restorers*
Rees, John ap 148
Reformation 6, *21*, 22–3, 27–8, 30, 93–4, 130, 144, 146, 167, 183, 188
restorers *see glaziers & restorers*
Royal Arms *see arms & heraldry*

saints
   Agatha *235*, 235
   Andrew 37, *38*, 89, 122, 128, 135, *136*, 138, 173, 185, 234, 237
   Anne (mother of Virgin Mary) 19, 53, 60, 88–9, 102, *139*, 178, *179*, *180*, 180–1, 238
   Anthony *46*, 48, 50, *166*, 168
   Armel 45–8, *46*, *47*
   Augustine 101–2, 111, 144–5
   Barbara 89, 145, 236
   Barnabas *11*, 77
   Bartholomew *136*, 138, 195
   Bernard *229*, 229–30, 237
   Catherine or Katherine (of Alexandria) 14, *17*, *18*, 18, 21, 25, 48, 51, 60, 82, 89, 100, 124–6, 129, 134–5, 144–6, 169, *170*, 170, 175, *182*, 184, 189, *193*, 193, 207, *219*, 220, 231–2, 234, 236, 240
   Chad 212
   Christopher *134*, 135, *171*, 172, *219*, 220, 247
   Dennis 92
   Dubricius 77
   Edmund (king and martyr) *206*, 206–7, 240, *243*, 243
   Edward the Confessor, King 26, 48, 110, 138–9, 144, 145, *179*
   Eligius 238
   Elizabeth 99, 144, 175, 240
   Ethelbert (king and martyr) 92, 101–2, 149, 178, *179*, 180–1
   Etheldreda 144
   Francis 86, 88–9, 117
   George 8, 26, 48, 50–1, *54*, 54–5, 101–2, 123, 128–9, 135, 145, 153, 163, 212
   Giles 128
   Guthlac 6, 197
   Helen or Helena 117, 144–5, 184, 236
   Hubert 238
   James the Great 37, *38*, 40, 89, 135, *136*, 138, 144, 235, 240–1
   James the Less 89, *136*, 138, 144
   Jerome 111, 128, 144, *236*, 236
   John of Bridlington 145
   John the Baptist 25, 31, *37*, 62, 86, 89, 99, 111, 134, 135, 141, 157, 175–6, *182*, 207, *211*, 211, 213, *223*, 224, 234, 240–1, 244
   John the Evangelist 6, 7–8, 24, 25, 37, *38*, 39–40, 41, 50–1, 57–8, 62, *63*, 74, 78–9, 84, 89, *98*, 122, 129, *136*, 138–9, 144–5, *152*, 153–4, 158, 162, 165, *166*–*7*, 168, 188–9, 202, 231, 233, 238–41, *239*
   Kenelm 166
   Lambert 232, 235–6, 238
   Laurence 23, 30, 57, 86, 89, 129, 130, 139, *140*, 141, 145, 172, 213, 214, *214*, 215, 258, 260, 265, 266, 270, 276, 277
   as Lawrence xiii, 52, 128, 130, 192, 266
   Leonard 145, 184
   Luke 35, 37, *38*, 144, 157–8, *232*, 232, *235*, 235, 238, 240–1
   Margaret of Antioch 15, *125*(?), 126, 129, 144–6, 167, 175, 184, *206*, 207, *211*, 212, 244, 247
   Mark 35, 37, *38*, *39*, 58–9, *157*, *232*, 232, 240–1, 248
   Martin 111, 128, 237
   Mary *see Virgin Mary*
   Mary Magdalene 101–2, *102*, 145, 175, 188–9, 232, 240, 247
   Mary Salome 240–1
   Matthew 37, *38*, 135, 138, 240–1
   Matthias 89, 128, 136, 138, 167, 239

saints cont.
   Michael *see archangels*
   Milburgha 148
   Nicholas 2, 197, 212, 233
   Owen 6, 69–70, 197
   Paul 122, 144, 173, 207, 236
   Peter *17*, 37, *38*, 60, *61*, 62, 89, 111, 122, 125–6, 135, *136*, 138, 145–6, 173, 185, *206*, 207, 234–7, 240, *243*, 243
   Philip the Apostle 86, 89, 135, *136*, 167
   Raphael *see archangels*
   Roch 128
   Sebastian 236, 247
   Simon 89, *136*, 138
   Stephen 86, 89, 135, 145, 155, 172, 202, 234–5
   Susannah 128
   Thaddeus (Jude) 135, 138
   Thomas the Apostle 135, *136*, 138, 144, 239
   Thomas Becket, of Canterbury 10, 26, 63–4, 88–9, 99, 117, 145, *166*, 207
   Thomas Cantilupe, of Hereford 10, 26, 63–4, 71, 77, 83, 92, 94, 146, 166, 178, *179*, 180–1
   Uriel *see archangels*
   Ursula *98*, 100
   Veronica 99, 162
   Vincent 145
   Virgin, The *see Virgin Mary*
   Werburgh 148
   Winifred or Winifreda 86, 88–9, 213
Sandford family 213, 224
Saviour *see Christ & Saviour*
Say family 175
Scudamore family ix, 7, 22, 25, *32*, 33, *37*, *39*, 39–42, *40*, *41*, 82, 88, 113, 164, 188–90
Scutum Fidei 167
seaweed background 67, 86, 213, 224, *241*, 241, *243*, 243, 254
seven sons, martyrdom of 247
Shadrach, Meshach and Abednego in the furnace 231
Shimei 231
Slaughter of the Innocents 8, *16*, 23, 58, 123, *124*, 205, *206*
Sorghelosse *127*, 127–8, 211
Sotheby, Barbara 43
Spofford, Bishop Thomas 5–6, 19, 21, 23, 83, 91, 93, *139*, 139, 141, 146, 177–8, *179*, *180*, 180–1
Straddell, Abbot *35*
Strange family 83, 212
sun, moon and stars 64–5, 102
sundial *124*, 124
Swinfield, Bishop 63–4
Swiss glass 22, 113, 210, *245*, 245–6
Symonds, Richard (d.1660) viii, *5*, 7, 27, 45, 53–5, 65, 92, 100, 148–9

Talbot family 7, 54–5, 63–4, 82–3, 151, 168
Taylor, Silas (d.1678) 44, 59–60, 63–5, 70, 74, 78, 82, 84, 90, 92–3, 102, 114, 148–9, 153, 159, 175, 177, 181–3, 197
Templars 92
tetramorphic symbols *see also animals* 35, 37, 104–5, 118, *157*, 158, 173, 194, 241

Thornton, John *see glaziers & restorers*
Throne of Mercy 25, 51, *140*, 189, *190*, *223*, 275, 276, 277
thuribles 35, 65, 185, 186
thurifers 27, *66*, *122*, 122
tiaras *see crowns & tiaras*
Tobit and Tobias *52*, 53, 116, 128, 233, *246*, 247
Tomkins family 163
Tracy family 122–3
Tree of Jesse *see Jesse Tree*
trellis 76, 80
Trinity 25, 28, 51, 94, 118, 141

Vaughan family 103, 182–3
de Verdon family 133, 197, 217
vestments *see garments & clothing*
Virgin Mary *ii*, 6–8, 13, 15, *17*, 19, 23–5, *24*, 28, 31, 40, *43*, 43, *48*, 48, 50–1, 53, 55, 57, 60, 63–4, 69, 74, 76, 78–9, 82, 84, 86–9, 91–4, *93*, 99–100, 108, 116, 123, 126, 129, 131, 133–5, *134*, *139*, 139, 141–2, 144–6, 148, 153–4, 157–8, 162, 165–9, *166*, *169*, 172, *176*, 176, 178, *179*, *180*, 180–1, 184, 187–91, 194–8, *195*, 202, 204–6, *205*, *215*, 215, *225*, 225–6, 231–2, *234*, 234, *236*, 236, 238–9, *239*, 240–1, *241*, *243*, 244, 249
   and Child *ii*, 8, 15, *18*, *24*, 24, *50*–1, 55, 76, 79, *93*, 93, *98*, 99–100, 123, 141, 144–5, 148, 157, 165–9, *169*, 189, *195*, 195–6, 204–5, *205*, 231, 234, *236*, 236, 238–9, *243*, 244
   and her mother Anne *see saints, Anne*
   Annunciation of *see Annunciation*
   Assumption of *see Assumption*
   Coronation of 25, *43*, 43, 50, 69, *114*, 115, 133, 145–6, *176*, 176
   life of the 86–7, 154, 249
   monogram of *see monograms*
   of the Seven Sorrows *234*, 234

Walwyn family 190–1
Warrene family 27, 111, 153
Warrington, William *see glaziers & restorers*
Women at the Sepulchre 154
Woodforde, Christopher 4, 9, 181

York School 5, 19, 21, 23, 48, 56, 60, 74, 77, 83, 91–4, 99, 103, 106, 120, 133, 144, 169, 173, 178, 181, 187, 196, 209, 214–6, 220–1, 224, 239–42, 244, 249, 254

Zouche family 67, 69, *191*, 192